State & Local Politics

State & Local Politics

JOHN A. STRAAYER
Colorado State University

ROBERT D. WRINKLE
University of Texas–Pan American

J. L. POLINARD
University of Texas–Pan American

ST. MARTIN'S PRESS
New York

Executive editor: Don Reisman
Development editor: David Estrin
Managing editor: Patricia Mansfield-Phelan
Project editor: Talvi Laev
Copy editor: Wendy Polhemus-Annibell
Production supervisor: Alan Fischer
Art director: Sheree Goodman
Text design: Celine Brandes
Photo research: Inge King
Cover design: Lisa Delgado
Cover art: Alex Zwarenstein

Library of Congress Catalog Card Number: 92-62739

For information, write to:
St. Martin's Press, Inc.
175 Fifth Avenue
New York, NY 10010

ISBN: 0-312-09104-4

We'd like to dedicate this book to seven special students— *to Keith and Sean, to Elizabeth and Tracie, and to Kathy, David, and Jeffrey.* We urge them to read it, even though it's not assigned.

Preface

State and Local Politics assumes that in order to understand U.S. politics one must know something about government — its purpose, its functions, and its organization. The text, therefore, has a distinct institutional and structural focus: It examines how the institutional arrangements of different state and local governments — and the different distributions of authority among the branches of state and local governments — affect issues in participation and public policy.

The first six chapters of the book detail the anatomy of government. Chapters 7 through 9 focus on political parties, interest groups, and elections, respectively. The remaining eight chapters cover local governments, selected public policy areas, and future trends in this country.

State and Local Politics emphasizes the importance of state and local governments in the daily lives of American citizens. Although the activities of the federal government are also important, what happens in state and local decision centers often affects people more directly and more frequently. For example, while Americans are affected by congressional and presidential decisions concerning the capital gains or income tax, they are more immediately affected by state and local government policies concerning public safety, clean drinking water, public health, and education.

In addition, the text combines several important and useful features. It is highly comprehensive in its coverage of state and local politics and government, thereby allowing students to see how the structure and organization of government can affect participation and decision making. In its focus on citizen interaction with government, the text shows how Americans are affected by government as well as how they can affect government decisions. Furthermore, the coverage of state and local governments is well balanced, with separate chapters on metropolitan areas (Chapter 10), local government (Chapter 11), and community politics (Chapter 12). Examples of citizen participation and citizen-initiated policy at the county, city, and local district levels are provided.

Several chapters on substantive policy issues are included to allow in-depth coverage of policy issues of interest (Chapters 13 through 16). Instructors and students may choose from chapters on fiscal policy, public education, social services, and crime and corrections. In addition, attention is given to state and local governments in various regions of the United States; for example, the models of city government employed in the older northeastern and midwestern cities are compared and contrasted with those of cities located in the Sunbelt states and the Northwest.

The book's language is clear, straightforward, and short on academic jargon. In other words, it is geared toward enhancing students' comprehension. The format of the book means that students and professors do not need to choose between comprehensiveness and cost, since the book is published in paperback and is reasonably priced.

Note to Instructors

Finally, we would like to note the availability of an *Instructor's Manual* that contains multiple-choice, true-false, and essay questions, as well as suggestions for student exercises. The manual is available both in print form and in formats for IBM-compatible and Macintosh computers. For more information, please write or call St. Martin's Press, College Desk, 175 Fifth Avenue, New York, NY, 10010 (**1-800-446-8923**); or contact your local St. Martin's sales representative.

Acknowledgments

We have worked with the editorial staffs of other publishing houses in the past, but none were as professional and competent as the staff at St. Martin's Press. In particular, we are grateful to executive editor Don Reisman and development editor David Estrin for their direction and support of this project and to project editor Talvi Laev and copy editor Wendy Polhemus-Annibell for working with us to bring the manuscript to its present form.

We would also like to thank our colleagues who reviewed the manuscript and offered many helpful comments and suggestions: John H. Baker, Southern Illinois University; Steve Mazurana, University of Northern Colorado; Angelo Messore, Manchester Community College; Charles H. Sheldon, Washington State University; and Joseph Stewart, Jr., University of Texas at Dallas.

Professor Straayer wishes to give special thanks to Earlene Bell for all her nearly successful efforts to keep him sane and functioning while this book was being written, and for her invaluable and professional assistance in the preparation of the manuscript.

Should the text contain any errors of fact or judgment, we'll likely blame each other by a succession of two to one votes.

John A. Straayer
Robert D. Wrinkle
J. L. Polinard

Contents in Brief

Contents

State & Local Politics

1

A Nation of State and Local Governments

The Arizona state capitol building *(foreground)* surrounded by a more recent extension. Phoenix, Arizona. *(Miro Vintoniv/Stock, Boston)*

Alice M. Rivlin, the first director of the Congressional Budget Office, commented in 1990 on the importance of state and local governments to the future of the nation:

> If the United States is to have a world-class economy for the twenty-first century, state governments have to take the lead. Infrastructure must be modernized, school systems drastically improved and public services, from child development to adult retraining, made dramatically more effective.
>
> The federal government is both broke and unsuited for the role of providing these services, which require diverse responses tailored to local conditions, active citizen participation and visible elected officials who can be held accountable for results. Washington is too far from the scene to handle these challenges flexibly and effectively.[1]

This book is about American state and local government and politics. It is about the governments that Rivlin sees as the key to the nation's future. More than 86,000 state and local government units operate in the United States. The text describes their organization, their institutions and institutional relationships, their politics, and their central role in our daily lives. Every one of us, every day, interacts in a variety of ways with state and local governments. We may hear or read about international affairs or the politics of Congress and the presidency in Washington, D.C., but we do so in a nation based on state and local government.

In its treatment of state and local government, the text emphasizes *institutions and their importance.* We cannot understand politics without first knowing how our system of government is organized. Institutional arrangements and the institutional allocation of authority determine the activities that can be undertaken by governments and politicians as well as the strategies and tactics for accomplishing goals. Federalism and the separation of powers give structure to the relationships among presidents, governors, judges, and legislatures, for example. The organization of the executive branch frames the working relationship of the attorney general and the governor. The particular form of local government dictates the respective roles of the mayor, council members, and, perhaps, the city manager. Scores of other examples will emerge throughout the book.

The importance of political behavior is also discussed (for example, in the treatment of voting, political parties, and interest groups). However, the political game is structured by institutional arrangements and procedural rules, and to these this book gives emphasis.

GOVERNMENT IN THE POPULAR MEDIA

In the broadcast and print media, we often see or read about government-related issues and events — in Washington, D.C., at the United Nations, on Wall Street, or in Moscow, Tokyo, or London. Problems in the Middle East, shortages of consumer goods in Russia, debtor nation difficulties in Latin America, and other international issues often make the headlines. In election years the news media perpetuate our preoccupation with national offices. Particularly in presidential-election years, the race for the nomination, the national party conventions, the presidential debates, and the preelection polls take center stage. During other years, the television, radio, and print media may focus on struggles for control of the Senate or a party's efforts to make gains in the House of Representatives.

Furthermore, when public policy issues make the news, they often involve such national matters as the federal deficit, the struggle to control federal spending, new or renewed civil rights legislation, and the latest revisions of the farm subsidy programs. Sometimes crises or spectacular events dominate the news (for example, the savings and loan scandal, the invasions of Panama and Kuwait, the movement of troops into Somalia, or floods and tornadoes that spawn local appeals for federal relief).

One might assume, given the media's focus on American government and politics, that these are inherently national entities, but this is not the case. Rather, American government and politics, as they affect us day in and day out, are largely state and local.

GOVERNMENT IN DAILY LIFE

Consider the experience that you may have had during your first few days as a college student. You pack up your belongings and leave home, driving first on a city street and obeying city traffic policies. You then travel on a county road, built with state and county funds, before moving onto a state highway, built largely with federal money but patrolled and maintained by state employees. You might, in your haste to get to school, be the sad recipient of a citation for a violation of the state speed laws and have to go to a state court. The court would be housed in a county building, which you would get to by traveling on city streets. You might park in a city parking lot while in court. In the county building you could "wash up," using facilities, for both water and sewerage, that are attached to city facilities. If you hired a lawyer, the attorney might be a graduate of the state university school of law. The attorney would have had to pass a state bar examination. Like other professionals, including funeral directors, hairdressers, architects, nurses, social workers, and teachers, lawyers are regulated by the state.

Assuming that you avoided jail, you would need to find housing at or near the university. When initially constructed, the housing had to be in conformance with city building codes. Such codes regulate the size and placement of the structure on the lot, the electrical and plumbing systems, and, perhaps, the size and condition of the rental unit. If you have a pet, you may have to deal with a leash law, purchase a pet tag, and secure required immunization shots for the animal. If your pet runs away or gets lost, it might end up in a city or county pound. If you run and play with your pet, you may do so on city streets on your way to a city park.

You may attend classes at a state university. If you are preparing for a career in teaching, you will need to obtain state certification and will likely teach in a local government school. If instead you have chosen a medical career, you will probably study at a medical school at a state university, intern in a city, county, state, or special-district hospital, and work with equipment purchased largely with federal, state, or local government money. When you practice, many of your patients may pay for your services with government money.

On weekends, you may retreat to the beach or mountains via state or local roads and may spend time in a state or local park. When you stop for a meal, the restaurant will have been inspected by a local government health agency. If you become sick or have an accident, you will likely end up in a state or local hospital. If you stumble into serious trouble with the law, you will most likely be led to a state court or a state corrections facility.

Yet students are not the only ones whose daily lives are affected by state and local governments. Consider the experiences of a homeowner, for example. When the person's house was built initially, the size of the home, the size of the lot, and the exact location of the house on the lot were controlled in part by city or town zoning codes. In addition, the contractor had to meet city building specifications for the framing, plumbing, electricity, window and door size and placement, and the like. The contractor also had to secure a building permit and pay a variety of fees. After the house is built, the homeowner must pay property taxes — a city tax, a county tax, a school district tax, and perhaps other government taxes (such as to hospital, recreational, police, or mosquito abatement districts). The family enjoys sewer, water, and maybe even electrical services provided by the city. The children use a city pool, city library, and city ice rink. They may go to a public school. They play in county parks. If the father is a lawyer, he is licensed by the state and practices in state courts. If the mother is an accountant, she is licensed by the state and works constantly with state laws. The couple's automobiles are licensed by the state. They get licenses at the county courthouse. Their gas is taxed by the state, which returns some of the money to the cities and counties for street maintenance. If the couple owns a boat, it too is licensed by the state. If any family members hold public office or politically support someone who does, the office is probably part of a city, school district, county, or state governing body.

Families with problems may have dealings with state and local governments. Welfare programs, though administered by counties, are funded in part by the states. Almost all incarcerated Americans are in state, city, or county corrections facilities. Marriage licenses are issued by the state. Divorces are granted by state courts. Child custody rights and support payments are likewise determined by state courts.

As you can see, even though the national government dominates the media and the American consciousness, state and local government affect our daily lives in numerous ways. The national government does touch our lives in many important ways—on April 15th, in times of war, when farmers and students receive federal subsidies, scholarships, or loans—but on a daily basis we are more likely to interact with and depend on the services of state and local government.

The vast scope of state and local government is particularly evident in the size of the public work force in the United States. As Figure 1.1 shows, state and local governments employ far more Americans than the federal government. Indeed, it is at the local level that most government-related work is done and it is there that most of the growth in public employment has occurred in recent decades.

FIGURE 1.1   Public Employment in the United States, 1950–1990

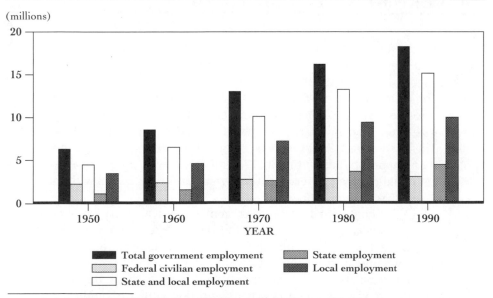

(millions)

Legend:
- Total government employment
- Federal civilian employment
- State and local employment
- State employment
- Local employment

SOURCE: *Statistical Abstract of the United States* (Washington, D.C.: Bureau of the Census, 1962), p. 431; *Statistical Abstract of the United States* (Washington, D.C.: Bureau of the Census, 1991), p. 304.

GOVERNMENT TODAY

The effects of state and local governments on Americans' lives may be even greater in the 1990s than they were in earlier decades. As Chapter 2 discusses in greater detail, in the 1980s President Ronald Reagan sought to reduce the scope of the national government's domestic programs and to give the states and localities more responsibility. Presidents Richard Nixon and Jimmy Carter had made similar attempts earlier. In some measure, their efforts have been successful; the proportion of state and local revenues from national government programs has declined from its high point in the 1970s. As a result, state and local governments are increasingly dependent on their own tax revenues.

During the past 20 years or so, state governments have gone through a process of reform and modernization that has made them more effective today. In the mid-1960s, for instance, state legislatures were reapportioned. As a result, there are now many more representatives from urban and suburban America, and the lawmaking process is no longer controlled by rural legislators representing numerical minorities. Many states have also streamlined their executive branch and courts. For these and other reasons, the state and local government units that operate today are more active and more effective problem-solving institutions than ever before.

STATE AND LOCAL GOVERNMENT IS POLITICAL

During the early decades of the twentieth century, reformers sought to alter the structure of America's cities in order to "remove politics from government." They fought, with considerable success, to replace elected mayors with hired professional city managers who would serve as the chief administrative officers, and to replace district council members elected on party tickets with council members elected from nonpartisan citywide districts. In the late 1800s and early 1900s, these so-called **Progressives** sought to curb rampant economic and political corruption by instituting multimember state-level boards and commissions that could oversee government programs and regulations without legislative or executive branch influence.

Today, the comment that "government should be run like a business," often made by newspaper editorialists and businesspeople, reflects essentially the same perspective as that embodied in the early municipal and state reforms — that government can and should function independently of politics. However, government without politics is not possible. Views such as this often fail to distinguish between that which is private and that which is public.

Governments are **public**, not private, **entities**. They belong to all of us. As individuals and groups, we differ in our opinions about what governments should do, how much governments should do, which governments should do what, and how their activities should be accomplished. We also disagree about who should pay for government. The resolution of these disagreements is necessarily political.

Politics, then, can be defined as the resolution of conflicts or disagreements over collective matters. Political questions focus our attention on the many conflicts present within government: Should cities tax and spend to build tennis courts and swimming pools or allow citizens to purchase the use of these luxuries privately at country clubs? Should cities spend public money to attract new industry through industrial parks and tax breaks or use their resources for day-care centers to help poor working families? Should schools spend more on education or on athletics and student clubs? Should state universities spend public money to support the national football and basketball leagues or should those tax dollars be spent on improving rural health care? What books should our children read in school? Should county health departments fight AIDS by giving away clean needles to drug addicts? Should the state regulation of taxi drivers, hairdressers, morticians, and teachers function to restrict entry into and competition in those fields?

These are all political questions. Government cannot be run like a business if doing so means avoiding such questions and the controversy they arouse. Nor should it be. Government's role — what it should do, when it should do it, how it should operate, whom it should serve, and whom it should tax — is based on political questions with political answers that are reached through political processes.

The political questions facing the school board members, county commissions, city councils, and legislatures of the nation's local and state governments are often difficult and contentious. Decision makers encounter unlimited demands but possess only limited resources, and face tough questions that have no readily apparent answers. State and local governments are political, for politics is the process of solving difficult conflicts. As later chapters point out, political conflicts range from questions about the structure of government and the use of public resources to who will pay the bill. Furthermore, the outcomes of the conflicts are influenced by many factors, including the organization of government itself. Governmental structures allocate public authority, public authority constitutes political power, and political power decides who gets what, when and how.

GOVERNMENTAL AUTHORITY IS DISPERSED

In the United States, there are approximately 20,000 cities, 3,000 counties, 15,000 school districts, 16,000 township governments, and 30,000 special districts (which handle, for example, sewage, trash, water, and park maintenance). These are all in addition to the 50 state governments and the national government. Clearly, the public's business is highly decentralized.

Even the existence of thousands of governing bodies does not tell the full story of political decentralization in America, as most of these governments are themselves divided. The states and many cities employ some form of separation of powers into the legislative, executive, and judicial functions. All states except Nebraska divide legislative authority between two houses. To varying degrees, the executive authority in the states is parceled out to several directly elected officials as well as to the governor. Some agencies are run by multimember boards and commissions that operate with substantial independence from gubernatorial or legislative control. Similarly, many cities and counties employ citizen boards to advise decision makers or to make authoritative decisions.

Reasons for Decentralization

The vast decentralization of public authority in the United States did not come about by accident. Our political forefathers, James Madison and others, harbored a profound suspicion of human nature. They believed that avoiding tyranny could be accomplished through a fragmented political system, one in which ambition could be countered with ambition. Thus, they viewed the concepts of federalism and separation of powers as not only comforting but convenient answers to political stalemates.

Toward the end of the 1800s, Progressive reformers sought safeguards against the political and economic abuses they had recently endured. They thus took steps to weaken the authority of legislatures and governors by creating boards and commissions. Similarly, in recent times, real estate developers and suburbanites who sought to reside outside of established city boundaries created special districts in order to provide city-type services.

U.S. government today is a highly decentralized political system. Although Americans did not at any one time choose a network of 86,000 authority-divided governing bodies, they did choose many of the features that characterize the system.

Consequences of Decentralization

The nature, extent, and consequences of institutional decentralization will become apparent in Chapter 2 and later in the text, but at this point it should be noted that certain consequences result from particular forms of decentralized organization. For example, when the separation of powers is combined with divided partisan control of the legislative and executive branches, conflict or stalemate between the governor and legislature often results. In large metropolitan areas with hundreds of semi-independent cities, counties, and special districts, providing for such services as housing and transportation can be chaotic. When cities employ nonpartisan, at-large election systems, upper-class businesspeople and professionals tend to gain more influence than voters lower in socioeconomic status. Finally, in older cities surrounded by new municipalities and special districts, discrepancies among the tax bases of the various governments often exist, so that some citizens enjoy services or levels of service that are unavailable to others.

Institutional decentralization thus has a variety of important consequences for Americans. Many of its consequences serve the intended function of decentralization—to prevent the power hungry from gaining too much power. Others do not—such as the existence of poor and wealthy school districts within the same state and the low levels of voter participation in special districts. The shape of U.S. institutions, especially their decentralization, has clear and significant impacts on the behavior of politicians and the content and consequences of public policies.

STATE AND LOCAL GOVERNMENTS: THEIR SIMILARITIES AND DIFFERENCES

The political environment and the political systems of the American states are alike in some respects and different in others. Since a detailed examination of the countless legal and political variations among the states is not possible, the book focuses on similarities and points out differences that are politically relevant. We will now consider briefly some of the characteristics that state governments share as well as some of their differences.[2]

Commonalities

American state and local governments share many historical, cultural, linguistic, and legal characteristics. All states are part of the constitutionally established federal system. They relate to the national government in the same legal fashion and are subject to the same constitutional restrictions (for example, restrictions on *ex post facto* laws and bills of attainder). Article IV of the Constitution requires each state to afford full faith and credit to the "public acts, records, and judicial proceedings of every other state."

The states also share many features related to their common northern European and British background. English, of course, is the dominant language for both written and spoken communications. British common law provides part of the basis for judicial decisions in all states except Louisiana, where French legal custom prevails. In addition, the state and local systems are structurally similar. Each state has a constitution with a bill of rights and separates the functions of government into three branches—the legislative, executive, and judicial. All states have an elaborate network of local governments and, except for Nebraska, a bicameral legislature. The states are similar in still other respects: Each state has two representatives in the Senate, spends more on education than any other activity, and encounters problems related to employment, schooling, poverty, race relations, and other issues.

The various similarities among American state and local governments make them politically alike in many ways. In these respects, it is possible to generalize about their functions.

Differences   Obvious differences exist among the states. In particular, differences in population size, population concentration, and ethnic distribution affect the politics of states and localities. In terms of population, the states differ considerably: California has 28 million inhabitants, New York 17 million, and Wyoming 500,000. As a result, public assistance programs such as welfare are more expensive in California than in Wyoming. In some states, including Illinois, Arizona, and Colorado, a large proportion of the population is concentrated in one or two major urban centers, but in other states, such as Wyoming and Vermont, the population is more scattered. In the former case, politicians need to be more concerned about urban transit, smog, housing, and the urban vote. Ethnic composition also varies among the states. For example, Hispanics are concentrated in the Southwest, while African-Americans are more likely to inhabit northern, eastern, and southern states. Some states and localities contain very small percentages of ethnic minorities.

In addition, industry, personal income, and taxes vary greatly among states and localities. In Michigan, particularly in the Detroit area, the automobile industry is critical, both politically and financially. In Montana the copper industry plays similar roles. Per-capita personal income in 1991 was nearly $22,000 in Connecticut and over $18,000 in five other states (Alaska, Hawaii, Maryland, Massachusetts, and New York), whereas it was less than $12,000 in Mississippi and under $13,000 in five other states (Arkansas, New Mexico, Oklahoma, Utah, and West Virginia). The per-capita taxes collected by the states of Alaska and Hawaii in 1991 amounted to nearly $3,000 and over $2,000, respectively, while New Hampshire collected just $538 and South Dakota a mere $699. The variations in income and taxes mean that some states can provide more services of higher quality, such as education and health care, than other states. Moreover, the states often differ in terms of election laws, in the structure of local governments, and in the nature of the tax system.

Just as the states vary in terms of their geography, industries, and wealth, so too do they differ in their political cultures, public attitudes, and public policies. According to Daniel Elazar, a professor of political science at Temple University, three political subcultures exist.[3] The **individualistic** subculture is comprised of groups that immigrated to America in search of self-advancement without government interference. They initially settled in New England and later migrated to the Midwest. The **moralistic** political subculture is made up of people who came to America with a more collective concern for their well-being and who demonstrated that concern by their community-oriented focus. They settled in the Great Lakes region and in the upper Midwest. Finally, settlers in the South brought with them a political subculture that Elazar refers to as **traditionalistic**. In a traditionalistic political culture, the status quo is the norm, while change is not. Those at the top of the social hierarchy are also dominant in government and politics.

As other sections of the nation were settled, the three political subcultures became somewhat mixed. However, recent studies by political scientists indicate that the subcultures tend to reflect regional variations in public attitudes about government and politics that translate into policy differences. (Chapters 13 through 16 examine the states' public policies in the areas of finances, education, social services, and corrections, making it clear that the American states are not alike and that their public policies vary considerably.)

The tradition, structure, and political style of state governments vary as well. In Louisiana, for example, certain instances of corruption were tolerated that would not have been permitted in North Dakota. In the South and West, most cities have adopted the city manager system and nonpartisan elections, both products of the early-twentieth-century reform movement. In eastern cities these reforms are much less prevalent. In some states, including Georgia and California, the governor derives considerable political clout from a major role in the budgeting process. In Texas and Colorado, however, the governor's role is much less central. In New Jersey, local governments and politicians strongly guard their independence from state encroachment. The funding of local government in Hawaii is largely centralized at the state level, as is political power.

Continuity and Change

In some respects American state and local governments are much as they were decades ago, whereas in other ways they have changed dramatically. All states still have three branches of government, and 49 states have had bicameral legislatures since statehood. In addition, local governments continue to be subordinate to the state government, and the states' constitutional relationship with the federal government has not changed. Finally, two major political parties still dominate U.S. politics.

However, state and local governments have undergone several major changes, many of which have had lasting and significant consequences. Following a period of economic growth, change, and corrupt politics as practiced by some wealthy industrialists in the late 1800s, populist and Progressive reformers successfully fought back with a host of political reforms, including the adoption by many state and local governments of the initiative and the referendum. These devices give the individual citizen a direct role in lawmaking. Civil service replaced the spoils system, in which government jobs were dispensed on the basis of political considerations. Locally, reforms brought the city manager system and nonpartisan, at-large elections, replacing the machine, the elected mayor, the political party, and the ward.

More recent changes of major consequence have involved state–nation relations and the vitality of state governments. Following several decades of increasing amounts of federal money being transferred to states and localities to support a variety of programs, the tide turned in 1980 when the Reagan administration required states to rely more on their own tax resources. The modernization of state institutions, particularly the legislature, began in the 1960s and has made state governments more active and more responsive to contemporary problems and needs. In these major ways, then, state and local government units operate differently than they did in the past.

SUMMARY

The United States has more than 86,000 governing bodies, including state, local, city, and county governments as well as school districts and special districts. The American political system is highly decentralized.

Most services are provided by state and local governments, and Americans are most likely to have contact with government at the state and local levels. These government units provide for such services as education, water, sewers, streets, police and fire protection, parks, and prisons. They regulate businesses, utilities, and the professions; maintain vital statistics; and conduct elections.

The highly decentralized nature of the U.S. government system has advantages and disadvantages. Dispersed power helps guard against tyranny and provides extensive citizen access to government as well as opportunities for participation. However, decentralization makes planning and problem solving difficult, can confuse citizens' understanding of the government system, and causes inequalities in the quality and quantity of services available to Americans.

What state and local government units do is necessarily political in nature. People want different things from their government, and disagreements must be worked out by government through political processes—debate, compromise, and voting.

The shape of the American institutional apparatus structures American politics. At the same time, politics helps to determine government structures. Institutions determine areas of authority and the processes by which decisions can be made. Power struggles over the shape of governments occur, and the particular configuration helps to determine who wins and who loses. The areas of power and the rules of the game, in turn, dictate appropriate political strategies and behavior. The structure of national–state–local relations, the division of authority through the separation of powers, bicameralism, the plural executive, boards and commissions, legislative committee systems, the proliferation of local governments, and still other structural characteristics of American institutions determine in large measure what governments do and how they behave politically.

This book pays special attention to U.S. institutions for two reasons. First, we cannot hope to understand the American political system without first knowing something about the governments that make up that system — their functions, their organization, and their structural relationship to one another. Second, an appreciation of the patterns of political behavior requires an understanding of why politicians and the public act in certain ways. Their behaviors are in large part determined by the organization of authority in government institutions.

KEY TERMS

Progressives
public entity
politics

individualistic political culture
moralistic political culture
traditionalistic political culture

NOTES

1. Alice M. Rivlin, "Wanted: A New State-Level Tax to Prepare Us for the Twenty-First Century," *Governing* (April 1990): 74.

2. A variety of statistical data on the American states is reported semiannually in *The Book of the States* (Lexington, Ky.: Council of State Governments). Data on the state and national governments can be found in various U.S. government publications; for example, the *Statistical Abstract of the United States* (Washington, D.C.: Bureau of the Census) is published annually and is available in the reference section of most libraries.

3. Daniel J. Elazar, *American Federalism: A View from the States*, 3rd ed. (New York: Harper & Row, 1984), chapter 5 especially.

2

The Organization of American Governments

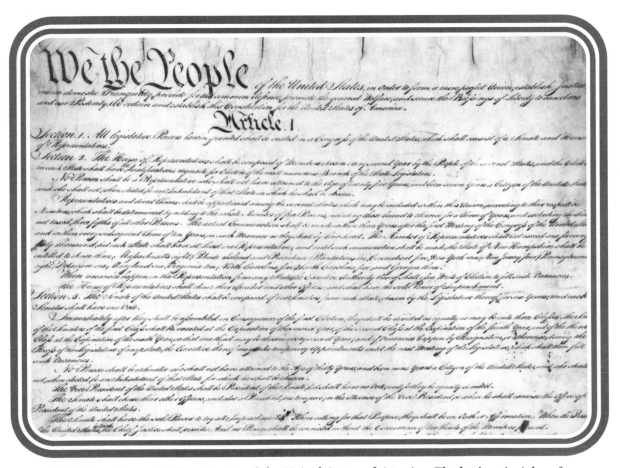

The Preamble to the Constitution of the United States of America. The basic principles of federalism are set forth in the Constitution.

In the summer of 1990, a Utah resident was wanted by the police for a robbery allegedly committed in Lawrence, Kansas. The fugitive was stopped by a Wyoming state patrol officer, who shot the suspect in the head as he emerged from his car carrying an AK-47 assault rifle. He was hospitalized in Laramie, Wyoming, but was later brought by a Wyoming county sheriff to a hospital with better facilities, in Fort Collins, Colorado. The hospital was operated by a special hospital district. The Wyoming authorities then left the fugitive, who was unconscious, unattended, and returned to Wyoming. The Fort Collins police and the sheriff of Larimer County, Colorado, had to guard him, and the local hospital had to pay for expensive medical treatment. Wyoming authorities washed their hands of responsibility. The Kansas authorities said they wanted the fugitive extradited to them, but not until his medical condition improved.

Every year in April, Kathy and Steve of Canyon Country, California, file their income taxes with the federal government. At the same time, they file their California state income tax returns. Also, each spring their mortgage company sends the Los Angeles County treasurer money to cover Kathy and Steve's property taxes (see Figure 2.1). They have paid a little of this money to the company each month as part of their total mortgage payment. The treasurer disperses portions of the property tax funds to the local governments within whose jurisdictions Kathy and Steve reside. These include, they have discovered, Los Angeles County, the schools, the city, a flood control district, a water district, and a sanitation district. In addition, Kathy and Steve pay special additional levies (voted for by the citizens) to the city for lighting, flood control, sewer maintenance, and sanitation.

ORGANIZING GOVERNMENT

When Americans talk about government it is often in the singular: The government did this or that; "government is necessary"; "the less government the better"; "a government investigation is needed"; or "the government should mind its own business." While opinions about government vary, often they are directed at *the* government. However, the United States has not one government but more than 86,000 governing bodies (see Chapter 1). As the preceding accounts demonstrate, the American system of government is highly decentralized; the authority and responsibility for public affairs are widely dispersed. The case of the fugitive involved four states, two counties, a city, a special district, and the question of who would pay the hospital bill. When Kathy and Steve pay taxes, they are interacting with a national government, a state government, a county government, a city government, and a host of other governments. Table 2.1 outlines the number and types of U.S. governments.

In the area of public policy especially, the decentralized institutional arrangement employed in the United States has far-reaching consequences. Levels

FIGURE 2.1 Sample Property Tax Bill—Los Angeles County, California

1992

JOINT CONSOLIDATED ANNUAL TAX BILL

CITIES, COUNTY SCHOOLS AND ALL OTHER TAXING AGENCIES IN LOS ANGELES COUNTY
SECURED PROPERTY TAX FOR FISCAL YEAR JULY 1, 1992 TO JUNE 30, 1993
SANDRA M. DAVIS, TREASURER AND TAX COLLECTOR

COUNTY OF LOS ANGELES

1992

OWNER OF RECORD AS OF MARCH 1, 1992
SAME AS BELOW

ACCOUNT NO	PRINT NO	REG	OPTION INFO BATCH NO	Year	Seq. No.	Map Book	Page	Parcel	TRA
				92	000				

PROPERTY LOCATION AND / OR PROPERTY DESCRIPTION

	CURRENT ASSESSED VALUE		TAXABLE VALUE
ROLL YEAR 92–93			
LAND	101769		101769
IMPROVEMENTS	106545		106545
FIXTURE			
		TOTAL	208314
		LESS EXEMPTION HOME	7000
		NET TAXABLE VALUE	201314

DETAIL OF TAXES DUE	RATE	AMOUNT
GENERAL TAX LEVY ALL AGENCIES	1 000000	2013 14
VOTED INDEBTEDNESS		
COUNTY	001409	2 84
SPECIAL WATER	037437	75 36
SANITATION DIST	001363	2 84
FLOOD CONTROL	003397	7 07
COMMNTY COLLEGE	002654	5 34
HIGH SCHOOLS	002627	5 29
DIRECT ASSESSMENTS		
CONS SEWER MAINT		14 50
SAN DISTRICT 26		59 40
MOSQUITO ABATE		2 10
STA CLARITA LTG		5 08
FLOOD CONTROL		30 18
CFPD-BENEFIT ASM		43 09
FIRST INSTALLMENT TAXES DUE		1133 08
SECOND INSTALLMENT TAXES DUE		1133 07
TOTAL TAXES DUE		2266 15

THERE WILL BE A $49.85 SERVICE CHARGE, FOR ANY CHECK RETURNED BY THE BANK.
KEEP THIS UPPER PORTION FOR YOUR RECORDS , YOUR CANCELLED CHECK IS YOUR RECEIPT

BEFORE CALLING A COUNTY OFFICE
SEE REVERSE SIDE FOR
IMPORTANT TAXPAYER INFORMATION

TABLE 2.1 American Governments

Type of Government	Number	
	1977	*1987*
Federal government	1	1
State governments	50	50
Local governments	79,862	83,186
Counties	3,042	3,042
Municipalities	18,862	19,200
Townships	16,822	16,691
School districts	15,174	14,721
Special districts	25,962	29,532
Total	79,913	83,237

Source: *Municipal Year Book* (Washington, D.C.: International City Management Association, 1990), p. xiii.

of taxes and of public service vary widely among states and among jurisdictions within states. The presence of thousands of governments means there are tens of thousands of opportunities for citizens to hold public office. However, it also makes coordinated problem solving difficult, and the large numbers of elections and offices can confuse voters. The division of authority between (1) a central (national) government and (2) the state governments and their tens of thousands of political subdivisions makes intergovernmental struggles for power an ongoing part of the U.S. political environment.

This chapter examines the institutional framework of the American political system. The relationship between the national government and the states has changed considerably over the years, and especially during the last four decades. In addition, the relationship of local governments to the states is unlike that which exists between the national government and the states.

ALTERNATIVE ORGANIZATIONAL FORMATS

The governments of nations around the globe are structured in a variety of ways. In some nations, decisions are made by a central government and carried out by a network of regional or local administrative departments. In other nations, decisions are both made and carried out by regional or local units. In still others, decisions are made centrally and administered locally, made locally and carried out locally, or made centrally and administered centrally. There are advantages and disadvantages to each of the three organizational patterns, which are termed *centralization*, *decentralization*, and *federalism*, a mixture of the other two.

In a **centralized**, or **unitary, system** of organization, decision-making **Centralization** authority, or sovereignty, is located in the central government. Most important decisions are made by the central government and are administered by its administrative arms — regional units (called states, prefects, or districts) or regional suboffices of an agency or department of the central government. However they are arranged or termed, the critical point is that decision-making authority resides in a central decision-making unit and the subunits exercise only those powers authorized by the main unit. In Great Britain and France, for example, the unitary system is employed. Although both countries have regional and local units of government, these subunits are not given the authority to make independent decisions. Their organizational structure, functions, duties, operating procedures, and personnel are controlled by the central decision-making unit. Alex N. Dragnich describes the arrangement in Great Britain in this way:

> The central government exercises three types of control over local authorities. The first is legal: Parliament can grant powers to local authorities and it can take them away. The second is financial: the national government provides over half the funds needed by local authorities and in large measure specifies the ways in which they are to be spent. The third is supervisory: various national ministries, through various statutory instruments, memoranda, inspectors and district auditors and also through their power to approve or disapprove local proposals in many areas of activity, influence and control the work of local government. The Home Secretary, for example, has significant supervisory powers over the police and the Minister of Education over the schools.[1]

Advantages of Centralization There are both advantages and disadvantages associated with the centralized or unitary system of government. On the positive side, centralization can be effective in solving problems that affect people in large geographic areas and in coordinating public programs. Air pollution, poor water quality, and unemployment are examples of problems that can affect many people in diverse areas; it is difficult to remedy such problems on a local or piecemeal basis. Thus, in these cases, an organizational scheme that permits decisions to be made by a central authority makes it easier for the government to develop and coordinate programs for dealing with the problems and for providing needed services. Centralization may also preclude the pursuit by various independent regional government units of contradictory policies on the same issue. (For example, without a centralized system, one government's policy may serve to increase unemployment whereas another government's policy may function to raise employment.)

Disadvantages of Centralization Centralization can create difficulties as well. Large centralized governments have the potential for becoming highly bureaucratic, impersonal, and unresponsive to local concerns. Although this is not always the case, for those who value small, proximate, and highly sensitive government, the vast size of the centralized government represents a definite disadvantage. When considerable discretion is not given to regional or local administrative units, for example, local problems (with sewer or water service, roads, parks, or public assistance, for example) may have to be communicated through numerous layers of the large bureaucracy before responses are received. This can be a time-consuming process; the time involved and the distant relationship can cause the main decision makers to see a distorted picture of the actual local problems and to give inappropriate responses. Some administrators may even deliberately use the complexity of the unitary system to delay or avoid responding. As a result, local citizens become frustrated and lose confidence in their government.

The centralized system is easier to establish and operate in some countries than in others. In countries with a common heritage, culture, and language, where racial, ethnic, and religious variations do not divide the population, and where people are not isolated geographically from others, centralization may be established and function with little or no difficulty. However, in countries where there are many segments of society and where people differ significantly in terms of language, race, religion, culture, and history, or where they are separated geographically, it is more difficult to unite the people under a centralized system of government. Centralization at the expense of local autonomy is not a problem in homogeneous societies. But in many nations, where regional or tribal ties are very strong, it is difficult to fabricate a new nation out of previously isolated or independent units. The recent struggles for regional independence within the former Soviet Union and what was once Yugoslavia illustrate the difficulty of politically centralizing diverse peoples. Still, the vast majority of the more than 150 nation-states in existence today are unitary, as are all 50 American states.

Decentralization

The **decentralized system** of government organization differs in many respects from the centralized scheme. Here, the sovereign authority to make policy decisions on most matters resides with the regional or local units. Like the Continental Congress of the formative years of the American Union, the central government in a decentralized system may represent the unity and purpose of member units and thereby have symbolic significance. It may also serve to enhance communication and program coordination among the member units. However, the local or regional units remain sovereign. Under a decentralized plan, the member units and the central unit relate to one another in a loose, leaguelike arrangement in which the central unit has no legally binding powers over the local or regional units.

The United States as it existed under the Articles of Confederation provides an excellent example of a decentralized nation. Following the American

War of Independence, neither public opinion nor the political alignment allowed government authority to be centralized. The best that could be achieved politically was a very loose, decentralized organization of the states. Today, the United Nations provides an example of a decentralized, or confederal, structure. Although its formation cannot be considered an attempt at global governmental unity, the use of the Security Council veto and the United Nations' limited success in its peacekeeping efforts illustrate the difficulties involved in combining peoples with different social, ethnic, and religious characteristics into a single system of government.

Federalism — A Compromise

Federalism represents a compromise between centralization and decentralization. It divides sovereignty between a central government and its subunits, such as states. A situation may arise, as it did under the Articles of Confederation, in which decentralization leads to unacceptable chaos but the formation of a strong central government remains politically infeasible. A workable compromise may be found by assigning to a central government those functions that cannot be conveniently performed on a local or regional basis (for example, national defense) and leaving certain other functions in the hands of the localities (for example, police and fire protection). Federalism may thus provide enough centralization and coordination to avoid conflict or chaos in domestic or international relations, as well as help to avoid political problems resulting from attempts to compromise the integrity of local or regional units. Although the compromise arrangement of federalism can blend degrees of centralization and decentralization, it can also make it difficult to resolve jurisdictional conflicts between the center and the regions. In many cases, the center gradually preempts the prerogatives of the regional units, and the system becomes centralized in a *de facto* sense.

THE AMERICAN ORGANIZATIONAL FRAMEWORK

Federalism is an important part of American political history. Today we have what is sometimes called **coercive federalism**, in which the central unit employs its fiscal and constitutional powers to subordinate the state and local units. However, this was not always the case.

For 150 years the states and the national government functioned in parallel fashion. Beginning in the 1930s and increasingly in recent decades, the central unit has wielded power over the states, while at the same time curtailing what had been a growing flow of federal dollars to help support state and local programs, many of which were begun with federal money as the stimulus (see Table 2.2).

TABLE 2.2 Three Brands of Federalism

	Basic Responsibilities		
	National	*State/Local*	*Characteristics*
Dual federalism (1789–1930s)	National defense Regulation of commerce Post offices and roads Immigration Currency Foreign policy	Public health Public safety (police, fire) Public utilities (sewers, water) Public education	National and state/local governments function in largely separate, independent fashion. Minimal interaction.
Cooperative federalism (1930s–1960s)	National defense Regulation of commerce Post offices and roads Immigration Currency Foreign policy	Public health Public safety (police, fire) Public utilities (sewers, water) Public education	More and more national programs are developed that provide financial support for state/local activities, with a few conditions attached to use of funds (e.g., for education, social services, highways).
Coercive federalism (1970s–)	National defense Regulation of commerce Post offices and roads Immigration Currency Foreign policy	Public health Public safety (police, fire) Public utilities (sewers, water) Public education	Flow of national government aid to states and localities slows; use of spending power to impose national policy objectives (e.g., speed limit, drinking age, drug use penalties, air and water clean-up) on states and localities accelerates greatly.

In order to understand the American organizational framework, we need first to examine the background and structure of that system as it was initially framed. We also need to trace the changes that have occurred over the years.

Background The relationship that exists between the national government and the states is federal in nature; that is, it represents a compromise between centralization and decentralization. In contrast, the relationship that exists between the states and local governments is unitary in nature; in other words, it is centralized.

The Articles of Confederation The first official organization of the American states was accomplished through the **Articles of Confederation**, which brought the thirteen American colonies together in a loosely knit confederation. Written in 1776 and legally ratified in 1781, the confederation plan remained in effect until it was replaced in 1789 by the current U.S. Constitution. However, the loose union created by the Articles of Confederation led to a host of organizational and operating problems for the thirteen states, and the perceived need to remedy many of those problems had a profound impact on the nature, formation, and adoption of the Constitution.

The Articles of Confederation established a unicameral Congress as the legislative or policymaking body for the loose union of the thirteen states. Each state had only one vote in Congress, though it could send a multiple-member delegation if it so desired. The unicameral body constituted the only branch of the central government—there were no executive and judiciary branches. From time to time the Congress set up *ad hoc* executive committees to administer programs, but there was no permanent executive branch to implement congressional decisions. Likewise, there was no judicial branch to resolve disputes between the states or jurisdictional quarrels between the Congress and the various states. Finally, the Congress did not have the authority to act directly on individual citizens but instead found it necessary to go through the states. Thus, to enforce laws or collect taxes, it had to gain the cooperation of the individual states—a situation that, in effect, gave each state the power to veto actions proposed by the Congress.

As in all confederations, the central organ of government was weak; and, in the case of the thirteen states, this weakness led to several problems. First, the Union was financially weak. Debts remained from the revolutionary war, and the Continental Congress found it hard to collect the taxes to pay the debts. In addition, its inability to regulate commercial relations among the states resulted in chaotic interstate commerce. States often refused to cooperate with other states and, in some cases, even erected interstate trade barriers. The lack of unity among the states and the weakness of the center made international dealings with such nations as England, France, and Spain difficult and placed the fledgling Union at a comparative political disadvantage—the Congress simply could not speak with authority for the consortium of states. On the western frontier there was dissatisfaction as a result of a perceived failure by the Congress to provide protection against the Native American population. The inability of the Congress to act directly upon citizens made tax collection and program implementation difficult. Finally, the operations of the Congress were hampered by certain requirements of the Articles of Confederation—that laws be passed by an abnormal majority of at least nine of the thirteen states and that amendments to the articles be made by unanimous vote.

The U.S. Constitution   The **U.S. Constitution**, written in 1787 and ratified in 1789, was in large part intended to remedy the problems confronting the Union. It contained provisions for the establishment of the executive and judicial branches of government, for more central and forceful conduct of international relations, for more orderly interstate trade relations, and for the direct enforcement of laws and implementation of programs by the central government vis-à-vis the citizen.

In many respects, however, the new Constitution was a compromise. The most important long-term compromise was the blending of centralized and decentralized government styles. The Constitution established a central government to perform one set of functions and left to the state governments the performance of other functions. Federalism thus emerged, characterized by dual, or divided, sovereignty.

The federal scheme was a workable compromise between two contending forces. On the one hand, there existed a clear need to centralize the power to conduct foreign relations, regulate interstate commerce, and collect taxes. On the other hand, the experience with British control, the prior existence of operating units of state government, and the desire for independence created by revolutionary war rhetoric made the abolition of the states in favor of a centralized scheme impossible. The states already existed, they had a structure, they carried on programs, and each had a battery of public officials and government employees — people who would not easily agree to the abolition of their government. Likewise, propaganda designed to whip up the revolutionary drive for independence and to support the war against England was not easily forgotten, and the colonists were highly suspicious of a centrally controlled government scheme. Thus, the federal arrangement provided a workable compromise. The states were retained, but certain critical functions, such as the regulation of interstate commerce and the conduct of foreign affairs, were transferred to a strengthened central government.

The Constitution became the supreme law of the land. It provided in general terms for the establishment of a central or national government, and it recognized the existence of the state governments. It established in skeleton form the structure of the national government. It specified in general terms the powers of the national and state governments, and it identified the activities in which neither the national nor the state governments could engage. As the supreme law of the land, the Constitution took precedence over any national government statute, any administrative edict, any action by public officials of the national and state governments, and any state constitutional provision, statute, or administrative edict.

Federalism: National and State Relations

The federal system that the Constitution established may be defined as follows: It contains two levels of government — national and state — that exist side by side, neither being a creature of the other but both being subordinate to the legal authority of the Constitution. Each level of government is sovereign; that is, each exercises authority that the other does not.

Figure 2.2 depicts the national government – state government relationship of the federal system. As the figure shows, the sovereign people acted to establish a basic law (or contract) known as the Constitution; the Constitution, in turn, legally established a dual system of government; and each level of government was designed to relate directly to each individual citizen. However,

FIGURE 2.2   The Federal System

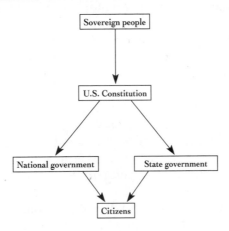

it should be noted that the Americans living today do not constitute the "sovereign people" who initially agreed to the federal arrangement. Figure 2.2 depicts, in theoretical terms, the relationships among the people, the Constitution, and the two levels of government.

Expressed Powers of the National Government   The Constitution explicitly details the legal or **expressed powers** of the national government and a number of activities in which the national government and the state governments may not engage. It is not as explicit, however, in detailing the legal powers of the states. The various powers and limitations outlined by the Constitution are shown in Table 2.3.

The Constitution established the three-branch structure of the national government. Article I established the **legislative branch**—a bicameral (two-house) legislature with representation in one house (the lower house) based on a state's population, and with each state, regardless of its geographic size or population, holding two seats in the upper house, or Senate. Article I also stipulates that representatives in the lower house be elected by the people and

TABLE 2.3
The U.S. Constitution: Legal Powers
of National and State Governments

National Government	State Governments	Intergovernmental Relations
Expressed powers	Reserved powers	National supremacy
Implied powers	Powers denied	Full faith and credit
Inherent powers		
Powers denied		

serve two-year terms, and that those in the upper house be selected by the legislatures of the various states and serve six-year terms. As a result of the Seventeenth Amendment, however, senators in all states are now popularly elected.

Article II of the Constitution established the **executive branch** of the national government. It also vests the power of the executive branch in the president and confers upon the president various powers and duties. Finally, the Constitution created a court system known as the **judicial branch**. Article III stipulates the establishment of the Supreme Court and empowers Congress to create lower courts as it deems necessary.

In most other respects, however, the Constitution does not provide much detail about the structure of the national government. As a result, congressional statutes and administrative orders have formed most of the vast national government apparatus.

The Constitution confers on the national government, in explicit terms, the authority to perform certain functions. For example, in Article I, Section 8, Congress is given the authority to lay and collect taxes, to borrow money, to regulate commerce with foreign nations and between the states, to constitute courts inferior to the Supreme Court, and to raise and support the armed forces, among a series of other expressly delegated powers. Also in Article I, the Constitution gives Congress the authority to "make all Laws which shall be necessary and proper for carrying into Execution the foregoing Powers, and all other Powers vested by this Constitution in the Government of the United States, or in any Department or Officer thereof."

Implied Powers of the National Government   The activities of the national government have expanded over time, in part because of technological advances and changing socioeconomic conditions, and in part because the Supreme Court has supported increased government activity in its interpretations of the Constitution. Historically, the Supreme Court has defined the constitutional authority of the national government broadly, thus giving rise to what are called the **implied powers** of the national government.

In the landmark case of ***McCulloch v. Maryland*** (1819), Chief Justice John Marshall, citing the "necessary and proper" clause of Article I, Section 8 of the Constitution, held that the national government could legally establish a national bank system because such a system would be an implied instrument for the implementation of the government's explicit authority to "coin money and regulate the value thereof." Further, Marshall said that the state of Maryland could not impose a property tax on the national bank property in Baltimore. Marshall, a federalist and an advocate of a strong central government, suggested that the expressed powers found in the Constitution be viewed as the ends or goals of the national government, and that any means necessary to reach those goals and not prohibited by the Constitution be considered constitutional. Although the *McCulloch* case is often cited in connection with the development of the national government's implied powers, changing conditions and a host of subsequent Supreme Court decisions that broadly interpreted the authority of the national government also contributed to the vast expansion of national activity.

Inherent Powers of the National Government　In addition to its expressed and implied powers, the national government exercises what are called **inherent powers**. The national government and the president in particular possess full constitutional authority to conduct foreign relations and enter into treaties. In the case of *United States v. Curtis-Wright Export Corporation* (1936), the Supreme Court strongly affirmed the inherent powers of the national government in foreign affairs, noting that such powers are inherent because of the United States' membership in the family of nations.

Interstate and State-National Relations　As noted earlier in the chapter, the Constitution does not include provisions for the structure of state governments or state authority. It does, however, deny certain powers to the states, address the subject of interstate and state-national relations, and provide a series of guarantees to the states. The one constitutional provision that deals affirmatively with the authority of the states is in the Tenth Amendment: "The powers not delegated to the United States by the Constitution, nor prohibited by it to the States, are reserved to the States respectively, or to the people." Because of the wording of this amendment, the states are generally said to possess **reserved powers**. Article I, sections 9 and 10 of the Constitution list a series of **powers denied** the states and the national government, including the power to enter into a treaty, to coin money, and to pass bills of attainder or *ex post facto* laws (criminal laws that are applied retroactively).

On the subject of interstate relations, Article IV of the Constitution is fairly elaborate. Section 1 of this article orders the states to grant "**full faith and credit**" to the public acts, records, and judicial proceedings of every other state. Section 2 commands each state to grant its "privileges and immunities" to the citizens of all other states and charges each state with the duty of rendering up to other states fugitives from the law (a provision with which states do not always comply).

Article IV is of considerable importance because it requires that states enforce their laws impartially, treating their own citizens and citizens of other states as equals in most areas. Deeds, contracts, wills, and other legal documents from one state must be honored in all other states. Although states can have their own legal provisions in such areas as residence requirements for voting, driver's licenses, out-of-state tuition rates for colleges and universities, and marriage laws, they nearly always administer them in a reasonable fashion. States allow, for example, drivers from other states to pass through with a driver's license and registration plates from their home state, and they recognize marriage and birth certificates from other states. From time to time problems may arise, however; for example, there was a time when North Carolina refused to recognize a Nevada divorce decree. In most cases, though, the states adhere to the requirements of "full faith and credit" and "privileges and immunities" stipulated in Article IV.

National Supremacy and Guarantees   Whereas Article IV of the Constitution structures the relationships among the states, Article VI specifies the relationship between the states and the national government. It reads, in part:

> This Constitution, and the Laws of the United States which shall be made in Pursuance thereof; and all Treaties made, or which shall be made, under the Authority of the United States, shall be the supreme Law of the Land; and the Judges of every State shall be bound thereby, any Thing in the Constitution or Laws of the State to the Contrary notwithstanding.

This provision, often referred to as the **national supremacy** clause, specifies that no state laws may conflict in any way with national government laws that are constitutional, with provisions of the Constitution, or with the provisions of treaties. For example, in *Missouri v. Holland* (1920), the Supreme Court held that the national government could write legislation based on the provisions of a treaty (in this case, a treaty related to the international protection of migratory birds), and that a state may not ignore or contradict such a law. Treaty-based legislation is, thus, constitutional even if the same legislation would be unconstitutional in the absence of the treaty.

Although the states have extensive authority through their reserved powers and their range of activity is very extensive, in a head-on clash of the laws of the national government and the laws of a state, Article VI of the Constitution provides for national supremacy if the Supreme Court deems the national law constitutional.

Finally, the Constitution provides a series of **guarantees** to the states in Article IV, which specifies that no state may be split so as to form another state without the consent of Congress and of both states involved. The article also commands the national government to protect the states from invasion and requires the national government to guarantee every state a republican form of government—that is, one based on the consent and representation of the people.

The Constitution as Compromise   As suggested at the outset of the discussion of federalism, the Constitution represents a compromise by its authors as they sought to cope with pressing problems. The states already existed, so their elimination was not politically feasible. At the same time, a lack of strong central direction caused the consortium of new states a host of irritating problems. The solution was to retain the states and let them continue to perform most of their traditional functions (such as the maintenance of local law and order), but at the same time create a central government to handle problems and services that demanded centralized decision making (such as the regulation of interstate commercial relations). Federalism, therefore, provided a mixture of centralization and decentralization and maintained the political integrity of both central and regional governments.

The process for amending the Constitution illustrates the legal relationship between the national government and the states. The amending process most often used involves the initiation of a proposed constitutional change by the national government—by a two-thirds vote in both houses of Congress and subsequent ratification by the legislatures of three-fourths of the states. Constitutional amendments may also be proposed by a national convention, called by Congress at the request of two-thirds of the states; again, ratification must be by legislative action or special conventions in three-fourths of the states. Whatever process is employed, both the national government and the state governments must be parties to the constitutional change. Neither unit of government can unilaterally amend the Constitution or increase or decrease the powers, duties, or limitations of the other. Rather, they are partners in the sense that they are equally bound to the legal authority of the Constitution.

A Unitary System: State and Local Relations

The legal relationship between state and local governments is very different from that of the national government and the states. Whereas the national government and the states are partners, both bound by the Constitution and both sovereign, all units of local government are part of and subordinate to the states. State governments create local governments; assign powers, duties, and limits to local governments; and, if they wish, may legally abolish local governments. In other words, local governments (counties, cities, townships) are subdivisions or administrative arms of the state.

State constitutions and statutes demonstrate this superior–inferior legal relationship. All state constitutions provide for the existence of local units. In some cases local governments are given some of their legal authority in constitutional home-rule provisions, but in most cases local governments are assigned their powers and duties and have limits imposed on them by state statutes— acts of the state legislature.

Legal Relations   A generalized model of the legal relations between the state and local governments is as follows: First, the constitution of the state provides for the existence of county governments, school district governments, special district governments (for example, water, sewer, and recreation districts), and city and town governments. It may specify the structure of county government, the number of members in and the terms of office for the county board of supervisors, and county duties (such as maintaining vital statistics and records). In addition, the state constitution may empower the legislature to grant home rule to cities and counties; that is, to allow them, by statute, to tailor their own government structure and range of functions. In reference to schools, the constitution may call for the establishment, by legislative statute, of a system of free and compulsory schools to be managed by local school districts and supervised by a state board of education. Regarding towns and cities, the constitution may instruct the legislature to classify towns and cities according to size, and to prescribe for each size its structure, powers, duties, and limitations. It may order the legislature to do likewise for special districts.

Furthermore, the state constitution may contain a variety of other provisions that affect the operations of local governments. It may, for example, restrict state and local governments by establishing in a bill of rights such basic freedoms as those of speech, press, assembly, and religion. In the area of taxation, the constitution may limit the kinds of taxes that local governments can collect and the rates they can impose. For example, the constitution may forbid local governments to impose an income tax or may limit the use of the property tax to a specified rate.

Other than providing for the creation and operation of local governments and the occasional prescription of structural features, state constitutions generally leave the detailed specifications of local government structure, powers, duties, and limits to the state legislatures. Thus, one must look to the statutes of a state for detailed descriptions of its local governments. Whether found in state constitutions or statutes, the laws regarding local governments tend to be restrictive.

Local Governments and Dillon's Rule   As noted earlier in the chapter, the federal courts tend to accord a broad interpretation of the constitutional powers of the national government. For local government, however, the tendency is in the opposite direction. The propensity for narrow court interpretations of local government powers is termed **Dillon's rule** after an Iowa judge named John F. Dillon, who stated:

> It is a general and undisputed proposition of law that a municipal corporation possesses and can exercise the following powers, and no others: First, those granted in express words; second, those necessarily or fairly implied in or incident to the powers expressly granted; third, those essential to the accomplishment of the declared objects and purposes of the corporation, — not simply convenient, but indispensable. Any fair, reasonable, substantial doubt concerning the existence of power is resolved by the courts against the corporation, and the power is denied.[2]

Although it is argued by some that the tendency of the courts to be strict in their interpretations of local government powers is shifting toward a liberal direction, there is no evidence of dramatic change. Local governments remain the legal children of the state. They were created by the state, they receive their instructions from the state, and they may do only what the state permits through its statutes and constitution. Occasionally, state courts interpret municipal home-rule laws, which grant cities greater discretion over governance, in ways that give cities some independence from their state. But even home-rule laws are state laws. State–local relations are still much as Judge Dillon described them.

Finally, whereas an amendment to the Constitution must be approved by both partners of the federal union—the national government and the states—local governments do not play a similar role in their relationship with the states. The constitutional powers, duties, limits, and geographic boundaries of the states cannot be altered without their consent. In contrast, local governments have no opportunity to alter proposed state constitutional changes. The state legislature plays a role, as do the voters of a state, but local governments do not.

INTERGOVERNMENTAL RELATIONS

The relationships that exist among the various levels of American government provide a legal picture of intergovernmental relations, but there are also many important modern-day realities to consider. From an examination of the legal nature of the federal system and the unitary relationship that exists between state and local governments, it may seem that each of the three levels of government operates independently of the other units. However, this is not how American government operates.

From the Founding to the 1960s

Intergovernmental relations in the latter half of the twentieth century have been characterized by the existence of an elaborate and complicated maze of legal and financial ties among national, state, and local units of government. By the 1970s this maze had become so complex that a succession of presidents—Nixon, Carter, Reagan, and Bush—sought to simplify it and restore some independence to the states.

The Impact of Federal Grants The instrument most responsible for the development of complex legal and financial ties is the national government's grants-in-aid program. **Grants-in-aid** are funds that the federal government makes available to state and local governments for support of state and local programs. Some grants are **categorical grants** and are used for narrowly defined purposes. Others are **block grants**, meaning that state and local governments have some discretion in the use of the funds. Today, almost every sphere of governmental activity—from the construction of sewer systems and golf courses to the training of police officers—involves cooperative programs among the different levels of government.

Intergovernmental relations have undergone dramatic changes over time, including, especially, increased interaction between the national government and the state and local units. The financial scope of national government grants-in-aid to state and local governments has increased over the past several decades, and cooperative programs now involve the national government in a wide array of activities and services (see Table 2.4).

Several observations may be made concerning grant-in-aid programs and their growth. It is clear that the dollar volume of the programs is large. Growth was especially dramatic between the 1930s and the 1970s but has since slowed. Moreover, not all national government money finds its way into state and local coffers in large blocks of cash. Instead, hundreds of categorical grant programs exist, each created by some act of Congress and each designed to help state or local government solve a particular problem or set of problems. There are programs to help local schools purchase student lunches, to help colleges and universities conduct research, and to help cities improve older neighborhoods, among hundreds of other programs designed to help the states and localities attack various problems.

A More Complex System   Not surprisingly, the federal grant system is confusing and unwieldy. The programs are so numerous and complicated that many colleges, universities, state agencies, and local governments employ people just to keep track of the programs that might be of benefit.

Most importantly, however, grant programs have brought the various levels of government together into a complicated set of legal and financial relationships. Unlike in the past, when the various units and levels of government could go about their business relatively unaffected by other governments, today's city, county, special district, state, and national bureaucracies must interact constantly with their counterparts in agencies of other governments. Moreover, federal money, or incentives, have the effect of speeding up states' adoption of new and innovative policies.[3]

TABLE 2.4
Federal Aid to State and Local Governments, 1970–1990

Type of Federal Aid	Dollars Spent (in $ millions)		
	1970	1980	1991
Total grants and shared revenues	$24,065	$91,451	$152,017
National defense	37	93	185
Natural resources and environment	411	5,363	4,040
Energy	25	499	457
Agriculture	664	569	1,220
Transportation	4,599	13,087	19,878
Community and regional development	1,780	6,486	4,273
Education, employment, training, social services	6,417	21,862	26,020
Health	3,849	15,758	55,783
Income security	5,795	18,495	36,856

Source: U.S. Bureau of the Census, *Statistical Abstract of the United States, 1992* (Washington, D.C.: GPO, 1992), p. 282.

Why the Change? A number of factors contributed to the development of the massive network of intergovernmental relationships that exists today. The historical propensity of the Supreme Court to interpret the authority of the national government liberally made it legally possible for Congress to create various kinds of grant programs. As noted earlier in the chapter, Chief Justice John Marshall began this trend with his ruling in *McCulloch v. Maryland* (1819). The grant programs are based on the constitutional authority of Congress to spend money, including money earmarked to support state and local activities.

In addition, the grant programs emerged as the national government sought to deal with problems related to the failure of the states to come to grips with urban issues during the Great Depression of the 1930s and the later period of rapid urbanization (from about 1950 to 1970). Whereas in 1790 only 5 percent of the U.S. population was classified as urban, in 1890, for the first time in American history, more people lived in cities than on farms. By 1970 that figure had soared to over 70 percent. The increasing U.S. population combined with greater numbers of urban dwellers meant that American society was becoming more crowded, more complicated, and less agricultural as millions of people moved into relatively small cities. All sorts of urban problems thus emerged — air and water pollution, poor and insufficient housing, mass-transit difficulties, increased crime, and others.

At the same time, political power remained in the hands of the rurally oriented and tight-fisted state legislatures (until the Supreme Court reapportionment decisions of the mid-1960s). The legislatures were thus unwilling to raise taxes or to address the growing needs of the urban areas.[4] In addition, cities were perceived negatively during the heyday of the urban political machines, so that state decision makers tended to ignore the problems of the burgeoning cities. Thus, with the woes of the urban areas increasing and the states somewhat indifferent to urban problems, the cities turned to Washington, D.C., for help. They received it in the form of grant programs approved by Congress.

Another factor contributing to the expansion of national government activity is the changing nature of many important public issues. Unlike the local problems that dominated the agendas of government in the past — such as wheat blight and potholes in county roads — today's decision makers must wrestle with more difficult issues — such as a polluted environment and rising unemployment — that are regional or national in scope.

Many contemporary problems, such as those associated with mass transit and clean air, plague entire metropolitan areas. As a result, they cannot be handled locally but require the help of the state and national governments. Their causes and consequences extend far beyond the jurisdictions of local governments. It is this pervasive quality of modern-day issues that keeps the national government on the scene. In addition, problems are increasingly national in character in that they tend to affect large areas of the country. They are thus perceived as national problems and are put on the agenda of the national government. Air pollution, for example, is a problem in Denver, Detroit, New York, Phoenix, and Los Angeles, to name only a few cities.

Finally, the technologically advanced and complicated nature of the U.S. economy and communication and transportation systems has contributed to national government involvement, particularly in urban areas. Modern communication technology makes it possible for the events and problems of one city or region to become known across the nation within minutes. The transportation system permits millions of people to move about throughout the country, making Americans more familiar with the conditions, events, and problems in other areas. Mass production and distribution systems have made various areas of the country dependent on one another.

Reasons thus exist for placing many modern problems on the agenda of the national government. Technology has made the nation smaller in a sense. It has created problems common to many regions. Politicians promise voters that national programs will be established to attack the problems, including urban slums, run-down schools, and air and water pollution.

A Layer Cake Becomes Marble Cake   Over 30 years ago Morton Grodzins first used what is now known as the **marble-cake federalism** analogy to describe the nature of intergovernmental relations, or cooperative federalism as it is often called.[5] According to Grodzins, the U.S. government system can no longer be viewed as a three-tiered layer cake of national, state, and local governments with each layer performing its own functions independently of the others. Through the grants-in-aid programs and cooperative federalism, intergovernmental relations now look more like a marble cake, with a maze of vertical financial and legal ties integrating the activities of the three sets of governments.

More recently, in an analysis of the expansion of national government programs and spending, Thomas Anton has characterized the contemporary federal system as composed of "coalitions of beneficiaries."[6] Private beneficiaries of congressional programs — such as farmers, water barge operators, students, the elderly, and public assistance recipients — are in league with the federal and state bureaucrats who administer the benefits programs. They are tied to the reelection-oriented members of Congress who sit on the committees that consider and review the programs and who seek to please their voting constituencies. These parties work together to advance their various personal and professional desires by protecting and expanding the programs from which they all benefit. Some call these mutually supportive networks **iron triangles**; others refer to them simply as subgovernments. In either case, it is these coalitions that make it politically difficult to cut spending by reversing what has already been established.

From the founding of the Union through the nineteenth century, fiscal **The 1960s** federalism—the financial interdependence of the national and state **and 1970s** governments—developed at a leisurely pace. Congress authorized financial aid to assist states with the construction of postal roads. The federal government also made funds available to assist with vocational education, aid the blind, and help universities conduct research. However, even as late as 1930, less than 3 percent of all state and local revenues came from the federal coffers.

The situation began to change significantly at the turn of the century, and the change accelerated in the mid-1960s and later. The adoption of the Sixteenth Amendment in 1913 legitimized the federal income tax, which greatly increased the amount of revenue available to the federal government. The Great Depression stimulated Congress to enact programs in states and localities designed to spur economic recovery and growth. In the decade or so following World War II, Congress authorized federal financial support of urban planning and renewal efforts in America's cities.

The Great Society   From the mid-1960s to the 1970s, the expansion of federal programs was enormous. Federal legislation made federal dollars available to states and localities through a wide variety of programs. Included were new or expanded funding programs in elementary and secondary education, higher education, the arts, mental health, drug and alcohol treatment, maternal and child health, family planning, legal services, highways, airports, job training, and wastewater treatment plants. Lyndon B. Johnson, a master of congressional politics, was president. Earlier, John Kennedy, elected president in 1960 and assassinated in 1963, had called on the nation's people to recognize their obligations to their fellow citizens. Johnson continued that theme and, with the help of Congress, expanded Kennedy's dream into the **Great Society**— countless domestic programs designed to fix our broken cities, educate our children, and train our unemployed. The period of the Great Society affected fiscal federalism dramatically.

But Congress wasn't finished. Just as the Great Society was in full swing, the nation developed a new consciousness with regard to both the environment and consumer protection. On the heels of domestic legislation—in areas such as education, jobs, and health—the administration in Washington began passing consumer and environmental protection laws, making even more money available to state and local governments.

The period of 1965 to 1975 transformed intergovernmental relations. But it was also significant for another, related reason. As Congress passed legislation making financial support available to state and local governments, it also accelerated the establishment of highly complicated and costly conditions that state and local governments had to meet in order to qualify for financial help. In other words, the programs came with strings attached. But this was not new to state and local governments. Congress had long imposed construction and accounting standards in such grant areas as highways, welfare, and education. For the most part, however, the guidelines were designed to ensure the responsible use of the funding.

Crossover Sanctions   The strings attached to federal funds took on a new dimension in the 1960s and 1970s. By this time many state and local units were dependent on federal dollars. Decision makers, both in Congress and in bureaucratic federal agencies, began to realize the extent to which they could impose national government policy objectives on state and local units by threatening to withhold federal funds. Washington decision makers thus imposed on state and local units, by means of congressional acts and agency guidelines, a wide variety of requirements, some of which were not directly related to the purposes for which the state and local units received funding. These became known as **crossover sanctions**. State and local governments, now "hooked" on Washington's financing, found themselves subject to requirements ranging from equal opportunity in women's athletics to the development of drug-free workplace programs. An example of the former occurred recently at Colorado State University when a federal judge ruled that CSU's 1992 decision to save money by eliminating its women's softball program violated Title IX of the Educational Amendments Act of 1972. The judicial order was quite specific, directing that CSU hire a permanent coach for the team, begin active recruiting, and offer an exhibition schedule by the fall of 1993. The judge left undisturbed a companion decision that eliminated the men's baseball program.

At stake is states' continued receipt of funding in such areas as sewerage, transportation, student aid, and research. Debates over national policy objectives raged in areas ranging from affirmative action and removal of barriers for the handicapped to consumer protection and clean waters. The costs, in time and dollars, to state and local governments accepting the aid grew. Intergovernmental relations became ever more complicated. Among the results were intergovernmental conflicts, a paperwork blizzard, and significant state and local dependence on federal money. Moreover, the stage was set for such political events as the passage of Proposition 13 in California in 1978, the election of Ronald Reagan to the presidency in 1980, and his "new federalism" of the 1980s.

Proposition 13 and the Taxpayer Revolt   The much-heralded Proposition 13, an initiative measure passed at the polls by California voters, reduced the levels of assessment on property (such as residential homes) and limited the permissible levels of property taxation. Most commentators viewed its passage as part of a national property tax revolt. In addition, however, voter support of Proposition 13 was interpreted as a statement by voters that they had had enough government and enough regulation and wanted relief. A vote on federal regulation was not available; a vote on state and local taxes was. Voters in other states responded to ballot initiatives in a similar antigovernment fashion.

Another factor or set of factors, one fundamentally associated with the nature of the U.S. political system, also lay behind these events. People were fed up with increased government intervention in their lives. The proportion of state and local revenues derived from the federal treasury had grown from less than 3 percent in 1930 to over 25 percent by 1978. This growth was accompanied (especially from 1965 forward) by a wide array of new mandates to state and local governments from Washington—some from Congress but most the product of bureaucratic interpretation. Private-sector federal contractors had similar experiences. The result, rightly or wrongly, was a growing sense of being bullied by Washington, of being caught in a paper tangle, of being helpless before the enormous federal establishment. Small businesspeople were angry, state lawmakers felt pushed around, state and local employees and public officials were pressured.

The 1980s: Reaganomics

The 1980 election of President Ronald Reagan was widely viewed as the product of widespread dissatisfaction with the state of the national economy, a troubled foreign policy, and an insufficiently forceful incumbent, Jimmy Carter. Following his election, President Reagan assembled a program designed to translate his campaign pledges into policy.[7] For Reagan, it was imperative that federal spending be brought under control, that state and local governments return to a financially more self-reliant status, that fiscal intergovernmental relations be simplified and made more efficient, and that the extensive network of federal regulations designed to push state and local governments into compliance with federal policy objectives be reduced. His program is referred to as **Reaganomics**.

Block Grants   Early in 1981 President Reagan presented Congress with proposals to consolidate 85 categorical grant programs into 7 block grant programs, among which were education, health, social services, urban development, and community development. He further proposed to reduce funding levels for the programs by one-quarter, with the programs to be "enriched" by the presumed savings of administrative efficiency. There were to be fewer strings attached to the blocked programs, allowing states and localities increased flexibility to reduce administrative costs. Reagan wanted the national government to assume full responsibility for Medicaid, while placing the cost of Aid for Dependent Children (AFDC) and food stamps on the states.

President Reagan did not get all he wanted from Congress, but he got some of it. In the Omnibus Budget Reconciliation Act of 1981, Congress consolidated 77 categorical programs and 2 existing block grants into 9 block grant programs. The newly created block grant programs were in the areas of community development; elementary and secondary education; preventive health and health services; alcohol, drug abuse, and mental health; maternal and child health services; primary care; social services; community services; and low-income home energy assistance. Funding was reduced in most areas, with the greatest reductions in employment and training assistance, child nutrition, public assistance, and low-income energy help.

The changes had a significant impact on state and local governments. They changed the nature of intergovernmental relations, with the role of the states strengthened and the role of local governments weakened. Many of the programs—in areas such as job training, community development, education, health, primary care, and community services—had been characterized by direct federal–local financial ties. With the blocking of formerly categorical programs, funds were targeted to the states and state officials had to play a larger role in distributing federal funds to local governments.

Less Federal Money The changes in the grant system also reduced the amount of federal money available to support state and local programs. In 1982 there was a reduction in the size of the grants-in-aid system for the first time in the history of the programs. In 1978 federal money constituted 9 percent of local government revenues and 22.3 percent of the revenues for the states; by 1987 these numbers had fallen to 4.2 percent and 18.5 percent, respectively (see Figure 2.3). The cutbacks, combined with other troublesome features of the economy and of state and local finances, created severe budgetary pressures for many states and localities.

FIGURE 2.3
Federal Funds as a Percentage of State and Local Revenues, 1978 and 1987

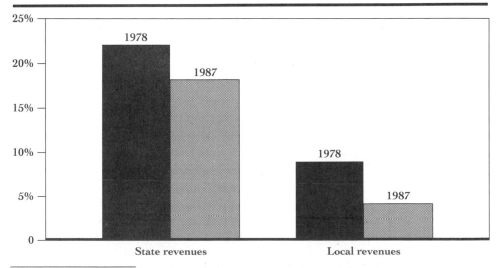

SOURCE: Robert Gleason, "Federalism's Fiscal Shifts," *ACIR Intergovernmental Perspective* (Fall 1988): 26.

The trends set into motion by Reaganomics in 1980 continued throughout that decade and into the next (see Figure 2.4). Presidents Reagan and George Bush restricted continued growth in the flow of federal money to the states and localities. Indeed, their goal was to shrink it. In addition, Reagan and Congress cooperated in running up enormous annual budget deficits in the 1980s, leading to constant pressure to control spending. That pressure continues to plague President Bill Clinton's administration. One clear result has been growing congressional resistance to spend more in support of state and local programs. This has caused more of the financial responsibility for many domestic programs to be placed on state and local units, as Reagan wanted. However, the flow of federal rules imposed on the states has not subsided.

Redistributing the Tax Burden   Reaganomics had redistributive effects. Programs targeting low-income people were hit quite hard, with reductions in education, job training, and community and regional development. At the same time, defense spending, Social Security, and Medicare, programs that primarily benefit the middle class, received significant support.

In addition, insofar as state and local governments replaced lost federal funds with revenues generated from their own sources, the overall tax structures of the states became more regressive. Today sales and property taxes, on which state and local governments rely heavily, take higher proportions of

---

FIGURE 2.4
The Rise and Decline of Federal Aid, 1958–1988
—and 1998? (as a percentage of state and local outlays)

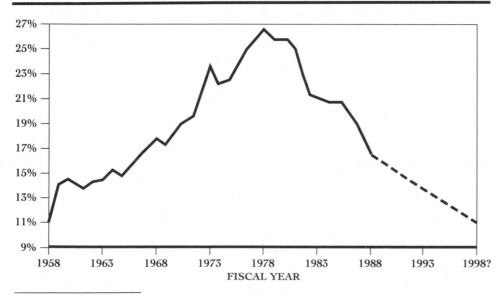

FISCAL YEAR

SOURCE: *ACIR Intergovernmental Perspective* (Winter 1988): 13.

income from low-income people than does the federal income tax. The new federalism thus did more than simply alter intergovernmental relations and shift policy responsibility to state and local governments; it also passed a larger part of the bill for government services to those in lower-income categories by shifting the cost of many programs to the states and localities, which rely heavily on regressive taxes.

The 1990s

The relationships among the national, state, and local governments today are different than were a decade ago in some important ways. Noted earlier in this chapter were the changed fiscal relations triggered by Reagan. State and local governments have had to rely on their own sources of revenue. As a result, the states emerged from the 1980s more self-reliant than they had been in the two preceding decades. State and local governments had to raise taxes to pay their own way. From 1982 to 1988, general fund spending increased by 51 percent for the states and by 62 percent for the localities.[8]

Local governments now rely more heavily on their political parents—the states. In 1988, for example, state aid to local governments totaled $143 billion, in contrast to only $17 billion in local aid from the national government.[9] Just as aid from the national government comes with strings attached, so does aid from the states. The flow of state money has grown together with state controls. For example, 9 states recently enacted legislation empowering the states to take over failing local school systems, and 20 others provide for some form of state intervention in troubled local schools.

Money Shrinks but Mandates Don't   Although one might expect national government influence to moderate or decline with the stabilization or reduction in federal financial help, this has not happened. Instead, government controls have increased to the point that in 1989 the governors called on Congress to stop placing mandates on the states. Congress, for example, has made continued state receipt of highway money contingent on compliance with congressional preferences as to the speed limit and legal drinking age, and the national government continues to impose clean air and water standards as well as wage and hour laws on state and local governments.

State and local officials do not like many of these mandates because they find them costly and unresponsive to regional and local conditions. But in numerous policy areas, Congress, through federal agencies, continues to tell state and local governments what to do. One observer puts it this way:

> State governments are required to develop programs, expend resources and participate in federal programs based on federal priorities instead of, or to the detriment of, state defined goals and missions.[10]

Federal Courts Side with Congress   However, Congress has not acted alone in altering intergovernmental relations. The courts have also participated in strengthening the hand of the national government over the states. In the 1976 case of *National League of Cities v. Usery*, the Supreme Court concluded that the commerce clause of the Constitution does not give the national government the authority to enforce the provisions of the Fair Labor Standards Act on the states and localities. In a 5–4 decision, the Court held that Congress may not "operate to directly displace the states' freedom to structure integral operations in areas of traditional governmental functions." The definition of a "traditional" function was difficult to define, however, and by 1985, in *Garcia v. San Antonio Metropolitan Transit Authority*, the Court reversed its ruling in *Usery* by allowing the imposition of the Fair Labor Standards Act on the states. Critics argue that this represents a damaging blow to the principle of federalism in that it strips away the semiautonomy of the states in the formerly dual system of federalism. The position of the Court is that if the states want to be shielded from the policy desires of Congress, they must seek their remedy through the political process (that is, they must lobby Congress).

Other cases have reinforced the *Garcia* ruling. In *South Carolina v. Baker* (1988), for example, the Court concluded that it is permissible for Congress to levy federal taxes on interest earnings on state and local bonds (previously, these bonds had been immune from such taxation). The 1987 case of *South Dakota v. Dole* is another example of the Supreme Court's approval of the congressional propensity to tell the states what to do. Shortly after it began providing financial help in 1921 to the states for the construction and maintenance of highways, Congress imposed conditions on the states for continued receipt of the money. These included creation of state highway departments, imposition of weight limits, highway maintenance to suit federal desires, imposition of heavy vehicle use taxes, billboard control, the visual screening of junkyards, speed limits, air-quality programs, and a minimum drinking age of 21 years.[11] Most recently, Congress required the states to revoke the driver's licenses of persons convicted of drug offenses, even if no driving was involved.

South Dakota and several other states challenged Congress's authority to impose the minimum drinking age, but the Court sided with Congress. One critic of the decision notes that "in *Dole* the Court effectively abrogated the notion that Congress is a government of delegated powers. . . ."[12]

Some federal requirements on the states and localities include forced uniformity in the keeping and reporting of information. It is argued that the requirements are necessary to provide Congress and federal agencies with comparable and reliable data for use in distributing funding and assessing program results.[13] However, they also add to the federal government's list of Supreme Court–sanctioned implied constitutional powers to influence state and local governments. Table 2.5 lists the regulatory statutes and amendments passed by Congress between 1982 and 1990 that significantly affected intergov-

TABLE 2.5
Major Enactments and Statutory Amendments
Regulating State and Local Governments, 1982–1990

Age Discrimination in Employment Act Amendments of 1986
Americans with Disabilities Act of 1990
Asbestos Hazard Emergency Response Act of 1986
Cash Management Improvement Act of 1990
Child Abuse Amendments of 1984
Civil Rights Restoration Act of 1987
Clean Air Act Amendments of 1990
Commercial Motor Vehicle Safety Act of 1986
Consolidated Omnibus Budget Reconciliation Act of 1985
Drug-Free Workplace Act of 1988
Education of the Handicapped Act Amendments of 1986
Emergency Planning and Community Right-to-Know Act of 1986
Fair Housing Act Amendments of 1988
Handicapped Children's Protection Act of 1986
Hazardous and Solid Waste Amendments of 1984
Highway Safety Amendments of 1984
Lead Contamination Control Act of 1988
Ocean Dumping Ban Act of 1988
Older Workers Benefit Protection Act of 1990
Safe Drinking Water Act Amendments of 1986
Social Security Amendments of 1983
Social Security: Fiscal 1991 Budget Reconciliation Act
Surface Transportation Assistance Act of 1982
Voting Accessibility for the Elderly and Handicapped Act of 1984
Voting Rights Act Amendments of 1982
Water Quality Act of 1987

Source: Timothy J. Conlan and David R. Beam, "Federal Mandates: The Record of Reform and Future Prospects," *ACIR Intergovernmental Perspective* (Fall 1992): 8.

ernmental relations. As you can see in the table, the legislation covers a diverse array of topics.

CONSEQUENCES OF INSTITUTIONAL DESIGN

Does it matter how a polity designs its institutions of government? Yes, for institutions are the foundation of the political system. According to the principle of federalism, both the setting and implementation of policy are left to the states and their local units. Public safety, for example, is a state and local matter. Police officers and fire fighters are local government employees. Public utilities — sewers, water, streets — are state and local matters, as are most parks and landfills. Public health programs and hospitals are state and local concerns. Most criminal laws, courts, and prisons are as well. If the founders had institutionalized a unitary relationship between the national government and the states, all of this would be different. Policies would be made centrally, and local options and state variations would not exist.

Variety does exist, for state and local governments differ widely (and sometimes wildly) in their priorities. Revenue systems vary among states and among cities. Some states and localities spend heavily on police and fire protection, whereas others do not. The tax burden is heavier in some states than others, as are levels of public assistance and health care benefits. Some states foot most of the bill for elementary and secondary education; others leave the tax collecting to local school districts. As Chapters 13 through 16 show, enormous variety exists in the policies of our 86,000 governments, and much of it is rooted in federalism.

The Design Provides Variety

The state–local relationship is unitary, not federal. Since local governments are creatures of the state, they do what their state dictates; within any single state, local policies are similar. Policies in all cities, counties, or special districts may not be identical because the states typically allow for local variation. But since state law establishes systems of local government, standardization is extensive. All cities in a given size classification, for example, employ the same form of government, and all counties are subject to state-specified powers, duties, and limitations.

The states must ratify proposed amendments to the Constitution, as they are partners in a federal relationship. No such role is provided within the states for their political subdivisions with reference to changes in state constitutions.

Both the behavior of interest groups and lobbyists and the organizational characteristics of political parties are heavily influenced by the shape of American institutions. Just a few decades ago, for example, civil rights proponents, unable to persuade state and local officials to eliminate racial segregation, shifted their focus to national decision makers. In *Brown v. Board of Education* (1954), the Supreme Court did what state officials would not do — outlaw the separate treatment of the races in public education. Congress enacted a number of significant civil rights laws in the 1960s.

The Design Affects Political Tactics

Recently, interest groups have been readjusting their focus on the states. This is the result of the devolution of program responsibilities to the states, of the states' undertaking some regulatory activities where national law is silent, and of a more conservative federal judiciary following 12 years of GOP presidential appointments. The design of our institutions thus provides the road map that guides and directs the activities of political interests.

The consequences of our institutional arrangements are evident in the electoral system as well. When we go to the polls, we are confronted with a formidable ballot featuring elections for national, state, and local offices. We may be able to vote on the same ballot for a

The Design Configures Elections

president, a U.S. senator, a congressional representative, a state governor, an attorney general, a secretary of state, a state senator and house representative, state judges, members of a state university governing board, and a host of local offices. Why? Because of the way our government is structured.

In a variety of ways, then, the shape of American political institutions affects the nature of our politics and policies. Election systems, policy and program variations, and political strategies and behavior are products of those institutions.

The Design Has Changed over Time

Over two hundred years ago America's political activists faced a serious problem. After difficult years under the thumb of the English crown and a revolutionary war, not many favored installing governmental institutions that centralized authority. Yet in the face of such pressing problems as interstate commercial squabbling and war debts, the existing decentralized scheme, wherein the states were autonomous, was not working. The political resolution was found in a federation. Some functions were handed over to a newly created national government, while most others remained with the states (and remain with the states today).

But times change, and over the years Congress, basing its decisions on the Constitution's commerce and tax clauses, the spending power, and the necessary and proper national supremacy provisions, has greatly expanded the scope of national government activities. Today, state and local governments find themselves forced to help implement a wide variety of national policy objectives and to comply with a host of national rules and regulations.

SUMMARY

In an attempt to resolve the differences between those in favor of a highly centralized government and those supporting a decentralized system, the framers of the Constitution developed a federal system. Federalism is a system of dual or divided sovereignty: The central government is sovereign in those policy areas with national impact, and the individual states are sovereign in those policy areas with more limited impact.

For the first 150 years of the Republic, there was some cooperation between the national and state governments; however, they were largely independent of each other. For the past half-century, there has been increasing interaction among the different levels of government. Most noticeably, the national government has used financial incentives to expand its influence over and to impose its policy preferences on the states.

As is evident throughout the book, the federal principle is pervasive in American politics. Almost every political institution is affected by this notion of divided sovereignty. Our system of justice, our political parties, and our elections of public officials all function the way they do because of the influence of federalism.

As this chapter has indicated, federalism is not a fixed principle. Rather, it evolves in response to changing political demands and values. There is no reason to believe this evolution will cease. James Madison might have trouble recognizing federalism in its current form, but if he could see it 10 years from now, who knows what he might think? Almost certainly, the federalism that characterizes American politics in the year 2004 will be different from that of today.

KEY TERMS

centralized system
unitary system
decentralized system
federalism
coercive federalism
Articles of Confederation
U.S. Constitution
expressed powers
legislative branch
executive branch
judicial branch
implied powers
McCulloch v. Maryland
inherent powers

reserved powers
powers denied
full faith and credit
national supremacy
guarantee
Dillon's rule
grants-in-aid
categorical grant
block grant
marble-cake federalism
iron triangle
Great Society
crossover sanction
Reaganomics

ADDITIONAL READINGS

Advisory Commission on Intergovernmental Relations. *Regulatory Federalism: Policy, Process, Impact and Reform.* Washington, D.C.: GPO, 1984.

Anton, Thomas J. *American Federalism and Public Policy.* Philadelphia: Temple University Press, 1989.

Beam, David R., and Timothy J. Conlan. "The Growth of Intergovernmental Mandates in an Era of Deregulation and Decentralization." In *American Intergovernmental Relations*, ed. Laurence J. O'Toole, 2nd ed. Washington, D.C.: Congressional Quarterly Press, 1993.

Conlan, Timothy. *New Federalism: Intergovernmental Reform from Nixon to Reagan.* Washington, D.C.: Brookings Institution, 1980.

Derthick, Martha. "American Federalism: Madison's Middle Ground." *Public Administration Review* 47 (Jan.-Feb. 1987): 66–74.

———. "The Enduring Features of American Federalism." *Brookings Review* (Summer 1989): 34–38.

O'Toole, Laurence J., ed. *American Intergovernmental Relations.* Washington, D.C.: Congressional Quarterly Press, 1985.

Walker, David. "Intergovernmental Relations and Dysfunctional Federalism." *National Civic Review* (Feb. 1981): 68–76.

Wrightson, Margaret T. "The Road to South Carolina: Intergovernmental Tax Immunity and the Constitutional Status of Federalism." *Publius* 19 (Summer 1989): 39–55.

NOTES

1. Alex N. Dragnich, "The Government of Great Britain," in *An Introduction to Political Science*, ed. Alex N. Dragnich and John C. Wahlke (New York: Random House, 1966), p. 71.

2. Quoted in Clyde F. Snyder, *American State and Local Government* (New York: Appleton-Century-Crofts, 1965), p. 353.

3. Susan Welsh and Kay Thompson, "The Impact of Federal Incentives on State Policy Adoption," *American Journal of Political Science* (Nov. 1980): 715–29.

4. Some observers challenge the notion that malapportionment was a major factor in the failure of states to tackle urban problems; see, for example, Thomas R. Dye, "Malapportionment and Public Policy in the States," *Journal of Politics* (Aug. 1965): 586–601.

5. Morton Grodzins, "The Federal System," in *Goals for Americans*, ed. the American Assembly (Englewood Cliffs, N.J.: Prentice-Hall, 1960), pp. 265–82.

6. Thomas Anton, *American Federalism and Public Policy* (Philadelphia: Temple University Press, 1989), p. 32.

7. Much of the material in this section is drawn from *ACIR Intergovernmental Perspective* (Winter 1982).

8. John Herbert, "The Growing Role of the States Is Greater Than We Knew," *Governing* (March 1990): 11.

9. Ibid.

10. Ali F. Seven, "Highway Sanctions: Circumventing the Constitution," *State Legislatures* (Feb. 1989): 28.

11. Ibid.

12. Thomas R. McCoy and Barry Friedman, "Conditional Spending: Federalism's Trojan Horse," *Supreme Court Review* (Chicago: University of Chicago Press, 1988), pp. 85–127.

13. Cheryl Arvidson, "As the Reagan Era Fades, It's Discretion versus Earmarking in the Struggle over Funds," *Governing* (March 1990): 22.

3

State Constitutions

The opening page of the Colorado state constitution. Every state has a written constitution that establishes the basic framework and procedures for collective decision making. In this case, the constitution also establishes the location and boundaries of the state. *(Colorado State Archives)*

The U.S. Constitution written in Philadelphia in 1787 is not the only American constitution. Every U.S. state also has its own written **state constitution**. Many states have had several constitutions. Indeed, over the course of U.S. history, Louisiana has had 11 constitutions, Georgia has had 10, South Carolina seven, and Alabama, Florida, and Virginia six each. Nineteen states have had just one constitution. State constitutions also differ in certain ways. The state constitutions of Connecticut, Indiana, Minnesota, New Hampshire, and Vermont are, like the U.S. Constitution, each less than 10,000 words in length. However, Alabama's constitution is about 174,000 words, New York's is 80,000 words, and Oklahoma's and Texas's each exceed 60,000 words. Furthermore, whereas the constitutions of Alaska, Illinois, Michigan, Montana, Pennsylvania, and Virginia have been amended fewer than 25 times, Alabama's constitution has more than 500 amendments and California's and South Carolina's constitutions have over 400 amendments each.[1] (See Table 3.1.)

Historically, many state constitutions have been long and full of detail, some of it outdated (prohibitions against dueling, for example). Constitutional reforms have been emphasized throughout the country over the past decades; when they have been successful, some of the length and detail of state constitutions have been eliminated. Although state constitutions contain common elements, they also display rich and interesting variety.

State constitutions are not nearly as well known as the U.S. Constitution. Most Americans have never read or seen a state constitution. General references to a "constitution," such as in a speech or a newspaper article, are almost always made in regard to the U.S. Constitution. Although people sometimes cite such foundational documents in claiming their "constitutional rights," they often do so inadvertently, rather than actually having consulted their state constitution.

STATE CONSTITUTIONS ARE IMPORTANT POLITICAL DOCUMENTS

From the lack of public attention that state constitutions receive, one might misjudge them as unimportant. However, in the U.S. federal system, it is these documents that establish the institutions of government within each state. State constitutions prescribe the structure, powers, duties, and limits of each branch of government. They lay the foundations for tax policies and systems of local government. Each state constitution contains a bill of rights; increasingly, the states' bills of rights are providing the foundation for legal decisions that affect American civil liberties.

The answers to a wide array of modern political questions lie in the constitutions of the American states. You and I may pay property taxes on our homes, but must the elderly, war veterans, and widows pay them too? Must churches that operate stores or day-care centers on their premises pay taxes? Can cities enact an income tax? Who dominates the state budget process—the governor or the legislature? How are state judges selected? Do citizens have the right to privacy and to a quality education? In the past, state constitutions also addressed important political questions: May women vote? May former Confederate soldiers vote?

State constitutions are inherently political in nature, and their execution often involves high-stakes politics. Power relationships between legislators and governors and between state and local governments are formed by state constitutions. Taxation policies are affected by state constitutional provisions. The institutional designs for state and local governments, as established in state constitutions, structure state–local political power relationships, provide the parameters for much political behavior, and in large part determine the content of public policy.

It is useful to think of the fundamental nature of state constitutions by considering by itself the word *constitution*. Constitutions "constitute"; that is, they form, create, or establish something. In the case of state constitutions, they establish the basic anatomy and procedures of government.

Constitutions Structure State Governments

A basic function of the state constitution is to establish the framework and procedures for collective decision making. Individuals and groups in any society find it necessary to accommodate their differences. One way to settle differences is to fight; another is to agree on a set of processes and establish an organizational arrangement through which disagreements may be resolved. Constitutions help perform this function. Generally, they spell out the fundamental organization of the governmental apparatus and specify procedures for proposing policy (the introduction of bills), implementing policy (the administration of bills that have passed), and settling disputes and interpreting laws (roles typically played by the courts). As noted in Chapter 2, the U.S. Constitution establishes for the national government organizational and decision-making procedures. The state constitution does the same for state and local governments. Many features of governmental structure and procedure are, of course, spelled out in detail by legislative acts and administrative agency decisions, but the basic framework is established in state constitutions.

Constitutions Impose Limits on States

Both the U.S. Constitution and state constitutions identify certain activities in which government may not engage. This feature is important because it identifies, for citizens, for the legislative and executive branches of government, and for the courts, those freedoms that are viewed as especially valuable and deserving of special protection from

TABLE 3.1   General Information on State Constitutions

State or Other Jurisdiction	Number of Constitutions*	Dates of Adoption	Effective Date of Present Constitution	Estimated Length (number of words)	Number of Amendments Submitted to Voters	Number of Amendments Adopted
Alabama	6	1819, 1861, 1865, 1868, 1875, 1901	Nov. 28, 1901	174,000	759	538
Alaska	1	1956	Jan. 3, 1959	13,000	32	23
Arizona	1	1911	Feb. 14, 1912	28,876 (a)	204	111
Arkansas	5	1836, 1861, 1864, 1868, 1874	Oct. 30, 1874	40,720 (a)	167	77 (b)
California	2	1849, 1879	July 4, 1876	33,350	800	480
Colorado	1	1876	Aug. 1, 1876	45,679	243	118
Connecticut	4	1818 (c), 1965	Dec. 30, 1965	9,564	27	26
Delaware	4	1776, 1792, 1831, 1897	June 10, 1897	19,000	(d)	121
Florida	6	1839, 1861, 1865, 1868, 1886, 1968	Jan. 7, 1969	25,100	83	57
Georgia	10	1777, 1789, 1798, 1861, 1865, 1868, 1877, 1945, 1976, 1982	July 1, 1983	25,000	44 (e)	32
Hawaii	1 (f)	1950	Aug. 21, 1959	17,453 (a)	98	82
Idaho	1	1889	July 3, 1890	21,500	188	108
Illinois	4	1818, 1848, 1870, 1970	July 1, 1971	13,200	12	7
Indiana	2	1816, 1851	Nov. 1, 1851	9,377 (a)	70	38
Iowa	2	1846, 1857	Sept. 3, 1857	12,500	51	48 (g)
Kansas	1	1859	Jan. 29, 1861	11,865	116	88 (g)
Kentucky	4	1792, 1799, 1850, 1891	Sept. 28, 1891	23,500	62	30
Louisiana	11	1812, 1845, 1852, 1861, 1864, 1868, 1879, 1898, 1913, 1921, 1974	Jan. 1, 1975	51,448 (a)	74	46
Maine	1	1819	March 15, 1820	13,500	188	158 (h)
Maryland	4	1776, 1851, 1864, 1867	Oct. 5, 1867	41,349 (a)	235	202
Massachusetts	1	1780	Oct. 25, 1780	36,690 (a,i)	144	117
Michigan	4	1835, 1850, 1908, 1963	Jan. 1, 1964	20,000	47	16
Minnesota	1	1857	May 11, 1858	9,500	207	113
Mississippi	4	1817, 1832, 1869, 1890	Nov. 1, 1890	24,000	140	108
Missouri	4	1820, 1865, 1875, 1945	March 30, 1945	42,000	119	76
Montana	2	1889, 1972	July 1, 1973	11,866 (a)	27	16
Nebraska	2	1866, 1875	Oct 12, 1875	20,048 (a)	289	193
Nevada	1	1864	Oct. 31, 1864	20,770	178	111 (g)
New Hampshire	2	1776, 1784	June 2, 1784	9,200	277 (j)	143 (j)
New Jersey	3	1776, 1844, 1947	Jan. 1, 1948	17,086	53	40
New Mexico	1	1911	Jan. 6, 1912	27,200	236	121

State	Number of constitutions	Dates of adoption	Effective date of present constitution	Estimated length (number of words)	Submitted to voters	Adopted
New York	4	1777, 1822, 1846, 1894	Jan. 1, 1895	80,000	277	210
North Carolina	3	1776, 1868, 1970	July 1, 1971	11,000	34	27
North Dakota	1	1889	Nov. 2, 1889	20,564	231 (k)	127 (k)
Ohio	2	1802, 1851	Sept. 1, 1851	36,900	248	147
Oklahoma	1	1907	Nov. 16, 1907	68,800	287 (l)	141 (l)
Oregon	1	1857	Feb. 14, 1859	26,090	375	192
Pennsylvania	5	1776, 1790, 1838, 1873, 1968 (m)	1968 (m)	21,675	25 (m)	19 (m)
Rhode Island	2	1842 (c)	May 2, 1843	19,026 (a,i)	99	53
South Carolina	7	1776, 1778, 1790, 1861, 1865, 1868, 1895	Jan. 1, 1896	22,500 (n)	648 (o)	463
South Dakota	1	1889	Nov. 2, 1889	23,300	190	98
Tennessee	3	1796, 1835, 1870	Feb. 23, 1870	15,300	55	32
Texas	5	1845, 1861, 1866, 1869, 1876	Feb. 15, 1876	62,000	499	339
Utah	1	1895	Jan. 4, 1896	11,000	128	79
Vermont	3	1777, 1786, 1793	July 9, 1793	6,600	208	50
Virginia	6	1776, 1830, 1851, 1869, 1902, 1970	July 1, 1971	18,500	27	22
Washington	1	1889	Nov. 11, 1889	29,400	156	86
West Virginia	2	1863, 1872	April 9, 1872	25,600	107	62
Wisconsin	1	1848	May 29, 1848	13,500	169	125 (g)
Wyoming	1	1889	July 10, 1890	31,800	101	61
American Samoa	2	1960, 1967	July 1, 1967	6,000	14	7
N. Mariana Islands	1	1977	Jan. 9, 1978	11,000	47 (p)	45 (p,q)
Puerto Rico	1	1952	July 25, 1952	9,281 (a)	6	6

*The constitutions referred to in this table include those Civil War documents customarily listed by the individual states.

(a) Actual word count.

(b) Eight of the approved amendments have been superseded and are not printed in the current edition of the constitution. The total adopted does not include five amendments that were invalidated.

(c) Colonial charters with some alterations served as the first constitutions in Connecticut (1638, 1662) and in Rhode Island (1663).

(d) Proposed amendments are not submitted to the voters in Delaware.

(e) The new Georgia constitution eliminates the need for local amendments, which have been a long-term problem for state constitution makers.

(f) As a kingdom and a republic, Hawaii had five constitutions.

(g) The figure given includes amendments approved by the voters and later nullified by the state Supreme Court in Iowa (three), Kansas (one), Nevada (six), and Wisconsin (two).

(h) The figure does not include one amendment approved by the voters in 1967 that is inoperative until implemented by legislation.

(i) The printed constitution includes many provisions that have been annulled. The length of effective provisions is an estimated 24,122 words (12,400 annulled) in Massa-chusetts and, in Rhode Island before the "rewrite" of the constitution in 1986, it was 11,399 words (7,627 annulled).

(j) The constitution of 1784 was extensively revised in 1792. Figures show proposals and adoptions since the constitution was adopted in 1784.

(k) The figures do not include submission and approval of the constitution of 1889 itself and of Article XX; these are constitutional questions included in some counts of constitutional amendments and would add two to the figure in each column.

(l) The figures include five amendments submitted to and approved by the voters which were, by decisions of the Oklahoma or U.S. Supreme Courts, rendered inoperative or ruled invalid, unconstitutional, or illegally submitted.

(m) Certain sections of the constitution were revised by the limited constitutional convention of 1967–68. Amendments proposed and adopted are since 1968.

(n) Of the estimated length, approximately two-thirds is of general statewide effect; the remainder is local amendments.

(o) As of 1981, of the 626 proposed amendments submitted to the voters, 130 were of general statewide effect and 496 were local; the voters rejected 83 (12 statewide, 71 local). Of the remaining 543, the General Assembly refused to approve 100 (22 statewide, 78 local), and 443 (96 statewide, 347 local) were finally added to the constitution.

(p) The number of amendments is from 1984–92.

(q) The total excludes one amendment ruled void by a federal district court.

Source: The Book of the States, 1992–93 (Lexington, Ky.: Council of State Governments, 1993), pp. 21–22.

government interference. State constitutions, like the U.S. Constitution, contain bills of rights, though the states' tend to be longer and more detailed.

MULTIPLE LEVELS OF LAW

Americans are frequently exposed to many different types of law—the Constitution, bills that have passed through legislatures, county zoning ordinances, parade permit rulings issued by city managers, and so on. But how these various types of law relate to one another, and especially when they come into conflict, may not be readily apparent. Before examining modern state constitutions in detail, let us consider briefly the relationship of the various levels of law in the American system.

The U.S. Constitution is the supreme law of the nation. Congress, in implementing the powers given to the national government by the Constitution, passes laws called **statutes**. But Congress may not pass just any statute. It may only pass laws and establish programs that are authorized by the Constitution. When questions arise about whether Congress has exceeded the authority given it by the Constitution, a Supreme Court interpretation, or **judicial review**, may take place. In judicial reviews of acts of Congress, the Court decides whether Congress has created a lower order of law that is beyond the range of activity authorized by the higher law—the Constitution.

Similarly, other lower levels of law cannot conflict with or involve the government in activities beyond the range authorized by the higher levels of law. Thus, state constitutions cannot in any way conflict with provisions of the U.S. Constitution or with congressional actions that are deemed constitutional. Furthermore, a state's legislative statutes cannot be in conflict with its constitution. State administrative agencies, such as the highway and fish and game departments, can engage in only those activities authorized by state statutes. Public officials may engage only in activities authorized by formal administrative procedures or guidelines, state statutes, state constitutions, congressional actions, and the U.S. Constitution. Figure 3.1 diagrams the relationships among the various levels of law.

These relationships are highlighted by Elder Witt in his characterization of Oregon's State Supreme Court Justice Hans A. Linde, a leader in what is known as new judicial federalism (see Chapter 6):

> The first question [Linde] asks when a state action is challenged in his court—whether it's a police request for a driver's license or a regulatory board's revocation of a dentist's license—is whether the action is authorized by law. If it is not, the government loses. If it is, he asks whether it is in line with the state constitution. If it is not, the government loses. If it is, only then does Linde look to a challenge based on the federal constitution.[2]

FIGURE 3.1   Levels of Law and Their Relationships

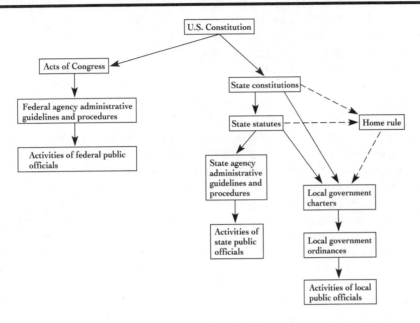

Although laws and official actions are not considered legitimate unless they are authorized by a higher law, it is important to recognize that laws do not define themselves or interpret their own legitimacy. People do so in courts of law. The legislature may pass laws that the Court may later declare unconstitutional. Moreover, state and local statutes likely contain numerous provisions that might be deemed unconstitutional if they were ever challenged in the courts. However, such provisions are treated as legal since they have not been challenged or found to be otherwise.

THE CONTENTS OF STATE CONSTITUTIONS

State constitutions establish the basic structure of state and local government systems. They allocate authority to various units and branches of government and prohibit state and local governments from engaging in certain activities. Although they vary along a number of dimensions, state constitutions are also similar in many respects. Most are long and detailed. They also tend to be restrictive, affording little flexibility to state and local governments.

Bills of Rights   Each state's constitution contains a bill of rights. The Bill of Rights in the U.S. Constitution affords American citizens protection from the national government, not from state and local governments. Although some degree of protection from the states does exist as a result of Supreme Court interpretations of the Fourteenth Amendment, most basic freedoms afforded citizens in state courts are established by **state bills of rights**. Although state bills of rights cover much of the same ground, they are typically longer and more detailed than the U.S. Bill of Rights.

California's constitution, for example, contains 28 provisions in its Bill of Rights. Included are the common provisions regarding the right of free speech, the right to petition government, the right of habeas corpus, and freedom from bills of attainder. However, also included are the right to fish and the right to post bond. Oregon's Bill of Rights protects freedom of religion, prohibits double jeopardy, and prohibits granting of titles of nobility. It also denies the state the power to prevent citizen emigration from the state. In Florida, the freedom from illegal search and seizure is spelled out more elaborately than it is in the U.S. Bill of Rights, and there is an explicit prohibition against the use of illegally seized materials as evidence against a defendant.

State bills of rights are not simple duplications of the national Bill of Rights. They are often much longer and contain protections that the U.S. Bill of Rights does not provide. For example, the elaborate Florida protection against illegal searches and seizures goes far beyond the U.S. Supreme Court's interpretation of the Fourteenth and Fourth amendments to the Constitution.

Provisions in state bills of rights have received considerable attention in recent years, as supreme courts in the states have often cited state constitutional provisions as providing individual rights more expansive than those established by the U.S. Supreme Court's interpretations of the Bill of Rights. In cases involving the rights to equal educational opportunity and privacy, for instance, state supreme courts have rendered decisions of significance based on state constitutional provisions. This trend has received increased attention as the U.S. Supreme Court's conservative members have become less receptive to civil libertarian claims. Federalism, the operation of dual systems, appears to be working well with respect to judicial politics. One commentator notes that "since 1980, dozens of state courts, in more than 350 cases, have declared their constitutions more protective of individual rights than the federal Constitution."[3]

The Framework of State Government   State constitutions also provide the basic framework for state governments. All 50 state constitutions create three branches of government—legislative, executive, and judicial. The legislature is divided into two houses in all states except Nebraska. In the executive branch, state constitutions typically establish the office of governor, specify the length of term, and describe the powers and duties of the office. These usually include the power to call the legislature into special session, to veto legislation, and to require written reports of executive agencies. Likewise, state constitutions specify legislative terms of office, some legislator privileges, and the lawmaking powers of the legislature itself. In judicial articles, state constitutions generally call for the establishment of a state supreme court and a system of lower courts, indicate the procedure by which judges are selected, and, together with state statutes, specify the powers and jurisdictions of the courts at each level of the judicial system.

In addition, state constitutions provide for the establishment of a variety of state boards, agencies, and institutions. These include such bodies as state boards of education, which oversee the operation of the elementary and secondary school systems in the state; public utility or "corporation" commissions, which license public utilities and other kinds of business corporations operating in the state; and boards of regents, which govern state colleges and universities. In some cases state constitutions establish elective governing boards for these agencies; in others board members are appointed by the governor.

Local Governments

State constitutions also establish elaborate systems of local government. These include cities, towns, counties, school districts, special districts, and in some cases township or parish governments.

Some state constitutions go into great detail about the structure, powers, duties, and limitations of local governments. Others are brief and leave the details of these matters to legislative bodies.

Control of State and Local Finances

Many state constitutions have highly restrictive fiscal provisions that earmark certain revenues for specified uses and place low ceilings on the permissible levels for state and local sales and property taxes. Some state constitutions allow, while others prohibit, income taxes.

State constitutions contain sections relating to numerous other matters as well, such as water and mineral rights, the conduct of elections, the allowable debt level for the state, and others. Table 3.2, which outlines the Illinois and Texas constitutions, illustrates the sorts of matters with which state constitutions deal.

THE LENGTH AND DETAIL OF STATE CONSTITUTIONS

As noted earlier in the chapter, many state constitutions are quite long. The constitution in effect in Louisiana until 1975 contained over 250,000 words, or

TABLE 3.2   Organization of Two State Constitutions

Illinois Constitution		Texas Constitution	
Article I	Bill of Rights	Article I	Bill of Rights
II	The Power of the State	II	The Powers of Government
III	Suffrage and Election	III	Legislative Department
IV	The Legislature	IV	Executive Department
V	The Executive	V	Judicial Department
VI	The Judiciary	VI	Suffrage
VII	Local Government	VII	Education — The Free Public Schools
VIII	Finance	VIII	Taxation and Revenue
IX	Revenue	IX	Counties
X	Education	X	Railroads
XI	Environment	XI	Municipal Corporations
XII	Militia	XII	Private Corporations
XIII	General Provisions	XIII	Spanish and Mexican Land Titles (repealed)
XIV	Constitutional Recisions	XIV	Public Land and Land Office
		XV	Impeachment
		XVI	General Provisions
		XVII	Mode of Amending the Constitution of This State

more than 400 book pages, with its amendments. It was said that the old Louisiana constitution weighed 36 pounds. Other states also have lengthy constitutions: Alabama's has over 174,000 words, New York's more than 80,000 words, Oklahoma's over 68,000 words, Texas's over 60,000 words, and Colorado's, Maryland's, and Missouri's more than 40,000 words each. In contrast, the U.S. Constitution, including its amendments, contains fewer than 10,000 words.

Although many state constitutions are long and detailed, they often lack clarity. Some are much more detailed than others, but most contain detailed provisions for taxing and spending; for the powers, duties, and limitations of local governments; and for bills of rights. The Texas Constitution, for example, contains detailed provisions on several issues: the teachers' retirement fund; rural fire protection districts; limits on state appropriation of anticipated revenue; the issuance and sale of bonds by the state to create the Texas Water Development Fund and Texas Water Development Board; a tax levy authorized for Confederate soldiers and sailors and their widows; compensation to persons fined or imprisoned for offenses of which they are not guilty; and land for psychiatric hospitals, among other provisions. Interestingly, these various issues, though subjects of law, are included in the state's constitution — the basic law of the state — rather than in state statutes or administrative provisions.

Numerous examples of highly detailed state constitutional provisions exist. Some are even humorous, such as the old Louisiana constitution that declared Huey P. Long's birthday a holiday forever. The Oklahoma Constitution requires all public schools to teach agriculture, horticulture, stock feeding, and

---

3.1 CITIZEN INITIATIVES IN COLORADO

On November 3, 1992, Colorado voters approved two highly controversial constitutional amendments, both of which were placed on the ballot through the citizen-initiative procedure. Amendment I limits both state and local taxing and state and local spending. Within months the impact was felt in the state's schools, which were hit with a 4 percent reduction in per-pupil spending for the next fiscal year.

Amendment II makes it unconstitutional for the state and local governments to enforce prohibition of discrimination against persons because of their sexual orientation. Existing antidiscrimination policies in Aspen, Boulder, and Denver were thus rendered unenforceable. The intended effect of the measure is to provide a shield under which private discrimination against persons because of their sexual orientation cannot, by law, be stopped. (The Colorado courts have temporarily halted enforcement of Amendment II.)

Both amendments remain highly charged, controversial matters. Amendment I triggered an immediate fiscal crisis in the school districts, many of which instantly prepared to lay off personnel, reduce or eliminate funds for busing and sports programs, and freeze salaries. Similar prospects are forecast for other Colorado cities and counties, as well as for the state government itself. Amendment II ignited nationwide efforts to convince tourists to boycott Colorado. A war of words continues between Colorado for Family Values, which promoted the measure, and its opponents, who view the amendment as a license to discriminate.

In Colorado, citizen groups altered their state constitution by way of direct democracy and seized the policy agenda of the state.

domestic science. In Alabama, the constitution provides for the continuity of the state legislature in the event of an enemy attack.

STATE CONSTITUTIONAL AMENDMENTS

Not surprisingly, long and detailed state constitutions are amended frequently. **Amendments** are modifications made to existing laws or bills. The **amendment process**—that is, the procedures used to make changes—varies among the states. However, it is typically a slow process that involves initiative through legislative action and popular ratification at the polls. Some state constitutions have been amended hundreds of times, whereas those drafted or redrafted recently have only a few amendments.[4]

Most proposals for state constitutional amendment begin in the state legislatures, and most proposed amendments pass. As of 1992, legislative proposal of an amendment required a simple majority in both houses in 17 states. In another 7 states a three-fifths majority is required, and in 18 others the required majority is two-thirds. Three states have procedures requiring either an abnormal (two-thirds, three-fifths, or three-fourths) majority in one legislative session or a simple majority in two sessions. In 17 states constitutional amendments may be proposed by way of a citizen initiative, a method requiring the signatures of a specified number of voters on a petition. These states are located in the midwestern or western United States, with the exception of Florida and Oklahoma. The inclusion of this **direct democracy** method of constitutional change in some states is a product of nineteenth- and early-twentieth-century Progressive and populist movements.

Table 3.3 lists the states with the most and fewest constitutional amendments. As one might expect, states that have recently adopted entirely new constitutions have the fewest amendments. Modifications to older constitutions that have been made through amendments are often incorporated into the revised documents.

In the 1980s alone, approximately 1,500 state constitutional amendments were proposed and 9 out of 10 were placed on the ballot by legislatures. Roughly three-fourths of the proposed changes met with voter approval. In 1990 and 1991, moreover, 226 amendments were proposed (197 of them by state legislatures) and 67.3 percent passed.

Although only a small number of proposed constitutional amendments reach the ballots by way of citizen initiative in the 17 states that authorize the process, the initiative is slowly gaining popularity. Whereas in 1982 and 1983 there were 16 such proposals involving 9 states, in 1990 and 1991 there were 29 citizen-initiated proposals in 10 states. Citizen-initiated amendments fare more poorly with the voters, with less than a 50 percent success rate.[5]

The subjects targeted for change in constitutional amendment proposals vary widely. Georgia voters recently rejected a proposal to lengthen the term of state representatives from two to four years. Voters in California, Colorado, and Oklahoma voted to limit the term for legislators in 1990, and a host of other limits followed in 1992. Texas voters defeated two proposals to raise legislator salaries. In Utah voters approved a change in the maximum allowable size of their state senate, from 30 to 29 (which was the actual number anyway), and in South Dakota a proposal to allow gambling in the city of Deadwood was approved. Colorado voters approved a similar limited gambling amendment in 1990, but defeated four others in 1992. California voters recently voted to increase the cigarette tax. In seven states—California, Colorado, Florida, New

TABLE 3.3   Constitutional Amendments in Selected States

State	Year of Most Recent Constitution	Number of Amendments
States with the most amendments:		
Alabama	1901	538
California	1879	480
South Carolina	1895	463
Texas	1876	339
New York	1894	210
States with the fewest amendments:		
Illinois	1970	7
Montana	1972	16
Michigan	1963	16
Pennsylvania	1968	19
Virginia	1970	22

Source: Data from *The Book of the States, 1992–93* (Lexington, Ky.: Council of State Governments, 1993), p. 20.

Jersey, New Mexico, Texas, and Washington—proposals to exempt veterans, widows, and the elderly from some taxes were endorsed. Colorado voters in 1992 approved a constitutional amendment prohibiting the state and local governments from protecting gays, lesbians, and bisexuals from discrimination in housing or employment.[6] (See Focus 3.1.)

CRITICISMS OF STATE CONSTITUTIONS

Over the past several decades, state constitutions have been attacked for their excessive length, detail, and restrictiveness. They also have been blamed for much of the inability of states and localities to cope with many contemporary problems.

Too Much Detail

For the sake of flexibility in changing times, it is argued that state constitutions, like all basic documents, should be brief and indicate succinctly general government principles. Although they should sketch the basic government structure and allocate authority in very general terms, the more detailed aspects of the law should be left to legislative statute. The excessive length and detail of state constitutions make change difficult. The hands of the governor, legislature, state agencies, and local governments are often tied, for enacting new laws or modifying old ones often requires constitutional amendment—a much more cumbersome and time-consuming process than the simpler enactment of a state statute or local ordinance.

Furthermore, much of the detail in state constitutions focuses on the limits and restrictions placed on state and local government, particularly in the area of finance. For example, the typical state constitution earmarks large proportions of the state's revenues for specified uses, severely limiting the ability of the legislature to allocate funds flexibly. Regarding local governments, state constitutions often place ceilings on the property tax and prohibit the use of an income tax, which restricts the ability of local governments to provide expensive services and attack costly problems.

Poor Design

State constitutions have also been criticized for the manner in which they organize the legislative and executive branches of state government. Until the Supreme Court reapportionment decisions of the early 1960s, some state constitutions provided for representation in one house of the legislature on a basis other than straight population—that is, not in terms of a "one person, one vote" formula. It is argued that this practice kept political control in the hands of rural interests, who were not likely to raise taxes and expenditures to fight growing urban and metropolitan problems.

In the executive branch, many state constitutions disperse authority to such a degree that firm executive leadership is difficult to achieve. For example, many permit the direct election of a series of executive branch officials (for example, attorney general, secretary of state, and tax commissioner), giving the officials an independent constituent base and allowing them to operate without control by the governor's office. Further, many state agencies are headed by multimember boards or commissions that maintain their autonomy from the governor.

Outdated

The perceived shortcomings of state constitutions are widely publicized. In 1968 James N. Miller began an article for the *National Civic Review* with this comment:

> In the next few years, Americans in as many as half the states will have a chance to vote on one of the most important government reforms facing the country: modernization of our ancient and ludicrous state constitutions.[7]

Miller added that if voters did not choose to modernize their state constitutions, "they [would] be missing one of their last good chances to pull our state and local governments out of their present rapid decline into senility and ineffectuality."[8]

Many state constitutions were written in the latter decades of the nineteenth century, when state and local governments were plagued by corruption. Attempts to thwart the chicanery led to the inclusion of many lengthy and restrictive constitutional provisions. For example, West Virginia's constitution, written in 1872 after a series of scandals involving the railroads, bars railroad officials from legislative office and devotes 6,300 words to functions in which the legislature *may not* engage. Miller argued that the excessive detail in constitutions encourages lawmakers to ignore or subvert the documents. Irrelevant passages designed to cope with problems of an earlier time are simply ignored. Provisions that are highly restrictive invite subversion. Very low debt ceilings, for example, have tempted states such as Pennsylvania to set up "public corporations," which borrow money for the state.

Former Pennsylvania governor William W. Scranton echoed the views expressed by Miller. Reflecting on his experience in office, Scranton stated:

> Hardly a day has passed when the attorney general or someone
> else has not told me of some constitutional restriction on proposed
> or needed action. My own frustrations have been only part of the
> problem. The restrictions placed on every executive department,
> the legislature, the courts and our more than 1,600 local
> governmental units, have been, if anything, even worse.[9]

The Reformers' Preferred Model

There have been demands in recent decades for constitutional revision in almost every U.S. state. In most cases the proposed changes follow a set pattern.

Proponents of constitutional revision typically seek shorter and less restrictive documents, a streamlined executive branch, a shortened ballot, a longer term in office for the governor, increased executive powers, and elimination of the mass of antiquated irrelevancies. These proposed revisions generally follow those of the model state constitution, first proposed by the National Municipal League in 1921. (The league proposed shorter and less restrictive state constitutions with increased powers for local governments.)

State Responses

Montana's constitution, adopted in 1972, provides for an apportionment commission, the election of the lieutenant governor and governor on the same ticket, and a maximum limit of 20 major executive branch departments. In addition, it lowers the age at which one is legally recognized as an adult to 18, provides for open legislative sessions, contains an environmental protection provision, and relaxes restrictions on state and local taxing and borrowing.

Many other states have also faced up to their constitutions' problems. Illinois, North Carolina, and Virginia adopted new documents in 1970, Louisiana adopted a new constitution in 1974, and Georgia did so in 1976 and again in

1982. But there have also been recent failures. In 1967 New York voters rejected a new document, as did voters in Arkansas, Idaho, and Oregon in 1970 and in North Dakota in 1972. Texas also failed in an attempt to revise its constitution in the 1970s.

During the 1980s (and early 1990s) the move to reform state constitutions subsided somewhat, as shown in Figure 3.2. The number of **constitutional conventions**, which are held to revise constitutions, declined, the number of new adoptions fell to just one, in Georgia, and voters' interest in conventions decreased. In 14 states the law requires that voters be asked periodically whether they want a constitutional convention to be called. In Hawaii this must occur every 9 years; in Alaska, Iowa, and Rhode Island it is done at 10-year intervals; and in the other 10 states it occurs less frequently.

State constitutional change is still difficult to implement despite reformers' efforts. Even those who seek change soon realize the difficulty of achieving it and tend to turn to the more successful tool of piecemeal constitutional amendment.

CONSTITUTIONAL POLITICS

Although it is tempting to view constitutions as higher laws that are somehow nonpolitical, they are the products of the same political processes from which other laws emerge. Many people associate the U.S. Constitution with the found-

FIGURE 3.2   Trends in Constitutional Change, 1940s–1980s

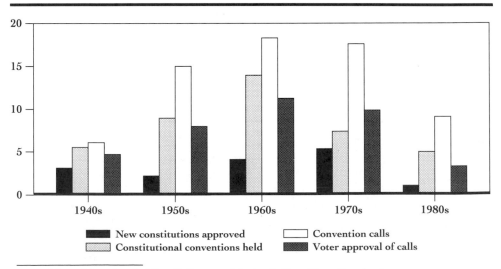

| | New constitutions approved | | Convention calls |
| | Constitutional conventions held | | Voter approval of calls |

source: Adapted from data in Albert L. Strum and Janice C. May, "State Constitutions and Constitutional Revisions: 1988–89," in *The Book of the States* (Lexington, Ky.: Council of State Governments, 1988), pp. 2–13.

ing fathers and the founding of the nation. As a result, the document is often viewed as a statement of "truths," rather than as a politically spawned set of laws. The propensity to hold constitutional documents in high esteem affects perceptions of state constitutions as well.

High-Stakes Politics

Constitutions are as political as any other law. They allocate authority, structure decision-making processes, specify rights and duties, and, as a result, help to determine who gets what, when and how. Examples of how state constitutions help to allocate scarce resources abound. To varying degrees, all state constitutions earmark tax revenues for specific uses: gasoline taxes for highway construction; hunting license fees for game, fish, and park programs; sales tax money for schools; and, in the case of Wisconsin, a portion of the property tax for the support of a statewide forestation program. Likewise, state constitutions provide a variety of tax exemptions for various special interests: veterans and the elderly may be exempt from part of the property tax; homesteads and certain classes of agricultural lands may receive a special tax break. Other examples include the granting of special water, mineral, and timber rights. Constitutions, like other laws, are not neutral —they favor some individuals and groups over others.

Special Interests

That state constitutions play a role in the allocation of scarce societal resources helps to explain why constitutional conventions are the site of hot debate and competition and why newly drafted documents are often rejected at the polls. When the subject of a new state constitution is raised, vested interests that receive special advantages under the existing document fight for its retention, whereas new interests fight for the inclusion of provisions that would benefit them. For example, veterans' groups support preference points on civil service examinations and property tax exemptions. Taxpayer groups push for the retention or imposition of very low ceilings on the property tax. The education lobby, made up of teachers and administrators, fights to earmark funds for the schools and to increase the level of state support for local school districts. Sporting groups insist that hunting and fishing license fees be constitutionally tagged for fish and wildlife programs. Churches lobby for property tax exemptions. At the Michigan convention in 1962, the Association of Township Government Officials successfully fought off an attempt to eliminate the township as a form of government. These and other vested interests seek to establish or protect, in their states' most basic law, special advantages for themselves.

Special private interests are especially vigorous in their efforts to influence the content of state constitutions because constitutions are more difficult to alter than are statutes or administrative rules and procedures. Administrative rules and procedures can be changed by administrative fiat, and statutes can be altered or repealed by a majority action in the legislature and the concurrence of the governor. It is much more difficult to change a constitution. In a majority of the states, the proposal of a constitutional amendment requires the consent of two-thirds or three-fifths of the members of both houses of the legislature, or the securing of a very large number of signatures of registered voters on a petition and ratification by a majority vote at the polls. It is, quite obviously, a long and difficult process; and, as a result, it is of great advantage to a special interest group to have its particular provision included in a document that is so difficult to change.

Vested Interests versus Reformers' Interests

Based on a 1970 study of constitutional conventions in three states, Elmer Cornwell, Jay Goodman, and Wayne Swanson suggested several trends regarding vested and reformers' interests. First, voting divisions in conventions tend to involve "good government" reformers versus groups that may be affected by changes in the constitution and thus have a stake in the status quo. Second, the methods by which constitutional convention representatives are chosen have an impact on the character of the document that is produced.

Finally, new documents that are either highly innovative or not at all innovative are not likely to receive public acceptance. A highly innovative document draws the wrath of "standpatters," whereas an uninnovative one is likely to be rejected by proponents of reform. A document promising incremental change, therefore, has the best chance of popular adoption at the polls.[10]

The Difficulty of Introducing Changes

Given that state constitutions are hard to change and tend to be long and detailed, one might infer that they are also conservative in nature. Provisions that favor special interests are hard to remove. New approaches that would allow government to move in new directions or attack new problems are difficult to secure. The hands of governors, legislatures, and state agencies are tied by constitutional restrictions on the earmarking of funds, the imposition of debt ceilings, and the exemption of properties from the tax rolls. In a period of rapid social, economic, and political flux, constitutional change is extremely difficult.

Enduring Issues

Some issues in state constitutional politics are universal and enduring, whereas others are more episodic in nature or the products of a particular state or region. Writing about the Virginia experience, for example, state constitutional expert A. E. Dick Howard points to several issues that he views as fundamental and common: To what extent should there be restrictions on popular preferences? How should legislative, executive, and judicial relationships be structured? What roles will state and local governments play? How much detail is appropriate in a foundational document? As Howard notes, questions such as these may never be fully answered.[11]

Other issues are less enduring or universal in nature. For example, in 1889 the Wyoming constitutional convention debated the issue of whether people need to be able to read in order to vote; the Wyoming convention resolved in the affirmative. The delegates also considered a tax on mined coal and the need for a civil service system. They decided not to tax coal and concluded that patronage "is one of the rewards of politics."[12] In a debate on the ownership of water, it was decided that all water belonged to the state of Wyoming. And, since there was no universal suffrage in 1889, the delegates discussed the wisdom of permitting only men to vote on ratification of the state constitution. They chose to have qualified electors of both sexes vote.[13]

During the late nineteenth and late twentieth centuries, certain issues became matters of constitutional politics. The last two decades of the nineteenth century witnessed widespread public and private sector corruption and abuse of power. These conditions spawned interest in the initiative, the referendum, and the recall as tools to control government and curb corrupt practices. The **initiative** is a process in which citizens sign petitions so as to place policy questions directly before the voters. The **referendum** is similar in that citizens vote directly on proposals that have been referred to them by the legislature. The **recall** is a process in which citizens vote on a proposal to remove (recall) a public official before the end of the normal term. More recently, in many of the 17 states that allow citizen initiative, it has been employed in efforts to enact constitutional limitations on taxes and spending. California, Massachusetts, Michigan, and Colorado are among the many states where such measures have appeared on recent ballots.

In the decades of the 1950s, 1960s, and 1970s, there was considerable interest in reorganizing state government by introducing some organizational features of the private sector. As a result, constitutional politics featured debates over such issues as centralizing executive branch authority and expanding the influence of governors in the budget-making process.

The political nature of state constitutional politics is illustrated vividly in Diane Blair's description and analysis of constitutional history and politics in Arkansas.[14] That state has had five constitutions. The **Arkansas: An Example**

first, ratified in 1836, was modeled after the U.S. Constitution. The second was adopted in 1861, when Arkansas joined the Confederacy at the start of the Civil War. References to the Union became instead references to the Confederacy, but not much else was changed. After the war between the states, the constitution was changed in 1864 as Arkansas was reassociated with the Union. In this third version, slavery was outlawed.

In 1868 Arkansas adopted what became known as the "carpetbag constitution" — its fourth. Blacks could vote but former confederates could not. State government power, including gubernatorial power, was centralized. Six years later, in 1874, a fifth constitution was ratified in Arkansas, this one in reaction to the 1868 document and the excesses and corruption of the postwar Reconstruction period. The 1874 document reflected widespread fear and distrust of the state government. It was long and went into detail to prescribe authority carefully and to limit the state. Many terms of office were shortened to two years and a number of appointed executive branch offices were made elective. In addition, many public office salaries were constitutionally set and the state's taxing and spending powers were limited. Clearly, each of the five constitutions reflects the politics of the day.

Arkansas continues to operate under the 1874 constitution, though there have been efforts to replace it. Between 1968 and 1980, when reformers nationwide were seeking to modernize state constitutions, reform efforts were launched in Arkansas. In one instance, the reform attempt was terminated when the Arkansas Supreme Court ruled that the directive given to the constitutional convention unlawfully tried to limit the scope of the delegates' agenda. Other attempts at reform failed to receive voter ratification at the polls, despite the apparent support of public officials, many interest groups, and the public.

In Arkansas, as in many other states, why do voters reject modern documents designed to streamline state government? Blair cites as reasons general voter indifference to constitutional reform, coupled with the opposition of many special interests. Voters for whom state constitutional reform is not a major concern may well decline to vote at all, or they may be easily persuaded by opponents. A few small special interest groups may favor much of the new arrangement but oppose one or two changes that would take away some special benefit. The opposition of small groups can add up to a negative majority. Blair describes the process by which many small objections to constitutional reform add up to the rejection of the entire proposal:

> In 1970, for example, county judges feared loss of power to a newly strengthened county legislature, chancery judges resisted their potential consolidation with courts of law, realtors feared potential increases in property taxes, and various professional associations opposed the rumored consolidation of their separate licensing boards with one administrative authority. In 1980 organized labor opposed removal of the 10 percent usury limit, the Arkansas Educational Association feared the loss of the Education Department's independent status to greater gubernatorial direction, some legislators resented the redistricting that mandated single-member districts would necessitate, and fundamentalists suspected an attempted backdoor to get an equal rights amendment into the constitution through reference to "sex" in the revised equal protection clause.[15]

It is no wonder that attempts at wholesale constitutional revision so often fail and that most constitutional change comes about through a piecemeal amendment process. When a host of special constitutionally anchored advantages are threatened with change, there is inevitably much opposition. However, when only one or two interests are threatened (as is usually the case with proposed amendments), the opposition is not as strong and the chances for passage are greater.

THE FUNCTIONS OF STATE CONSTITUTIONS

Does it matter what the people of a state include in their constitution? Does it matter how constitutions "constitute" the institutional apparatus of state and local government? Judging from the interest that political groups have in defeating reforms, in Arkansas and elsewhere, the answer to both questions clearly must be yes.

Constitutions Distribute Power

Consider again the functions and content of state constitutions; it is the features of these documents that are often the targets of reform. The relationships between the legislative and executive branches are set forth. In the critical process of budget making, it is determined whether the governor or the legislature will play the dominant role, and whether the governor will have veto authority over legislative actions. In Wisconsin, for example, the governor's role in the budget and the governor's authority are strong. Recently, and to the consternation of the legislature, Wisconsin Governor Tommy Thompson went so far as to rearrange some numbers and words in the budget, thus altering legislative intent. In North Carolina the governor has no veto power.

The state constitution structures state executive branches. It determines whether the attorney general, secretary of state, treasurer, highway department director, and others will work for the governor or be directly elected by the voters and thereby possess an independent constitutional base and freedom from gubernatorial control.

Constitutions Govern Finances

Unlike the federal government, which struggles with huge budget deficits, especially in recent years, all states except Vermont are required by law to balance budgets annually (Vermont does so as a matter of practice). In most states this is a constitutional requirement, though in a few it is a statutory one.

The balanced budget requirement is of no small consequence—it keeps the states out of the type of deficit trouble that plagues Washington. However, it also makes budgeting difficult for states. Matching expenditures with revenues during 12-month fiscal-year cycles is not an easy task. Revenues must be forecast well over a year in advance, often in the context of an unsettled economy. The potential for agency spending overruns in program areas that are not easily controlled, such as social services and health, is always a danger. As a result, states maintain reserve accounts. But there is constant political pressure to reduce or raid reserve accounts to meet one spending demand or another. Overall, though, state constitutional barriers to deficit spending provide effective parameters to the budget process.

Summary

Each of the 50 states has its own state constitution. Some states have had many different constitutions over the years. State constitutions are important because they organize the branches of state government, distribute powers and privileges among agencies and officeholders, and impose limits and restrictions on government activities. Although most state constitutions are excessively long and detailed, modern reformers are emphasizing a shift to briefer, more basic documents. Most attempts at sweeping reform have failed; the groups that benefit from the existing provisions often work together to defeat the changes or the new documents. State constitutions embody high-stakes politics; like all laws, they help to determine the distribution of power and material resources.

When reformers seek to reorder or modify institutional arrangements, groups whose current interests are best served by the status quo resist the changes. Legislators, judges, governors, agency heads, universities, cities, and counties all seek maximum constitutional authority and flexibility. Similarly, teachers, realtors, morticians, lawyers, and taxpayers want support of their endeavors addressed by the state constitution, with the cost or a good portion of it paid by the government. The most basic rules of the political game — including the structure of the playing field and the tools needed to work the system successfully — are thus set forth in the constitutions of the 50 American states.

KEY TERMS

state constitution	direct democracy
statute	constitutional convention
judicial review	initiative
state bill of rights	referendum
amendment	recall
amendment process	

**ADDITIONAL
READINGS**

The Book of the States (Lexington, Ky.: Council of State Governments), published biennially. Each issue contains information updates on state constitutions as well as a wealth of statistical data.

Miller, James N. "The Dead Hand of the Past." *National Civic Review* (April 1968): 183–88.

National Municipal League. *Model State Constitutions*. 6th ed. New York: NML, 1968.

Witt, Elder. "Hans A. Linde: The Unassuming Architect of an Emerging Role for State Constitutions." *Governing* (July 1989): 58.

NOTES

1. Up-to-date information, statistical and otherwise, may be found in the biennial issues of *The Book of the States* (Lexington, Ky.: Council of State Governments).

2. Elder Witt, "Hans A. Linde: The Unassuming Architect of an Emerging Role for State Constitutions," *Governing* (July 1989): 58.

3. Ibid.: 56.

4. See *The Book of the States, 1992–93* (Lexington, Ky.: Council of State Governments, 1993), p. 20.

5. Janice C. May, "State Constitutions and Constitutional Revision: 1990–91," in *The Book of the States, 1992–93* (Lexington, Ky.: Council of State Governments, 1993), p. 2.

6. See ibid., pp. 8–9; and Janice C. May, "State Constitutions and Constitutional Revision, 1988–89 and the 1980s," in *The Book of the States, 1990–91* (Lexington, Ky.: Council of State Governments, 1991), p. 21.

7. James N. Miller, "The Dead Hand of the Past," *National Civic Review* (April 1968): 183.

8. Ibid.

9. William W. Scranton, "A National Movement," *National Civic Review* (Jan. 1967): 7.

10. Elmer E. Cornwell, Jr., Jay S. Goodman, and Wayne R. Swanson, "State Constitutional Conventions: Delegates, Roll Calls and Issues," *Midwest Journal of Political Science* (Feb. 1970): 105–30.

11. A. E. Dick Howard, "Constitutional Government," in *Virginia Government and Politics*, ed. Thomas R. Morris and Larry Sabato (Charlottesville, Va.: Institute of Government Research, University of Virginia, 1984), p. 11.

12. Tim R. Miller, *State Government: Politics and Wyoming*, 2nd ed. (Dubuque, Iowa: Kendall/Hunt, 1985), p. 13.

13. Ibid.

14. Diane D. Blair, *Arkansas Politics and Government* (Lincoln: University of Nebraska Press, 1988), p. 130.

15. Ibid.

4

The State Legislature

The house of representatives of the Texas state legislature in session. Texas has a bicameral legislature, modeled on the U.S. Congress, as do all states except Nebraska. Austin, Texas. *(Bob Daemmrich/The Image Works)*

INSTITUTIONAL DESIGN

Central characteristics of the institutional design of state government include the separation of powers in all 50 states and bicameralism in all states except Nebraska. Voters in Indiana provided a striking illustration of the effects of such institutional arrangements in November 1988. They elected Democrats as governor and lieutenant governor, and a senate with a Republican majority of 26 to 24 over which the Democratic lieutenant governor would preside. For the house of representatives the voters selected 50 Democrats and 50 Republicans.[1]

The stage was thus set for conflict—within each house, between the house and the senate, and between the legislative and executive branches. Yet Indiana was not alone in this regard. In recent years, well over one-half of the American states have had split party control either between the house and the senate or between the legislative and executive branches. Following the November 1992 elections, 30 of the 50 states were split. Only 4 states featured Republican party control of both legislative chambers and the governorship, and 16 others were dominated by the Democrats. The states of Alabama, California, Maine, Massachusetts, Mississippi, and South Carolina had Democratic legislatures but Republican governors in 1992. Divided government and its attendant conflict are no longer the exception but the norm.

To those who cherish neatness, order, and speed in decision making, this combination of institutionally dispersed authority and political competitiveness must be a nightmare. For others, who fear concentrated power and cherish representation above all, the carnival that such divided government is certain to produce is a small price to pay. But no one should fail to see the impact of a state's institutions on its politics.

INSTITUTIONAL TRANSITION

Legislatures are the centerpieces of the institutional arrangements in the American states. The legislature is where U.S. policies are made. Elected legislators decide how much to spend on schools, how much zoning power cities may exercise, which professions will be regulated, what acts will constitute crimes, and who will pay for it all. The legislature is also the institution that produces most of the nation's laws.

American state legislatures have had a varied and interesting history. During the early decades of the Republic, they were the dominant branch. Later they fell into disrepute and became, quite often, subservient and sometimes corruptible rubber stamps for state governors and lobbyists. More recently, the state legislatures have been reformed and have reasserted themselves as the central institution of state government, although they are still not free of problems and criticism.

Legislative Supremacy

Following the revolutionary war, public fear and dislike for executive authority was high, and thus representative bodies — legislatures — were fashioned as the dominant institutions of government. The Virginia constitution of 1776, for example, provided for a strong legislature and a weak executive. The governor was elected by the legislature itself for a term of just one year and could serve no more than three years in a row. There were few limits on the power of the legislature. Indeed, Thomas Jefferson, who served as Virginia's second governor, commented on the extent of legislative power by observing that "173 despots would surely be as oppressive as one."[2]

Trouble in the Legislature

The later years of the nineteenth century witnessed widespread political corruption and a decline in trust of government. State legislators, like many governors and both local and national officials, joined hands with big-money interests to enrich themselves at public expense. Such behavior fueled the Progressive and populist movements and led to efforts to restrict government. For example, in 1901 the state of Alabama adopted a constitution that allowed the legislature to meet for just 50 days once every 4 years. Other states instituted similarly limiting reforms. Public confidence in the legislative institutions of the time was not high.

Throughout much of the period from World War II to the reapportionment revolution of the mid-1960s, however, state legislatures remained under the dominance of special interests and rural-oriented lawmakers. They teamed up with their lobbyists (see Chapter 8) to work out public policy in "capitol hill" pubs like the Bull Ring in Santa Fe, the Broken Spoke in Austin, Clyde's in Tallahassee, and the Galleria Tavern in Columbus, Ohio.[3] (See Focus 4.1.)

The Reformers Triumph

In the 1960s the U.S. Supreme Court kicked off a revolution of sorts with its decision in the case of *Baker v. Carr* (1962). In *Baker* and subsequent related decisions, the Court declared that state legislative districts must contain approximately equal numbers of people. These decisions broke many old patterns of power and many old habits. The **reformed legislatures** have not been the same ever since.

FOCUS

4.1   ALCOHOL AND LEGISLATORS

The political "watering hole" is as old as American politics and American legislatures themselves. Over two hundred years ago, Thomas Jefferson and Patrick Henry met at the Raleigh Tavern in Williamsburg, Virginia, to complain about the actions of King George III. For years, legislators and lobbyists in Denver bought each other hamburgers and beer at the Congress lounge—called Nick's—or French dip and martinis nearby at the Quorum as they exchanged information and lobbied each other. Stories have it that at Santa Fe's Bull Ring, a state senator named "Diamond Tooth" Miller wore a button advertising himself as "the Best Goddamn Senator Money Can Buy" as he filled himself with drinks bought by lobbyists. In Texas, tax bills were written over lunch and drinks in the Deck Club. Florida's lobbyists used to supply food and drinks to legislators in rooms near the capitol, compliments of the "booze fairy."

The situation has changed in recent years. Modern post-reapportionment, career-oriented state legislators drink less. The media are more apt to report on off-the-floor behavior. The public is impatient with lawmakers. So today it's less booze, more soft drinks and coffee. Some say that the modern legislature is cleaner and better. Others lament the trend, arguing that better policy emerges from an environment in which elected officials can cut deals away from the glare of the press, and without constant concern for the impact of their frank discussions and their compromises on their reelection fortunes. We may have fewer barroom and back-room deals than before, but do we have better public policy?

SOURCES: Jonathan Walters, "A Night on the Town Isn't What It Used to Be in Jefferson City," *Governing* (July 1989): 26–31; and Alan Ehrenhalt, "An Embattled Institution," *Governing* (Jan. 1992): 28–33.

America's state legislatures have continued to change in many ways over the past three decades. Years ago they were roundly criticized for being malapportioned and exhibiting a rural bias in an urban age; for not offering members decent staffing, space, equipment and pay; and for being internally undemocratic and rife with cronyism. Pundits said that the legislatures should modernize and become more like the U.S. Congress, with good salaries and ample staff and space, that they should meet every year in long sessions, that they should open up and clean up internally, and that they should be reapportioned so as to be more representative of the population. Much of that has happened, and now the state legislatures are sometimes criticized for being too well endowed with pay, staff, and space. The members are becoming careerist just like — some say unfortunately like — members of Congress.

Prior to *Baker v. Carr*, state legislatures were heavily dominated by rural interests. Legislative leaders and majorities had little interest in expanding tax bases so as to raise money to deal with growing urban problems. **Legislative turnover**, the election of new freshman lawmakers, in states was quite high, running near and sometimes over 50 percent following some elections. As a result, novice lawmakers could be tightly led by old-hand leaders and effectively coached by special interest lobbyists. Sessions were short, often running just 30, 60, or 90 days, and in many states legislators met just every other year. Session-end **logjams** or deadlocks were frequent, and some legislation was sloppy and hastily adopted. Alan Ehrenhalt describes these old-time legislators as "racist, sexist, secretive, boss-ruled, malapportioned, and uninformed."[4]

The 1960s and 1970s were periods of major change. In the wake of Watergate and Vietnam, and in the context of the civil rights, consumer, and environmental movements, the nation was ripe for reform, and the reformist sentiment touched state legislatures. Following the *Baker* case, the legislatures were reapportioned and thus came to represent urban and suburban interests more fully. Sessions in many states were lengthened and some were changed to annual meetings. Pay was increased, expense accounts expanded, new offices built, and staffs enlarged. (In many states now, staff help is available for committees, party caucuses, leadership, members, and even members' home offices.) State after state passed laws requiring members to report their finances and lobbyists to report their income, expenses, and clients. The media began to watch legislators more closely.

The modernization of state legislatures proceeded unevenly across the country. The states of California, Florida, Pennsylvania, Michigan, New York, and Wisconsin led the way. Others, such as Wyoming and Kansas, moved more slowly. A number of states remain unreformed today, preferring to stay with the **citizen legislature** model, in which lawmakers do not make a career out of politics; New Hampshire is an example.

As many state legislatures became more like Congress, legislators became more like the representatives in Congress, looking at their position in careerist terms and gearing more of their behavior toward reelection. Campaigns became increasingly expensive, political consultants were hired more often, and running for reelection became a full-time enterprise for many. Legislative leaders took on the role of fund-raisers to help members' campaigns.[5] (See Table 4.1.)

Did Reform Backfire?

Today, state legislatures are again the subject of criticism, but, ironically, often because they did what the pre-1960s critics asked of them. The opening of all legislative decisions to public scrutiny makes it more difficult for members to sit down and work out compromises. Like Con-

TABLE 4.1
State Legislatures before and after Modernization

Before Modernization	After Modernization
Malapportioned	One person, one vote
Rural dominance	Improved pay
Internally undemocratic	Expanded staff help
Strong leaders	Better facilities
High turnover of members	Longer sessions
Short sessions	More independent of governor
Limited staff	Conflict of interest laws
Low pay	Sunshine laws
Many conflicts of interest	More costly elections
Strong influence by governor	More PAC money
Strong interest group influence	Careerist legislators
Sometimes corrupt	More independent legislators
	Weakened leadership

gress, some state legislatures are faulted because they are heavily staffed and the staffers devote energy to the reelection of their bosses. High pay has made the job so attractive that some members want to stay in office forever. The preoccupation with reelection, critics say, drives members to endless pandering to district interests—to the neglect of statewide problems and needs. All the while the costs of running a campaign have escalated, from $25,000 to over $1 million in some cases. Members now must devote far too much of their time to fund-raising and to interest groups' political action committees (**PACs**), which are the political arms of professional associations, unions, corporations, and other groups. (See Chapter 8 for a more detailed discussion of PACs.)

Perhaps, some say, the states would be well served by a return to the citizen legislature. Others suggest that the answer lies in an intermediate position, with fair representation and reasonable but limited staffing, pay, and so forth. In any case, the state legislatures have undergone significant change in recent years (see Table 4.1). For better or worse, they have been modernized, or professionalized, as early critics wanted.

LEGISLATIVE FUNCTIONS

All 50 states follow the national pattern of instituting a formal separation of the lawmaking, the law-implementing, and the law adjudication functions through the establishment of three branches of government. Separation of powers does not, of course, completely compartmentalize these three governmental functions, but it does place most of the responsibility for each function with a specified branch of the government. One of the major tasks of state legislatures, then, is the enactment of statutes, or state laws. In the process of fulfilling their formal responsibilities of lawmaking and budget review, state legislatures interact closely with the other two branches of government—the executive and the judiciary—and perform the critical function of legitimizing public policy.

Thus, laws are passed—an almost endless string of national, state, and local measures that place limits on behavior and establish public service programs. State constitutions allocate to legislatures the authority to pass laws. In some cases, constitutions specifically restrict behavior and establish public programs. But it is in the statutes—the laws enacted by the legislature—that most of the provisions that authoritatively restrict behavior and establish public programs are found.

The range of subject matter contained in the flood of legislative proposals considered by state legislatures is considerable. They have to do with such weighty matters as agriculture, health, roads, education, local governments, state agencies, water rights, the environment, taxation, motor vehicles, insurance companies, children's codes, and others. Some bills are of much less consequence than others, and still others are, in fact, patently silly. But by and large the business of legislatures is serious.

Another important function of state legislatures is controlling the budget. This is the oldest legislative function and predates the enactment of laws. In a sense, the budgetary powers of legislatures are part of their overall policy formation role and, again, this is a role that legislatures share in a *de facto* sense with the executive branch. But legislative control of the public purse is important for both real and symbolic reasons. Most state legislatures must approve state budgets annually: They have the authority to review, revise, or eliminate any or all items, and they may add new items if they wish. In reality, of course, modern state budgets are so voluminous and complicated that the legislatures' role is often one of reviewing and making minor alterations in the budget as it is proposed by the governor. But the legislature does retain the final legal budgetary sanction, and this fact alone conditions the contents of the budget that the governor submits.

THE LEGISLATIVE PROCESS: AN OVERVIEW

The **legislative process** is that by which a bill becomes a law. In most states, the process is similar both to that of other states and to that of Congress. (The legislative process in Nevada is shown in Figure 4.1.) Although there are variations among the states, in general terms the process goes like this: A bill is introduced, in either the house or the senate, by one individual or a group of the members of that particular chamber. A bill might have been sketched out by the legislator, but it is as likely to have originated with an administrative agency,

FIGURE 4.1   The Legislative Process in Nevada

Initial Steps by the Author

Idea

Sources of ideas: government, elected officials, businesses, lobbyists, citizens.

Drafting

Request for bill draft made by legislators, legislative committees, the governor, or state and local governments. Formal copy of bill prepared by legislative counsel.

Introduction

Bill submitted by senate or assembly member. Numbered and read for first time. Assigned to committee. Printed.

Action in the House of Origin

Committee

Testimony taken from sponsor, proponents, and opponents. Typical actions include: "Do Pass"; "Amend and Do Pass"; "No Action"; "Indefinitely Postpone (kill)"; "Amend and Refer to Same Committee"; "Refer to Another Committee"; "Redraft as Interim Study Proposal." Bills with any fiscal implications, if approved by policy committee, are referred to Committee on Finance in the senate and to Committee on Ways and Means in the assembly.

Second reading

Bills given "Do Pass" recommendations are read a second time, and placed on the general file for debate and vote. Bills given "Amend and Do Pass" recommendation are read a second time, amended and reprinted prior to being placed on the general file for action.

Floor debate and vote

Bills are read a third time and debated. A roll call vote follows. For passage of bills or joint resolutions, 11 votes are needed in the senate and 22 in the assembly. If these numbers are not reached, the measure is defeated. Any member voting on the prevailing side may serve notice of reconsideration to request a second vote. If passed or passed with amendments, the measure is sent to the second house.

Action in the Second House

Reading

Bill is read for the first time and referred to committee.

Committee

Procedures and possible actions are identical to those in the first house.

Second reading

If cleared by committee, the bill is read a second time and placed on the general file (agenda) for debate and vote.

Floor debate and vote

The procedure is identical to that in the first house. If a bill or joint resolution is passed without having been amended in the second house, it is sent to the governor. (Other types of resolutions are sent to the secretary of state.) If amended in the second house and passed, the measure is returned to the house of origin for consideration of the amendments.

Resolution of Two-House Differences, if Necessary

Concurrence

The house of origin decides whether to accept the second-house amendments. If accepted, the bill goes to the governor. If the amendments are rejected, the bill is returned to the second house for a decision whether to withdraw the proposed changes. If the second house does not recede, the bill is referred to a two-house conference committee.

Conference

If the conferees fail to agree, the bill dies. If the conferees present a recommendation for compromise (conference report), both houses vote on the report. If the report is accepted by both, the bill goes to the governor. If either house rejects the report, a second (and final) conference committee may be formed.

Role of the Governor

Sign or veto?

Within 5 days excluding Sundays (10 days if session has ended) of receiving a measure, the governor may sign it into law, allow it to become law without his signature, or veto the bill. A vetoed bill returns to the house of origin for reconsideration. An override of the governor's veto requires a two-thirds majority vote of both houses. If a bill is vetoed after the session ends, it returns to the next legislative session for reconsideration. A measure becomes effective on the following October 1st unless otherwise specified in the bill.

SOURCE: State of Nevada, *Legislative Manual*, Bulletin no. 92–23, 1993.

the governor's staff, or a special interest group. Usually, the formal bill is drafted by a legislative bill-drafting office. Next, the bill is sent by the presiding officer or a clerk to a **legislative committee** that usually considers that particular type of bill. The bill is then considered by that committee, and hearings may be held.

In some states all bills must be given a hearing; in others the chairperson can kill a bill by simply ignoring it. At the hearings testimony is heard from both proponents and opponents of the bill. After consideration, the committee may send the bill to another committee, or back to the floor of the full house with the recommendation that it be voted either up or down. As in Congress, many bills never make it out of the state legislative committee. However, it should be noted that some bills, in some states, do not go to committee but are instead handled directly by a caucus of the majority party.

If a bill is placed on the agenda of the full house — an event that is not always automatic — and if the bill is passed, it is then sent to the other house, where it runs through roughly the same process. If a bill makes it through both houses, it is sent to the governor for signature or veto, whichever the governor chooses.

In many cases, bills passing both houses have some amendments attached at some point in the process. Therefore, the wording of the house version of a bill may differ from that of the senate version. In such cases, the first chamber may accept the amendments of the other chamber. If it does not, a **conference committee** comprised of a few members of each house may meet to iron out the differences between the two versions and send a uniform bill back to the two houses. Researcher Donald Gross suggests that in conference committee negotiations, senate conferees generally come out best.[6] It is customary, then, for each house to approve bills in the compromise form suggested by the conference committee. The bill is then sent to the governor for signature or veto.

Death Traps for Bills

The state legislative lawmaking process is, of course, more complicated than the preceding brief sketch suggests. As many commentators correctly suggest, the legislative process, as it currently operates in American national, state, and local governments, has a strong conservative bias. As a result, it is much easier to use the procedures to stop a bill from becoming a law than it is to secure its passage. The legislative process thus lends itself to obstructionism. As in Congress and many city councils, there are several critical points in the legislative process, called **power pockets**, whereby a strategically placed individual or minority coalition in a state legislature can kill or radically alter a bill.

The speaker of the house of representatives and the president of the senate are sometimes able to affect the fate of a bill through their power to refer bills to committees. As we will see later in the chapter, all state legislative bodies are broken down into subject-matter-oriented committees. Some bills, however, may properly be sent to more than one committee. An education bill, for example, might legitimately be sent to either a committee on local government or a committee on education. The chair and members of one of these committees might be inclined to look favorably on the proposed law, whereas the chair and members of the other committee might be hostile to the bill or to some of its provisions. In Colorado, for example, House Speaker Carl "Bev" Bledsoe, a cigarette smoker and a rancher, opposed no-smoking laws and daylight savings time. A fellow Republican introduced bills to curb smoking and institute year-round daylight savings time in the state. Bledsoe sent the bills to Colorado's House Committee on Agriculture. His friends on that committee "smoked" both bills, and neither one saw the light of day.

Legislative committees themselves exercise extensive control over bills. Committees always have more work than they have time for; as a result, some bills are considered and others are left to die. If a committee chairperson is opposed to a certain bill, that committee chair can, within limits, refuse to schedule hearings or delay them. In some states the committee chair can send the bill to a subcommittee that the chair knows will ignore it, amend it to the point where it loses its original intent, or recommend that it not be passed upon favorably by the full committee and the full house. Full committees can do likewise: In some states they can ignore bills, amend them to death, postpone them indefinitely, or report them out to the full house knowing that the bills will be defeated. As one would expect, the degree of influence that such committees have over proposed legislation varies greatly among the states. For example, according to Malcolm Jewell, committee influence is weak in Illinois, due in part to the strength of political parties, but strong in Minnesota. As a general rule, though, committees, their members, and their chairpersons are in a position to critically affect the fate of bills.[7]

The governor is obviously in such a critical position. Governors in every state except North Carolina possess some sort of **legislative veto** power, and many have a **line-item veto** over specific items in the budget.[8] Since a two-thirds or three-fifths vote in both houses of the legislature is typically needed in order to override an executive veto, the governor is in a position to thwart the enactment of laws that are found displeasing. In most states the veto power is strengthened further by the tendency of legislators to rush the most important and most controversial bills (for example, education, welfare, taxation, budget) through the legislature in the final few days of the session, for legislatures in most states cannot call themselves back into special session. Therefore, critical legislation sometimes appears on the governor's desk toward the end of a session; should the governor decide to veto or pocket veto a measure, the legislature is left without enough time to reconsider the bill or attempt to override the veto.

Some legislative houses have powerful agenda-setting committees of some sort, often called **rules committees** or **calendar committees**. They become powerful, in many cases, because of the voluminous flow of bills sent to the floor, especially during the final few days of a session. The extensive flow of proposed legislation means that if bills are considered on the floor in the order in which they emerge from various committees, the most important legislative proposals may never be considered. Thus rules committees often have the authority to restructure the legislative calendar, giving priority to certain bills and ensuring their consideration. Clearly, this makes the rules or calendar committee a powerful body, for it can, in many instances, determine the fate of a bill.

In short, there are many stages in the lawmaking process at which an individual or group may sabotage policy proposals. To become law, a bill must successfully make its way through a process rife with pitfalls. It is no wonder, then, that in most states fewer than half of the bills introduced ever make it all the way through the legislative process; in some states the rate is below 20 percent.

Is the Process Effective?

It has been implied here that the slow, cumbersome, and hazardous state legislative process is not effective. Given the ability of individuals and small groups to use the procedures to thwart majority rule, it is difficult for some to come to a different conclusion. Others argue, however, that the process works to serve the public interest in that it mitigates potentially rash and hasty action. Supporters of the slow legislative process suggest that there are times, especially during crises, when the temptation is great to rush a host of new bills through the process. Its slow-moving nature forces legislators to take the time to reconsider, dispassionately, the proposed laws that at first may seem wise and necessary. Bicameralism, the committee system, the gubernatorial veto, and other factors that slow down the legislative process are, therefore, considered effective.

Recent Improvements

During the recent era of state legislative modernization, many states instituted a variety of procedures to streamline the process. In most states today legislators may pre-file bills; that is, they may have bills prepared, and submit them, before the legislative session actually begins. In about half the states, a bill that has not passed in the first year of a two-year session may be carried over into the second year.

Most state legislatures also now operate with a calendar that sets deadlines for the introduction of bills, for the completion of committee work on bills, and for action on bills in the two chambers on second and third readings. All of these innovations in procedure are designed to expedite the work of committees and to relieve some of the pressure of the old end-of-session logjam.[9]

INFORMAL RULES AND STRATEGIES

In addition to the formal rules and procedures that govern the lawmaking activities of state legislatures, there are a number of informal yet powerful rules that guide behavior. Informal rules tend to exist, of course, in almost all types of organizations.

In a classic study of four state legislatures, John C. Wahlke and his associates identify several informal rules that expedite the operations of state legislatures and make the legislative process reasonably coordinated and predictable for the lawmakers:

> Keep your word; abide by commitments; support another member's local bill if it doesn't affect you or your district; don't make personal attacks on other members; oppose the bill, not the [person]; observe common courtesies; be friendly and courteous even if you disagree; take a stand, don't be wishy-washy; notify in advance if you are going to change your stand or can't keep a commitment; be willing to compromise; don't fight unnecessarily; follow caucus or conference decisions; keep your temper; don't introduce too many bills or amendments; don't divulge confidential information; defend legislature and members against outsiders; be fair, show good judgment, maturity, responsibility.[10]

Sanctions can be applied against individuals who violate these and other informal rules of the game. The most commonly applied sanctions include obstructing the violator's own bills, applying the "silent treatment," indicating mistrust by cross-examination, and stripping away political tools such as patronage, good committee assignments, and the support of local organizations and constituencies.

Similarly, lawmakers have access to a wide variety of tactics that they can use to political advantage. One way to help ensure passage of one's bills is to seek well-placed co-sponsors. It doesn't hurt a bill's chances, for example, to have as a co-sponsor the chairperson of the committee that hears the bill or a legislative leader in either or both houses. It also doesn't hurt to have multiple co-sponsors, for any lawmaker willing to add his or her name to a bill is unlikely to oppose the measure.

All sorts of other informal strategies are employed in state legislatures. Lawmakers sometimes lean on lobbyists to help sell a bill or an idea to other legislators—a sort of reversal of the lobbying role. Presiding officers selectively send bills to certain committees, depending on whether they want a bill supported or killed. Legislators and lobbyists collaborate to generate home-district pressure on committee chairs to bring bills up for hearings. The tactics are endless, spurred at times by purely partisan or personal motives and at other times by a genuine desire to get the votes needed to convert good ideas into public policy.

TABLE 4.2
**Membership in the Five Largest
and Five Smallest State Legislatures**

State	Number of Members		
	House	*Senate*	*Total*
Largest:			
New Hampshire	400	24	424
Pennsylvania	203	50	253
Georgia	180	56	236
New York	150	61	211
Minnesota	134	67	201
Smallest:			
Hawaii	51	25	76
Delaware	42	21	63
Nevada	41	21	62
Alaska	40	20	60
Nebraska (unicameral)	—	—	49

Source: The Book of the States, 1992–93 (Lexington, Ky.: Council of State Governments, 1993), p. 141.

LEGISLATIVE ORGANIZATION

Forty-nine of the fifty states have a **bicameral legislature**—one composed of two houses. The lone exception is the state of Nebraska; it shifted to a **unicameral legislature**—the single-house system—in 1937 because of a desire to save money on lawmakers' salaries and the conviction that this is a more efficient system than the two-house body. As Table 4.2 shows, the 99 state legislative houses vary greatly in size, ranging from a senate of 20 members in Alaska to a house of representatives of 400 in New Hampshire. Senators in all except 12 states serve four-year terms, and house members in every state except Alabama, Louisiana, Maryland, and Mississippi serve two-year terms.

Division of Labor

Like sizable organizations of almost any kind, state legislatures find it both convenient and necessary to organize and divide the labor in order to get the work done. Although the nature of the organizational scheme varies among the states and legislative houses make their own operating rules, three common features include party or factional caucus formation, a leadership structure, and a committee system.

Party Caucuses

Organization in state legislative houses usually begins with the formation of majority and minority **party caucuses**. In most two-party states, caucus formation follows party lines; thus, in each house at the start of the session, a Democratic caucus and a Republican caucus form and meet.

In some states, however, such as the one-party Democratic states in the South and the nominally nonpartisan state of Nebraska, caucus formation, if it exists, is based on factions rather than party. The Mexican-American caucus in Texas is an example. On occasion, caucuses cross party lines, particularly when there is a move to dump party leadership. This occurred fairly recently in a number of states, including California, Connecticut, Florida, and Oklahoma.

Leadership Positions

Once formed, majority and minority party caucuses make decisions regarding the organization of the house or senate and, in some cases, membership on committees. Where they are operative, majority caucuses decide whom they will support for the offices of speaker of the house and presiding officer of the senate where there is no presiding lieutenant governor. Since, in most cases, voting on matters of organization is according to strict majority–minority lines, the nominees of the majority caucus prevail. The selection of presiding officers is critical, especially in the house of representatives, because the speaker in most states has the power to appoint committee members and to refer bills to the various committees.

In addition to the selection of presiding officers, majority and minority caucuses usually select their own informal leadership. This may consist of a floor leader, who guides the activities of the majority in its attempt to control procedure and to secure or thwart the passage of legislation on the floor, and perhaps one or more assistants or "whips" to assist the floor leader in communicating with members and counting votes. In some states, the majority or minority caucus meets periodically to identify its position and strategy on particular pieces of legislation.

The number of leadership positions and their degrees of authority vary from house to senate and from state to state. Typically, the presiding officer in the house, the speaker, has greater power than does the senate counterpart, the president or president *pro tempore* (pro tem). State senates are smaller and more informal than state houses; senate members usually serve four-year terms, whereas a two-year term is the norm for state houses of representatives; and many senators have had previous experience in the house. In general, then, individual senate members tend to be less inclined than their house colleagues to take orders from leadership. In some state legislatures, New York being an extreme case, a large number of leadership slots exist. They carry a little extra pay and prestige for those who hold them, and can be parceled out in exchange for the support of top leaders.

Table 4.3 outlines the most common state leadership structure. However, it is important to remember that state-to-state variation is extensive and the relationships among leaders are not necessarily hierarchical or authoritarian.

TABLE 4.3   State Legislative Leadership Positions

House of Representatives		Senate	
Majority Party	*Minority Party*	*Majority Party*	*Minority Party*
Speaker (presiding officer)		President (presiding officer)	
Majority floor leader	Minority floor leader	Majority floor leader	Minority floor leader
Assistant majority leader (whip)	Assistant minority leader (whip)	Assistant majority leader (whip)	Assistant minority leader (whip)
Caucus chair	Caucus chair	Caucus chair	Caucus chair

Powers of Leadership

Legislative leadership positions are prized, and for good reason—they generally bring with them considerable power and sometimes serve as launching pads for higher office. For example, house speakers and senate presidents in many states appoint committee members and committee chairs. Since committee positions are highly valued, members may be willing to support a leader in exchange for a desired committee assignment. Furthermore, the power to direct bills to the various committees provides presiding officers with opportunities to affect the fate of bills. Some state legislative leaders are empowered by the rules to waive certain other rules, such as bill introduction deadlines and bill limits. This, too, gives them influence over members. Following an election, minority party leaders may become majority party leaders; therefore, members generally want to remain in their good graces. The floor leaders, whips, and caucus chairs are close to the presiding officers and may at some time succeed them. Members are aware of this and as a result often pay them deference as well.

For a variety of reasons, then, including their ability to win leadership contests in the first place, legislative leaders wield considerable **leadership powers**. Yet the powers, roles, and perils of legislative leadership have changed significantly in recent decades. Improved pay, staff help, and facilities as well as longer, annual legislative sessions have attracted more career-oriented politicians who want a share in the power and the action. Many of today's state legislators have no other job. They use questionnaires, newsletters, constituent service, and often their own state-paid staffers to campaign year-round. They look to their legislative leaders to help them raise money to secure reelection.

Trends in Leadership

Contemporary legislative leaders in the states are weaker than their historical counterparts. The new members want to share power. In exchange for their support of the leadership, they expect to receive help with their fund-raising efforts and legislative agendas. Legislative committees are stronger now, and they too sometimes become little centers of power able to rival that of the leadership.

When modern legislative leaders seek to exert their influence, they may be deposed. In 1989 in Connecticut, for example, Speaker of the House Irving Stolberg was deposed after serving two terms in that position and shortly after having been selected to serve a third. Stolberg met his demise at the hands of a **bipartisan coalition** in which many of his former Democratic supporters joined Republicans in a cross-party alliance. One of Stolberg's younger colleagues described the context of the situation this way:

> We were a new generation of professional legislators. . . . We had our own staff, our own offices. And there was a sense among the younger generation that Irving was just not allowing any upward mobility.[11]

Regarding the trend toward weaker leaders, legislative scholar Alan Rosenthal notes that a more professionalized legislature leads to more careerists in office, which leads to more ambition on the part of more members, which leads to challenges of strong leadership.[12] Legislative leaders in California, New Mexico, Florida, Oregon, Vermont, New York, and elsewhere also have been deposed in recent years, often by bipartisan coalitions. In 1992, in the context of a general anti-incumbent and antigovernment mood, the American voters joined in: Some 85 state legislative leaders chose not to seek reelection and another 8 were defeated.[13]

As the ability of strong-armed leaders to survive declines, traditions of short-tenure rotation in leadership slots are dissolving in some states, too. As Malcolm Jewell notes, strong one-term traditions are practiced in Arkansas, Florida, Wyoming, Alaska, North Dakota, and South Dakota, but two-term terms are in place in Connecticut, New Jersey, Kansas, Montana, Nevada, and Utah.[14]

There seem to be changes, then, in two directions. Rotation is giving way to some continuity in many states, and long-term, strong leaders are increasingly at risk in others. It appears that in the modern state legislature, a successful leadership strategy increasingly must include the provision of opportunities and assistance for members as well as broad consultation and inclusion in decision making.

Legislative leaders are playing a larger role as fund-raisers to support the election and reelection of members of their party. Leaders require the support of their members, and they cannot be influential speakers, senate presidents, or majority leaders if their party is in the minority. Therefore, more legislative leaders are hosting fund-raisers and leaning on the lobby corps to build election war chests for their legislative candidates.[15]

In the 1960s California's house speaker, Jesse Unruh, pioneered the practice of building leadership campaign funds. One of his modern-day successors, House Speaker Willie Brown, has raised and spent between $2 million and $4 million per election. This has helped to keep Brown's Democratic party in the majority in California's house and also to keep house Democrats beholden to Brown. In the same vein, writer Rob Gurwitt describes the fund-raising process in Ohio:

> House Speaker Vern Riffe will throw a birthday party for himself. . . . There will be a small combo playing jazz off in the corner as guests spread through the huge hall, stopping to fill up at the bar or graze the buffet tables of fried chicken legs, egg rolls, pasta, vegetables, broad trays of cheeses. . . . As many as two thousand politicians, union officials and corporate executives will have come by to pay their respects to the Democratic speaker at a cost of $300 each.[16]

How can we characterize such practices and events? Lobbyists with interests in policy decisions are squeezed for money by legislative leaders who make the decisions and also have an interest in staying leaders. These leaders in turn help members who have an interest in reelection. The money that changes hands is used, legally, to purchase mostly issueless propaganda designed not to inform the public but to persuade it to vote in a particular way.

LEGISLATIVE COMMITTEES AND THEIR ASSIGNMENTS

State legislative organization is characterized by the committee system. As noted earlier in the chapter, division of labor is necessary because committees consider hundreds of bills covering a wide range of subject matter. Further, the chambers can range in size from 20 to 400 members. Thus, the work of American state legislatures is divided among a number of committees organized by subject matter. Table 4.4 lists the 24 senate committees in operation in California. The typical state legislative chamber includes committees on education, highways, health and welfare, state institutions, local government, judiciary, finance, interstate relations, and others.

However, as Table 4.5 shows, the number of committees varies among the state legislatures. Whereas Missouri has 81 legislative committees, Maryland has only 15 committees. The states also vary in terms of their use of **joint committees** — that is, committees made up of members from both the senate and the house of representatives. Connecticut, for example, has 22 committees, all with joint membership. The typical state legislator serves on two or three committees, though this also varies, as some lawmakers in certain states serve on more than a half-dozen committees. Like many other aspects of state government structure and procedure, the committee system is in a constant state of flux.

TABLE 4.4
Standing Committees in the California Senate, 1989–1990

Agriculture and Water Resources
Appropriations
Banking and Commerce
Bonded Indebtedness and Methods of Financing
Budget and Fiscal Review
Business and Professions
Constitutional Amendments
Education
Elections
Energy and Public Utilities
Government Organization
Health and Human Services
Housing and Urban Affairs
Industrial Relations
Insurance, Claims, and Corporations
Judiciary
Local Government
Natural Resources and Wildlife
Public Employment and Retirement
Revenue and Taxation
Rules
Toxics and Public Safety Management
Transportation
Veterans Affairs

Source: State Legislative Leadership, Committees and Staff, 1989–90 (Lexington, Ky.: Council of State Governments, 1990), pp. 10–11.

The method by which committee assignments are made in state houses of representatives is fairly standard, but in state senates the committee assignment process varies considerably. In 39 states the speaker makes the committee assignments for both parties in the house of representatives. In four states the speaker appoints majority party members and the minority leader appoints minority party members. Three other state houses use a committee called a **committee on committees**. In Hawaii a party caucus appoints members to committees.

TABLE 4.5   Legislative Committees in Selected States

State	Number of Committees			
	House	*Senate*	*Joint*	*Total*
Missouri	46	27	8	81
Illinois	38	23	0	61
California	25	23	10	58
Connecticut	0	0	22	22
Alaska	9	9	2	20
Maryland	7	6	2	15

Source: The Book of the States, 1992–93 (Lexington, Ky.: Council of State Governments, 1993), p. 191.

In the senates of most states, committee assignments are made by a committee on committees, by the president of the senate, or by the president *pro tempore*, who presides in the absence of the senate president or lieutenant governor. There are certain variations in procedure, of course. In California, committee assignments in the senate are made by the committee on rules, whereas in Virginia they are determined by election.[17]

In a study of the U.S. House of Representatives, Nelson Polsby concludes that the House has become increasingly "institutionalized" over time—that is, legislative turnover has declined, committees have become more important and more autonomous, and their operations have become more routine.[18] Using these same measures, it appears that state legislatures are relatively uninstitutionalized, for personnel turnover is high, the committees are sometimes weak, and the seniority principle is not followed rigidly. In a study of selected committees in six state legislatures, Keith Hamm found that committee members tend to have a special interest in the type of legislation considered by their particular committee. This special interest, in turn, translates into an advantage for the interest groups, which also have a special stake in the bills. The same phenomenon is, of course, very pronounced in the committees and subcommittees of the U.S. Congress.[19]

The organizational and procedural features of state legislatures thus affect the distribution of power and influence among legislators. The speaker of the house is usually quite powerful, given the speaker's power of recognition in floor debate, power to refer bills to committee, and power to appoint committee members and, in some cases, committee chairs. Given their role in the appraisal of bills, state legislative committees are influential, though they are not as strong as their congressional counterparts.

LEGISLATIVE SUPPORT

Legislators cannot function without help. They need clerical assistance, researchers, some type of income, financing for their housing and transportation expenses, and a place to work. Before the modernization of many state legislatures in the 1960s and 1970s, both staff and financial help was minimal in most legislatures. In some states there was no staff assistance at all, and many legislators received no salary. Some had no place to work, save for their desk on the floor of the chamber itself. In addition, many legislatures met in very short sessions, some only every other year.

There have been significant changes in state legislative support in recent years. As in the case of Congress, staffing in the more professionalized state legislatures is becoming increasingly decentralized. Some legislatures, including those in California, Illinois, Michigan, and New York, now provide staffing for

T A B L E 4.6   Legislators' Salaries in Selected States, 1992

Highest (yearly)		Lowest (daily)	
New York	$57,500	Rhode Island	$ 5
California	52,500	Alabama	10
Pennsylvania	47,000	Kansas	60
Michigan	45,450	Utah	65

Source: The Book of the States, 1992–93 (Lexington, Ky.: Council of State Governments, 1993), pp. 151–52.

individual members, leaders, committees, party caucuses, and, in a few instances, home district offices. Legislator salaries are still low in some states but substantial in others, exceeding $20,000 a year in most cases and reaching $50,000 in some others. New Hampshire pays its legislators just $100 a year, whereas New York lawmakers receive almost $60,000 annually. (See Table 4.6.) Allowances for housing, per diem, and travel expenses are much more generous than they were formerly. Space and equipment have also improved in many states.

Expanded staffing can affect state legislatures in many ways. It can make legislators much more self-reliant and less dependent on lobbyists for information. Lawmakers must cast votes on hundreds of complicated measures every year and must turn somewhere for information and advice. To the extent that they have their own staff members, they are able to discount, or at least supplement, the information fed to them constantly by representatives of interest groups. Better staffing can also give the state legislature a measure of strength and independence in its relationship with the governor, particularly in the area of budgeting. If the legislature and its committees (which bear the responsibilities of budget preparation and review) lack their own cadre of analysts, they will be largely captive to the numbers, projections, and estimates of consequences given them by the governor's staff. In recent years many reformed and resurgent state legislatures have become increasingly free of gubernatorial influence, in part as a result of improved staffing.

Staffing levels also have implications for legislative careers. Even though staffers on state payrolls technically should not perform partisan work to advance the political careers of their superiors, much of what they do has that effect. Staff members handle constituent inquiries and help solve constituent problems. They send out questionnaires and newsletters, all of which bear the name and picture of the lawmaker and thereby advance his or her name recognition and chances for electoral success. As in Congress, a few states now provide staff help for district offices, which functions to maintain the incumbent's presence in the home district. Some critics argue that expanded staffing reinforces the trend toward career-oriented politicians, whose major objective then becomes repeated reelection, and who eventually lose touch with their workaday-world constituents.[20]

REPRESENTATION

In large and complex communities such as the American states, it is not possible to pursue the democratic dictum of "government of, by, and for the people" through direct democracy. There are simply too many people and complicated issues to make collective decisions in that fashion. Thus, out of necessity, the states resort to some form of representative government, and state legislatures are among the nation's most representative institutions.

Apportionment

To establish and operate any representative system, an important normative, or value, question must be resolved regarding **apportionment**: On what basis shall representatives be selected? Should the seats in state houses and senates be apportioned on the basis of local government units, just as those in the U.S. Senate are doled out on the basis of two per state? Should they be apportioned on the basis of land area, with each legislative district containing the same number of square miles or acres? Or should districts be drawn so as to include roughly the same number of people within each district? Selecting the criterion by which to apportion legislative seats is a normative issue because there is no absolutely right or wrong way to do it.

A search for historical precedent in the United States on the matter of apportionment is of relatively little help. The Constitution provides for representation on the basis of population in one house of Congress and for equal representation for political units (the states) in the other. The situation is different in the states, however, because local units of government (for example, counties and townships) are not legally related to the states in the same way that the states are to the national government.

Likewise, a search for precedent in the states themselves is of no help in the apportionment selection. Some states entered the Union with representation in both houses based on population. Others based representation in one house on population and employed other criteria, such as local governmental unit, in the other house. Before the one person, one vote decisions of the 1960s, many state constitutions provided for representation in at least one house on a basis other than straight population. In Vermont, for example, each organized town received at least one seat in the lower house; in seven other states, each county was given at least one seat in the senate.

Although there are no clear-cut clues to proper apportionment criteria in the history of apportionment schemes in the United States, a fairly obvious suggestion is implicit in democratic theory. Democratic decision making at its best provides for political equality. Influence is not, of course, equally distributed throughout society, but democratic theory still insists that this be the case—or at least that no overt attempts be made to enforce political inequality.

Malapportionment Develops

In the past many states deliberately employed apportionment schemes in which the one person, one vote criterion was violated. However, the drive for **reapportionment** did not become a salient political issue in America until the massive population shifts of the twentieth century, which created dramatic imbalances in the number of individuals in the legislative districts of many states. Then, throughout the early decades of the twentieth century and into the 1960s, malapportionment was increasingly criticized as inherently undemocratic and the cause of many of the social, economic, and political ills of the cities. Thus, **malapportionment** — gross imbalances in the number of individuals residing in state legislative districts — emerged as a by-product of twentieth-century population shifts. As Figure 4.2 demonstrates, astounding rural and urban population shifts occurred in the United States between 1910 and 1990. In the nineteenth century, state legislative houses, whose membership was based on population, were regularly reapportioned to match population shifts, in accordance with state constitutional requirements. Throughout the first half of the twentieth century, however, when much of the U.S. population moved from farms to cities, state legislatures became increasingly reluctant to redraw their district lines in accordance with the movements of the people.

Yet state legislatures' reluctance to obey the provisions of state law regarding the redrawing of district lines was understandable. Typically, the task of

---

FIGURE 4.2
Urban and Rural Populations in the United States, 1910–1990

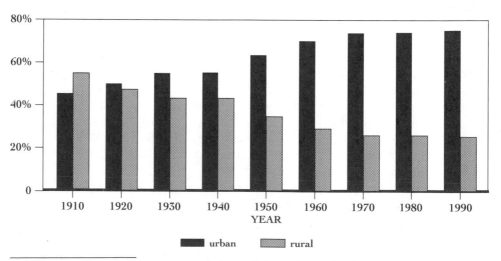

source: U.S. Bureau of the Census, *Statistical Abstract of the United States* (Washington, D.C.: GPO, 1981 and 1992).

reapportioning state legislatures has long been that of the legislatures themselves. Therefore, if representatives and senators had supported reapportionment, they would have been voting to eliminate their own seats, to combine
their own districts with other districts, or to create additional districts in the
urban and suburban areas, thus diminishing their own relative political power.
Like most people and nearly all politicians, state legislators sought self-preser-
vation, which almost invariably meant their refusal to reapportion, despite the
demands of state law.

The existing political power arrangements and the American grass-roots
ethic supported the persistent refusal of state legislatures to reapportion themselves. Malapportionment itself meant that legislative control remained in the
hands of the rural representatives. They could, and did, thwart most attempts to
redraw district lines. Their refusal to act received substantial support from a
deeply rooted American notion about the romantic character of the hinterland.
Rural people themselves opposed reapportionment. Many claimed a need for an
inflated rural vote so as to protect the farming and cattle economy against the
antirural onslaughts of urban politicians, which, it was feared, would lead to
reapportionment.

Many urban people, too, supported malapportionment. In Colorado in
1962, for example, a "federal plan" for apportionment that did not comply with
the one person, one vote principle carried by better than three to two in a
statewide election. In addition, the plan received a majority of votes in every
county in the state, including the highly populous counties in and around
Denver. The Supreme Court later voided the Colorado federal plan, even though
thousands of urban and suburban voters seemed willing to help their rural
neighbors diminish the value of the urban vote.[21]

The Extent of Malapportionment   While the extent of malapportionment varied among the states, at least one house in nearly every state was
seriously out of balance by the 1960s. The Arizona senate, for example, was
composed of 28 members—two from each of its 14 counties—even though 75
percent of the people in that state lived in just two counties (Maricopa County,
which contains Phoenix and its surrounding suburbs, and Pima County, where
Tucson is located). Similarly, in California in the 1960s, one senate district
contained over 6 million people whereas the population in another barely
exceeded 14,000. In Vermont the largest house district had a population of
33,155 and the smallest a scant 38. It was not unusual for states to have at least
one chamber in which fewer than 20 percent of the state's voters could elect
enough representatives to constitute a voting majority in that house. Table 4.7
displays the extent of malapportionment in selected states in the 1960s.

Complaints about malapportionment and its ill effects grew in number and
intensity throughout the 1950s and into the early 1960s. Some of the criticism
was ideological in nature, asserting that it was unfair and undemocratic to
minimize the value of the urban and suburban votes. Other observers blamed
malapportionment for the growing ills of the cities.

TABLE 4.7
Selected States' Legislative Apportionment in the 1960s

State	District Population		Minimum Popular Vote for Majority
	Largest	*Smallest*	
California senate	6,038,771	14,294	10.7%
Connecticut house	81,089	191	12.0
Florida senate	935,047	9,543	12.3
Kansas house	68,646	2,069	18.5
Montana senate	79,016	894	16.1
New Jersey senate	923,545	48,555	19.0
Rhode Island senate	47,080	486	18.1
Vermont house	33,155	38	11.6

Source: National Municipal League, *Compendium on Legislative Apportionment,* 2nd ed. (New York: National Municipal League, Jan. 1962).

Yet there was no universal agreement as to the impact of malapportionment on state politics, and some observers were skeptical about the supposed ill effects brought about by it. In 1964, for example, Herbert Jacob warned that reapportionment would not have a dramatic impact on the behavior of state legislatures.[22] Similarly, in a study of the public policies of states with varying degrees of malapportionment, Thomas Dye concluded in 1965 that:

> On the whole, the policy choices of malapportioned legislatures are not noticeably different from the policy choices of well-apportioned legislatures. Most of the policy differences which do occur turn out to be a product of socio-economic differences among the states rather than a direct product of apportionment practices.[23]

However, Allan Pulsipher and James Weatherby argued in 1968 that malapportionment depressed spending in some service categories in the states, whereas party competition elevated it.[24] Thus, while we cannot lay a major portion of the blame for urban woes on state legislative behavior resulting from malapportionment, it may have had some impact on state policy.

A Remedy for Malapportionment   The remedy for malapportionment came in the early 1960s by way of Supreme Court decisions. Until 1962 the federal courts had steadfastly refused to involve themselves in the apportionment question, arguing that the selection of a criterion for the drawing of representative boundaries was essentially a policy or "political" question, not a legal issue. The subject of apportionment criteria was not considered a judicial matter based on the constitutionally established separation of powers doctrine, which gives the legislative branches of government the chief responsibility for matters of public policy and specifies that the courts concern themselves only with legal questions.

The pre-1962 position of the Supreme Court is often illustrated by its decision in the 1946 case of *Colegrove v. Green*, in which the malapportionment of congressional seats in the state of Illinois was challenged as constituting a denial of the Fourteenth Amendment guarantee of equal protection of the law to everyone. In *Colegrove*, the Supreme Court ruled that the federal courts did not have jurisdiction over apportionment cases and that the remedy for malapportionment should be sought in the legislatures. But the Court was minus two members when the *Colegrove* decision was rendered, and one of the majority judges wrote an independent decision. Thus, the four-to-three decision was rather "soft." Nevertheless, the federal courts refused jurisdiction in apportionment cases until 1962.

The Supreme Court's decision in *Baker v. Carr* in 1962 overturned the *Colgrove* ruling. In the *Baker* case, which involved a Tennessee apportionment controversy, the Supreme Court decided that the federal courts did have jurisdiction in apportionment cases, since malapportionment violated the Fourteenth Amendment guarantee of equal protection of the laws. The *Baker* decision quickly led to many other suits in nearly every state challenging the apportionment schemes of state houses, state senates, and congressional districts. For example, in *Wesberry v. Sanders* (1964) the Supreme Court ruled that all congressional districts must contain substantially the same number of people, and in *Reynolds v. Sims* (1964) the Court applied the same principle to both houses of state legislatures. Several decisions rendered by the Court in the early 1970s indicated that, while the one person, one vote principle need not be realized with absolute precision, districting must be fair and deviations may not be extreme.

One Person, One Vote   Through reapportionment cases the Supreme Court firmly established the principle that one person's vote must count substantively as much as another's. Before the end of the 1960s, reapportionment had been accomplished in all states, either by the legislatures themselves or, when the legislature was unable or unwilling to do so, by the federal courts. Chief Justice Earl Warren, speaking for the Supreme Court majority in *Reynolds v. Sims* (1964), indicated clearly the position of the Court on districting:

> Legislators represent people, not trees or acres.
> Legislators are elected by voters, not farms or cities or economic interests.
> Weighting the votes of citizens differently, by any method or means, merely because of where they happen to reside, hardly seems justifiable. . . .
> Our constitutional system amply provides for the protection of minorities by means other than giving them majority control of state legislatures. . . .[25]

In some instances, however, the one person, one vote dictum has not translated into equal apportionment. The Court has insisted on strict equality when states are districted for the U.S. House of Representatives. But in terms of the states themselves, the Court has said that when a substantial state interest in some small deviation from perfect apportionment exists, such deviation is allowed.

Room for Flexibility   Through a series of decisions in the 1970s, the Supreme Court arrived at what some have called a "*de facto* plus or minus 10 percent" rule. That is, when the deviation in population between a state's most populous and least populous house or senate districts is less than 10 percent, any plaintiff challenging the plan carries the burden of proof as to why it should be disallowed. When a plan exceeds the 10 percent variance and is challenged, the state must show a clear state interest to justify the departure from strict equality.

The Court has allowed several states, including Wyoming, Virginia, Connecticut, and Texas, to operate with plans containing some departure from precise population equality. In a truly unique instance the Court allowed Wyoming in 1983 to employ a districting plan in which one district contained such a small population that there was a difference of 89 percent. The extreme deviation occurred because of a longstanding state constitutional rule that provided for at least one house member from each county. The Court found a state interest in preserving that historical condition (*Brown v. Thompson*, 1983). By and large, however, the Court has held the states to substantially equal population in legislative districts.

Many early critics had hoped that the end of rural domination of state politics would mark the start of a period of revitalization in state government and the allocation of increased public resources to urban problems. There is little evidence that this has happened, however. While rural influence has diminished in state legislative politics, it has not disappeared. Perhaps more important, there are signs of considerable friction between the urban and suburban blocs. Although the twentieth century has been marked by tremendous urban population growth, it was the suburbs, not the cities, that experienced the greatest growth between 1950 and 1970.

Gerrymandering

The phenomenon of gerrymandering is related to the apportionment issue. Although the Supreme Court now demands that all districts in a given state legislative or congressional chamber contain roughly the same number of people, it also indicates a willingness to invalidate apportionment schemes when districts are formed with the clear purpose of assigning certain people to one or another district on the basis of their party identification or race (*Davis v. Bandemer*, 1984; *Gomillion v. Lightfoot*, 1961). The opportunity still exists, however, for subtle manipulation of district lines to favor one group or party over another.

A **gerrymander** is an attempt to draw district lines in such a way as to maximize the voting power of one faction and minimize that of another. It often results in the creation of odd-shaped districts. A district may be perfectly apportioned and even have a rather normal shape, yet be horribly gerrymandered. While the term *gerrymander* often suggests very odd-shaped districts, it is also used to refer to attempts by political parties to draw district lines so as to maximize the electoral impact of their voters and minimize those of the opposition party.

A Hypothetical Case   Suppose that Congress and the Census Bureau entitle our hypothetical state to four seats in the House of Representatives. It is the task of the legislature of our state to come up with a plan to divide the state into four districts. Given the ruling of the Supreme Court, each of the districts must contain substantially the same number of people. Our state has 800,000 registered voters—485,000 registered Democrats and 315,000 registered Republicans. (Let us suppose, unrealistically, that these 800,000 registered voters are the only people in the state and that they all vote for their registered party.)

It is possible for the legislature of our hypothetical state to draw the four districts in any number of shapes, including plans A–F as suggested in Figure 4.3. Just as the shape of congressional districts can vary, so too can the distribution of registered Democrats and Republicans within the various districts, with a highly significant impact on the electoral outcome. Table 4.8 shows the

FIGURE 4.3   Six Hypothetical State Districting Plans

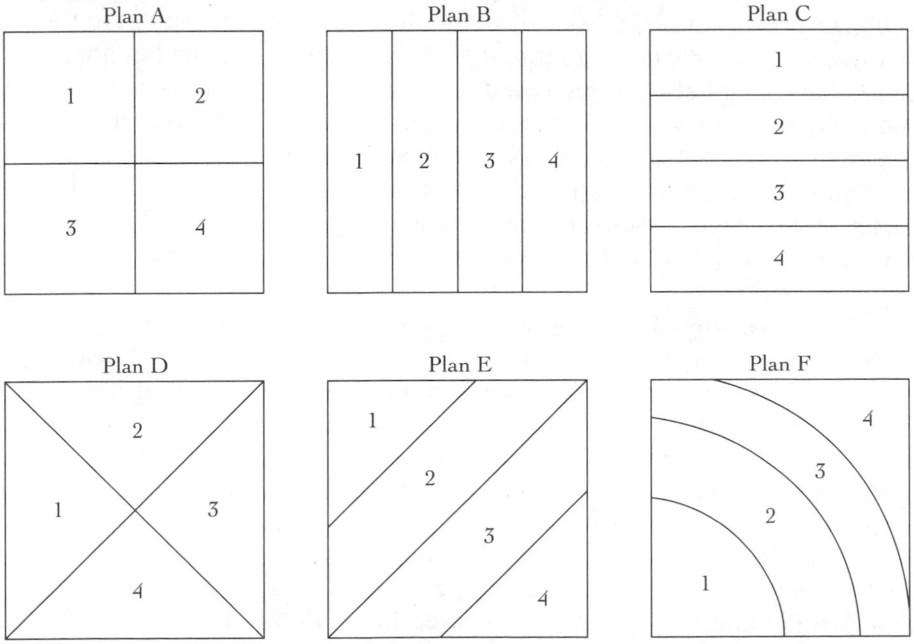

TABLE 4.8
Hypothetical Districting Plans and Electoral Outcomes

	Plan A		Plan B		Plan C	
District	Democrats	Republicans	Democrats	Republicans	Democrats	Republicans
1	120,000	80,000	150,000	50,000	200,000	0
2	120,000	80,000	150,000	50,000	95,000	105,000
3	120,000	80,000	90,000	110,000	95,000	105,000
4	125,000	75,000	95,000	105,000	95,000	105,000
Total	485,000	315,000	485,000	315,000	485,000	315,000

electoral outcomes of districting plans A, B, and C in the figure. Note how partisan distribution can vary and change the outcome of elections without violating the Court's one person, one vote dictum. Although each district in the three hypothetical plans contains the same number of persons — 200,000 — the electoral outcomes would clearly differ. Under districting plan A in Table 4.8, the Democrats would have a significant edge in statewide voter registration and would likely win all four congressional seats. However, if we shuffled the voters around according to plan B, the Republicans would capture two of the four seats even though they are the minority party. Under plan C (which is admittedly absurd), the minority party would capture three of the four congressional seats, and the Democrats would have a 200,000 to 0 landslide victory in district 1.

The hypothetical districting options suggested here and in Figure 4.3 and Table 4.8 are, of course, grossly oversimplified. Even so, they point to the kinds of advantages a party can gain through manipulation of district boundaries. The courts have long held that gross and obvious tinkering with district boundaries and the creation of contorted district shapes will not be tolerated when it can be shown that such districting results in the denial of equal protection of the law to someone. But the door is still open to all sorts of subtle maneuvering to gain partisan advantage. It obviously matters very much, then, which political party is in the majority in a state legislature at reapportionment time.

The Position of the Courts The voting rights legislation of 1982 requires that any jurisdiction with a history of denying electoral political equality to racial minorities secure clearance from the U.S. Department of Justice or the U.S. District Court in Washington, D.C., before altering district boundaries or making any other election system changes. The legislation also prohibits states from using voting systems that result in discriminatory practices or that reduce the political role of racial minorities.

In addition, recent Supreme Court decisions may affect the ability of parties to gerrymander for political purposes. In *Davis v. Bandemer* (1984), for example, the Court ruled that gerrymandering is within the Court's jurisdiction when it functions to harm the other party. In this Indiana case Democrats accused controlling Republican legislators of unconstitutionally depriving them of equal protection of the law. The Court consented to hear the case but found insufficient evidence to justify the claim. More recently, in the California case of *Badham v. Eu* (1988), Republicans accused Democrats of districting California's U.S. House seats so as to reduce their fair share of members. Here the Court found that the Republicans' claim of being shut out of the political process could not be sustained.

Today the Court has yet to disallow a districting plan just because it has the effect of advantaging one or the other party. But the Court is quick to void plans that, by either intent or results, diminish the voting and representative power of minorities.[26]

Control of state houses, state senates, and the governorship is always important to political parties, but especially so at the start of each decade, when state legislatures and U.S. House district lines are redrawn. Both houses of a state's legislature and the state's contingent of congressional seats must be reapportioned after each census. As is the case with legislative bills generally, new congressional districting plans are developed and passed by the legislature and signed by the governor—unless, for some legal reason, the courts must step in. In many states, the reapportionment of state legislative seats is handled in the same fashion.

Once district lines are set, they remain for 10 years. In the 1990 elections, for instance, the biggest prize to be won was generally considered that of the governor's chair, especially in such large and growing states as California, Florida, and Texas. Because of the 1990 census, those three states gained 13 new U.S. House seats and, for the final decade of the twentieth century, would be sending 105 members to the 435-member U.S. House. In all three states Democrats controlled the legislatures. Democratic governors, thus, could work with Democratic legislators to devise districting schemes that would help their party. Republican governors, possessing the veto, could bargain with the Democrats and press for districting plans that helped Republicans or were somewhat neutral in their impact. As it turned out, Democratic governors won in Texas and Florida, while a Republican prevailed in a close contest in California.

REPRESENTATIONAL ROLES

The selection of a criterion for legislative districting involves in part a normative judgment and, because of recent Supreme Court decisions, a primary focus on population. However, other matters related to the question of representation also merit attention. What should the role of the representative be? How does the representative actually view that role? What might the role of the representative also encompass? There are three different views on the role of the representative in a democracy.

Representatives as Mirrors

Some critics argue that the representative should only strive to function as a link between constituents and public policy decisions. In the **mirror role**, the representative "mirrors" the preferences of the people. The representative is a device for simplifying the problem of achieving government by the people.

For those who support this view, direct democracy is preferable to representative government because the individual is the best judge of his or her own values and does not need others in the legislative chambers or in the courtroom to make decisions. But since direct democracy is an impractical way to arrive at collective judgments in a crowded and complex world, people must resort to representative government and try to make it reflect voters' wishes.

Representatives as Oracles

Others argue that representatives should use their superior insight and access to information to benefit the people. This is called the **oracle role** because lawmakers predict rather than attempt to figure out constituents' needs.

Supporters of the oracle role prefer it over the mirror role because they believe that the electoral processes seek out the best people to serve in communities. Others support the oracle role for a more practical reason: Given legislators' access to information and their proximity to the seats of power, they are privy to facts and problems unknown to the average voter and, therefore, can make informed judgments.

Representatives as Brokers

Another view of the legislator's role is termed the **broker role**. Here lawmakers neither try to transfer constituents' preferences into law nor follow their own wisdom. Rather, legislators' major task is to play the game and make the trades that will benefit constituents' interests. The broker role is actually a combination of the mirror role, the oracle role, and a little crass self-interest.

Knowing that public policy results in the allocation of scarce societal goods and services, legislators make the trades and deals necessary to ensure that their district is the beneficiary of a fair share of what is available. Of course, legislators must make judgments about what their district wants and needs, and they may be assisted in making these judgments by consulting constituents. In general, though, these legislators do what is necessary to bring into their district public benefits for schools, roads, parks, and so on. Supporters of the oracle role might call a broker an immoral dealer. The broker might reply that the real world is composed of conflicting interests and many diverse images of the public good, and that as such it requires compromise. It also requires that members stick with their party and party leaders much of the time if they wish to be successful.

THE DEMOGRAPHICS OF LEGISLATORS

If being a representative means possessing the characteristics of one's constituents, then American state legislators are unrepresentative in many ways. Compared to the larger population, state lawmaking bodies are overly populated with men, whites, older people, people with higher-than-average incomes, better-educated Americans, and lawyers and businesspeople.

Not everyone has the desire or resources to run for public office, and not everyone can afford to take time away from other pursuits to sit in a legislature from 60 to 200 days a year. Young people often lack the money, experience, and occupational flexibility to serve. Poor people are too busy trying to support themselves. Working people seldom have the occupational flexibility needed to run a campaign and trot off to the state capitol. Large numbers of Americans, thus, cannot serve in public office for a variety of reasons.

Over the years, legislatures have had relatively few women and minority members. Until recently there were few women and minorities who possessed all or most of the resources needed for successful pursuit of a state legislative seat—interest, education, money, and flexibility. They may have had the interest but lacked the money or occupational flexibility. Or they may have had the ability, money, and time, but no interest. In addition, deeply rooted attitudes among voters often worked to discourage either the candidacy or the electoral success of women and minorities. For years the laws and political practices in some southern states made it difficult for blacks to vote, much less run successfully for public office.

Many of these patterns have been changing. The heavy representation of lawyers in state legislatures is receding, though the number of businesspeople and other professionals (educators, for example) is growing. In addition, while the number of minorities remains low, with only 407 African-Americans and 128 Hispanic-Americans among the 7,461 state legislators in 1989, their numbers are growing.[27]

The number of women legislators is increasing as well. Whereas in 1969 only 4 percent of the states' lawmakers were women, by 1990 that figure had grown to over 17 percent and by 1993 to 20 percent (see Figure 4.4). The states with the highest percentages of women legislators are New Hampshire, Arizona, Colorado, Vermont, and Washington. States with the most modernized legislatures rank well in this area.[28]

Women are making their presence known in positions of leadership, too. In 1989, fifteen women held the position of either presiding officer of a chamber or majority or minority floor leader. One such leader, Vera Katz, a speaker of the Oregon house of representatives and a Democrat, was first elected to the Oregon house in 1972. Over the years she joined forces with other women in the chamber, members of both parties, to press issues of concern to women.[29]

There is some evidence that changing legislative demographics can lead to changing public policy. A study conducted by the Center for American Women

FIGURE 4.4   Women in State Legislatures, 1969–1993

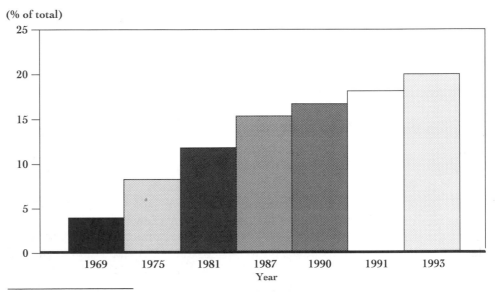

(% of total)

SOURCES: Data from Susan Biemesderfer, "Political Women Give Even Cowboys the Blues," *State Legislatures* (Oct. 1990): 21–23; *The Book of the States, 1992–93* (Lexington, Ky.: Council of State Governments, 1993), p. 130; and *Rocky Mountain News*, 25 Nov. 1992, p. 4.

and Politics at Rutgers University indicates that women legislators are more apt than their male counterparts to resist state laws banning abortion. For example, 38 percent of the men polled and 26 percent of the women polled strongly supported laws banning abortion. The study also suggests that Republicans of both sexes are more favorably disposed than Democrats to such legal prohibitions.[30]

Various factors influence the voting behavior of state lawmakers — for example, political party, constituents' desires, advice from other legislators or the leadership, and personal values.[31] Gender and race, like schooling, age, and economic and occupational circumstances, also shape attitudes and behavior. As the demographics of state legislatures continue to change, albeit slowly, public policy will shift as well.

TENURE AND TURNOVER

Legislative turnover is both a problem in and of itself and a reflection of undesirable conditions within state legislatures. Before modernization, the chambers were internally undemocratic and often under the thumb of one or a few heavy-handed veterans. With little chance of playing a meaningful role in the process, the newly elected soon left. Of course, the poor or nonexistent pay and the absence of staff assistance and adequate office space contributed to high turnover as well.

With high turnover, most pre-modernized legislatures were composed primarily of novices — lawmakers unfamiliar with many issues, with the arguments on two sides of an issue, and with the probable consequences of proposed legislation. Their lack of background knowledge, coupled with the absence or shortage of staff, tended to force lawmakers to rely on the lobby corps for information and voting cues. Although lobbyists had to be honest and reliable to be effective in the long run, they were also in the employ of interests that had special and self-serving stakes in legislative outcomes.

The remedy, critics argued, was longer tenure. Indeed, with the improved pay, staff help, and facilities that came with the reforms of the 1960s and 1970s legislative turnover declined significantly (see Table 4.9). For example, whereas in 1978 at least 30 percent of the membership in state legislatures was new in 34 of the 99 chambers, by 1988 the number had dropped to just 9. The decline in legislative turnover was especially high in the most modernized states. In California, for example, new membership fell from 25 percent in the senate and 31 percent in the house in 1978 to just 8 percent and 10 percent, respectively, in 1988. The decline in Ohio in the same period was from 15 percent to 6 percent in the senate and from 18 percent to 7 percent in the house.

Scholars who study state legislative turnover link the increasing stability of legislative membership to modernization. In a 1988 study of 25 states, Squire Perverill indicates that improved salaries and opportunities for advancement lead to membership stability.[32] In a related finding, legislative experts Malcolm Jewell and David Breaux document the growth in the winning electoral margins of state legislative incumbents — an indication that legislators are finding careers in state houses and senates more to their liking and are replicating the political strategy of members of Congress when they attempt to maintain their positions.[33] In a 1986 study on why state legislators voluntarily leave office, Wayne Francis and John Baker note that one common reason given is the

TABLE 4.9   Legislative Turnover Rates, 1978 and 1988

	Year	New Membership (as a percentage of total membership)					
		−10%	*10−19%*	*20−29%*	*30−39%*	*40−49%*	*+50%*
Number of Legislative Chambers*	1978	1	19	41	22	9	3
	1988	13	40	28	7	2	0

*Number of chambers does not total 99 because not all states held elections shortly before 1978 and 1988.

Source: Calculated from data in *The Book of the States, 1980-81* and *1990-91* (Lexington, Ky.: Council of State Governments, 1981 and 1991), pp. 103 and 124, respectively.

pursuit of other political ambitions.[34] It appears, then, that the recent era of modernization has produced meaningful changes in legislative membership.

In an ironic turn of events, the extension of legislative tenure called for by early critics is now producing complaints of a different sort. Many contemporary critics argue that a growing number of state legislators are behaving like their counterparts in Congress. With better pay and working conditions, it is claimed, many legislators are looking to make elective office a career and thus spend an increasing portion of their time solidifying their electoral base. Newsletters, questionnaires, and constituent service—anything that keeps the incumbent's name in the forefront—become the agenda, it is argued. At the same time, the costs of election campaigns are soaring and the role of political action committees in financing them is growing. It is argued that career advancement is displacing effective governing as the legislator's main objective.

Disillusionment with some of the consequences of a modernized, or "congressionalized," legislature was recently expressed in citizen-initiated efforts to limit the legal tenure of lawmakers. In 1990 voters in three states—California, Colorado, and Oklahoma—had the opportunity to approve constitutional amendment proposals to impose tenure limits. All three proposals passed. In California, house members may serve 6 years and senate members 8 years. Service in the affected legislative and executive public offices is limited to 12 years in Oklahoma and to 8 years in Colorado. In 1992 voters in 14 other states followed suit and adopted term limits. Opponents argue that tenure limitations deprive the voter of a full range of choices, saddle legislators with a constant flow of inexperienced lawmakers, and spell a return to the troublesome days when lobbyists were informed and experienced but elected officials were not. Whatever the pros and cons of tenure restrictions, it appears that voters do not fully support all of the results of the modernized, professionalized legislatures. The virtues of the citizen legislature are thus receiving renewed attention.

SUMMARY

Today's state legislatures are arguably the centerpieces of the institutional arrangement of American state government. The state legislature writes the laws and controls the purse strings. The shape of much of the executive and judicial branches is determined by legislatively drawn statutes. The size of the budget and the configuration of tax laws are set by the legislature. The shape, roles, and powers of local governments are products of legislative action.

Early in U.S. history, the legislature was indeed the supreme branch. The founders feared concentrated executive authority. Over the years state legislatures fell into some disrepute and were often manipulated by governors and special interests. The public good suffered. More recently state legislatures reformed themselves to varying degrees, and they are now more effective and reputable institutions.

The manner in which state government in general and state legislatures in particular are organized has significant political consequences. The deliberate separation of the legislative and executive functions builds into the system the potential for conflict. So does the division of the legislature into two chambers. In recent years well over half of the states experienced divided government, in which one political party controlled one or both legislative chambers while the other party held the other chamber, the governorship, or both. This combination of institutional design and split party control leads to conflict.

The states have modernized their legislative institutions, and this too has had consequences. Better pay, enhanced staffing, longer sessions—these and other changes have freed legislatures from some gubernatorial and interest group influence, thus addressing some of the criticisms of decades past. But modernization has also created more career politicians. Many citizen legislators still serve, but there are fewer of them. Institutional modernization, contemporary observers argue, has led to increased power of incumbency and lower electoral competition, more costly elections, greater reliance on interest group money, weakened legislative leadership, and greater internal decentralization and fragmentation. In their heightened concern for reelection, legislators may tend to worry more about their district and less about the larger statewide good.

The powers of legislatures, governors, courts, and local governments, the levels of conflict and cooperation among the branches of government and chambers of a legislature, the behavior of politicians and the strategies they employ—these are all determined in large measure by the shape of the institutions within which they operate.

KEY TERMS

reapportionment
reformed legislature
legislative turnover
logjam
citizen legislature
legislative process
legislative committee
conference committee
power pocket
legislative veto
line-item veto
rules committee
calendar committee

bicameral legislature
unicameral legislature
party caucus
leadership powers
bipartisan coalition
joint committee
committee on committees
apportionment
malapportionment
gerrymander
mirror role
oracle role
broker role

ADDITIONAL
READINGS

Chasen, Daniel J. *Speaker of the House: The Political Career and Life of John L. O'Brien.* Seattle: University of Washington Press, 1990.

Ehrenhalt, Alan. "An Embattled Institution." *Governing* (Jan. 1992): 30.

Hanson, Royce. *Tribune of the People: The Minnesota Legislature and Its Leadership.* Minneapolis: University of Minnesota Press, 1989.

Jewell, Malcolm E., and Penny Miller. *The Kentucky Legislature: Two Decades of Change.* Lexington, Ky.: University of Kentucky Press, 1988.

Rosenthal, Alan. *Governors and Legislatures: Contending Powers.* Washington, D.C.: Congressional Quarterly Press, 1990.

———. *Legislative Life: People, Process, Performance.* New York: Harper & Row, 1981.

Straayer, John A. *The Colorado General Assembly.* Niwot, Colo.: University Press of Colorado, 1990.

NOTES

1. Robert X. Browning, "Indiana Elects Democratic Governor and Equally Divided House," *Comparative State Politics Newsletter* (April 1989): 1–2.

2. Quoted in Thomas R. Morris and Larry Sabato, eds., *Virginia Government and Politics* (Charlottesville: Institute of Governments, University of Virginia, 1984), p. 79.

3. Jonathan Waters, "A Night on the Town Isn't What It Used to Be in Jefferson City," *Governing* (July 1989): 26–31.

4. Alan Ehrenhalt, "An Embattled Institution," *Governing* (Jan. 1992): 30.

5. For an excellent discussion of the modernization of state legislatures since the mid-1960s and its consequences, see Alan Rosenthal, "The Legislative Institution: Transformed and at Risk," in *The State of the States*, ed. Carol E. Van Horn (Washington, D.C.: Congressional Quarterly Press, 1989), pp. 69–101.

6. Donald A. Gross, "House-Senate Conference Committees: A Comparative State Perspective," *American Journal of Political Science* (Nov. 1980): 769–78.

7. See Malcolm E. Jewell, *The State Legislature* (New York: Random House, 1969), ch. 3.

8. *The Book of the States, 1992–93* (Lexington, Ky.: Council of State Governments, 1993), pp. 49–50.

9. See *The Book of the States, 1990–91* (Lexington, Ky.: Council of State Governments, 1991), pp. 151–56.

10. John C. Wahlke, Heinz Eulau, William Buchanan, and L. C. Ferguson, *The Legislative System* (New York: Wiley, 1962), pp. 146, 147, 154.

11. Quoted in Alan Ehrenhalt, "A Coup in Connecticut: The Unmaking of a Leader—and Its Consequences," *Governing* (Aug. 1990): 74–79.

12. Alan Rosenthal, "A Vanishing Breed," *State Legislatures* (Nov.–Dec. 1989): 30–34.

13. Karen Hansen, "Elections 1992: The Message Is Mixed," *State Legislatures* (Dec. 1992): 13.

14. Malcolm Jewell, "The Durability of Leadership," *State Legislatures* (Nov.–Dec. 1989): 10–11, 21.

15. Alan Rosenthal, "There's Power in Campaign Bucks," *State Legislatures* (Nov.–Dec. 1989): 34.

16. Rob Gurwitt, "How to Succeed at Running a Legislature: Pack a Mighty Wallet," *Governing* (May 1990): 26–31.

17. *The Book of the States, 1992–93* (Lexington, Ky.: Council of State Governments, 1993), p. 191.

18. Nelson Polsby, "The Institutionalization of the U.S. House of Representatives," *American Political Science Review* (March 1968): 144–68.

19. Keith Hamm, "The Role of Subgovernments in U.S. State Policy-Making: An Exploratory Analysis," *Legislative Studies Quarterly* (Aug. 1986): 321–52.

20. For discussions of consequences of well-staffed professional legislatures, see William T. Pound, "Legislatures: Our Dynamic Institutions," *State Legislatures* (Jan. 1993): 22–25; and Rich Jones, "The Legislature 2010: Which Direction?" *State Legislatures* (July 1990): 22–25.

21. Susan W. Furniss, "Reapportionment in Colorado" (M.A. thesis, Colorado State University, 1967).

22. Herbert Jacob, "The Consequences of Malapportionment: A Note of Caution," *Social Forces* (Dec. 1964): 256–61.

23. Thomas R. Dye, "Malapportionment and Public Policy in the States," *Journal of Politics* (Aug. 1965): 599. See also Richard I. Hofferbert, "The Relationship between Public Policy and Some Structural and Environmental Variables in the American States," *American Political Science Review* (March 1966): 82; and John C. Grumm, "The Effects of Legislative Structure on Legislative Performance," in *State and Urban Politics*, ed. Richard I. Hofferbert and Ira Sharkansky (Boston: Little, Brown, 1971), pp. 298–322.

24. Allan G. Pulsipher and James L. Weatherby, Jr., "Malapportionment Party Competition and the Functional Distribution of Governmental Expenditures," *American Political Science Review* (Dec. 1968): 1207–19.

25. *Reynolds v. Sims*, 377 U.S. 533 (1964).

26. Task Force, "Reapportionment Law: The 1990s" (National Conference of State Legislatures, Denver, Colorado, Oct. 1989).

27. Rich Jones, "The State Legislatures," in *The Book of the States, 1990–91* (Lexington, Ky.: Council of State Governments, 1991), p. 111.

28. Ibid. See also *Women in Elective Office*, fact sheet (Rutgers University, Center for American Women and Politics, Eagleton Institute of Politics, 11 July 1988), p. 2.

29. Foster Church, "Just Like a Woman," *Governing* (Sept. 1990): 26–30.

30. "Lawmakers' Abortion Votes Are Influenced by Gender," *Governing* (Aug. 1989): 17.

31. See Cole Blease Graham, Jr., and Kenny J. Whitby, "Party-Based Voting in a Southern State Legislature," *American Politics Quarterly* (April 1989): 181–93; Gregory A. Calderia and Samuel C. Patterson, "Political Friendship in the Legislature," *Journal of Politics* (Nov. 1987): 953–75; Warren E. Miller and Donald E. Stokes, "Constituency Influence in Congress," *American Political Science Review* (March 1963): 45–56; Herbert McCloskey, Paul J. Hoffman, and Rosemary O'Hara, "Issue Conflict and Consensus among Party Leaders and Followers," *American Political Science Review* (June 1960): 406–27; and Herbert McCloskey, "Consensus and Ideology in American Politics," *American Political Science Review* (June 1984): 361–79.

32. Squire Perverill, "Career Opportunities and Membership Stability in Legislatures," *Legislative Studies Quarterly* (Feb. 1988): 65–82.

33. Malcolm E. Jewell and David Breaux, "The Effects of Incumbency on State Legislative Elections," *Legislative Studies Quarterly* (Nov. 1988): 495–514.

34. Wayne L. Francis and John R. Baker, "Why Do U.S. State Legislators Vacate Their Seats?" *Legislative Studies Quarterly* (Feb. 1986): 119–26.

5

The State Executive

L. Douglas Wilder is sworn in as the 66th governor of Virginia during a ceremony outside the state capitol in Richmond (January 13, 1990). Wilder became the first elected black governor in U.S. history. *(AP/Wide World Photos)*

THE MODERN STATE GOVERNOR

Two days before the November 1990 elections, a *New York Times* article reported that:

> From New England to California, the fiercest battles of the 1990 election are being fought for governor, as voters pick the men, and perhaps women, who will shape everything from taxes to the political districts that [U.S.] House members will serve for the next decade.
>
> The political stakes are so high that when all the accounts are tallied, more than a quarter of a billion dollars will have been spent.[1]

In recent years the post of governor has been an increasingly attractive political position. Just as recent modernization has changed the state legislative institution, so too has it affected the state executive branch. A number of states have lengthened their chief executive's term of office from two years to four years; today only the governors of New Hampshire, Rhode Island, and Vermont serve for two years.[2] Several states that previously had not permitted a governor to serve two consecutive terms have now relaxed that restriction. In addition, there has been some reduction in the number of other directly elective executive branch slots, positions from which the incumbents could operate independently of the governor.

Governors have been given broader powers to reorganize their bureaucracies without having to await legislative action. In many states the governor's staff has been expanded, which has enhanced the chief executive's capabilities with respect to budgeting and planning.[3] Together, these recent changes have strengthened state governors and enhanced their political roles and visibility.

Increased Responsibility

The devolution of responsibility from the national government to the states for funding many domestic programs over the past decade or so has contributed to the expanded, more visible role of the state governor. Increasingly, the states have had to fend for themselves in the underwriting of environmental, health, and educational programs. As the national government has imposed more and more requirements on the states as conditions for continued federal funding, governors have had to become involved in the tasks of complying with the requirements and paying the bills.

The combination of enhanced executive authority and the states' expanded policy responsibilities has dramatically transformed the position of state governor—from one of mild importance to one at center stage in American politics. Several widely respected scholars of the American governorship recognize the modern role of the state chief executive. According to Thad Beyle and Lynn Muchmore: "During the mid-twentieth century, the American governorship has grown in importance not only within the states themselves, but also within the context of our federal system of government."[4] Similarly, Coleman Ransone observes that "During the last thirty years the American governor has emerged as a policy leader of no mean proportions."[5]

The increased importance of the position of governor in the states is evident both in the credentials of individuals who seek the post and in the fact that past governors have recently been presidents or presidential candidates. In 1990, for instance, former U.S. senator Lawton Chiles of Florida and sitting U.S. Senator Pete Wilson of California ran for governor of their respective states. Both won. Cecil Andrus of Idaho served as governor, left to become U.S. Secretary of the Interior, and then returned to run successfully for his old slot as governor. Others have served once as a state's chief executive, left that office, but then sought it again, including Orval Faubus of Arkansas, George Wallace of Alabama, Michael Dukakis of Massachusetts, John Y. Brown of Kentucky, and Richard Snelling of Vermont. Jimmy Carter and Ronald Reagan both served as state governors before winning the presidency. Dukakis, California's Jerry Brown, Michigan's George Romney, and Wallace of Alabama have all sought the presidency. In 1992 Bill Clinton won the presidency while serving as governor of Arkansas.

Of course, not all governors have been former U.S. senators or are destined to become presidents or presidential candidates. Many have had political careers as state legislators, state treasurers, or state attorney generals, or in some other elective position. One study shows that among the governors serving between 1970 and 1989, just over one-half had served in the state legislature at some time and 38 percent had held some other statewide office.[6]

Greater Visibility

The growing importance of state governors is also evident in the changing public roles they are playing. The National Governors Association (NGA) has emerged in recent years as an increasingly visible and respected voice for states and governors alike. In late 1990, for example, the NGA joined other groups in publicly criticizing a new federal policy that would have withheld highway funds from states refusing to revoke the driver's licenses of drug offenders. Governors do not always get their way, but they do constitute a meaningful and respected collective voice in American politics.

Modern governors are also increasingly visible policy leaders within their own states. Wisconsin's Governor Tommy G. Thompson describes the expanded role of the modern American governor in this way:

> American governors consider two of their most vital tasks to be
> broadening their state's economic base and providing opportunities
> for their citizens. Thus, governors have led efforts to guide and
> stimulate economic development and job creation for more than 20
> years. As the world has become smaller, so governors' economic

development strategies have become more far-reaching. Now that economic opportunities are more international in scope, governors' efforts must extend beyond state and national borders.[7]

Not all governors employ the same strategies in their public life, and for some the highly public role can compensate for shortcomings in other areas of gubernatorial responsibility. Marc Landy describes the style of two Kentucky governors, Happy Chandler and John Y. Brown:

> Chandler was widely considered to be the best storyteller in Kentucky political history. He campaigned for office by tirelessly traversing the state, regaling and beguiling audiences, in every little crossroad and rural hamlet with his songs, jokes and tales.
>
> Brown's skills have proven themselves to be more appropriate to the onset of the television age. He skillfully exploited the same marketing flair that he had used to develop his Kentucky Fried Chicken empire.[8]

Today's more public gubernatorial role can often be a major political resource, for the accompanying visibility allows governors to keep their faces and names continuously before the voters. But the center-stage position can sometimes be damaging as well. Following the U.S. Supreme Court's decision in the 1989 *Webster* abortion case, Florida's Governor Bob Martinez led a charge to press the legislature to enact antiabortion policies. The failed attempt contributed to Martinez's November 1990 defeat. Similarly, Kansas Governor Mike Hayden and Nebraska Governor Kay Orr were associated with unpopular tax increases, and both lost in 1990. In 1990 Texas's Clayton Williams lost his first and only bid to become governor, and his defeat is widely attributed to the extensive publicity he received. Williams assumed a "good old boy" posture and took a host of "six-shooter tough-guy" positions on issues such as drugs. Polls showed that the voters loved it at first, but became increasingly uneasy the more they saw of it. In a $17 million campaign, Williams spent $8 million of his own money — too much, it appears, for in his case familiarity bred the contempt of voters. The spotlights that focus so intensely on governors and would-be governors and that work most often to their political advantage were hard on Martinez, Hayden, Orr, and Williams.

Tight Competition for the Job

It is not surprising that as the post of governor of the American states has become more important and more desirable, so too have the contests become increasingly expensive and, in some instances, contentious or downright nasty. In 1956 the average cost of a gubernatorial election was $100,000 (or $418,410 in 1987 dollars) and the costliest races in the largest states averaged $300,000 (or $1.3 million in 1987 dollars). For the 1986 elections, however, the average cost had soared to $7.4 million (in 1987 dollars). The Texas campaign alone ran to $35 million in 1986 and over $40

FOCUS

5.1   MUDSLINGING IN MINNESOTA

In Minnesota a particularly nasty gubernatorial campaign developed during the 1990 elections. Republican candidate Jon Grunseth called incumbent Governor Rudy Perpich "the supreme liar." Stories about Grunseth also circulated—it was rumored that he had had extramarital affairs and had invited teenage girls to swim naked in his pool. Grunseth eventually withdrew from the race, and Perpich lost to an eleventh-hour Republican replacement candidate.

SOURCES:"Road to Governor's Mansion in California Is Paved with Mud," *Rocky Mountain News*, 4 June 1990; "Mud Gets Thick in Minnesota Race," *Denver Post*, 21 Oct. 1990; and "Minnesota Governor Candidate Quits," *Rocky Mountain News*, 29 Oct. 1990.

million in 1990.[9] The enormous amount of money spent on gubernatorial elections parallels the escalating costs of all types of elections, particularly statewide races. The objectives of the modern campaign—building an image and gaining media coverage—involve the use of consultants, polling, mass mailings, and especially television, which are prohibitively expensive.

Negative campaigning also seems to be a popular modern strategy in gubernatorial races, as it is in American elections generally (see Focus 5.1). Incumbents who have been in office during any form of tax increase are sure to be blamed. In the 1990 California Democratic primary, for example, the advertisements of John Van de Kamp blasted Dianne Feinstein as "a Republican in Democratic clothing." In Texas, candidate Clayton Williams refused to let voters forget about his opponent's earlier personal problems with alcohol, while the opponent and eventual winner, State Treasurer Ann Richards, blasted Williams for spending $8 million of his own money on the campaign and for failing to pay 1986 income taxes.

Incumbents enjoy a large advantage in gubernatorial elections, just as they do in virtually all American elections. Beyle reports that incumbents win more than 70 percent of the time.[10] Voters are increasingly crossing party lines and generally lack detailed information about candidates and their positions on the issues. Name identification and image, then, are important cues for most voters. Therefore, the public stage that governors enjoy during their term in office later provides them with a significant edge in election years.

Modern governors are usually very deliberate and purposeful in their use of the public spotlight. Writer Paul West captures the essence of their electoral life in a 1990 article entitled "They're Everywhere! For Today's Governors, Life

Former New Jersey governor Thomas Kean poses for photographers as he works on his annual message to a joint session of the legislature. An incumbent's "look" — in this case, rolled-up sleeves, no jacket — is carefully managed to enhance his or her political image. *(AP/Wide World Photos)*

Is a Never-Ending Campaign," in which he describes former New Jersey governor Thomas Kean's early days in office as "such a disaster that his pollster, Robert Teeter, said privately that Kean's career might already be over."[11] In response, Kean's handlers set about to change his image. They manufactured televised town meetings that aired on cable television in all New Jersey counties. Kean appeared with actors Bill Cosby and Brooke Shields in advertisements geared toward promoting tourism in the state. The governor hosted a televised talk show. In short, Kean's image changed, and he became an enormously popular governor.

Colorado's Governor Roy Romer employs a different but equally successful approach to image building. Romer works constantly to project an image of energy and identification with the common folks. During an election in which the construction of Denver's new airport was a central issue, the governor had breakfast in small cafés with early risers on their way to work — his so-called oatmeal circuit. The image carried constantly in the media is one of a hardworking, shirt-sleeves governor who associates with the average working person. When, in 1990, the eastern Colorado town of Limon was devastated by a tornado, Romer was there on local streets and on televised news shows, dressed in an ordinary jacket and promising state help.

However, even with the media focus, the contemporary state governor is not unbeatable. The more than 70 percent success rate that gubernatorial incumbents enjoy is not as strong as the 97 percent or 98 percent success rate enjoyed by incumbent members of the U.S. House of Representatives. Governors and senators run statewide. During campaigns, as during their service in office, they receive considerable media exposure. Though usually an advantage that sitting governors can exploit, media exposure can be a liability at certain times, such as when a scandal breaks out or when unpopular policies (tax increases, in particular) must be adopted.

In addition, the intense media attention given gubernatorial contests can in some cases help the challengers. As in U.S. Senate contests, which are also statewide, challengers enter the race without the advantage of extensive name recognition enjoyed by the incumbent. But media coverage can narrow that gap and thereby diminish the incumbent's initial advantage. For the governor who remains visible, stays out of trouble, and either ducks or shares the blame for unpopular actions or policies, though, the political future remains reasonably secure.

ROLES OF THE GOVERNOR

The range of formal authority that a governor possesses varies among the 50 states. In some states, such as Kentucky and Wisconsin, the governor has extensive power to appoint top-level state administrators, to veto legislation, and to influence the size and shape of the budget. In other states, including Texas, the governor's formal powers are more limited. Indeed, governors in most states share some executive branch authority with other directly elected officials and may be politically constrained by the legislature or by interest group power. At the same time, they are often able to augment their institutional authority with political clout, derived variously from exploitation of the media, hard work, force of personality, intelligence, and, perhaps, a central position in the political party.

One factor common to all states, however, is the public expectation that the chief executive officer play a host of roles. Some **gubernatorial roles** are formal and institutional, whereas others are symbolic and ceremonial. In virtually all cases the responsibilities that fall on the shoulders of the state governor are not matched by a parallel allocation of formal authority. Thus, successful governors often combine their formal authority with personal political skills and effective exploitation of public opinion.

Chief Administrator

Perhaps the most important and best-known role played by governors is that of chief administrator. Although not the only high-level position in the executive branch of state government, the office of governor is generally considered the top job because it carries the most authority, responsibility, and visibility. At the same time, the legal authority and political power of governors vary among the states and are in some cases fairly limited. Still, the public image is that the governor "runs" the state. If things go well the governor takes the credit, and if things fail the opposition party or faction sees to it that the governor takes the blame. When the legislature passes a law, it is the governor's duty to enforce it. If an agency is not doing its job, the governor is expected to investigate. In the event of a scandal in state government, the governor has to explain and rectify it. The media demand it and so does the opposition party.

Although the authority and power of the governor vary among the states, and although in some states the governor's powers are few and relatively weak, the public's image of the chief administrator remains constant. The governor is widely viewed as a state's chief administrative officer and as ultimately responsible for conducting the state's affairs.

Party Leader

The governor is frequently looked upon as a party leader, though here there are also great variations among the states. In one-party states, such as those in the South, the governor may be the leader of just one faction of the majority party. Or, with the Republican party enjoying growing success in southern states, the governor may be someone who has bucked traditional partisan trends and built political success via party organization and extensive media play. In other states the governor may be a maverick personality, having obtained a party's nomination for office by challenging the choice of the party regulars in the statewide gubernatorial primary. Party mavericks and governors in one-party states may still be viewed as the most significant and most visible members of their party, but they may not be widely considered the true leaders of their party.

The governor's role as party leader may also depend on the composition of the legislature. When the governor's party has a majority in both houses, the governor may well be the acknowledged rallying point for party maneuvers. When the opposition party controls the legislature, which is increasingly the case, the governor may be the opponent of the legislature rather than a source of direction and strategy.

Regardless of the chief administrator's status in the political party or the composition of the legislature, the governor remains the most visible elective official in the state and is almost always an asset to the party. Governors command vast amounts of television, radio, and newspaper attention. They speak at hundreds of social and political gatherings. They are asked to campaign for and support members of their party who are candidates in legislative contests. And they are the key attraction at their party's fund-raising affairs.

State Symbol

Chief executives, including mayors, governors, and U.S. presidents, are automatically visible symbols of their community and its government, and as such they perform a wide range of ceremonial functions. In effect, then, the governor is a state symbol.

Governors welcome dignitaries from other states and nations. They dedicate new bridges, highways, and public buildings. They make speeches on holidays, march at the head of parades, and warn children not to experiment with drugs or eat the apples they collect on Halloween until the fruit is checked by their parents. They express alarm at the growing number of highway deaths and appeal to motorists for caution on holiday weekends. And often governors, like the president, are, in the minds of children, the personification of government itself.

The symbolic role that governors play can be both a liability and a political asset. It can be a liability because of the tremendous demands it places on the people who serve as governors. However, the widespread visibility of the role translates into a significant advantage at the polls.[12]

Policy Leader

Another role of the governor, one of growing significance and importance, is that of policy leader. Like other chief executives, governors are increasingly involved in policy-related activities—anticipating and identifying problems and issues, proposing goals and programs for the states, as well as fabricating and implementing legislative policy.

Three critical factors have combined to increase the salience of the policy role of the governor. First, the growing need to attack such problems as air and water pollution, crime, and illegal drugs through public policies has increasingly involved state government programs and spending. Second, twentieth-century developments in mass communications have increased the visibility of such politicos as state chief executives. Third, the growing number and complexity of the problems with which state governments wrestle, and the web of ties with local units of government and the national government, have made it increasingly necessary to coordinate public policies and programs; this has been done increasingly through the office of the governor.

As a result, party leaders, legislators, bureaucrats, and the public expect governors and gubernatorial candidates to act like policy leaders. They are expected to identify issues and anticipate public problems. When they run for office, they are expected to do so on platforms that call for specific policy options. Once in office, governors are expected to help determine the legislative agenda, to bring to the legislature a program (a set of specific policy recommendations as well as some written legislation), and to play the political game to secure passage of that program. Governors can work with and cajole their own party and legislative leaders. They can appeal to the public for support. Through patronage and other devices, they can pressure various interest groups and individual legislators so as to gain their support of a program. Their ability to push certain policies also gives governors great power. The role of policy leader, therefore, is a source of power for most governors.

Policy Coordinator

Closely related to the governor's role as policy leader is that of **policy coordinator**. Governors are often in a position to coordinate and integrate public policy—in preparing party platforms and legislative program proposals, in preparing and reviewing state budgets, and in acting as the state's chief administrative official. Bills are introduced in the legislature on a variety of subjects and from a variety of sources; they are considered in a variety of committees; and, if passed, they are administered by a variety of disparate departments and agencies of the state government.

All the ingredients are present, then, for an incremental and totally undirected and uncoordinated implementation of public policy. Some duplication, waste, and lack of coordination are inevitable, but the governor, like other executives in U.S. government, is in a position to maintain a degree of perspective on state government activities.

SOURCES OF GUBERNATORIAL POWER

Like the roles of a governor, **gubernatorial power** can be both formal and informal. **Formal powers** are institutional; that is, they come with the position. **Informal powers**, such as the ability to influence public opinion, are derived in part from a governor's personality and in part from the visibility of the position itself.

Visibility

Governors' policy role and symbolic position provide them with an almost continuous public platform. They can command front-page newspaper coverage and radio and television time almost at will. If they wish to generate an issue, argue on behalf of pending legislation, indicate their displeasure with someone's actions, or focus public attention and thereby put pressure on some legislator or committee, governors can call on their publicity resources and gain visibility faster and more effectively than perhaps any other state official. Of course, this does not always guarantee governors success in all endeavors, but it is one of many tools in their collection of political resources.

Although some degree of power accrues to all state governors by virtue of their formal authority, many governors are restricted by constitutional and statutory limitations on budgetary, appointive, and veto powers, as well as by the establishment of several other elective executive posts. Nevertheless, all governors retain some power to appoint executive personnel, influence the content of the budget, demand written performance and progress reports from executive departments, and issue administrative orders. Formal executive authority, though it varies among the states, adds significantly to the governor's political powers.

Executive Authority

The political party of a governor is usually a source of political power, though to varying degrees. It is a strong source of power for governors who have been active within their party, who have built a network of political alliances, and whose party controls both houses of the legislature. In this case, the legislature is likely to look to the governor for policy direction, to consult the governor throughout the legislative session, and to be supportive of the governor's policy preferences.

The Political Party

However, divided government is more prevalent than ever before. As a result, governors often do not enjoy a united and supportive legislative party. Following the 1990 election, only 19 states had governments in which the party of the governor also controlled both legislative houses. A similar pattern emerged after the 1992 elections. Partisan division can reduce governors' powers, whereas unity can mean significant legislative support of their major policy objectives.

The political party can also help gubernatorial candidates at the polls. In most states the two major parties are organized at the precinct, county, and state levels, which helps candidates raise funds, get potential voters registered, and disseminate political propaganda. Party identification is the single most reliable predictor of an individual's vote, and a candidate's firm identification as a Democrat or a Republican automatically guarantees the candidate an electoral base. (However, some states are dominated by one party; as a result, political contests can be based on factional fights rather than party competition.)

The governors in all states except North Carolina possess some sort of veto power over legislative action, and in over 90 percent of the states governors are empowered to use the line-item veto (usually in regard to appropriations, or budget, bills). The veto is a significant political tool for the chief executive. Given the nature of the legislative process, important and controversial bills tend to be reported out of committee and placed before the

The Veto

full house late in the session. Therefore, governors can appraise and veto critical bills when the legislature is about to adjourn and after it has disbanded. A few states allow governors to **pocket veto** legislation; that is, the governor may neglect to sign bills after the legislature has adjourned. In addition, it takes an abnormal majority of two-thirds or three-fourths to override an executive veto in most states (the former majority is more common). Some states do not allow the legislature to call itself back into session. As a result, it is difficult for the legislature to override a gubernatorial veto.[13]

The potential for executive veto can affect the governor's powers in two very different ways. First, the fact that the governor has the opportunity to void legislation means that the legislature is apt to keep controversial provisions out of bills. The governor thus can have an impact on legislation even without acting. Second, there are ways of structuring legislation so as to minimize the risk of a veto. Provisions that a governor is known to favor may be tied to other unfavorable ones, making it difficult for the governor to eliminate a provision without voiding the entire legislative package. For example, a legislature might effectively avoid a budget item veto by lumping endangered items with other appropriations. As in all areas of politics, the outcome tends to be one of compromise.

The veto powers of governors vary among the states. Although in a few states a veto can be overridden by a simple majority vote in the legislature, a majority of two-thirds is the norm in most states. Some governors have only a limited time period in which to sign or veto legislation; others are granted extended periods of time. Indiana, for example, has no line-item veto, so the governor's veto can be reversed by a simple majority. North Carolina's governor has no type of veto power. In contrast, the governor in Wisconsin may veto parts of items of bills. Governor Tommy Thompson has employed that authority to alter legislative intent. Despite legislative protest, Wisconsin's supreme court has upheld his actions, stating that the governor can apply his or her veto authority to individual words, letters, and punctuation marks in bills.[14]

Appointment Power

The power of governors to appoint administrative personnel varies considerably among the states. However, for those with a significant degree of appointment power, it is an important executive tool. When an official in the executive branch is popularly elected or appointed by a board, has civil service protection, or is appointed by the governor with the confirmation of the senate, that official is in a position to exercise considerable independence from the governor. In contrast, when an official is appointed by the governor and may be dismissed by the governor, that official is likely to remain closely attuned to and to comply with the chief executive's preferences. Similarly, the agency head who can be fired by the governor and whose paycheck depends on courting the governor's wishes is more apt to cooperate with the governor than the agency head who is appointed by a multimember board and has a degree of independence from the chief executive. In short, appointment power is of immense value to governors in their efforts to get members of the state executive branch to comply with their directives.

However, as with veto powers, the degree of executive appointment power varies. The governors of Oklahoma, Mississippi, Georgia, and Texas, for instance, have only weak appointment power; the heads of many agencies in those states are elected or appointed by a board, a commission, or another state official. In contrast, the appointment power of the governors of Alaska, Colorado, Delaware, Indiana, Kentucky, Massachusetts, and Tennessee is strong.

Budget Power

Playing a major role in the development of the state budget and in the dispersal of appropriated funds can give governors power in their relations with the legislature and administration. Governors in all 50 states play some role in the budget-making process, but the degree of their power varies considerably. In some states the governor and staff members solicit requests for funds from various state agencies, review the funding requests (in terms of, for example, their reasonableness and the degree to which they reflect the governor's goals and legislative program), and make upward or downward monetary adjustments on the basis of their compatibility with the governor's program and the anticipated state revenues.

In other states the governor's role in the budget-making process is more limited. The governor may participate in budget formation along with a state budget director, a state comptroller, or a state finance director. Such a situation exists in Texas, for example, where the lieutenant governor and the speaker of the house share most budget-making powers. The individual with whom the governor shares the budget preparation role may also be an elected state officer, a civil service employee, or an officer chosen by the legislature; in these cases the individual is less influenced by gubernatorial control. In all states, however, governors' budget powers, like those of the legislature, are restricted by state constitutional or statutory earmarking of certain tax revenues.

Budget preparation is an extremely critical function of state politics. The greater the governor's role in budget making, the more likely it is that the legislature and the administration will respond positively to the governor's proposals. Legislators know that modern-day state budgets are large and complex and that legislative time is limited; as a result, the legislature often reviews the governor's budget and makes some incremental adjustments. Similarly, the heads of administrative agencies know that if they cross the governor they may be shortchanged in the next budget. The legislature's role tends to be one of budget review rather than of budget formation, which gives the governor the power to make budget cuts.

The power to control the distribution of money is an important political resource for state governors. Lawmakers and bureaucrats alike tend to be more responsive to governors who possess a high degree of control in budget making.

Tenure   In earlier decades many governors served only two-year terms and were prohibited by law from serving consecutive terms. This has changed in recent years. Today the governors of 47 states serve four-year terms, and in 18 of these states the governors may serve an unlimited number of consecutive terms as long as they win the elections. Four states prohibit consecutive terms, and in some other states the governor may serve only two consecutive terms (a restriction similar to that imposed on the U.S. presidency).

The appointment power of governors is quite restricted. Often governors find that a majority of the members of executive boards and commissions serve longer terms than does the governor. Obviously, the longer a governor stays in office, the more appointments he or she can make. Longer tenure may also give the governor greater political freedom and a stronger hand in exercising other gubernatorial powers.

Lobbying   Straightforward lobbying is an important political tool for state governors both within their own states and in their collective interactions with the national government. At home, governors must deal with their own state legislature in getting bills passed, appropriations made, and measures vetoed. It is thus critical for governors to maintain ongoing contact with the legislature. In order to do so, governors have on staff a **legislative liaison** — a person who lobbies the legislature on a daily basis and keeps legislators informed of the governor's preferences (including, for example, unacceptable provisions of bills that will be vetoed). As noted earlier in the chapter, the threat of a veto can influence the content of bills and the behavior of lawmakers.

Governors and other elected state officials have now become important lobbyists in their own right. Much of a governor's time is spent in lobbying within the intergovernmental system. Governor Ann Richards of Texas, for example, spent a considerable amount of time lobbying President Clinton and Congress on a host of issues, including NAFTA (the North American Free Trade Agreement) and the Supercollider, both issues of importance to the Texas economy.

LIMITS ON EXECUTIVE POWER

Although the governors of the American states derive political power from a variety of legal and other sources, their executive power is limited by a host of legal and practical restrictions. Governors bear the responsibility for, but often lack the power to control, large and unwieldy state bureaucracies. They frequently lack strong veto, appointment, and budget powers. Since many of their counterparts in the executive branch are independently elected, governors must often bargain for what they want for their states. Some of the severest limitations on executive power have been the target of recent reform proposals geared toward strengthening the governor's power.

In many states the governor is a member of a **plural executive**—in other words, one of a number of directly elected members of the executive branch. It is not uncommon for states to elect at the polls

The Plural Executive

the lieutenant governor, the secretary of state, the attorney general, the treasurer, the auditor, other top state officials, and, of course, the governor. The governors of all 50 states are popularly elected. However, 43 states directly elect the attorney general, 38 elect the treasurer, 37 elect the secretary of state, and 42 elect the lieutenant governor. Voters in some states also elect an assortment of other executive branch officials, including the comptroller, the insurance commissioner, the land commissioner, and the mining commissioner. In addition, most states have a host of boards and commissions whose members are sometimes elected at the polls. In Arizona, for instance, the three members of the state's corporation commission are directly elected; in Michigan the governing boards of three state universities (University of Michigan, Michigan State University, and Wayne State University) are directly elected in statewide elections.

Some elective executive posts are established by constitutional provision; others are provided for in legislative statutes. However they are created, elective posts exist in every state and, as a general rule, executive authority is widely dispersed. The plural executive model diagrammed in Figure 5.1 is similar to that of most states. A number of implications of the plural executive approach to administrative organization are immediately apparent. Since several major executive officials are directly elected and possess independent constituent bases, they may not have much incentive to follow the governor's directives or preferences. Because the governor does not hire and cannot dismiss the secretary of state, the attorney general, the treasurer, or many other executive branch officials, they are free to choose whether or not to cooperate with the governor. However, such executive branch officials are required by constitutional and statutory provisions and encouraged by public opinion to cooperate with other public officials and to assist in the smooth and effective conduct of public affairs. Still, they owe their jobs to the voters who elected them. As a result, elected officials tend to be much less indebted to the governor than those who are appointed by the chief executive.

Many gubernatorial candidates campaign while holding another state office, such as that of state treasurer, attorney general, or secretary of state. It is not unusual for one of these statewide officeholders to see political advantage in embarrassing the incumbent governor while keeping his or her own name in the headlines. When Governor Jerry Brown of California, for example, was out of

FIGURE 5.1   **The Plural Executive Model**[*]

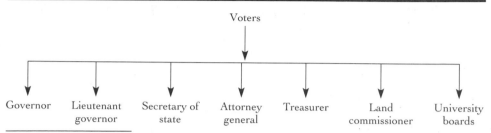

*This figure shows a hypothetical sampling of offices; the actual selection varies from state to state.

the state, his lieutenant governor, as acting governor, often countermanded the executive orders Brown had issued.

The diffusion of executive authority and responsibility in the American states not only weakens the political power of governors but also adds to voter confusion. As every voter knows, American ballots are extremely long. It is difficult for even the most conscientious voters to make informed choices from such a wide and diverse list of candidates and offices. Voters dissatisfied with their state government, and with the executive branch especially, must attempt to choose from among dozens of individuals running for election and reelection to executive branch posts.

In addition, the plural executive model in state government makes it difficult to maintain administrative coordination of responsibilities. Most of the functions performed by state government departments and agencies are related in some way to the functions of other departments and agencies. Under the plural executive model, many functions and duties are performed semi-independently with no overall coordination. The governor can create some degree of coordination through persuasion, and the legislative budget committees, unwieldy as they often are, through budgetary threat and intimidation, but no comprehensive approach to the coordination of responsibilities exists.

Reform Proposal: The Integrated Executive   The elimination of the plural executive is among the countless administrative reforms that have been proposed over the course of American history. Most reformers propose replacing the plural executive with a strong **integrated executive** model. An organizational arrangement borrowed from the business world, the integrated executive model would eliminate several elective posts and increase the governor's appointive and administrative powers. Heads of cabinet-type departments, such as the secretary of state, the attorney general, and the treasurer, would no longer be selected in statewide elections but would be appointed by the governor instead.

They would also be responsible to the governor and subject to removal by the governor.

The governor in the integrated executive approach would serve as chief executive in both fact and theory. Like the U.S. president, governors would have the power to select department heads and, together with cabinet members, would be responsible for the administration of their departments. Governors would also be able to remove department heads whose performance was lacking. Lines of authority and responsibility would be more clearly established than in the plural executive model. Figure 5.2 diagrams a hypothetical integrated executive model of state government.

Progress in securing adoption of the integrated executive model has been slow but steady. *The Book of the States* reports that in the last decade, nearly one-half of the states underwent some form of reorganization.[15] However, reorganization does not necessarily reduce the number of bureaucratic units or strengthen the power of the chief executive. In some cases reorganization may be little more than a rearranging of existing units, with no reduction in the proliferation of those units.

In none of the 50 states does the actual organization of the executive branch perfectly match the model of either the plural or the integrated executive. Some tend toward one side or the other. Each state's organizational scheme is the product of the political history of the state and the success or failure of reform movements. Figures 5.3 and 5.4 show the contemporary organizational schemes in Oklahoma and Alaska, respectively. Oklahoma's institutions were

FIGURE 5.2   **The Integrated Executive Model**

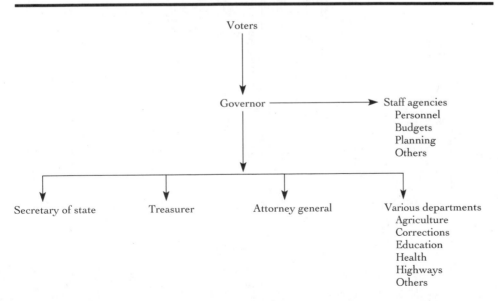

FIGURE 5.3   Oklahoma's Executive Branch

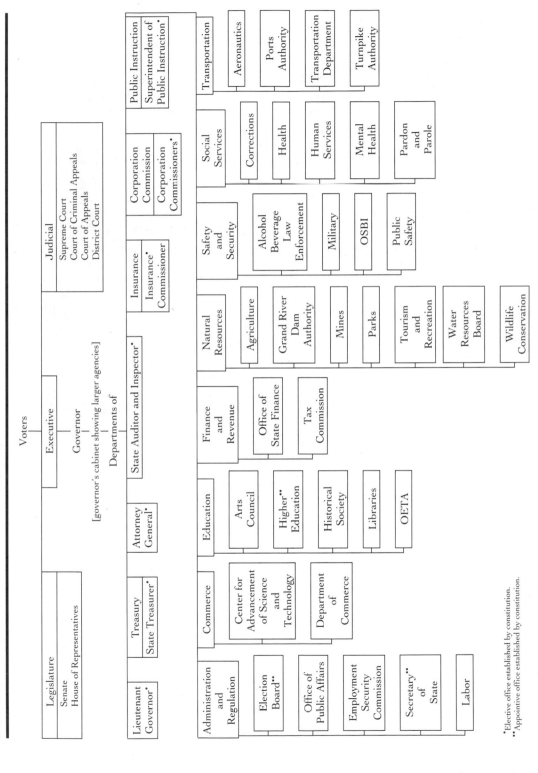

SOURCE: *Oklahoma 1989–1990* (Oklahoma City: Oklahoma Department of Libraries, 1990).

*Elective office established by constitution.
**Appointive office established by constitution.

created initially when it entered the Union in 1907, a time of Progressive reforms designed to disperse power and thus weaken corrupt institutions. Today formal authority is still widely dispersed in Oklahoma. In contrast, Alaska became a state in 1959, in the midst of the executive reform movement. Not surprisingly, the Alaska executive branch resembles the integrated executive model.

The Bureaucratic Organization

The structure and operation of most state bureaucracies further reduce the political strength of many governors. It is not uncommon for states to have well over a hundred agencies, many headed by multimember boards or commissions, existing in dispersed fashion in sprawling bureaucracies. It is also not unusual for much of the activity of the agencies to be uncoordinated or to overlap with that of other agencies. The results of this lack of coordination are clear. It makes it difficult for the governor or other state officials to exercise meaningful coordination and control over the state's activities. When administrative units are headed by multimember boards or commissions, the governor may be able to exert only little influence because the members' terms are longer than the governor's. Moreover, the governor can neither appoint nor dismiss many members of boards and commissions.

In addition, governors may find it impossible to keep track of the numerous individuals and functions for which they are responsible. Further, the various administrative units, especially those headed by boards and commissions, may respond to a variety of different "publics."

Development of Bureaucracies   American state governments attained their present bureaucratic structure through the combination of several circumstantial factors over a long period of time. The nineteenth-century Jacksonian penchants for representativeness and maximum public participation in decision making provided the initial impetus for multiple membership on governing boards of state and local administrative agencies. Boards and commissions became even more popular in the late nineteenth and early twentieth centuries, when there was rampant corruption in state government. State legislatures were viewed, often correctly, as the tools of such special interests as the railroads and big corporations; and governors, it was thought, could be persuaded by the rich and powerful. The remedy offered by reformers involved the insulation of government in general and of public administration in particular from corrupt public officials in the legislative and executive branches. Thus emerged the widespread use of multimember boards and commissions with representation from a variety of economic sectors, terms that exceeded those of the governors, and nonpartisan or bipartisan membership. Of course, in the process of insulating state agencies from corruption, the reformers also may have insulated them from the control of the public.

Another factor contributing to the bureaucratic state of administrative affairs in state government was the constant need for government to respond

FIGURE 5.4 Alaska's Executive Branch

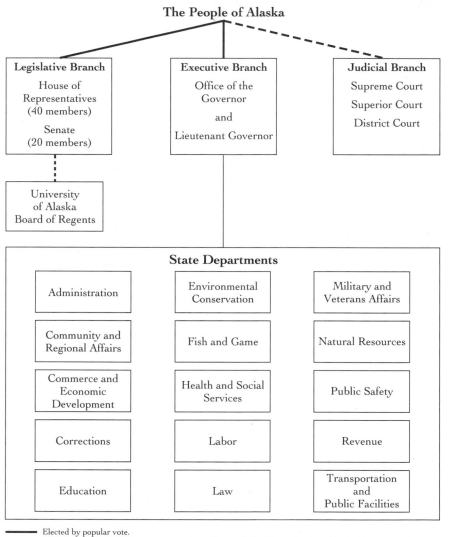

The People of Alaska

Legislative Branch
House of Representatives
(40 members)

Senate
(20 members)

Executive Branch
Office of the Governor
and
Lieutenant Governor

Judicial Branch
Supreme Court
Superior Court
District Court

University
of Alaska
Board of Regents

State Departments

Administration	Environmental Conservation	Military and Veterans Affairs
Community and Regional Affairs	Fish and Game	Natural Resources
Commerce and Economic Development	Health and Social Services	Public Safety
Corrections	Labor	Revenue
Education	Law	Transportation and Public Facilities

——— Elected by popular vote.
– – – Justices and judges of the courts are nominated by the Judicial Council, selected by the Governor, and thereafter subject to voter approval.
——— Department heads are appointed by the Governor and confirmed by the Legislature.
▪ ▪ ▪ ▪ ▪ Regents are appointed by the Governor and approved by the Legislature. The University's budget is subject to legislative approval.

SOURCE: *Alaska Blue Book, 1989–90* (Juneau: Alaska Department of Education, Division of State Libraries and Archives, 1990).

130

incrementally to an increasing number of emerging problems associated with the new programs and new agencies. In no state did the present administrative structure take shape overnight. Rather, like all public and private bureaucracies, state bureaucracies are the product of numerous decisions—made incrementally at various points in time—to take on new public programs and to create new departments for implementing those programs and policies.

Bureaucratic Reform   There have been attempts in almost every state to reform the bureaucratic organization in order to facilitate assignment of authority, accountability, and responsibility as well as to increase the economy and efficiency of state government. Figure 5.2, which diagrams the integrated executive model, also shows the envisioned shape of the reformed administrative structure. No state bureaucracy, whether reformed or unreformed, is exactly like the model depicted in the figure, and no two state bureaucracies are exactly alike. But the reform proposals, which have been adopted in many states, call for a restructuring of the administration along the lines shown in Figure 5.2. The numerous existing agencies are grouped according to function into a few departments. Internally, these departments are organized along hierarchical lines, with authority flowing downward and responsibility upward. Each department is run by a department head who is appointed by and responsible to the governor. Because the number of departments is reduced, the governor's span of control—the number of individuals the governor supervises directly—is reduced to a more manageable level. The governor is better able to perform in an informed manner, and the voter knows that the governor is responsible for poor government. The governor, in turn, can easily identify the responsible department head, and so on. The lines of authority and responsibility are, in other words, simplified and clearly fixed.

In addition, the governor is given the needed staff to manage the tasks of budget making, personnel hiring, and planning. The governor's powers are strengthened and the bureaucracy is more logically arranged. The governor can administer the affairs of the state with more order and dispatch, and the people can better evaluate their government in action.

One must not overestimate the effect of reorganization on human behavior. All organizations tend to develop elaborate informal authority and communication systems, quite apart from the formal channels. Employees tend to become acquainted with their counterparts in other agencies and departments; the work of the organization is then expedited as communication is conducted laterally throughout the organization by phone, by note, or in person. When the law changes the formal structure of the organization, it does not immediately or necessarily eliminate personal acquaintances or change behavior and communication patterns.

Researchers disagree about the impact of government structure on behavior and performance. Some studies suggest that government structure may be of secondary or no importance in determining output and performance.[16] The efficiency objective is questioned as well. Kenneth Meier reports that:

> The conventional wisdom that executive reorganization along the principles of classical organization theory introduces economies into bureaucracy is not supported by major American state government reorganizations from 1965 to 1975.[17]

Scholar James Conant, in a review of the arguments and evidence supporting the push for a streamlined, more efficient executive branch structure, concludes that the ultimate effects of reorganization remain largely unknown.[18]

At the same time, however, it is clear that the current complicated government apparatus makes it difficult for the average voter to remain informed. There is also some debate over the assumption that economy, efficiency, and simplicity in government are good. Some critics argue that, in light of democratic theory, it is more important for government to be responsive to the people than efficient and economical. Questions about the impact of government structure on policy output are subject to some degree of empirical measurement, but questions that focus on values in decision making are normative and thus subject to debate.

Among the requirements of any successful reorganization are (1) reducing internal and external resistance to and (2) developing support for the proposed changes. An example of the skillful achievement of these ends is described by Phillip Foss in his case study of the reorganization of the highway patrol in California.[19] Foss points out that the proponents of the plan to reorganize took great pains to "reduce the costs of change." Employees who were to be affected by the changes were consulted before the plan was announced. Great efforts were made to avoid demotions or cuts in pay and to avoid moving employees against their will. And the reorganization did not necessitate a change in state statute, which could have precipitated trouble with or in the legislature. The reorganization, in short, was successful because the political groundwork was carefully planned.

Bureaucratic Control   Modern bureaucracies, whether state, local, federal, or private, provide their administrative subunits with multiple opportunities to develop autonomy within the larger organization and some degree of immunity from executive and public control. As organizations become larger and more complex, as communication systems become more elaborate and impersonal, and as employees master increasingly specialized skills, administrative departments and agencies and the offices within them become harder to control. As a result, the problems of executive leadership also increase.

State bureaucracies and other large organizations share a number of characteristics. Perhaps among the most important features are specialization, division of labor, and elaborate systems of communication and authority. The massive technological advances of recent decades have created ever-increasing specialization. The jack-of-all-trades who could adequately perform a number of functions has been replaced by the expert who is skilled in a narrow range of activities. Modern bureaucracies are full of them — accountants, attorneys, computer programmers, mechanics, typists, engineers, and a variety of other technicians. These individuals are usually adept at their trade but may be unable to understand or perform other organizational tasks. Likewise, their functions may be beyond the comprehension of their co-workers.

The same sort of specialization characterizes entire administrative units, such as libraries, research services, budget offices, data-processing centers, and motor pools. The organization is dependent on its specialist employees and departments; indeed, they may increase its productivity considerably, providing they function properly. It makes sense, of course, to staff public administration with the best experts available — to employ skilled typists, computer programmers, biologists, and mechanics instead of people with relatively low skill levels. However, the widespread use of expertise can also create problems of coordination and control. Experts and specialized administrative units can derive considerable autonomy from their expertise. Motor pools can structure their regulations, procedures, requirements, and schedules and demand compliance from any state employee who wants the use of a vehicle. Libraries on university campuses can make their own rules. Data-processing personnel can insist on compliance with the information-collecting and -reporting procedures that they prefer. It should not be implied that large organizations or state government bureaucracies are typically in a state of chaos and rebellion, for this is clearly not the case. But the possession by an individual or department of an expert skill on which the organization depends and that cannot be easily replaced gives that individual or department a base of independence. In this case, it is no easy task for an administrator or chief executive to obtain the performance desired of subordinates just because he or she has formal authority over them.

Agency–Clientele Ties   Another factor that can reduce the ability of the governor to control an administration is the tendency for government agencies to forge links with private interests, often called **clientele groups**. Such ties can prove advantageous to both the agency and the clientele group. The latter may be given opportunities to appraise agency programs and plans before they are implemented. The agencies and groups may even swap personnel. It is common, for example, for the relevant clientele groups to be contacted before administrative appointments are made to the boards that govern the agencies with which they interact, or before a department head is selected. As a result, an individual who is not acceptable to an interest group rarely wins appointment to the state agency with which that group deals.

The collective result of agency–clientele ties is that government agencies tend to be staffed with personnel who share the values and goals of the private interests with which they interact. Indeed, the agencies are often staffed with persons who formerly worked for those interests and who may work for them again in the future. Private interests, in short, are formally plugged into the official decision-making apparatus (see Focus 5.2).

5.2   WHO OWNS GOVERNMENT?

One obvious result of our style of governance is that many administrative units are responsive to private interests. The hunting and fishing department may become the servant of the wildlife conservationists; the highway department may become tied to the trucking interests; the liquor control department may become a close friend of the industry that it is supposed to regulate; and the many licensing agencies may come under the control of, and become tools of, the professionals whom they are supposed to license—be they lawyers, barbers, or pharmacists. Each administrative unit, in other words, is responsive to various lobbies and may be responsive to the governor or the public only incidentally.

Sunk Costs   The money, staffing, and physical facilities that a government, an industry, or another type of organization has already invested in ongoing programs are referred to as **sunk costs**. The widespread existence of sunk costs—in terms of money, staffing, buildings, institutions, programs, behavior patterns, and expectations—restricts the political power and decision-making options of both the governor and the legislature. As a result of decisions made in the past, of policies already adopted, of programs presently in existence, and of staff already employed, a widespread network of public expectations exists and policy options are thus restricted.

The drastic reduction of ongoing programs in areas such as education, public health, parks, or highways is not a politically feasible option for a governor or a legislature. In the area of education, for example, millions of dollars' worth of buildings and materials exist; thousands of people have been trained, licensed, and employed; millions of children are involved in the school programs; and millions of parents expect educational programs. The most a governor can hope to accomplish under such circumstances is to seek small and incremental adjustments in the programs and the budget.

Similar conditions exist in other policy and program areas. Budgets for highways, mental health care, and other social services can often be adjusted upward or downward by up to 10 percent. The political climate is sometimes ripe for the institution of new programs or the reduction of others, but wholesale reversals are almost never feasible policy alternatives. Consideration of new mass-transit programs must recognize the existence of billions of dollars of investment and thousands of miles of expressway systems; new building plans must include strategies to deal with existing structures; plans to close or relocate recreational facilities must anticipate citizen expectations and behavior;

and plans to expand or move an airport must accommodate existing physical facilities, citizen resistance to expansion or relocation, and the networks of communication and transportation that service existing facilities.

Thus, it is clear that public programs and annual budgets are not drastically transformed by governors or legislatures. Decisions made earlier restrict the powers of governors and legislators.[20]

GOVERNORS' POWERS: A COMPARISON

Scholars who study state governors have developed numerical indices that they use to evaluate levels of formal gubernatorial authority. One recent study conducted by the National Governors Association (NGA) examined six areas of gubernatorial power: (1) the governor's ability to run for repeated reelection, (2) the extent of the governor's authority to appoint and remove the heads of executive branch departments, (3) the governor's role in the budget-making process, (4) the legislature's prerogatives to change what the governor proposes, (5) the nature of the governor's veto power, and (6) the extent of legislative control exercised by the governor's political party.[21] Each state was assigned a score in each category, and from that a combined point total was computed (see Table 5.1).

Although the NGA study cannot account for the political clout enjoyed by a governor as a result of political savvy, hard work, intelligence, a powerful personality, or skill in the use of image and the media, its measures do display the range of authority that exists among state governors. As shown in the table, most states received a score in the 19 to 24 range, although some were at the high or low end. The two extremes — Rhode Island and Maryland — show, for example, that not all governorships are created equal in terms of authority. Some governors enjoy extensive formal authority, whereas others have only weak authority and may need to compensate for it through informal sources of power.

EXECUTIVE STRENGTH AND LEADERSHIP

It is clear from our discussion of gubernatorial roles, powers, and limitations that executive strength and leadership are enormously complicated and can vary widely. Institutional structure, formal authority, executive and legislative branch partisan line-ups, the governor's personality and political savvy — these and other factors all contribute to executive strength and leadership.

Kentucky's governors have historically been leaders in their political party

TABLE 5.1
Degrees of Formal Gubernatorial Authority among the States

Degree of Authority (on a scale of 15–29)	States
29	Maryland
27	Massachusetts, West Virginia
26	New York
25	Minnesota
24	Arizona, Connecticut, Hawaii, Kansas, Nebraska, New Jersey, Oregon, Tennessee, Utah
23	Arkansas, Delaware, Illinois, Iowa, Louisiana, Michigan, North Dakota, Ohio, Pennsylvania, South Dakota, Virginia
22	California, Colorado, Georgia, Mississippi, Montana, Washington, Wisconsin, Wyoming
21	Arizona, Florida, Idaho, Kentucky, Missouri
20	Indiana
19	Alabama, Maine, Nevada, New Mexico, Oklahoma
18	New Hampshire, South Carolina, Vermont
17	North Carolina
16	Texas
15	Rhode Island

Source: National Governors' Association data from Thad L. Beyle, "Governors," in *Politics in the American States*, 5th ed., ed. Virginia Gray, Herbert Jacob, and Robert B. Albritton (Glenview, Ill.: Scott, Foresman/Little, Brown Higher Education, 1990), p. 228.

and have enjoyed extensive appointment powers as well as a political environment conducive to a strong leadership role. Government has not been divided, since the Democrats have controlled both legislative chambers and the executive. The Kentucky governorship has been quite strong with respect to both formal institutional authority and informal political powers.[22]

In Georgia governors have also been quite strong, but not because of their formal authority. The governor's appointment powers are only moderate, due to the direct election of many department heads, including the lieutenant governor, the secretary of state, the attorney general, the commissioners of insurance, agriculture, and labor, and the superintendent of schools. The governor in Georgia does play a major role in the budget process and has strong veto powers. Both tradition and one-party Democratic domination of state legislative and executive elections provide the governor with a strong political base from which to operate. Until the 1960s Georgia's governor could select legislative leaders, and there is still a tradition of gubernatorial appointment of people to judicial and other elective offices. For example, the incumbent resigns voluntarily before the end of the term, the governor fills the vacancy, and the appointee can then seek reelection running as an incumbent. Clearly, this strengthens the governor's hand by helping to ensure that the governor's appointee stays on the job.[23]

Texas's governor enjoys neither strong appointment powers nor a central role in budget making. Texas has a host of boards and commissions, including the Railroad Commission, which regulates state oil and gas leases. The lieutenant governor presides over the senate and, together with the house speaker, plays a large role in the budget process.[24] Recent Republican governor Bill Clements faced a Democratic house and a Democratic senate headed by long-term and powerful Democratic lieutenant governor Bill Hobby. Limitations such as these restrict the ability of the governor to forge a strong electoral base.

California's governor enjoys extensive institutional authority but may encounter political problems. The governor's budget, appointment, and veto powers are extensive, and there are no limits on reelection. However, during much of the recent past, the state government has been politically divided, with a Republican governor and a Democratic majority in the legislature.[25]

OTHER STATE EXECUTIVES

As noted earlier in the chapter, the governor is not the only elected administrative official in state government. In most states voters also elect a lieutenant governor, an attorney general, a secretary of state, and a treasurer; some also elect a state auditor, a comptroller, and commissioners of education, agriculture, labor, and insurance (see Table 5.2). Although reformist efforts to stream-

TABLE 5.2
Directly Elected State Executive Officers

Position	Number of States
Governor	50
Attorney general	43
Lieutenant governor	42
Treasurer	38
Secretary of state	36
Auditor	25
Comptroller	9

Source: Calculated from data in *The Book of the States, 1992–93* (Lexington, Ky.: Council of State Governments, 1993), pp. 74–75.

line state government and centralize authority have included proposals to make some of these positions appointive by the governor, the array of directly elected posts has remained substantially unchanged in recent decades.

The Lieutenant Governor

All executive offices are of some administrative and political importance. The lieutenant governor may preside over the state senate (28 states), cast a vote in cases of ties (28 states), assign bills to senate committees (15 states), or appoint members to senate committees and committee chairs (7 states). The lieutenant governor functions as the governor when the latter is disabled (in 42 states) and when the governor is out of state (27 states).[26]

Typically, the lieutenant governor has no direct administrative duties other than special tasks assigned by the governor. Further, lieutenant governors whose duties include presiding over the state senate often decline to do so much of the time. There are exceptions, however, as in Texas, where the lieutenant governor's role in the senate is of major political importance. Some critics argue that the lieutenant governor position is not needed, and there has been a movement in several states to eliminate the position.

The position of lieutenant governor can be a launching pad for mischief, for a run at the position of governor, or both. In states where the governor and the lieutenant governor are not elected on a single ticket, they may be from different political parties. In Massachusetts, for example, a lieutenant governor, an announced candidate for the governorship, proposed a new state budget during the governor's absence from the country.

The Attorney General

The attorney general performs important administrative functions for the state and the position is often used to advance the political ambitions of the incumbent. The job of the attorney general is to defend the legal interests of the state. This involves providing legal services to the governor and state agencies when needed, defending the state and its employees in legal actions, and enforcing state laws (for example, prosecuting cases against environmental polluters or false advertisers). Sometimes the attorney general offers advisory opinions on the constitutionality or proper legal interpretation of a state law or regulation. Sometimes, too, the attorney general's office handles time-consuming cases by contracting them out to private law firms.

Because the office of attorney general is a statewide elective office, a candidate wins it by building a statewide constituency. The attorney general can then easily use the office to gain the visibility needed to launch a run for some other office, such as governor or U.S. senator. Not infrequently, the attorney general and the sitting governor are members of different political parties, which can lead to friction within the executive branch.

Other executive branch officials elected directly by voters include the secretary of state and the state treasurer. State treasurers are elected in 38 states and secretaries of state in 36 states. The secretary of state oversees elections and administers election laws, lobbying laws, and campaign finance laws. In addition, the secretary's office generally administers state laws regarding the filing and establishment of corporations.

The Secretary of State and the State Treasurer

The state treasurer is the custodian of the state's money. The flow of tax revenues and state spending does not occur at a constant pace throughout the year, and revenues may not flow in at exactly the rate at which expenditures flow out. Thus, the state must sometimes spend what it does not have, while at other times it can bank its revenues until they are spent. The treasurer handles the funds, borrowing for short periods in some instances and seeking a good interest return on short-term surpluses in others. The treasurer's position, like other statewide slots, can lead to higher office. Three recent governors — Ann Richards of Texas, Roy Romer of Colorado, and Joan Finney of Kansas — served as state treasurer before being elected governor.

Here again the importance of institutions and institutional design is clear. The relationship of the state executive branch to the other branches, especially the legislature, is one of both cooperation and tension.

THE GOVERNOR AND SEPARATION OF POWERS

The governor and the legislature are rivals for control of the budget process. Governors can and do employ the veto, and they threaten its use to coax from the legislature policies that they prefer. Governors also use their visibility in the media to press on the legislature those parts of their agendas that are supported by public opinion. But the legislature ultimately controls the lawmaking process; it can exert control over the authority, the resources, and the shape of both the executive branch and the courts.

The internal structure of a state's executive branch can have a pronounced impact on state politics. When executive authority is dispersed among a variety of directly elected officials, the governor's power is weakened somewhat. The governor may even face public political opposition from other executives, especially if they belong to the other party. But U.S. institutions do divide authority. When the various parts of the institutional apparatus are controlled by different parties — which is the case in the vast majority of states — implementing a particular political philosophy is difficult. A Democratic legislature may thwart a Republican governor and vice versa. A Republican attorney general may give a Democratic governor a rough time with unwanted advisory opinions, investigations, or prosecutions. Boards and commissions that govern regulatory bodies or large educational institutions may pursue policies and priorities—with respect to environmental pollution or tuition rates, for example—that both the governor and the legislature dislike.

The hallmark of executive branch organization in the American states is, clearly, decentralization. Like federalism and legislative bicameralism, executive branch decentralization disperses power and, when combined with partisan division, creates a political system characterized by extensive conflict. Of course, there are some centralizing features in the system as well. With a mixture of available budgetary, appointment, and veto powers, as well as skillful use of the media and political party connections, some governors can overcome the effects of institutional decentralization and push their preferred policies into public law. Such successes are the result of the triumph of informal gubernatorial power over formal fragmentation.

The place of the states in the federal system has changed over the years, most recently with an increase in their role and importance. Within that context, the nature of the governorship has changed as well. Today's governorship is a prized position. Some past governors want the job back. Many already successful politicians are willing to surrender their U.S. House and Senate seats to seek the position of state governor. Many attorney generals, state treasurers, legislative leaders, and individuals with successful records in the private sector want to be governor. As formally instituted, the governorship is not all that powerful a position, and the increasingly prevalent party-divided government makes the job more difficult than ever before. But the states are major actors in the contemporary federal system, and, with skillful supplementation of formal authority with public relations and political savvy, an energetic politician can indeed make a difference.

SUMMARY

The modern state executive system is one in which the governor occupies a primary place, often among a host of other elected executive officials. Governors play a variety of formal and informal roles, many of which contribute to the expansion of executive power. However, today's governors also face limitations. The plural executive system was designed to limit executive authority and continues to do so. An established bureaucracy with strong agency–clientele ties also limits the power of the governor. While most modern governors are not formally endowed with extensive powers, there are ways to create a stronger gubernatorial office. Some states continue to amend the executive structure by placing additional formal powers in the hands of the governor. Informal powers and bureaucratic expertise can add to the power of the governor who possesses the political expertise and public support to make effective use of them.

KEY TERMS

gubernatorial roles

gubernatorial power

formal powers

informal powers

pocket veto

legislative liaison

plural executive

integrated executive

clientele group

sunk costs

ADDITIONAL READINGS

Beyle, Thad, and J. Oliver Williams, eds. *The Governor in Behavioral Perspective.* New York: Harper & Row, 1972.

Beyle, Thad L., and Lynn R. Muchmore, eds. *Being Governor: The View from the Office.* Durham, N.C.: Duke Press Policy Studies, 1983.

Rosenthal, Alan. *Governors and Legislatures: Contending Powers.* Washington, D.C.: Congressional Quarterly Press, 1990.

Sabato, Larry. *Goodbye to Goodtime Charlie.* 2nd ed. Washington, D.C.: Congressional Quarterly Press, 1983.

NOTES

1. Michael Oreskes, "Governors' Races, Close and Costly, Are Richest Prize," *New York Times*, 4 Nov. 1990.

2. *The Book of the States, 1990–91* (Lexington, Ky.: Council of State Governments, 1991), pp. 85–86.

3. See Thad L. Beyle, "From Governors to Governors," in *The State of the States*, ed. Carl E. Van Horn (Washington, D.C.: Congressional Quarterly Press, 1989), pp. 33–45.

4. Thad L. Beyle and Lynn R. Muchmore, eds., *Being Governor: The View from the Office* (Durham, N.C.: Duke Press Policy Studies, 1983), p. 3.

5. Coleman B. Ransone, Jr., *The American Governorship* (Westport, Conn.: Greenwood Press, 1982), p. 3.

6. Thad L. Beyle, "Governors," in *Politics in the American States*, 5th ed., ed. Virginia Gray, Herbert Jacob, and Robert B. Albritton (Glenview, Ill.: Scott, Foresman/Little, Brown Higher Education, 1990), pp. 201–51.

7. Tommy G. Thompson, "Going Global: A Governor's Perspective," *Intergovernmental Perspective* (Spring 1990): 15.

8. Marc Landy, "Kentucky," in *The Political Life of the American States*, ed. Alan Rosenthal and Maureen Moakley (New York: Praeger, 1984), p. 206.

9. Beyle, "Governors," pp. 208–9.

10. Beyle, "Governors," p. 214.

11. Paul West, "They're Everywhere! For Today's Governors, Life Is a Never-Ending Campaign," *Governing* (March 1990): 51–52.

12. The symbolic role of the U.S. chief executive develops in Americans' minds at a very early age. See David Easton and Jack Dennis, "The Child's Image of Government," *Annals of the American Academy of Political and Social Science* (Sept. 1965): 40–57.

13. *Book of the States, 1990–91*, p. 119.

14. Tony Hutchinson, "Legislating via Veto," *State Legislatures* (20 Jan. 1989): 20–22.

15. Thad L. Beyle, "The Executive Branch: Organization and Issues, 1988–89," in *The Book of the States, 1988–89* (Lexington, Ky.: Council of State Governments), p. 75.

16. Thad L. Beyle, "The Powers of Governors," in *State Government*, ed. Thad L. Beyle (Washington, D.C.: Congressional Quarterly Press, 1990), pp. 124–25.

17. Kenneth J. Meier, "Executive Reorganization of Government: Impact on Employment and Expenditures," *American Journal of Political Science* (Aug. 1980): 396–412.

18. James K. Conant, "In the Shadow of Wilson and Brownlow: Executive Branch Reorganization in the States, 1965–1987," *Public Administration Review* (Sept.–Oct. 1988): 892–902.

19. Phillip O. Foss, *Reorganization and Reassignment in the California Highway Patrol* (Indianapolis: Bobbs-Merrill, Inter-University Case Program, 1962), case no. 75.

20. Ira Sharkansky suggests that the best predictor of the content of a new budget is the content of past budgets. See his "Agency Requests, Gubernatorial Support and Budget Success in State Legislatures," *American Political Science Review* (Dec. 1968): 1,220–31.

21. Reported in Beyle, "Governors," pp. 201–51, esp. pp. 217–30.

22. Landy, "Kentucky," pp. 208–13.

23. Lawrence R. Hepburn, "Georgia," in *The Political Life of the American States*, ed. Alan Rosenthal and Maureen Moakley (New York: Praeger, 1984), pp. 191–93.

24. Anthony Champagne and Rick Collis, "Texas," in *The Political Life of the American States*, ed. Alan Rosenthal and Maureen Moakley (New York: Praeger, 1984), pp. 144–47.

25. Charles G. Bell, "California," in *The Political Life of the American States*, ed. Alan Rosenthal and Maureen Moakley (New York: Praeger, 1984), pp. 53–54.

26. *Book of the States, 1990–91*, p. 56.

6

State Judicial Systems

Most judicial activity in this country occurs in the state and local courts, not at the federal level. Minnesota's supreme court, the highest court in that state, has seven justices: *(seated, from left)* Justice Rosalie E. Wahl, Chief Justice A. M. (Sandy) Keith, Justice John E. Simonett; *(standing, from left)* Justice Sandra S. Gardebring, Justice M. Jeanne Coyne, Justice Esther M. Tomljanovich, Justice Alan C. Page. *(Courtesy of the Supreme Court of Minnesota)*

MOST JUSTICE IS ADMINISTERED BY STATE AND LOCAL SYSTEMS

JUDGES ARE HUMAN BEINGS

THE COURTS ARE POLITICAL ENTITIES

THE STRUCTURE OF STATE JUDICIAL SYSTEMS

State Courts and Federal Courts / Federal versus State Cases / State Supreme Courts / Intermediate Appellate Courts / Trial Courts / Lower Courts / Special Courts / Legislative Control of the Courts

JUDICIAL REFORM

SELECTING JUDGES

Judge Selection Varies among States / Should Judges Be Elected or Appointed? / Choosing the Best Judge Selection Method / The Methods Are Political / *FOCUS 6.1:* Judicial Selection and the Voting Rights Act

DEMOCRACY AND THE COURTS

Political Equality / *FOCUS 6.2:* Religion, Sexual Orientation, and Parades / Legal Precedent

CONTEMPORARY PROBLEMS IN THE COURTS

Attitudes and Values / Judicial Delay / Bargain Justice / *FOCUS 6.3:* Crowded Dockets and Their Consequences / Unequal Resources / Lack of Diversity / Searches for Remedies

STATE COURTS AND CIVIL LIBERTIES

State Bills of Rights / The Fourteenth Amendment / Rights by Case Law

RECENT DEVELOPMENTS IN THE STATE COURTS

New Judicial Federalism / Alternative Dispute Resolution / Other Approaches to Expediting the Courts' Business / Gender and Ethnic Fairness

SUMMARY

Like the legislative and executive branches, the judicial branch makes authoritative decisions and allocates scarce goods and values in the states. That is, the judiciary is a political as well as a legal institution. This may be the single most difficult characteristic of the judiciary for most of us to understand. The conventional view is that the courts, and the judges who preside over them, are somehow removed from politics. We like to believe that justice is indeed blind, and so we embrace a **cult of the robe** — the notion that when an individual puts on the robe of a judge, he or she sheds all biases and prejudices and becomes an impartial dispenser of justice. In reality, the cult of the robe is based on a myth — but a functional myth, because it helps us to accept judicial decisions with which we disagree.

In order to maintain respect and support for the judicial system it may be important that the image of judicial impartiality be preserved. Still, the courts, like the legislative and executive branches of government, are highly politicized. As in most other areas of government and politics, opinion and prejudice help to determine who wins and who loses in the courts. This is not to suggest that the judicial environment is the same as the legislative and executive environments; it is not. But it is a political environment nonetheless.

The principle of **judicial review** — the determination by the judiciary of the constitutionality of the actions of public officials — operates at the state as well as the federal level. Through this principle, state courts hear thousands of cases every year, and in the process they settle disputes, interpret the law, and help to shape public policy. Many cases that come before the courts involve minor events (for example, the prosecution of individuals for disorderly conduct or traffic violations); others are more serious (murder trials or million-dollar lawsuits). Some cases may have implications for just one individual, while others may involve an interpretation of a statute or of the powers and duties of a local government or state agency and may affect many people for years to come. Whatever the nature of the case — whether it involves an intergovernmental dispute over the powers of local governments, a contest for the custody of children, a suit for land or money, or a prosecution of an individual accused of a crime — the courts are involved in the creation and application of law and in the authoritative resolution of conflict.

MOST JUSTICE IS ADMINISTERED BY STATE AND LOCAL SYSTEMS

Most of the courts, judges, and criminal and civil cases in the United States are in the state and local systems, not in the federal courts. The reason is simple: Most of our laws are state-made laws. Virtually all property, contract, domestic relations, and criminal law is embodied in state-made common law, state statutes, or local ordinances. The federal laws and federal courts deal with matters of federal taxation, bankruptcy, racketeering, and civil rights and liberties, as well as a host of other matters. The bulk of the action involving crime, property, families, children, and the general health, peace, and safety of the public, however, is in the state and local domain.

Most legal matters, criminal and civil, are not settled as a result of lengthy and full-blown judicial proceedings. Rather, criminal cases are often settled before they ever go to trial, through plea bargains struck between defendants and prosecutors, deals that are then accepted by a judge.

JUDGES ARE HUMAN BEINGS

Judges, like the rest of us, have sets of attitudes and policy preferences—and these creep into their decisions. Prosecutors in most states possess broad discretionary powers, with the result that some people are prosecuted and others are not. As we will see later in the chapter, decisions are made and political equality is violated through a system of bargain justice. Prosecutors are actually a part of the executive branch of government, but their roles have obvious implications for the court system. Some judges have widely known reputations as being "hanging judges" (meaning that they are tough on crime). Other judges are more sympathetic than some of their colleagues to the defense or the prosecution, to citizens or corporations, to women or men. In some courts, students, blacks, or poor people may be at a definite disadvantage. After all, the courts are called "courts of law," not courts of justice.

Some judges also enjoy reputations for being hard-working, knowledgeable, and fair. Unfortunately, the process of selecting judges in many states (discussed more fully later in this chapter) sometimes produces judges whose abilities are widely disparaged by the local members of the bar. In one Texas jurisdiction there is a district judge whose nickname among practicing lawyers is "Reversible Error"; the attorneys know that this judge is likely to make an error during a trial that will lead a higher court to reverse the decision on appeal. Unfortunately, this type of judge is hardly unique.

This chapter describes the structure and operation of the judicial systems in the American states. It also outlines the structure of the state courts, including their relationship to the federal judiciary, a few of the more salient characteristics of the judicial process, the various methods that are employed to select judges, a number of problems that continue to plague state courts, and the role of the courts in the maintenance of political equality and civil rights.

THE COURTS ARE POLITICAL ENTITIES

As was noted earlier, we often think of courts as nonpolitical institutions, and this is understandable. Formulating public policy is normally perceived as a function of the legislative and executive branches, not of the courts. Judges often take great pains to maintain judicial restraint and to avoid the appearance of judicial activism by claiming to look to statutes and legislative intent rather than their own preferences when making decisions. (The terms **judicial restraint** and **judicial activism** describe the relationship between the courts and the elected branches of government. Advocates of judicial restraint believe that the courts should defer to the elected branches on questions of public policy. Proponents of judicial activism view the courts as equals of the elected branches and believe that the courts should be directly involved in the policymaking process.) In our explanations of democracy we call for equality for all before the bench. In many ways, then, our understanding of the role of the judiciary in the separation of powers, our assumptions about democracy, and judges' stated intention to exercise restraint all seem to picture a court system that is not political.

But, of course, the judiciary is political. If the term *politics* refers to the determination of public policy, then the courts are very much political institutions. No matter how detailed and specific our constitutions and statutes are, judgments about their meanings in specific situations must be rendered. What does prohibition of "cruel and unusual punishment" mean when it comes to living conditions in some state prisons? What does it mean to provide equal educational opportunity in elementary and secondary education? How much money may one recover as "damages" in a case of personal injury? How far does "due process" go in preventing a city or state agency from firing an employee? The courts end up making many of these decisions, and their choices often have enormous policy consequences. When a court disallows "double-bunking" or requires a certain number of square feet in living space per inmate in a state prison, it can set off a capital construction program with major fiscal consequences for a financially beleaguered state. A court decision that finds a state's educational funding system to be an impediment to equal educational opportunity among school districts can do the same. Texas, for instance, has been grappling with the latter problem for several years now, with increasing costs to the taxpayers, while at the same time failing to resolve the problem to the satisfaction of the state courts.

Courts also have a political character as a result of the backgrounds and attitudes that judges bring to their jobs. Judges, like governors, legislators, and lobbyists, come to their job with a set of values and preconceptions, and, try as they may (and some do not try), they are never able to shed their prejudices and apply the law objectively. Thus, while the courts may try to be fair, while they may attempt to minimize partisan considerations in their judgments, and while they may be the least political of the three branches of government, they remain political institutions.

No one can deny that the choices made by judges have major impacts on public policies or that the preferences of judges find their way into decisions, just as attitudes and values affect the way legislators vote. But at the same time, while the avowed responsibility of legislators is to translate voter preferences into public policy, it is often argued that the duty of judges is to minimize the impact of political preferences in general and try instead to "discover" what the people want, as evidenced in the words and intent of constitutions and statutes. This task may not be feasible, or even desirable according to some, but the very perception on the part of the public that this is the proper role of the judiciary is a constraint on judicial behavior.

THE STRUCTURE OF STATE JUDICIAL SYSTEMS

While the judicial systems of all states share many characteristics, there is also extensive diversity. By and large the courts are, like much of the U.S. government system, highly decentralized. Some courts handle minor cases, while others deal with more serious ones. Courts may have original jurisdiction, appellate jurisdiction, or both. In general, however, all states have a three-tiered judiciary made up of trial courts, appellate courts, and a supreme court (although not all states call their top court a "supreme" court). In most states various parts of the court system operate independently of one another. Sometimes more than one set of courts has jurisdiction over similar cases. Often the administration of the courts is decentralized, too. As we will see later in the chapter, methods of selecting judges vary among the states and even among the courts within individual states.[1]

State Courts and Federal Courts

The judicial systems in the American states are structurally separate from the national court system. Here again we see the influence of the federal principle. As in American government generally, decision making in the judiciary is widely diffused—both between and within the national and state court systems. The output of the judicial system is the cumulative result of thousands of decisions made in literally thousands of courtrooms.

Our use of the federal system results in the parallel existence of two sets of government—the national government and the 50 state governments. As a result, there are actually 51 sovereign governments and 51 court systems. The national courts (or federal courts, as they are usually called) have **jurisdiction** over matters involving national laws and personnel, and the state courts deal with state matters. When the national government, an employee of the national government acting in an official capacity, or a national law is involved, the case is heard in national court. If the state government, a state employee acting in an official capacity, or a state law is involved, the state courts have jurisdiction. Since local governments are legally a part of the state governmental system, matters involving local governments, their official representatives, or their ordinances are usually heard in the state courts as well. The major exception involves U.S. constitutional issues; that is, under some circumstances when there is a question as to the constitutionality of a law or act of a state or local government, the U.S. Supreme Court may hear the case.

There are a few other exceptions to the various jurisdictional rules. For example, if a state employee breaks a federal law by violating someone's civil rights, he or she may be tried in a federal court. There are even some criminal actions that run afoul of both federal and state laws (for example, bank robbery); a person accused of such crimes may be tried in both federal and state courts (there is no double jeopardy violation, as the accused is not being tried twice under the same law). The highly publicized Rodney King case in Los Angeles is an example. The police officers accused of beating King were first tried in a local court under California law; they were acquitted. Then, they were tried in a federal court, on the charge of violating King's federal civil rights, and here two of the officers were found guilty.

Federal versus State Cases   At one time or another we have all heard the quip, "Don't make a federal case out of it." The intended implication, of course, is that somebody is making a "big deal" out of a minor matter. But the unintended implication is that the issues before the national courts are always more significant than those addressed by the states. Not so. Jurisdiction between the national and state courts is determined by the government, the public official, or the law that is involved, not by the seriousness of the case. Murder, rape, assault, and reckless or drunk driving, for example, are all serious matters, but they are state cases because they involve violations of state law. Likewise, disorderly conduct and illegal parking or drinking after hours are state cases because they involve violation of local ordinances, and local governments are legally a part of the state government. However, the theft or purposeful destruction of a mailbox is a federal offense; it involves obstruction of the U.S. mail, a violation of a federal (national) law, and a person accused of such an act would be tried in a federal court.

In some cases, both state and federal courts have jurisdiction in a particular civil matter. If an individual chooses to sue a firm engaged in interstate commerce, he or she may bring the case in federal court. If the firm is engaged in intrastate commerce only, the suit will be heard in a state court (unless the matter involves a U.S. constitutional issue, such as alleged civil rights violations or a breach of federal law). Sometimes the case can be brought in either court, if there is concurrent jurisdiction. For example, some years ago a serious automobile accident resulted in a case in which the injured party brought suit for personal injury against a consortium of a railroad and two construction companies. In this particular case, the suit could have been brought in either a state or federal court. The incident was a crash involving an automobile and a train at a construction location where highway work was being done by two construction companies, each of which maintained its central office in a different county of the state. The individual injured in the accident actually had a choice of five courts in which to bring an injury suit. Since the railroad was involved in interstate commerce, suit could have been brought in federal district court — the lowest major court in the federal judicial hierarchy. But suit could also have been brought in any one of four trial courts in the state in which the accident occurred. It could have been brought in the state court in the county where the accident happened, or it could have been brought in state court in the county where the plaintiff (the person filing the suit) resided. Finally, the suit could have been brought in state court in either of the two counties where the construction companies maintained their home offices.

Figure 6.1 illustrates the dual nature of the legal structure. It should be kept in mind that the figure is only a rough model; as we will see shortly, the court systems in many states are much more complicated than the model suggests.

The national judiciary is structurally uncomplicated, consisting of three levels of courts plus a group of special courts. State court systems are often not so simple. All states have a supreme court, an intermediate appellate structure, and a group of trial courts. Some states have a number of other courts as well. No two states have identical court systems. In some states, such as Wyoming, the judiciary consists of just three tiers. In other states, such as New York, the judiciary contains a host of special purpose courts in addition to the major trial courts and the supreme court.

State Supreme Courts

At the top of every state court system is a court of last resort, usually called the **supreme court**. Two unusual deviations are found in Oklahoma and Texas, where there are two courts of last resort — one for civil cases and another for criminal matters. State supreme courts typically are composed of five or seven justices, although Alabama, Iowa, Mississippi, Oklahoma, Texas, and Washington each have nine. In some states the justices are

FIGURE 6.1   Federalism and the Courts

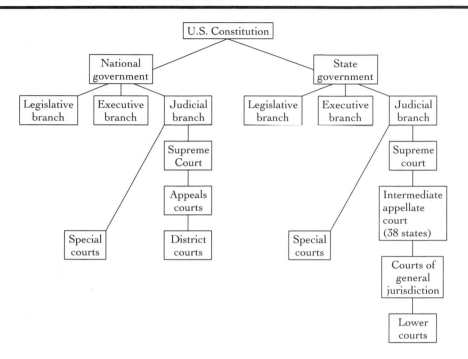

appointed by the governor or legislature; in others they are elected on either partisan or nonpartisan ballots. In a few states the judges serve life terms on the top court, while in others they are elected to 2-, 6-, 8-, or 10-year terms. (The methods of judicial selection are examined more fully later in the chapter.)

Most of the business of state supreme courts involves hearing appeals from lower court decisions; in a few states the supreme court has original jurisdiction (that is, can be the court in which the case originates). Decisions by these courts are made by majority rule and usually are recorded in written opinions. In considering appeals from lower court decisions, state supreme courts play an important role in the political process. Often cases that reach the appellate court are controversial and hinge on disagreement about the interpretation of a law. When the court renders a decision, therefore, it sets a precedent that the lower courts are expected to follow. As a result, state supreme courts play a critical role in the actual establishment of the law, and, since their decisions bind the lower courts, the decisions of the supreme courts may affect large numbers of people.

State supreme court dockets have become extremely overloaded in recent decades. As a result of the serious and growing problem of delayed justice, nearly two-thirds of the states now have some form of **intermediate appellate court**. These appeals courts are higher on the judicial totem pole than the major trial courts, but lower than the supreme court. Their task is to relieve the supreme court of some of its burden and to reduce the long delays that have become such a serious problem in cases under appeal. With few exceptions, such as death penalty cases in some states, cases that eventually reach the supreme court must be heard by the intermediate appeals court first. The number of judges on intermediate appellate courts varies from 3 in Alaska, Hawaii, and Idaho to 8 in Texas. In most states appellate judges are selected for terms ranging from 5 to 12 years.

Intermediate Appellate Courts

Below the supreme court and the intermediate appellate courts (in states where they exist) are the **trial courts**, or the courts of general jurisdiction. The names and numbers of courts of general jurisdiction vary considerably, but they handle the bulk of the most serious cases in every state. These trial courts go by several names, the most common of which are district, superior, circuit, county, and common court. In some states there are just a few such courts, and in others there are dozens of them. In some states each county has one or more major trial courts, whereas in other states one court may serve several counties. In the most complex systems there are trial courts of record (that is, courts whose proceedings are recorded) as well as trial courts, usually addressing minor issues, that do not keep a written record.

Trial Courts

Courts of general jurisdiction possess both original and appellate jurisdiction. They may hear appeals from such lower courts of limited jurisdiction as probate, municipal, or magistrate courts, and, while they possess original jurisdiction in both serious and petty matters, most of their work entails civil cases involving large sums of money and criminal cases involving large fines or lengthy jail sentences. Felony cases, for example, are heard for the first time in the major trial courts. When these major trial courts hear appeals from the lower courts of limited jurisdiction, the case is heard *de novo* (literally, "anew"); that is, since many lower courts are not courts of record, the cases that are appealed are heard all over again, from the beginning.

Unlike appellate courts, where there are no juries, major trial courts may use juries in both criminal and civil cases. As is the case with state supreme courts and intermediate appellate courts, trial court judges are appointed in some states and elected in others for terms ranging from 4 to 15 years.

Lower Courts   At the bottom of the judicial hierarchy are the **lower courts**, or courts of limited jurisdiction. These may be county, municipal, or justice of the peace courts, depending on the exact structure of a state's system. These lower courts process the thousands of minor cases involving traffic violations, misdemeanors (such as disturbing the peace), and suits involving small amounts of money. Compared to the courts of general jurisdiction and state supreme courts, the lower courts are less significant politically because the cases they handle affect only the immediate parties. Unlike supreme court decisions, the actions of the trial courts do not set precedents that are followed by other courts.

Special Courts   Finally, many states include certain types of **special courts** in their judicial systems. States with heavy urban concentrations, such as Michigan and New York, may make constitutional or statutory provision for special municipal courts for the large cities. Other states have established special purpose probate, juvenile, small claims, tax, or domestic relations courts.

As noted earlier in the chapter, no two states have identical judicial systems. The names of the courts, the methods of selecting judges, the length of judges' terms, and other features of the judicial system vary among the states. Most states employ one or more courts that handle specialized cases of one sort or another. Table 6.1, which outlines the relatively simple court structure of Hawaii, the moderately complex system of Iowa, and the highly complicated arrangement of New York, illustrates the variations that can exist among state judicial systems.

TABLE 6.1   **Judiciary Structure in Three States**

Hawaii	Iowa	New York
Supreme court	Supreme court	Courts of appeals
Intermediate courts of appeals	Court of appeals	Appellate divisions of supreme court
Circuit courts	District courts	Supreme court
District courts	Superior courts	Court of claims
	Municipal courts	Surrogates' courts
	Judicial courts	Family courts
	Magistrate courts	County courts
	Police courts	Civil court (New York City)
		Criminal court (New York City)
		District courts
		Justice courts
		City courts
		Town and village courts

Sources: Adapted from data in *State Court Systems* (Chicago: Council of State Governments, 1962); and *The Book of the States, 1988–89* (Lexington, Ky.: Council of State Governments, 1989).

Although some of the basic features of state court systems are established in state constitutions, the state legislatures make most of the decisions that shape the structure, jurisdiction, and operation of the courts. What constitutes a felony or a misdemeanor, and what shall be the penalties for conviction? How much sentencing latitude shall judges have? What shall be the salaries of judges? Will there be a public defender system and, if so, what will it look like? How many courts and how many judges will there be in the state? These are the types of questions answered by state legislatures.

Legislative Control of the Courts

Each year state legislative agendas contain many bills related to the judiciary. Often the bills are pushed to change or clarify laws in direct response to a court decision with which the legislature may have disagreed. Sometimes legislators, angry with a court decision, may seek to remove jurisdiction from a court. Of course, it is the legislature that writes the statutes that the courts apply and interpret. It is also the legislature that creates most of the court system. And, while to some degree the courts are supported by fees, it is the legislature that appropriates much of the money needed to run the judicial system.

JUDICIAL REFORM

Reformers have been busy in recent decades pressing for structural changes in the courts. The criticism of and recommendations for the courts follow much the same line as those targeted at other parts of the government. The state judicial systems are faulted for instances of overlapping jurisdiction and for their generally decentralized character. Critics accuse the court systems of being inefficient and confusing. They should be restructured and centralized, it is argued.

The reformers often advocate what is called a **unified court system**. In theory, a unified system would be hierarchical, with the supreme court at the top, serving both as a court of last resort and as the body that possesses final administrative power over the entire court system. The rest of the courts would be subordinate to the supreme court. The jurisdiction of each set of courts would be clearly defined, with no overlapping or conflict. Procedures would be the same in all courts that share similar responsibilities and jurisdiction. Personnel and pay systems would be standardized and centrally administered or controlled. The benefits of such an orderly system, reformers argue, would include greater public understanding of the courts, increased speed in the processing of cases, and financial savings.

However, like reformist campaigns in government generally, court reforms have not been universally adopted. As is the case with any existing organizational arrangement, many people have a stake in the existing system. Judges and lawyers develop useful routines that they do not want disturbed. Many of the people most closely associated with the court system oppose any type of radical change. In addition, proposals for unified court systems often require that the state assume more of the costs of running the courts, with perhaps less reliance on support from local governments or from fees. This could create problems for legislators, especially in times of tight budgets. It is the legislature that must modify state statutes to reorganize the judicial system, and legislatures are reluctant to do so if there is a significant price tag associated with the changes. Although there has been some modernization of the structure and operation of state courts in recent years, it has not been as sweeping or as extensive as reform advocates would like it to be.[2]

SELECTING JUDGES

All federal judges are appointed by the U.S. president, but considerable variation exists among the states in the procedures of judicial selection. Indeed, some states employ one system of selecting judges for some courts and a different system for other courts. Still, there are five general patterns of judge selection:

1. appointment
2. election in nonpartisan elections
3. election in partisan elections
4. a combined appointment–election plan
5. legislative selection

The appointment–election plan, often called the **Missouri plan** or the **merit plan**, has enjoyed some popularity recently. Although the details vary among states, basically the Missouri plan involves the appointment of judges by the governor from a list of nominees submitted by a judicial nominating panel. The nominating panel is supposedly made up of experts—knowledgeable attorneys and laypersons who are considered capable of identifying candidates who will make good judges. After appointment by the governor, the judge serves a brief term in office and then runs for election against his or her record (that is, the judge faces no opposition). The voters determine whether to retain the judge for another specified term or to reject the judge and have the governor appoint a replacement.

Judge Selection Varies among States   Although changes in judge selection procedures are constantly being made, the state variations are as follows: 19 states elect all or some of their judges in partisan elections; in 3 states all or some judges are elected by the legislature; 20 states elect judges in nonpartisan elections; 9 states permit the governor to appoint all or most judges; and 23 states employ the Missouri plan.

The judge selection scheme of each state can be classified as one of the five general types, but there are many variations among the states in terms of the details of the selection plans. For example, Ohio has partisan primaries but nonpartisan general elections. In Rhode Island the legislature elects the members of the state supreme court but the governor makes the appointments to the trial courts. In Arizona the selection process varies by the population of the county in which the court is located, with still other variations for certain local jurisdictions.[3] Maryland's judge selection process varies not only with the level of the court but also with the county involved. New Mexico employs a hybrid system in which a nominating convention provides the governor with a list of judicial nominees, the governor makes the appointment, the appointee runs in a partisan election in a first retention attempt after a period on the bench, and thereafter runs unopposed in a typical Missouri plan fashion.[4]

However, most judges in Alabama, Arkansas, Texas, Illinois, Mississippi, New Mexico, North Carolina, and West Virginia are elected on partisan ballots, and all judges in Kentucky, Michigan, Minnesota, Montana, Nevada, North Dakota, Ohio, Oregon, Washington, and Wisconsin are elected in nonpartisan elections. A number of other states elect most, but not all, of their judges in either partisan or nonpartisan elections.

The method of judge selection utilized by any given state is usually the result of decisions made at the time the state entered the Union. It is often conditioned by the precedents set in and around that state in pre-statehood days as well as the reform movement that was in vogue at the time of statehood. This explains the widespread use of the elective procedure in the western states, for example. In a few states, though, later reform movements brought about the adoption of new judge selection methods. The complex mixture of procedures that exists in some states today may well be the result of incremental modification of the basic system brought on by such changes in the environment as rapid urbanization, which led to the addition of municipal courts in some cities.

Should Judges Be Elected or Appointed?

Arguments have been made both in support of and in opposition to the various methods of selecting judges. An old saying has it that the appointment process makes judges out of politicians and the electoral process makes politicians out of judges.

Elections It is argued that direct election, the most widely used method, is effective because it subjects judges, who clearly play policy-related roles in the governmental process, to direct control by the sovereign public. Governors, legislators, mayors, and other public officials are held accountable for their behavior in public office and, the argument continues, the same level of accountability should be required of judges, since their actions, like those of other public officials, affect large numbers of people.

A counterargument contends that, although it makes sense in a democracy to maintain a popular check on all public officials, elections can tempt judges to "bend the law" in order to muster political support at the polls. The goals of the courts are to apply the law and to administer justice in an impartial and nonpolitical fashion. However, this counterargument continues, elections may subject judges to a host of political pressures and make it difficult for them to remain impartial on the bench. The contention is that the judiciary should be kept out of politics; that the courts and judges are, or at least should be, "above the law."

As noted earlier in the chapter, the courts are very much a part of the political process. Still, in the name of judicial impartiality, opponents of the popular election of judges would rather minimize the political pressure to which judges may be subjected. The use of nonpartisan elections in many states represents an effort to avoid the "taint" of partisan politics. While the removal of party designations from the ballot may reduce the overt role of the political party in the judicial selection process, it does not purge the process of its partisan nature. Elections, by their very nature, are political affairs because they involve contestants for designated positions.

In addition, judicial elections are usually down-ballot races; that is, the candidates' names appear near the bottom of the election ballot and thus attract a relatively low voter response because most voters are not likely to be familiar with them. A few years ago, for example, Texas voters elected a candidate whose last name was identical to that of a well-known candidate from the recent past. There is little doubt that most Texas voters mistakenly assumed the current and past candidates were the same person. They were not, and the public was dismayed to learn that they had elected an individual whose personal legal problems led eventually to his fleeing the state to avoid imprisonment.

Another criticism of the electoral method of judge selection is that money can taint the process. It is not uncommon for successful judicial candidates at the district court level to hold receptions for the purpose of paying off their campaign debt shortly after winning an election. Obviously, local law firms feel strong pressure to contribute to a judicial campaign or risk alienating a judge before whom they may appear in court. This is hardly "blind" justice.

Appointments   Some argue that the gubernatorial or legislative appointment of state judges removes the worst of partisan politics from the courtroom. It is considered important that judgeships not be given to political hacks as a reward for party support. The judicial system, the argument continues, needs both qualified people and the highest possible degree of objectivity; thus, it is important to insulate judges from the political combat of elections. However, opponents of the appointment method reverse this argument. Judges, they contend, are public officials and an integral part of the government apparatus. Because their decisions affect the public, judges, like all other public officials, should be subject to public oversight and public control. And, of course, there is nothing about the appointment process that is any more likely than the electoral process to filter out political hacks.

There is widespread agreement as to the goal that should be pursued: Judges should avoid partisanship and favoritism in their official decision-making capacity, but as public servants they should be responsible to the people. The disagreement hinges on the methods that best achieve that goal. Are judges best made impartial and accountable when they are periodically forced to encounter the judgment of the people at the polls? Or is justice best served by appointing judges and thus insulating them from the pressures of elective politics?

The Missouri Plan   As noted earlier in the chapter, the Missouri plan is a "merit" system that combines aspects of the elective and appointment methods of judge selection. It is intended to eliminate the worst and preserve the best of both the appointment and elective systems. Various forms of the method are employed in almost two dozen states. Advocates of the Missouri plan argue that it ensures the selection of competent judges, reduces the political nature of judge selection, and sees to it that judges remain accountable to the people.

Critics of the Missouri plan, however, contend that it combines the worst, not the best, of the appointive and elective methods. First, they argue, it eliminates much of the public accountability that is supposedly inherent in the elective system. The popularly elected governor is restricted to the choices proposed by the nominating commission, so that the public cannot justifiably hold the governor responsible for the appointment of an incompetent judge. Second, once a judge has served a short initial term, reelection is almost guaranteed for two reasons: (1) the judge is not likely to face serious opposition and (2) the public's knowledge of the affairs of the court is all but nonexistent. One of the ways in which voters become informed about the record of incumbents seeking reelection, and one of the ways in which incumbents are replaced by new officeholders, is through the debate and publicity that accompany most contests for public office. The contention is that when judges are allowed to run without opposition, they face no opponent whose campaign rhetoric might inform voters about the incumbent judge's past record. As a result, Missouri plan judges are almost never voted out of office.

It is important here to qualify the word *never* with *almost*, for occasionally voters do decline to return certain Missouri plan judges to the bench. Usually reelection fails when a judge runs afoul of the law or otherwise does something extreme and widely publicized. Perhaps the best-known example of the popular ouster of a judge in a retention election occurred in California in 1986, when Chief Justice Rose Bird and two of her associates failed to be retained. Bird had voted repeatedly against imposition of the death penalty and she and her colleagues were painted as liberal and soft on crime in a sophisticated $4 million television campaign.

Another criticism of the Missouri plan is that the informal role of state bar associations is enlarged and strengthened by its use. Attorneys are officially given a role in the selection of the short list of nominees from which the governor must appoint judges, since they are given a number of slots on the judicial nomination commissions. Critics of the Missouri plan argue that the courts belong to the people and not to a privileged set of lawyers.

In addition, critics note that the jockeying for appointment to the recommending panel is very political, for attorneys campaign for these positions. The result is that the formal process of the merit system may mask a highly politicized informal process of selection.

Choosing the Best Judge Selection Method

The debate over which judge selection method is best hinges in part on the assumption that it makes a difference which plan is used — that better judges or better decisions can be achieved by using one plan instead of another. Research addressing this issue is inconclusive. While the various plans may result in the selection of different kinds of judges, it is not certain whether better decisions are also a result. One reason for this, of course, is the difficulty of determining what "better" decisions are. In addition, there are other factors that tend to standardize the selection processes and minimize the potential differences.

In a study of 12 states, Herbert Jacob found that the various systems lead to the selection of judges with different social and political backgrounds (though his evidence is not considered conclusive).[5] Jacob compared judges selected through partisan, nonpartisan, and legislative election as well as by gubernatorial and Missouri plan appointment, according to their localism (roots in the state), education, and previous political experience. While he found slight variations, no clear patterns emerged. And, of course, the larger question remains unanswered — whether any one of the plans produces better judicial decisions.

The Methods Are Political

At the same time, differences among the various judge selection methods are lessened somewhat because they are all political and because gubernatorial appointment plays a major role in all of them. Both partisan and nonpartisan elections are obviously political. Partisan elections more overtly bring the political parties into the selection process, but even in nonpartisan elections many candidates have had previous political experience. In fact, Jacob's study indicated that over one-half of all judges elected on nonpartisan ballots had held previous political office.[6] In addition, contestants in any election, whether labeled partisan or nonpartisan, are involved in a struggle for funds, visibility, popularity, and, most importantly, votes.

Judge selection by way of legislative election, gubernatorial appointment, or the Missouri plan is a political process as well. Nearly 60 percent of the judges selected by gubernatorial appointment, over 90 percent of those selected by state legislatures, and almost one-third of the Missouri plan judges studied by Jacob had held previous political office.[7] Appointments to the bench have always been a popular way for governors and legislatures to reward staunch party supporters, and so it is unlikely that an individual with little or no earlier participation in partisan activities would attract the attention of a governor, a legislature, or even a Missouri plan nominating commission. It is difficult, in other words, to demonstrate that some judge selection methods are political whereas others are not.

The differences among the plans are also minimized by the fact that the gubernatorial appointment of judges plays a major role in judge selection even when elective systems are employed. Judges may die or retire from the bench in the middle of their terms, giving governors numerous opportunities to appoint replacement judges. Since incumbent judges are defeated in bids for reelection less than 10 percent of the time, gubernatorial appointments turn out to be extremely significant, even in elective states. It is likely that as many as one-half of the judges in elective states come to the bench by way of executive appointment.

Craig Emmert and Henry Glick have also pursued the question of the differential impact of judicial selection methods. Like Jacob, they found that the method used makes little difference. Their work focused on state supreme court justices, and, while they found background differences among the judges, they concluded that the variations were best explained by region of the country, not by the selection method.[8]

In general, we can say that variations in judge selection plans may have some impact on the kind of person who ends up on the bench. However, we cannot say with certainty that any one selection plan removes politics from the courtroom or that it leads to better judicial decisions than do the others.

It may well be that judicial elections are becoming even more political as voters become more aware of the political impact of judicial decisions, especially those at the supreme court level. In 1980, for example, a candidate for the bench in Texas campaigned on an avowedly political platform, calling for prayers in the schools, elimination of pornography, and lower taxes. Texas supreme court races of late have been major battlegrounds concerning tort reform, with one slate of candidates (usually Republicans) receiving strong support from insurance companies and the medical profession, and another slate of candidates (usually Democrats) drawing a major portion of support from trial lawyers' associations. In short, judicial selection involves issue politics, ethnic politics, party politics, and personal politics just as do all other contests for positions of authority. (See Focus 6.1.)

6.1   JUDICIAL SELECTION AND THE VOTING RIGHTS ACT

The courts themselves have been used to attack judicial election systems in certain jurisdictions. For some years now, courts have employed the 1965 Voting Rights Act to declare that at-large city council elections have discriminatory impacts on ethnic minorities. Recently, judicial elections have been attacked on the same basis in Alabama, Florida, Georgia, Louisiana, Mississippi, Ohio, and Texas.

The position of the courts on this matter remains unsettled. In 1987 one U.S. District Court found that the at-large system did indeed have a discriminatory impact, and in 1989 a U.S. court of appeals agreed. In addition, the U.S. Department of Justice, which has some direct enforcement powers for the Voting Rights Act, found in 1990 that the Georgia at-large system of choosing state judges disadvantaged African-American voters. However, also in 1990, a U.S. district court held that because judges are not "representatives," the Texas system of electing judges was not subject to challenge under the provisions of the 1965 act. Next, a divided three-judge panel on the Fifth Circuit Court of Appeals reversed this decision in 1992, and the Texas attorney general recommended that the state adopt a plan for judicial districts in selected urban areas. In August 1993, the full Fifth Circuit Court of Appeals reversed the three-judge panel and ruled that the Voting Rights Act should not be applied to judicial selection in Texas.

DEMOCRACY AND THE COURTS

The relationship between democratic theory and the courts has long been a focus of scholars. This is especially true at the federal level, where judges are appointed and therefore are not directly accountable to those affected by their decisions. It is also true with respect to state and local courts. Historically, the courts have been viewed as the defenders of basic American values, especially those associated with civil liberties. A realistic appraisal of this role, however, must acknowledge an "accordion" effect; that is, the protection of civil liberties expands when the courts are staffed with liberal judges and contracts when the courts are staffed with conservative judges. This is yet another indication of the political role of the judiciary.

There are several important aspects of the courts' role in protecting civil liberties. First, one of the most basic assumptions underlying democratic thought is that people should be politically equal, and judicial precedents have been a critical device for the maintenance of political equality. Second, the courts are currently plagued with a host of serious problems that make the maintenance of political equality all but impossible. Third, civil liberties, such as free speech, free press, and **due process** of law (which includes such procedural rights as the right to counsel and the right to a jury trial), are considered necessary for democracy, and historically the courts have played a major role in the protection of these rights.

Political Equality

In some totalitarian states elitist theories of government advance the notion that some people should rule others because they are inherently superior in terms of race, religion, wealth, gender, family, knowledge, or some other ascriptive characteristic. Political equality does not and cannot exist, it is contended. Rulers in some totalitarian states purposely undermine political equality by programming a sort of randomness into public decision making. The prospect of an unpredictable midnight "knock on the door" is used to terrorize the population. Due process of law and equal protection of the law are nonexistent. One person, one vote at the polls is a joke, although the myth may be maintained.

Things are supposed to be different in a democracy. Here special claims to rule are rejected, and, supposedly, all people are politically equal. Nobody gets two votes at the polls; traffic tickets are not supposed to be fixed just because one has a friend or relative in city hall; contracts for the construction of public buildings are supposed to be let on the basis of competitive bidding, not on the basis of "who you know"; and every person is supposed to be treated like every other person before the law.

We all know that this is not really how things work, but most of us agree that this is what a democracy should strive for. The use of legal precedent and the rule of law—both matters deeply involving the courts—are critical in the effort to achieve the goal of political equality. The **rule of law** means that public decisions affecting such activities as the establishment and enforcement of traffic regulations, the issuance of parade permits, and courtroom trials for everything from disorderly conduct to rape are to be made and conducted according to known legal provisions, and not on the basis of the preferences of some individual or group (see Focus 6.2). In short, a democracy is supposed to be a government of laws, and no one person is supposed to be "above" those laws.

FOCUS

6.2   RELIGION, SEXUAL ORIENTATION, AND PARADES

In the spring of 1993, New York City's annual St. Patrick's Day parade spawned lawsuits aimed at forcing the event's sponsors to allow a gay Irish group to join the parade. A federal court ruled that the permit to parade should be issued and that the sponsors were under no legal obligation to admit the gay organization. The sponsors argued that the parade was a religious event, venerating a Roman Catholic saint, and that, since homosexuality violates Catholic teaching, the sponsors could exclude gay organizations from the parade.

A group of lawyers then filed suit in state court, asking for a court order barring New York City from issuing a parade permit. They argued that, under the constitutional separation of church and state, the parade could not be sanctioned by the city or take place on a public street with police officers serving at public expense.

Legal Precedent   **Legal precedent** means that the procedures used and the decisions rendered in one situation should match those in other situations involving similar circumstances. In other words, it is assumed that there is value in maintaining some degree of predictability in the application of law.

The decisions of the higher courts, usually the federal and state supreme courts, establish legal precedents that bind the lower courts. Such precedents are intended to standardize the decisions and procedures followed throughout the federal and state judiciaries and thereby increase the probability that individuals will receive equal treatment before the law regardless of the courtroom they find themselves in. However, the standardizing effect of higher court precedents is reduced somewhat by judges' different perceptions of the meaning of decisions as well as by the intrusion of judges' individual values. But any judge who systematically deviates from the decisions and interpretations of the higher courts will be overruled with considerable frequency. Thus, the use of legal precedent—the similar interpretation and application of the law in similar circumstances—is critical for the maintenance of political equality.

Precedents are often borrowed from other states. It is not unusual for attorneys to seek to bolster their arguments and nudge the local court in one direction or another by citing cases decided by supreme courts in other states.

CONTEMPORARY PROBLEMS
IN THE COURTS

It is important to acknowledge that numerous real-life conditions lead to something less than total political equality in the courts. Ideally, for example, courts in a democracy would provide citizens with speedy and impartial justice. Individuals arrested for a crime would be swiftly charged, arraigned, and brought to trial. Persons who suffer injury as a result of an accident or breach of contract would be able to file suit and have the courts reach a quick and just decision. This ideal comports with the familiar saying that "justice delayed is justice denied." Unfortunately, however, this is not the way our courts work today. Rather, clogged dockets and large backlogs of cases are the norm, and swift justice is the exception.

Attitudes and Values

The values of judges and juries reduce objectivity and equal treatment before the law. The combination of delayed trials and the availability of plea bargaining may have unfortunate consequences. For example, an innocent person may be advised to cut a deal with the district attorney by pleading guilty to a lesser offense in order to expedite the process and avoid the vagaries of a jury trial. This is not to say that most judicial decisions make a mockery out of equal protection of the law, or that there is no attempt to run the judicial process according to democratic norms. Rather, the conditions in the courts are such that there is a gap between the reality of the courtroom and the goal of equal and impartial justice.

Judges, like everyone else, are in part products of their past. Their attitudes, values, and ways of looking at the world are partly the result of their life experiences. Thus, it is to be expected that different judges, having had different sets of experiences, will vary in terms of their attitudes and values. It may also be expected that these variations will lead to different patterns of judicial decisions.

In the 1960s several studies of state supreme court justices conducted by Stuart Nagel found differences in the behavior patterns of Democratic and Republican judges, Catholic and non-Catholic judges, liberal and conservative judges, and white and nonwhite judges.[9] For example, Nagel found that, compared to Republican judges, Democrats more frequently decided in favor of the defense in criminal cases, of the tenant in landlord–tenant cases, of the consumer in sale-of-goods cases, of the injured in motor vehicle accident cases and of the employee in employee injury cases. They were also more likely to find a constitutional violation in criminal cases. Judges of color, compared to white judges, more often found in favor of the defense in criminal cases and of the wife in divorce cases, and they more often found a violation of procedure in criminal-constitutional cases. Catholic judges were more likely to find in favor of the defense in criminal cases, of the wife in divorce settlement cases, of the debtor in creditor–debtor cases, and of the employee in employee injury cases than were non-Catholic judges. Finally, liberal judges were more apt than conservatives to side with the defense in criminal cases, with the injured party in motor vehicle accident cases, and with the employee in employee injury cases.

Although not usually systematically gathered and reported, additional evidence of the intrusion of personal attitudes and values into judicial decision making is available in almost any city or county courthouse. For example, following an extensive "drug bust" in Colorado in the late 1970s that culminated in scores of arrests, large numbers of young people appeared for arraignment in a state district court. Some were released on personal recognizance bonds, pending trial. Others, appearing before a different judge in the same court, were required to post cash bonds of up to $2,500 — an event that led the district attorney to complain that the propensity of the more lenient judge to release the accused without a cash bond was extremely discouraging to the local police. The district attorney was probably correct; the behavior of the more lenient judge regarding the bonds was probably discouraging to the police. Furthermore, the obvious dual standard created by the two judges' behavior was doubtless discouraging to those who did not have the $2,500 for bail and who may have spent time in the county jail awaiting trial. The behavior of two sincere judges, trying to do their best, led to inequality before the law.

Gender Issues   Studies of gender differences show that male and female judges share most characteristics. Male and female judges are nearly equal in terms of percentage of convictions, imposition of prison terms, and length of hard time sentenced. However, female judges tend to be harsher than male judges on convicted women defendants.[10]

Jurors' Prejudices   Jurors come to the jury box with their own preconceptions. This unfortunate fact is illustrated at its extreme by the comments of a male juror who had been dismissed on a peremptory challenge by the defense attorney in a Colorado courtroom in 1975. In reference to the case, which involved a convicted felon then being tried for rape, the juror commented to a fellow juror, "If they hadn't kicked me off that jury, I'd have saved the taxpayers some money by getting a short trial. I could have told you that son-of-a-bitch was guilty by just looking at him."[11] The use of dismissals from the jury both for cause and by peremptory challenge (the prerogative of both the defense and the prosecution to remove a specified number of potential jurors for no stated cause) is designed to minimize the intrusion of this sort of overt prejudice into judicial decisions. Although attorneys are allowed considerable discretion in exercising peremptory strikes during the *voir dire* ("to speak the truth") phase of jury selection, recent court decisions have held that peremptory challenges may not be used to exclude jurors because of their race.

Juries are one of the most important links between democracy and the judicial process. Although they are instructed by judges to consider only the law and the facts entered into evidence, virtually all studies of jury behavior reveal that jurors view their role as that of dispensers of justice rather than interpreters of law and facts. For example, juries often refuse to convict, regardless of the evidence, when they view the law being applied as silly or unjust.

As might be expected, jury practices vary from state to state. Several states permit nonunanimous verdicts, especially in civil trials. The trend among the states now is toward 6-person rather than 12-person juries.

There are two types of juries: grand juries and petit juries. A **grand jury** does not determine guilt or innocence; rather, it decides whether sufficient evidence exists to warrant an indictment (that is, to bring the accused to trial). The determination of guilt or innocence is left to the **petit jury**, or trial jury.

Judicial Delay

Another serious problem that makes the administration of impartial justice difficult is the tremendous case backlog of many state courts. Tens of thousands of cases are handled by the courts each year and, as a result, delays of up to five years between filing a case and final resolution are not uncommon in civil cases. (Criminal cases, in contrast, must be brought to trial within three months in most states.) Although there are many reasons for the growing case backlog, appeals of lower court judgments and the growing interdependence and general complexity of our society are among the most basic reasons. Delays of this sort are serious in both civil and criminal matters. Some civil suits, for example, involve the attempts of individual citizens to recover damages from insurance companies for injuries or losses suffered in accidents. When such a case drags on for months or years, evidence gets old, witnesses forget what they saw, and injured parties must get along without payment for the injury or loss. Families who have lost their homes, widows and widowers who have lost their spouses, or breadwinners who have become disabled as a result of an accident may be seriously hurt by long delays. The case of the insurance company, however, may be aided by the aging of evidence. Also, the plaintiff may tire of waiting and be willing to settle for less than stipulated in the original claim. Some research suggests that the failure of some judges to manage their dockets, and the dilatory habits and tactics of many lawyers, also contribute to the delays.[12] (See Focus 6.3.)

Bargain Justice

Crowded court dockets and uncertainty about the behavior of judges in many instances lead to what is called **bargain justice**, or the making of deals — **plea bargaining** — between the district attorney's office and a defendant. Indeed, most civil and criminal cases are settled without ever coming to trial. Every year defendants in literally thousands of criminal cases agree to

---

FOCUS

6.3 CROWDED DOCKETS AND THEIR CONSEQUENCES

Attempts to address the crowded dockets of state courts sometimes have less than desirable consequences. In 1992 the chief justice of the Texas supreme court acknowledged that almost one out of every eight state district court cases was being heard by an ex-judge through a state-based visiting judge program. The chief justice conceded that some infirm or controversial ex-judges, despite having been rejected by the voters, were still adjudicating cases around the state. These ex-judges included individuals who had been reprimanded by the state's Commission on Judicial Conduct, one ex-judge whose family life was such a scandal that his own children endorsed his opponent during the latter's successful election campaign, and an ex-judge so feeble that he was cited for lacking the basic vision and hearing needed to make competent decisions.

---

plead guilty to a less serious crime than the one for which they were first indicted. District attorneys often promote such deals when they are not sure their case is strong enough to ensure a conviction on the first, more serious offense, or when they are simply too busy to follow through with full trials on every indictment. Bargains of this sort often benefit the defendant in that they expedite the processing of the case and ensure a much lighter sentence than if the defendant had been convicted on the original indictment. At the same time, however, plea bargaining may also influence the innocent defendant to plead guilty to a lesser charge in order to avoid the risk of conviction.

A study of New Orleans area courts illustrates the political nature of the prosecution process. Over a six-year period fewer than 40 percent of the defendants pled guilty to their original charge. Over 5 percent of the others pled guilty to a reduced charge, roughly 10 percent pled innocent and were tried, and nearly 45 percent had their case dismissed for a variety of reasons.[13]

One might logically ask why bargain justice is a problem, especially since it expedites the business of the courts. Even though plea bargaining only recently became a public topic, it dates back over a hundred years. Measured against the democratic demand for political equality, however, it can become a serious problem, for it places tremendous judicial power in the hands of the district attorney's office — an office the people did not establish to pass judgment on citizens. When district attorneys are in a position to make deals with defendants, inequality before the law is almost ensured. District attorneys make deals in some cases but not in others. They are most likely to deal when the case is weak, when their office is overly busy, when the court dockets are full, or when they are on familiar terms with the defendant's attorney. This means, then, that the fate of many accused persons rests not with the facts and merits of the case but with such circumstantial factors as the business load of the court and the mood and prejudices of the district attorney.

Sometimes district attorneys with future political ambitions press a case because it may bring them great publicity and the opportunity to create a favorable public image. At other times they may drop a case because a rash of new and serious crimes demands their attention. The result is inequality in the application of law. Some people are subjected to the full weight of a state's laws. Other people who should be prosecuted are not, and the public loses.

Unequal Resources

A problem that is not peculiar to the courts is the unequal distribution of benefits that results from gross inequities in wealth. Rich people are better equipped than poor and moderate-income people to influence politics — from the county and states to the federal government. They are also in a better position to employ skilled legal help, thereby increasing their chances of success in the courts. The services of a skilled attorney are essential to success in the courtroom. The legal process and the law itself are extremely complicated. Since the average citizen is understandably overwhelmed and confused by what goes on in a courtroom, the services of a lawyer or a public defender are necessary. The wealthy can avail themselves of the best legal services; the poor cannot. Although certain Supreme Court decisions have helped to eliminate some of the most serious disadvantages that formerly haunted the poor in terms of legal representation, inequities still exist. Generally, the rich continue to receive better-quality legal representation than the poor. In death penalty cases especially, a disproportionate number of poor defendants in capital cases find themselves represented by inexperienced and overworked public defenders or court-appointed counsel.

Lack of Diversity

Ethnic minorities and women are underrepresented in the state judicial system. The number of judges of color is low and is growing only slowly. The same is true, of course, of the number of minority lawyers and minority law school students. Although the number of women lawyers and judges is on the upswing, the judicial system is still dominated by men. These imbalances are an ongoing problem, for it is difficult to maintain the legitimacy of any government institution when one group disproportionately controls the seats of power.

The lack of diversity in the judiciary became a source of concern in two states recently. In 1990 the U.S. Department of Justice found that Georgia's system of electing judges in large judicial districts by majority vote conflicted with the law. The Justice Department claimed jurisdiction over the matter based on the 1965 Voting Rights Act, which requires states to clear their electoral processes with the department under certain circumstances. It was argued that the election system in Georgia worked to discourage the election of African-American judges. Similarly, in Colorado in 1991, minority spokespersons addressed the issue of their underrepresentation when a judicial selection panel sent a list of six nominees—all white—to the governor. The critics further noted that only 13 of the state's 248 trial court judges were Hispanic (even though Colorado has a significant Hispanic population) and 9 of those 13 had been appointed within the previous three years.

Searches for Remedies   Little can be done about the personal attitudes of judges; lawyers can only try to choose jurors whose personal attitudes make them sympathetic to the lawyer's position. There is a growing awareness of and concern about the crowded dockets, delayed justice, inequities in quality of legal representation, and minority underrepresentation of the American state judicial system. In efforts to deal with the volume of cases and the resulting backlog, many states, including California, Pennsylvania, New Jersey, and New York, are experimenting with alternative methods of dispute settlement.[14] These include arbitration and mediation, which are methods of settling disputes without a trial. Both involve a third party who serves as an "umpire" between the two opposing sides. The major difference between the two methods is that decisions reached through arbitration are legally binding, whereas decisions reached through mediation are not. Mediation services are sometimes called citizen dispute settlement programs and are sometimes provided in locations known as neighborhood justice centers.

The quality of justice is a matter of increasing concern in the states. Since it can be affected by the abilities and integrity of judges and attorneys, nearly a dozen states have established continuing legal education programs, or CLEs. Other states are exploring methods of monitoring the performance of judges.

It is clear that the courts face many problems, but the judicial system does have many relatively unbiased and competent judges and district attorneys. While some judges may be biased and incompetent and some district attorneys may engage in questionable tactics, the sources of these problems lie in the system itself. Perhaps the primary purpose of the law and the judiciary in any society is to give people's lives and the application of law some degree of regularity and predictability—to eliminate unnecessary uncertainty and randomness in interpersonal, intergroup, and government relations. Hence, the system emphasizes the rule of law, the use of precedent, and the general attempt to make every person equal before the law in a democracy. At the same time, however, differences in interpretations of the law are inevitable, as is inequality before the law. Caseloads are such that delayed justice must often be taken for granted.

STATE COURTS AND CIVIL LIBERTIES

The American state courts are deeply involved in protecting **civil liberties**—the freedoms of speech, press, and religion; due process of law; and apportionment. Most contact that citizens have with their government is at the state and local levels, and most serious cases addressing civil liberties arise in the localities and the states.

State Bills of Rights

Civil liberties are specified in the national Bill of Rights, in the states' bills of rights, and in U.S. Supreme Court interpretations of the Fourteenth Amendment to the U.S. Constitution. These documents typically guarantee the freedoms of religion, speech, and press, protection against capricious deprivation of property, and a variety of other civil liberties. In addition, there are procedural rights, generally categorized under the umbrella of due process, which include the *Miranda* warnings, the right to have counsel provided, and the right to have evidence that is seized in violation of one's constitutional rights excluded from use in trials. The latter is called the **exclusionary doctrine**.

Perhaps the best-known statement of freedoms in the U.S. legal system is contained in the First Amendment to the Constitution:

> Congress shall make no law respecting an establishment of religion, or prohibiting the free exercise thereof; or abridging the freedom of speech, or of the press; or the right of the people peaceably to assemble and to petition the Government for a redress of grievances.

The legal application of civil rights to the states by the courts is complex. In 1833 in *Barron v. Baltimore*, the U.S. Supreme Court held that the Bill of Rights afforded citizens protection only from the national government, not from the states, and that state bills of rights restricted the states. The Court held to that interpretation until the twentieth century. This meant that systems of justice varied greatly among the states, as well as between states and the national government.

The Fourteenth Amendment

In the twentieth century, Supreme Court interpretations of the Fourteenth Amendment have had the effect of expanding and standardizing citizen rights in the states. The Fourteenth Amendment states that:

> No State shall make or enforce any law which shall abridge the privileges or immunities of citizens of the United States; nor shall any State deprive any person of life, liberty, or property, without due process of law; nor deny to any person within its jurisdiction the equal protection of the laws.

Note that the opening line of the First Amendment reads, "Congress shall make no law . . . ," but that the opening line of the Fourteenth Amendment speaks specifically of the states. In 1925 the Supreme Court began what is known as **selective incorporation**—giving specific meaning to the Fourteenth Amendment's concepts of liberty, due process of law, and equal protection of the laws by linking the protections found in the Bill of Rights to the Fourteenth Amendment's due process clause.

In *Gitlow v. New York* (1925), the Court held that the freedoms specified in the First Amendment (speech and press) were among the liberties that, according to the Fourteenth Amendment, could not be compromised by a state without due process of law. In *Palko v. Connecticut* (1937), Justice Benjamin Cardozo held that the Fourteenth Amendment required states to protect those rights "implicit in the concept of ordered liberty" and basic to an "enlightened system of justice." He went on to suggest that the freedoms of speech, press, assembly, and religion were among the rights selectively incorporated through the Fourteenth Amendment in order to ensure ordered liberty. In subsequent cases the Court has, through the Fourteenth Amendment, applied numerous other restrictions on the states, most of them similar to those of the national Bill of Rights. They include the use of the exclusionary principle (*Mapp v. Ohio*, 1961), the right to counsel (*Gideon v. Wainwright*, 1963), and several others. Indeed, most of the liberties of the Bill of Rights have been effectively incorporated. The application of many Bill of Rights freedoms to the states via the Fourteenth Amendment has helped to standardize justice among the states.

Rights by Case Law

In essence, the Supreme Court has built a body of case law that establishes the parameters for the states in a host of policy areas. Reading much of the meaning of the U.S. Bill of Rights into the words of the Fourteenth Amendment, the Court has circumscribed the ability of state and local governments to restrict speech, the press, and rights of assembly. It has given definition to the concept of freedom of religion, and it has told states and localities how to handle those accused of crimes. The Court has forced desegregation of schools. State courts, as well as all state and local governments, are obligated to obey the "supreme law of the land," and that law is what the Supreme Court determines it to be.

RECENT DEVELOPMENTS
IN THE STATE COURTS

There have been several interesting developments in the state courts in recent years. One is the emergence of **new judicial federalism** — that is, the expanded use by state supreme courts of provisions in state bills of rights as the legal bases for decisions. The courts in California and Texas, for example, cited their own state constitutions in decisions requiring modification of school financing schemes so as to achieve more equity in educational opportunity. Some state courts have restricted the employer's right to fire employees "at will." The courts have also relied on their state bills of rights to anchor such civil liberties as free speech, sexual equality, and freedom from illegal search and seizure, often going beyond the protections outlined by Supreme Court decisions.

New Judicial Federalism

Many of these developments occurred in the 1980s. It was in this decade that the U.S. Supreme Court retreated from its earlier tendency to base decisions on interpretations of the Fourteenth Amendment. The shift toward new judicial federalism has led to some expansion of civil liberties and diversity among the states.[15]

Utah's Supreme Court Justice Christine Durham explains the trend toward new judicial federalism as a result of the emergence on the bench of a new generation of judges. Many of today's justices grew up and received their legal training during a period of general social activism in the late 1960s and the 1970s, when the courts, like other institutions, were used strategically to press political agendas in such areas as civil rights, consumer rights, and environmental protection. State judges today bring to their cases the perspectives and understandings that they learned and internalized during that earlier era. They thus tend to be active and innovative in the search for and use of fresh sources of judicial guidance and precedent.[16]

In a related trend, the state courts have shifted the perspective of some laws through judicial decisions. State courts have long played a major role in the development of policy in areas not addressed by or not fully covered by state statute, including tort (legal wrongs), contract, and property law. Thus, the cumulative impact of the decisions of state judges has been the basis of law.

Historically, the judge-made law was conservative, protecting the holders of money and property and providing substantial protection to businesses from product liability. This has changed some in recent years, for state courts have begun to side more often with injured plaintiffs in cases involving such matters as medical malpractice and product liability. In some instances state legislatures have responded by placing into statutes limits on liability. Physicians and businesses push for such limitations, of course, whereas trial lawyers are opposed to them. This particular issue, referred to as **tort reform**, was a central campaign theme in the Texas judicial elections in the late 1980s and early 1990s. The willingness of some citizen interest groups throughout the nation to seek relief through the state courts has increased as the effects of the conservative Reagan and Bush appointments to the federal court system have begun to assert themselves. Whereas during the 1960s and 1970s the federal courts were viewed as relatively friendly to litigation involving civil rights or consumer protection, today the state courts are considered the safer havens because of the more conservative federal bench.

Alternative Dispute Resolution

In response to the continuous high volume of legal activity, many states have experimented with alternatives to full-blown courtroom litigation. Although the approaches vary, they are often referred to generally as **alternative dispute resolution (ADR)** and include mediation, binding and nonbinding arbitration, short "mini-trials," court-mandated arbitration, and summary jury trials. The abbreviated proceedings are binding only when both parties agree to them in advance. Roughly one-half of all ADR schemes were developed in the 1980s or later. They are employed in various forms and combinations by the states.[17]

Other Approaches to Expediting the Courts' Business

Approaches geared toward speedier and more effective processing of the legal business of the states also include automation of fines, jury selection, judge access to case law and child-support payment records; videotape recording of court proceedings; long-distance audio and video communication in certain court proceedings; the use of more specialized courts (for example, drug case courts); and a general tightening of procedures so as to reduce the number of postponements and delays.[18] The public, in turn, has been made more aware of the judicial process through the televising of state and local trials. Although not all states permit televised trials, and no federal trials are televised, the Supreme Court has held that there is no constitutional prohibition against televising courtroom proceedings.

There is widespread opinion that many contemporary problems facing the courts are the result of a litigation explosion. But at least one study disputes that claim. An investigation conducted by the National Center for State Courts in

1986 found no evidence of such an explosion.[19] The need for ways to expedite the courts' business seems to be a longstanding problem caused by many factors.

More than one-half of the states have recently established commis- **Gender and** sions or task forces to investigate and seek remedies for gender bias **Ethnic Fairness** in the courts. Their recommendations include changes in procedures, modified law school curricula, and the use of gender-neutral language.

Some states have also established bodies to look into the problem of racial and ethnic bias. A New York group, for example, found that the domination of the legal system by whites leads to distrust of the system by nonwhites. The courts will continue to change, albeit incrementally, as a result of the findings of such study groups, as well as in response to political pressures (such as those now challenging judicial election systems).

SUMMARY

The role of state courts in the American judicial system is complex. Because of federalism, both the national government and the state governments have courts. Because of the separation of powers, the judiciary is only one of three branches within each state.

Courts are often viewed by the public as removed from politics, handing down legal decisions that have little policy import. But this view of the courts, based on the cult of the robe, is a myth. In reality, courts make policy through decisions that are influenced by the attitudes and worldviews of the judges who make them. Thus, state and local judicial systems are actively involved in the political process because they render decisions that have an impact on public policy.

Perhaps the most striking characteristic of state judicial systems is their diversity; no two state court systems are alike. Unfortunately, they are also characterized by overloaded dockets, which often means that justice is not served swiftly. The states use various methods of selecting judges, although studies indicate that there is little substantive difference in the types of judges selected.

Finally, the diversity of state courts also results in inequities in the quality of justice that is dispensed. Nonetheless, contemporary state judicial systems have been willing to extend state rights beyond those guaranteed by the U.S. Constitution, in a trend called new judicial federalism.

KEY TERMS

cult of the robe
judicial review
judicial restraint
judicial activism
jurisdiction
supreme court
intermediate appellate court
trial court
lower court
special court
unified court system
Missouri plan
merit plan

due process
rule of law
legal precedent
grand jury
petit jury
bargain justice
plea bargaining
civil liberties
exclusionary doctrine
selective incorporation
new judicial federalism
tort reform
alternative dispute resolution (ADR)

ADDITIONAL READINGS

Glick, Henry R. *Courts in American Politics: Readings and Introductory Essays.* New York: McGraw-Hill, 1990.
———. *Courts, Politics and Justice.* New York: McGraw-Hill, 1993.
Grilliot, Harold J., and Frank Schubert. *Introduction to Law and the Legal System.* 4th ed. Dallas: Houghton Mifflin, 1989.
Rosenberg, Gerald N. *The Hollow Hope: Can Courts Bring About Social Change?* Chicago: University of Chicago Press, 1991.
Wice, Paul. *Judges and Lawyers.* New York: HarperCollins, 1991.

NOTES

1. See *The Book of the States, 1990–91* (Lexington, Ky.: Council of State Governments, 1991), pp. 210–22; and Lawrence Baum, *American Courts: Process and Policy*, 2nd ed. (Boston: Houghton Mifflin, 1990).

2. See, for example, U.S. Department of Justice, *Court Unification* (Washington, D.C.: GPO, April 1988).

3. Baum, *American Courts*, pp. 100–101; and *The Book of the States, 1992–93* (Lexington, Ky.: Council of State Governments, 1992), p. 233.

4. See Dixie K. Knobel, "The State of the Judiciary," in *The Book of the States, 1990–91* (Lexington, Ky.: Council of State Governments, 1991), p. 200.

5. Cited in Kenneth Vines, "Courts as Political and Governmental Agencies," in *Politics in the American States*, ed. Herbert Jacob and Kenneth Vines (Boston: Little, Brown, 1965), pp. 239–87.

6. Ibid.

7. Ibid.

8. Craig F. Emmert and Henry P. Glick, "The Selection of State Supreme Court Justices," *American Politics Quarterly* (Oct. 1988): 445–65.

9. See Stuart Nagel, "Political Party Affiliation and Judges' Decisions," *American Political Science Review* (Dec. 1961): 843–51; Stuart Nagel, "Ethnic Affiliation and Judicial Propensities," *Journal of Politics* 24 (1962): 92–100; and Stuart Nagel, "Off-the-Bench Judicial Attitudes," in *Judicial Decision-Making*, ed. Glendon Schubert (Glencoe, Ill.: Free Press, 1963), pp. 29–55.

10. See John Gruhl, Cassia Spohn, and Susan Welch, "Women as Policymakers: The Case of Trial Judges," *American Journal of Political Science* (25 May 1981): 308–22.

11. Witnessed by one of the authors.

12. James H. Bradner, Jr., ed., *Advancing Justice: May We Approach the Bench?* (Schaumburg, Ill.: Alliance of American Insurers, 1987).

13. Herbert Jacob, "Politics and Criminal Prosecution in New Orleans," in *Studies in Judicial Politics*, ed. Kenneth Vines and Herbert Jacob (New Orleans: Tulane University, Studies in Political Science, 1963).

14. *The Book of the States, 1988–89* (Lexington, Ky.: Council of State Governments, 1989), p. 148.

15. See Elder Witt, "Hans A. Linde: The Unassuming Architect of an Emerging Role for State Constitutions," *Governing* (July 1989): 56–60; and Stanley Mosk, "The Emerging Agenda in State Constitutional Rights Law," *Annals of the American Academy of Political and Social Sciences* (March 1988): 54–64.

16. Lawrence Baum and David Frohnmayor, eds., *The Courts: Sharing and Separating Power* (New Brunswick: Rutgers University, Eagleton Institute of Politics, 1989).

17. Bradner, *Advancing Justice.*

18. Knobel, "The State of the Judiciary," pp. 194–203.

19. National Center for State Courts, *Court Statistics and Information Management Project* (Williamsburg, Va.: NCS, April 1986).

7

Political Parties

Partisan politics is everywhere. This booth and the political activity it stimulated were photographed at the Monterey County Fair in California. *(David Conklin/Monkmeyer)*

Chapters 7–9 focus on the organizations and activities within the political system that link citizens to the formal institutions discussed in earlier chapters. This chapter addresses political parties; Chapters 8 and 9 cover interest groups and elections, respectively. In a democracy, public policies are intended to reflect the preferences of the people, and it is through political parties, interest groups, and elections that the people most often make their desires known. The links between institutions and citizens are not perfect, of course, but collectively parties, interest groups, and elections help to keep decision makers informed of voter preferences.

THE FUNCTIONS OF POLITICAL PARTIES

The major goal of political parties is to win elections in order to organize the government and make public policy. Indeed, parties must win elections with some degree of regularity or endless defeats will make it extremely difficult to maintain a cadre of party regulars and a viable party organization. But in their search for success at the polls, political parties perform a number of functions considered essential to the successful operation of democratic political systems. These **latent functions** include contributing to the political education of the public, increasing citizen involvement in politics, recruiting people for political office, organizing the government, partially fusing a government fragmented by federalism and the separation of powers, forming the majorities necessary for the fabrication of legitimate public policy in a democracy, and serving as vehicles that negotiate conflict into compromise.

Educating the Public

Without the participation of an informed citizenry, democratic government is meaningless. Scholars of democracy agree that informed citizen participation is an important check on political leadership. In this regard Americans have traditionally assigned a major educational role to the mass media, arguing that a free press and free speech are necessary to the full and free flow of ideas and information. Without such a flow it would be impossible for the voter to participate intelligently in the decision-making processes.

The media must have something to report to the people, and it is here that the parties play a critical role. Much of our political news is party news — news of the controlling party in the legislature doing battle with the governor who is of a different party; news of the minority in the state senate struggling to block the passage of a bill; news of the entry of new candidates into an upcoming race for governor; or news of the leadership of the minority party blaming the majority party for bad roads, prison riots, or rising taxes.

It is the political struggle that the media report, and it is the parties that have organized much of it. The political parties create and publicize platforms. They search for and create issues. They criticize the opposition party's policies and offer alternative policies. And they publicize all of this through the mass media as well as through other traditional campaign channels. During election campaigns, the parties consciously seek to inform the public through their influence with the media, giving rise to the use of **spin doctors**, whose task is to offer the media the party's interpretation of campaign events. Most of the activities in which parties engage in their search for electoral success have the effect of disseminating information throughout the system.

Increasing Political Involvement

When an individual becomes involved in politics, the chances are that the person is affiliated with one of the two major political parties — the Republican party or the Democratic party. Of course, there are other ways to be politically active. One can work with an interest group or be politically active in nonpartisan city elections. But it is more likely that an individual's involvement in politics is defined largely through contact with a major party.

Thus, it is the major parties, with their permanent and ongoing organizations, that more than any other single factor inform political activism. One may be active in a precinct or the county organization, or even be a candidate for local, state, or national office. Whatever the nature of an individual's involvement in the political process, political parties are useful vehicles in enhancing the political activism considered essential to a democratic decision-making process.

Recruiting Candidates

State constitutions and statutes provide for the establishment and assignment of powers, duties, and limitations to public offices. But they have little to say about who will fill these offices. In part, this is deliberate; the legislatures are organized by the parties and it is to the parties' advantage to retain discretion over the recruitment of candidates. As we will note in more detail later in the chapter, the laws in most states govern the formation and operation of the parties, but the laws fail to provide the informal routines for the recruitment of candidates for public office. This role is filled by the parties.

Obviously, screening devices of some sort must operate to select from the vast general public those few who will contend for office in public elections. Some people will run for office but most will not; some procedures, either formal or informal, must operate to form the selection process. With rare exceptions, an individual with aspirations for public office must start by affiliating with and working for a political party. This alone does not ensure success, but it almost always is a prerequisite to political success. Again, it is the political party that recruits most of the people needed to fill elective public offices in the states.

Organizing the Lawmaking Process

Although much of the formal structure of American governments is prescribed by law, the law is largely silent concerning other organizations that are equally necessary to the smooth functioning of government. For example, the laws of a state may establish three branches of government, but may say nothing about how the three branches will relate to one another or how the hundreds of members of the legislature will conduct business. To expedite the operations of an otherwise unwieldy legislature, committees must be formed, leadership selected, and procedures established. Working relationships among the three branches of government, and between the legislative and executive branches especially, must be forged. Political parties generally perform these functions.

Most legislatures divide into majority and minority factions, usually along party lines. The majority faction controls the selection of formal leadership for each house, and both the majority and minority select their own floor leadership. Likewise, the parties usually play major roles in the selection of personnel for legislative committees and in the maintenance of communications with the governor—matters about which the law is generally silent. But this is not always so. In Texas, historically, ideology has been more important than partisanship in organizing the state legislature; conservatives have battled liberals more than Republicans have battled Democrats. However, this is changing in the 1990s, and increasingly Texas mirrors most other states in that the dominant political party in the legislature (currently the Democrats) controls the leadership positions. The essential point here is that government bodies, like all organizations, do not run themselves—people run them. The political parties play a major role in organizing the government so that issues may be identified, alternatives proposed, bills introduced and processed, and public programs effectively administered.

Fusing the Fragmented System

One of the most salient features of American government is the extent to which it is structurally fragmented. Federalism divides authority between the national and state governments. The separation of powers, which is employed at both the national and state levels, further divides authority. So do bicameral legislatures, the plural executive model (employed to some degree in all of the states), and the vast systems of local government.

Most of the factors that divide decision-making authority were adopted purposefully to reduce the opportunities for individuals and groups to exert excessive influence on public decisions; federalism and the separation of powers are examples of such intentionally adopted institutional features. Other fragmenting structures, such as the proliferation of governments in many metropolitan areas and the expansion of bureaucracies at all levels, have been the result of changing social and technological circumstances and purposeful design. Whatever their cause, however, the fact remains that decision-making power is widely dispersed in the American government system.

To a degree the political parties glue the fragmented system back together. Sometimes the two houses of a bicameral state legislature are controlled by different political parties, or one party may control the legislature while the other party occupies the governor's chair. In the latter case, the effects of structural fragmentation may be further aggravated by interparty wrangling. A Republican legislature, for example, may refuse to help a Democratic governor push a legislative program; or the governor may refuse to place items on the call (agenda) of a special legislative session that the majority leadership in the legislature wants to consider. In many other cases the same party controls both houses of a legislature, or even the entire legislative branch and the governorship as well. Under these circumstances the controlling party may fuse what the structure has fragmented. The governor and the legislative leadership may work closely as a team to propose, enact, sign, and implement a package of policy proposals.

The capacity of the political parties to transcend structural divisions can also link the states with the national government. Although communication may not be extensive, the congressional representation of a given state usually maintains contact with the party and its elected officials back home. Senators and members of Congress return for reelection campaigns as well as for a variety of other reasons, and their agenda almost always includes a round of meetings and speeches involving members of the party. Problems are discussed, information is exchanged, and promises are made. Since more and more programs at all levels of government involve cooperative efforts, discussions almost always include some consideration of how the Washington representatives can be of assistance to the home state. The existence of linkages of this sort can be seen in the frequent announcement by senators and members of Congress of federal grants to such state institutions as universities and to local governments in the representative's home state.

In the United States, two seemingly contradictory truths operate simultaneously. On the one hand, we profess to adhere to the concept of majority rule, and in most cases actually live up to it (majorities, not minorities, pass legislation in city councils, state legislative committees, and state supreme courts). On the other hand, we experience and often encourage considerable social, cultural, and political diversity. How, then, do we get anything done? How can effective public programs be designed to attack our numer-

Forming Majorities

ous pressing problems if, in the face of a culturally, socially, and politically pluralistic system, we require majority approval of public actions?

The political parties help answer these questions by creating voting majorities out of a maze of minorities — both at the polls and in legislative bodies. The parties assist their members who are aspirants for political office, and in return they expect some loyalty from those who are successful (though their loyalty is not always forthcoming). In addition, the parties play a key role in the organization of legislative bodies, and those who occupy such critical posts as committee chairperson or house speaker owe some of their success to the party. Ideological commonalities provide another basis for party unity. This is not to say that American political parties are tightly knit and disciplined organizations, for they clearly are not. But they do provide an organizing and rallying point for politicians.

When majorities form to pass laws, therefore, the parties more than any other single factor are responsible. Studies of legislative behavior indicate that the single best predictor of legislative voting behavior is party affiliation. On most legislative proposals, those lawmakers who lack a vital interest in the particular issue up for a vote frequently rely on party direction to govern their vote. This is not to say that all votes are determined by the party line, that parties are the only institutions to which lawmakers are loyal, that all divisions fall along party lines, or even that a majority vote invariably indicates widespread agreement on the issue at hand. On many occasions different individuals favor an item for quite different reasons. Nevertheless, the democratic expectation of majority rather than minority rule demands that public measures be passed by majority votes. The political parties thus play a critical role in assembling majorities out of what is often a vast network of minorities.

Resolving Conflict

For a political party to select a nominee for public office, put together a platform, or come to a party position on a legislative proposal, it must successfully negotiate a number of compromises. There are few issues on which all the members of a party can agree. Differences of opinion between party members often are of a lesser magnitude than the differences between the party itself and the opposition; but differences are almost sure to exist within the party as well. Sometimes the parties, both national and state, can unite and pull together after ironing out their internal differences; at other times the differences run too deep and the party is weakened by internal division.

The capacity of political parties to make compromises has implications for the political styles found in legislative bodies and for the relationships between governmental branches and agencies. Some commentators argue persuasively that there exists a widespread consensus in the United States on such political fundamentals as the proper institutions and procedures for decision making, but few claim that a majority of the people, be they leaders or followers, can agree on such narrow and specific issues as the proper level for the property tax, the best expenditure levels for parks or roads, or the wisest approach to addressing the problem of crime. When we move from the general, such as the need for better schools, to the particular, such as the best way to achieve better schools, consensus rapidly gives way. Thus, if the parties did not effect compromises, if all the differences of opinion that exist on nearly every issue were fed into legislative deliberation, if all of the latent points of disagreement had to be fought out in the official decision-making arenas, it would be difficult to accomplish anything at all.

The preceding description of the functions performed by political parties is necessarily generalized because in no two states are the political systems exactly alike. Indeed, rarely does a given party have exactly the same political stance and agenda in one state as it does in another. And, within the larger states, it is not uncommon for Democrats and Republicans in one region of the state to differ ideologically from their counterparts in another region. Whatever their shape or style, parties do have in common the fact that they perform a number of significant functions in the political system. It is important that some individual or organization inform the public, nominate candidates, publicize issues, organize the legislatures, facilitate communications among the branches of government, effect compromise, and put together the majorities needed to pass bills. For these reasons the political parties are vital components of the political system.

Political scientist John Bibby suggests that modern-day political parties may be "likened to public utilities in the sense that they perform essential public functions."[1] They nominate and run candidates for office and do much of the work to organize U.S. governments. And they perform these public functions within the confines of state law.

POLITICAL PARTY ORGANIZATION

There are laws in every state that control various aspects of political parties and elections. In all except a few states, the statutes speak to the structure and organization of the parties. They control party finances. State laws specify the means by which parties can place candidates for office on the ballot, and they do so in ways that make it easy for the two major parties to run candidates, but difficult for third parties to enter the game (the two major parties control the legislatures that pass these laws, so they have no desire to facilitate the emergence of a third party). In some instances the states establish in law the dates for such party functions as precinct caucuses. To varying degrees, then, the political parties operate within parameters established by state law.

Three Levels of Party Organization

There are basically three levels of party organization in most states —the *precinct*, the *county*, and the *state*—though the law in many states also provides for organization along such lines as congressional districts.

The **precinct** is the basic unit of party organization. There are hundreds of precincts in every state, and a total of over 100,000 in the entire country. A precinct typically takes in an area covering several blocks and contains hundreds of individuals. In competitive two-party areas, each party may have viable precinct organizations. Periodically—once a year in some cases—a meeting called a **caucus** is held in the precinct and is open to anyone who lives within that precinct and who wishes to affiliate with the party. Officers called precinct captains are chosen. In areas where one party is dominant, the weaker party may find it difficult to maintain an effective organization in many precincts; even in competitive states, one party may dominate an area with the result that the other party has no effective organization in that area. In addition, the activity of many precinct organizations tends to surge around election time and grow dormant between elections. The precinct level is where much of the hard and unrewarding work is done, but it is also the level at which elections often are won or lost. Precinct workers typically do much of the legwork in getting people registered, peddling campaign materials, and hustling the voters to the polls on election day.

The next unit of party organization is the county. The typical county has a Democratic party organization and a Republican party organization. Each party periodically holds a county convention, sometimes once a year or perhaps just in election years. Representatives to the county convention usually are selected by the precincts. The convention elects a set of permanent officers, including a county central committee, a county chair, a county vice-chair, and a secretary-treasurer. In some years the convention also nominates candidates for such offices as county board of supervisors and sheriff, as well as delegates to the state convention, if there is one that year. In some states there is a party organization in each congressional district, and the county conventions may elect delegates to that unit as well. Party organization at the county level tends to sustain more continuity and vigor than it does at the precinct level. This is true in large part because the county is larger, containing dozens or hundreds of precincts.

The third and top level of party organization in the states is the state party itself. Just as the parties hold countywide conventions, so they also periodically hold statewide conventions, at which they may nominate or endorse candidates for statewide office and select officers for the state central committee. In most states candidates for statewide office are selected in direct statewide primaries, but in others the convention can endorse a candidate or give him or her top-line designation on the ballot, thus providing the candidate with an advantage in the primary.

In addition to the party organizations at the precinct, county, and state levels, other organizations may exist to serve the purposes of individual candidates. Senators and members of Congress, for example, typically maintain some sort of home organization of their own.

One-Party States

In one-party states or regions, there may be organizations linked not to a particular office but to a particular agenda. There is a county in south Texas, for example, that has never elected a Republican to a district or countywide office. The county is a key player in statewide politics because of its monolithic Democratic vote. There are two longstanding organizations that operate within the county as **vote brokers**. During the Democratic primaries, those seeking statewide nomination attempt to lock in the endorsement of these two organizations as a key to success in the primary. If one organization endorses one candidate, the other supports an alternative candidate. Whichever candidate wins the primary is expected to reward the appropriate organization with patronage.

Variety among States

There are tremendous variations within and among the states as to the shape and operating procedures of the parties. Some states have many more precincts and counties than others, and thus their party organizations are more expansive. Some states, and even regions within them, are two-party competitive, with the result that there is vigorous organization and competition within most of the precincts and counties. In one-party dominant areas, however, the party that chronically loses may be unable to sustain any organization at all in some precincts and counties.

The procedures for selecting delegates to national presidential nominating conventions and the ways in which members of county and state executive committees are selected also vary among the states. But again, in most states the parties are organized at three levels (see Table 7.1).

TABLE 7.1   Political Party Organization

Nation	States	Counties	Precincts and Wards
National chairperson	State chairperson	County chairperson	Precinct and ward chairs
National committee	Other officers	Other officers	Precinct committee members
	State central committee	County central committee	

An Untidy Structure

One major characteristic, and perhaps the defining characteristic, of American political parties is that they are structurally untidy, from the precinct to the national level. This is a gentle way of saying that each level of party organization enjoys considerable autonomy. Charles O. Jones, commenting on the degree of cohesion and unity characteristic of American parties, aptly refers to them as "non-things."[2] Unlike the political parties in certain Western European nations, those in the United States are relatively undisciplined, for it is rare that one level of organization is able to control the activities of those below it. Precincts are free to operate independently of the county; county officials, when they do accede to the wishes of state or national party officials, do so because they want to, not because they have to; and state officials are similarly independent of the national party. Neither U.S. presidents nor state governors can instruct county organizations on how to conduct their campaign activities or how to spend their money. American parties tend to be loosely knit confederations of largely independent fiefdoms, especially at the state and national levels.

The loosely organized nature of American political parties can be explained in part by the structure of the U.S. government. Here, again, the federal principle is at work. The government structure disperses decision-making authority. Federalism permits the existence of one national and fifty state governments. The separation of powers and bicameralism further divide authority within these and other local units. In most states there exist hundreds of local government units. Because many of the officials of these governments are elected on partisan ballots, political parties compete for the offices. The structure of the parties, thus, follows the structure of the government. The government is decentralized and so are the parties.

The decentralization of government is also reflected in the great diversity of the American polity. The Republican party in Alabama, for example, is very different from the Republican party in Oregon. A Democratic governor in Texas is likely to pursue quite different policy goals from his or her counterpart in Massachusetts.

In addition, the loose and rather unstructured nature of American political parties is a product of reforms adopted during the twentieth century. Until the early twentieth century, the parties, at the local level especially, were tightly organized and exerted significant control over nominations, elections, and the behavior of elected officials. Nominations for political office were made in caucuses of the party "big cheeses." Government jobs were passed out by the winners to the party faithful. As a result, there were powerful incentives for people to associate with one of the two major parties and to work to keep their party in power.

This was an era of great **political machines**, which were highly disciplined, hierarchical organizations controlling precinct, ward, city and sometimes county politics with an iron hand. They were headed by such well-known individuals as Boss Crump in Tennessee, Tom Pendergast in Kansas City, and the late Richard Daley in Chicago, perhaps the last of the classic machine bosses. Tammany Hall in New York City controlled patronage with an iron hand, and the *patrons* in South Texas likewise dictated electoral outcomes through their grip on the local vote. Political organizations still exist, of course, but the reduction in immigration combined with the impact of World War II and various reform movements have made the old-style political machines a relic of the past. Immigration restrictions reduced the steady flow of people on whom the machines depended for votes and day-to-day political work in exchange for patronage appointments. Similarly, the end of World War II brought with it the G.I. Bill, which provided a college education to thousands of individuals who otherwise might have remained dependent on the machines for their livelihoods.

Weakened Political Parties

Civil Service   Most state government employees today are part of a civil service system wherein employment is based in large measure on training and merit, rather than on patronage. It is one's education, training, and skills, not one's contributions to a political party, that lead to a job. There are some exceptions to this rule, most notably in policy-level positions, wherein devotion to a victorious governor's or mayor's policies is required, and in many county and municipal governments, where longstanding traditions of patronage have won out over reformist sentiment. Even here, personnel turnover often is a function of personalized, nonpartisan political organizations that are not identified with either of the two major political parties.

Therefore, control over most public employment is no longer in the hands of the political parties. As a result, the parties are weakened by their inability to distribute rewards to the party faithful.

Direct Primaries   Similarly, the introduction of the **direct primary** in the early twentieth century deprived the parties of control over a major set of political prizes. The direct primary allowed voters the opportunity to choose a party's candidate for the general election. Before the 1920s, long-term service to one of the two major parties was the necessary route for anyone seeking a place on the ballot. In contrast, the direct primary now allows politically ambitious persons to launch a drive for a party's nomination by appealing directly to the voters. The laws governing primaries and nominations vary somewhat among the states, but the direct primary has universally loosened party control over nominations.

Candidate-Centered Campaigning   Another development that has weakened the American political parties is the candidate-centered campaign.

Prior to the 1960s, the parties were the major source of the money and staffing that candidates needed to run their campaigns. Today, however, without the patronage, jobs, and control over nominations needed to entice large numbers of people to stay involved and loyal, the modern parties can seldom provide such support. Rather, political action committees (PACs) now provide much of the money needed to fuel campaigns, and political consultants increasingly run sophisticated campaigns featuring computer-supported polling and targeted mailing as well as fund-raising.

The candidate is at the center of the campaign and is supported by money and skills obtained outside of the political party. The party role has thus become one of assisting, not directing, political campaigns. Furthermore, at the municipal level, the trend toward nonpartisan elections has rendered the parties irrelevant to most local governments.

A RESURGENCE IN PARTY VITALITY?

The various reforms—civil service, direct primaries, and candidate-centered campaigning—coupled with such sociological factors as immigration patterns, have steadily reduced the influence of political parties over the course of the twentieth century. However, there are recent signs of renewed vitality, primarily as a result of changes in the financial relations between the national parties and the state parties.[3] In particular, the Republican and Democratic National Committees are increasingly resourceful in raising money, and both are pumping some of the funds into state party organizations and state-level elections.

At the state and local levels, the parties are using the additional resources to add more permanent staff. Previously, many state and local political units would fold up their tents between elections or maintain a minimal presence, perhaps only in the town or the home of the party chair. Today, more money is coming to mean more organizational permanency. In addition, increased resources allow the parties to be more vigorous and regular in their polling, in their get-out-the-vote efforts, and in developing mailing lists for fund-raising and targeted campaign mailings. The infusion of national money into state parties and to state candidates is drawing the different levels of party organization closer. It is also putting the national committees in a position to exert previously nonexistent leverage on the state parties.

PARTY COMPETITION

Before the 1970s, political scientists often addressed such issues as voters' tendency to inherit their parents' political leanings, the tendency of Americans to identify with one of the two parties, and the frequency of voting straight party-line ballots. They also wrote about the "solid South," where after the Civil War the southern and border states were solidly in the Democratic party camp.

Contemporary political scientists focus on an array of very different issues because so much has changed. A growing number of voters are **ticket-splitting** — that is, not voting a straight party ticket, but rather choosing one party's candidates for some offices and the other party's candidates for other offices — as the bonds that once held them tightly to one of the two major parties continue to dissolve. The extensive use of television in statewide contests — for governor, for example — fueled with enormous sums of money gives today's candidates the opportunity to promote an attractive personality instead of party loyalty. The South is no longer solidly Democratic, and such traditional Republican strongholds as Vermont, Arizona, and Idaho are showing some Democratic successes.

Divided Government

Table 7.2 demonstrates the extent to which solid party control of regions has dissolved throughout much of the nation. In 1992, for example, three states in the formerly solid Democratic South had Republican governors — Alabama, Mississippi, and South Carolina. The Republican-leaning states of Colorado, Idaho, Kansas, and Wyoming all elected Democratic governors in 1992. Indeed, in only 20 of the 50 states did voters that year elect a fully united government with both legislative chambers and the governorship in the hands of the same party. Conversely, 60 percent of the states were operating with divided government.

Furthermore, at various points during the 1980s, eleven southern or border states chose Republican governors. These included Alabama, Arkansas, Florida, Louisiana, Missouri, North Carolina, Oklahoma, South Carolina, Tennessee, Texas, and Virginia. The South, then, is no longer solidly Democratic.

It is interesting to observe the actual divisions of state governments in 1992 (see Table 7.2). While control in 30 states was split in some fashion, 34 states had both houses of the legislature under one party's control; of these legislatures, 25 were Democratic and 9 Republican. Much of the divided control came in the form of united legislatures with governors from the opposite party (14 states were split in this way).

Divided party control has deep roots in American history. The results of the Civil War affected American elections for a hundred years after the conflict ended. In reaction to the activities of the postwar Republican president and Congress, the southern and border states embraced the Democratic party. Indeed, they did so with such tenacity that the Republican party was all but nonexistent in those states and all meaningful political competition took place within the Democratic party. Virtually all local and state officeholders were Democrats, the Democratic primaries constituted the only meaningful elections, and Democratic presidential candidates could count on the support of the solid South. The economic disaster of the 1930s, the Great Depression, began during

TABLE 7.2
Divided Party Control: State Legislatures and Governors in 1992

FULLY UNITED (20 states)		
Democratic Legislature and Governor (16)		**Republican Legislature and Governor (4)**
Arkansas	North Carolina	Arizona
Georgia	Oklahoma	Michigan
Hawaii	Rhode Island	New Hampshire
Kentucky	Tennessee	Utah
Louisiana	Texas	
Maryland	Virginia	
Missouri	Washington	
New Mexico	West Virginia	

SPLIT CONTROL (30 states)		
Democratic Legislature/Republican Governor (9)		**Republican Legislature/ Democratic Governor (5)**
Alabama	Minnesota	Colorado
California	Mississippi	Idaho
Illinois	South Carolina	Kansas
Maine	Wisconsin	New Jersey
Massachusetts		Wyoming

Split Legislature (13 states)	
Democratic Governor (8)	**Republican Governor (5)**
Delaware	Iowa
Florida	Montana
Indiana	North Dakota
Nevada	Ohio
New York	South Dakota
Oregon	
Pennsylvania	
Vermont	

Other (3 states)
Alaska — split legislature; independent governor
Connecticut — Democratic legislature; independent governor
Nebraska — independent legislature; Democratic governor

the tenure of another Republican, Herbert Hoover, and thereby served to reinforce the Democratic solidarity.

Beginning in about the 1960s, however, the situation gradually changed. The civil rights movement of the 1960s and 1970s, which was pushed by Democratic presidents and Congress but opposed by many political leaders in the South, weakened the loyalty of many white southern voters to Democratic presidential candidates. Indeed, from 1968 to 1988 Republican candidates (Richard Nixon, Ronald Reagan, and George Bush) enjoyed widespread southern support. At the same time, the considerable southward migration of many easterners and midwesterners with Republican party affiliation or leanings also helped to expand the Republican electoral base in the South.

In 1992, however, the Democrats broke through the Republican southern stronghold at the presidential level with the election of Bill Clinton. This was aided in part by the presence of two southerners on the Democratic ticket.

The style of campaigning, especially in statewide contests, also has changed in recent decades. As noted earlier in the chapter, elections are increasingly expensive candidate-centered media events, and money, television, and personality have diminished the importance of political party affiliation as a factor in voters' choices.

Electoral success and organizational strength go hand in hand. When one party dominates elections for a long period of time, it is difficult for the minority party to remain active. People simply are not motivated to contribute their time, money, and energy to losing causes. But a few victories can change that situation. Thus, when Republican presidential and gubernatorial candidates enjoyed some success in the solid South, new life was given to the Republican party organization. Democrats continue to win most local and state contests, but both parties are active, functioning organizations.

Local One-Party Control

One-party dominance, and thus the absence of competition, is the norm in local contests and state legislative district politics. Similarly, the level of competition within many legislative districts is weak. In the 1988 state legislative elections in Colorado, for example, the outcomes in just 11 of the 65 house seats and 3 of the 19 senate seats up for reelection were closer than 45 to 55 percent (see Table 7.3).[4]

In the American states, then, there is two-party competition but one-party dominance. Voters in most states provide some support for both major parties. Hence, divided government is common. At the same time, many state legislatures remain under extensive control of one party, most often the Democratic party. In addition, within the states many local offices and state legislative seats belong to the same party after repeated elections.

TABLE 7.3
The Competitive Status of Colorado House and Senate Seats, 1988

Status	House	Senate
Seats up	65	19
Only one candidate	18	6
Outcome closer than 45–55%	11	3
Not that close	36	10

Source: John A. Straayer, *The Colorado General Assembly* (Niwot, Colo.: University Press of Colorado, 1990), p. 30.

Perspectives on Political Competition   In addressing the issue of whether competitive politics or one-party dominance is best, political scientists generally advocate two-party competition. It is argued that in states with one-party control, there is a tendency for factions to form within the dominant party. This was particularly true in the South when the Democrats long controlled elections.

In an extensive study of politics in the South conducted in 1949, V. O. Key suggested that some characteristics of factional politics may be unhealthy for a democracy.[5] In representative democracies, the political parties provide the link between the mass of voters and the seats of power. They nominate candidates, publish policy platforms, organize and run the government, and, in periodic elections, take the credit or blame for what has gone on. In addition, organized political parties are like most other organizations in that they provide assistance to their members, command a degree of loyalty in return, and operate according to sets of rules and norms that help to control and direct the behavior of their members.

The Downside of Factional Politics   When political struggles among factions replace interparty competition, problems result. For example, without the parties there is no highly organized and visible "in-group" or "out-group" for voters to hold responsible for successes and failures. Voters cannot easily or accurately decide whether the party in power has done a bad job and on that basis proceed to vote for the other party; in fact, there may be no "other" party, and the voter may be unaware of the other faction. In addition, parties operate according to sets of rules and norms that factions do not employ. Without the parties it is possible for candidates and politically active types to behave in an irresponsible, freewheeling, and self-serving fashion. Furthermore, without viable political parties candidates are much more "on their own" in their search for campaign funds and other forms of political support. As a result, they may be more susceptible to the influence of special interest groups. There are other problems as well. Without party support and the need to conform to party norms, candidates may be tempted to resort to demagogic tactics, focusing their attention on such factors as personalities or race.

Therefore, when political parties are weak, or when legislative competition revolves around a series of factions within a single dominant party so that policy leadership is not provided by the parties, influence will flow elsewhere. It will flow to dominant personalities, to committees and their chairpersons, and to the lobbies.

The Advantages of Competition   Political parties, of course, are not perfectly representative of the American public or even of the American voting public. The highly educated, financially well-off, occupationally prestigious, and politically involved "elite" tends to dominate the voting, candidate, and decision-maker ranks. Nevertheless, political parties are more reflective of popular preferences than the alternatives—single dominant individuals, small legislative committees, and narrowly focused lobbies. In its search for some person or institution to represent its values and views, the American public is better off casting its lot with the party than with any of the available alternatives. But the option of the party is available only so long as the political environment remains competitive.

In short, vigorous interparty competition is healthy in a representative democracy. The parties broaden the base of support for candidates, freeing them from the possible control of special interests. The out-party criticizes the in-party, thus helping to keep the public informed. The out-party also provides a ready, visible alternative for a dissatisfied public. Where effective two-party competition exists, party organization in the legislature tends to be more cohesive, with the healthy result that public policy is more heavily influenced by the parties than by strong committee chairs or special interest groups. With competition, the quality of candidates offered by the parties is higher, whereas the absence of competition allows the dominant party to nominate anyone it wishes. (This absence of competition in the South led to the term **yellow-dog Democrat**, which was used to identify voters who would vote the Democratic ticket even if the candidates were yellow dogs.) The parties articulate and press for the interests of large numbers of people. Factions, in contrast, are not nearly as effective or responsible as links between the people and their government. Without healthy two-party competition, the preferences of the unorganized and the inarticulate often are ignored in public policy.

Competing Views A number of studies question Key's suggestion that the level of party competition has an effect on the public policies of a state. Studies conducted by Dawson and Robinson,[6] Hofferbert,[7] and Dye[8] conclude that differences in the taxing and spending patterns of the states are affected more by social and economic variations than by differences in political factors (such as party competition, apportionment, and government structure). Yet studies conducted by Cnudde and McCrone[9] and Sharkansky and Hofferbert[10] modify this suggestion that political variables and policy outcomes may be causally unrelated. They point out that political factors may have a greater effect on policy outcomes in some policy areas than in others. For instance, Cnudde and McCrone suggest that in the policy areas of greatest concern to society's less well-off, such as aid to dependent children and unemployment compensation, increased party competition works to their benefit, whereas in policy areas of less concern to this group, the level of party competition has little or no impact. One explanation for this tendency is that the less well-off often lack access to the decision makers, money, positions, and status needed for placing their concerns on the public agenda. Thus, in areas of concern to them, they take advantage of the potential of the political party to champion their needs.

Similarly, Sharkansky and Hofferbert contend that political factors such as party competition and governmental structure affect policy in the states but to varying degrees according to the particular policy:

Welfare-education policies relate most closely with the competition-turnout dimension of state politics and with the affluence dimension of the economy. Highway–natural resources policies show their closest (inverse) relationships with the industrialization dimension of the state economy.[11]

It might also be argued that two-party competition, insofar as it leads to divided government, makes it difficult to assign responsibility for government actions. When a legislature is divided, or when a governor is from one party and the legislature is controlled by the other, each party tends to blame the other for problems (a pattern not uncommon at the national level as well) and both parties seek to take credit for accomplishments. Governors may argue that their state's legislature ignored their priorities or failed to fund their programs adequately. The legislature, in turn, may blame the governor for budget shortfalls or scandals in state agencies.

Third Parties   The preceding discussion of political parties has referred only to the Republicans and Democrats, for the American party system is typically described as a **two-party system**. However, there have been many more parties in the history of American politics, and even today there are several so-called **third parties** offering choices to voters (see Focus 7.1). Still, only two parties—Democrats and Republicans—have a realistic chance of winning the vast majority of elections in the U.S. political system. Therefore, competition is defined in terms of the two-party system.

FOCUS

7.1 SELECTED THIRD PARTIES IN THE UNITED STATES

Farmer-Labor Party
  (Minnesota)
La Raza Unida Party (Texas)
Conservative Party of
  New York State
Libertarian Party
Socialist Labor Party
Socialist Workers Party

Theocratic Party
New Alliance Party
Consumer Party
Right-to-Life Party
Peace and Freedom Party
Populist Party
American Independent Party
Worker's League Party

CRITICISMS OF THE POLITICAL PARTIES

Political parties have long been the topic of heated discussion regarding both their performance as conduits of public preferences and their proper role in the political system. The first question is an empirical one, for it simply asks whether political parties are effective links between the people and their government. The second question is normative, addressing the question of what parties should try to do.

Through the years American political parties have been criticized for being insensitive to the desires of the masses and insufficiently cohesive to allow the voters to make meaningful choices. These twin critiques may appear contradictory, and to some extent they are.

Do Elites Control the Parties?

It has been argued that the parties—from county organizations to presidential nominating conventions—are controlled by a few party leaders. Scholar Robert Michels[12] suggests that there is an "iron law of oligarchy" operative in parties, a sentiment echoed by Phyllis Schlafly,[13] who asserts that both major American parties are controlled by a big-money eastern establishment.

Are the Parties Directionless?

The parties are also criticized for being so incohesive that the public is not given a clear-cut choice at the polls. From the county to the national level, it is argued, the parties lack tight organization. As a result, they cannot effectively articulate and institute a "party line" and the voters cannot effectively hold any party fully responsible for the public decisions that are made.

This criticism has some merit, for the fragmented nature of the political system works against party cohesion. Governors, state representatives, others elected to the executive branch, and the various boards and commissions all respond to slightly different constituencies. Thus, the parties are both controlled by an elite group and, at the same time, insufficiently cohesive to present the voters with as meaningful a set of choices as some would like. As Samuel Eldersveld suggests, the parties constitute a multiplicity of oligarchies.[14] On both counts, then, it is argued that the preferences of the masses are slightly obscured.

Are the Parties Too Much Alike?

In addition, the two major parties are criticized for being too much alike in that they both seek middle-of-the-road candidates and platform stands designed to alienate as few voters as possible. As a result, the voter ends up with a choice between Tweedledum and Tweedledee—a rather meaningless differentiation at best. In common terms, as many observe, "there's not a dime's worth of difference between the two major parties."

Although there is some merit in this observation, it should not be carried too far. It is true that the two major American parties lean toward the middle of the road on issues, but they must do so if they hope to win votes and elections. A radical stance, whether to the far left or far right of the political spectrum, would prove suicidal for the parties. Moreover, the parties are not exactly alike, and one study even suggests that they offer more choices than voters want. In a study of political leaders and followers conducted by Herbert McCloskey in 1960, it was found that, on most policy issues (for example, education, economics, and natural resources), Democratic party leaders were more liberal and Republican leaders were more conservative than the followers of either party. The study did not find a large number of voters far to the left or the right of the existing party leadership in search of a more meaningful alternative.[15]

McCloskey's findings lend some support to what several other political observers argue—that the parties reflect, rather than create, the political leanings of the American people. Thus, both major parties are in the middle of the political spectrum because that is where most of the people are.

American society is, in a sense, consensual; people tend not to want or need more extreme choices at the polls. While there is division on specifics, there is consensus on basics. Indeed, if Americans were presented with more radical choices, a host of changes could lead to the development of a potentially dangerous situation. For example, great ideological divisions would exist within society, which radical parties would exploit in search of votes. The lack of consensus would, in turn, create widespread disagreement on fundamental questions and make it difficult to arrive at compromise decisions. Decision making would likely be characterized by rigid factional adherence to ideological and policy positions, and thus by immobility. As a result, it would be relatively easy to form a majority to stop something from happening but impossible to generate majority support to get anything done. In other words, our political parties serve the central functions of creating consensus in our system, balancing the system between the extremes, and helping us, as a people, to "agree to disagree."

SUMMARY

Political parties perform many important functions in the political system. These include nominating candidates for office, contributing to the political education of the public, maintaining a check on those in office, drawing people into political activities, organizing the government, and bridging some of the gaps created by federalism and the separation of powers.

The United States is characterized as having a two-party system, but there are great variations among the states, some of which are dominated by one party. In addition, some are predominantly Democratic, whereas others lean toward the Republican side. The parties vary in terms of their organization as well. Although they are governed by law in nearly all states, the exact pattern of party organization varies. So do the number of elective offices, the frequency of elections, and the time of year at which elections are held.

Finally, the two major parties have been the subject of much criticism. While some of the criticisms have a degree of merit, effective counterarguments can be made. Although both parties tend toward the middle of the political spectrum and to avoid radical positions on issues, it can be argued that this is a reflection of the political leanings of the American people. Therefore, parties do not create political beliefs but mirror those of the masses.

KEY TERMS

latent functions
spin doctor
precinct
caucus
vote broker
political machine

direct primary
ticket-splitting
yellow-dog Democrat
two-party system
third party

ADDITIONAL READINGS

Frendreis, John P., James L. Gibson, and Laura L. Vertz. "The Electoral Relevance of Local Party Organizations." *American Political Science Review* (March 1990): 225–35.

Hawley, Willis D. *Non-Partisan Elections and the Case for Party Politics.* New York: Wiley, 1973.

Jewell, Malcolm E., and David M. Olson. *Political Parties and Elections in American States.* Chicago: Dorsey, 1988.

Keefe, William. *Parties, Politics and Public Policy in America.* Washington, D.C.: Congressional Quarterly Press, 1987.

NOTES

1. John F. Bibby, "Party Organization at the State Level," in *The Parties Respond*, ed. L. Sandy Maisel (Boulder, Colo.: Westview Press, 1990), p. 22.

2. Classroom comment by Charles O. Jones, professor of political science.

3. See Bibby, "Party Organization," p. 22. See also Samuel C. Patterson, "The Persistence of State Parties," in *The State of the Party*, ed. Carl E. Van Horn (Washington, D.C.: Congressional Quarterly Press, 1989), pp. 153–74; and John F. Bibby, Cornelius P. Cather, James L. Gibson, and Robert J. Huckshorn, "Parties in State Politics," in *Politics in the American States*, 5th ed., ed. Virginia Gray, Herbert Jacob, and Robert B. Albritton (Glenview, Ill.: Scott, Foresman/Little, Brown Higher Education, 1990), pp. 85–122.

4. John A. Straayer, *The Colorado General Assembly* (Niwot, Colo.: University Press of Colorado, 1990).

5. V. O. Key, Jr., *Southern Politics* (New York: Knopf, 1949).

6. Richard E. Dawson and James A. Robinson, "Interparty Competition, Economic Variables and Welfare Politics in American States," *Journal of Politics* (May 1963): 265–98.

7. Richard I. Hofferbert, "The Relation between Public Policy and Some Structural and Environmental Variables in the American States," *American Political Science Review* (March 1966): 73–82.

8. Thomas R. Dye, *Politics, Economics and the Public: Policy Outcomes in the American States* (Chicago: Rand McNally, 1966).

9. Charles F. Cnudde and Donald J. McCrone, "Party Competition and Welfare Policies in the American States," *American Political Science Review* (Sept. 1969): 858–66.

10. Ira Sharkansky and Richard I. Hofferbert, "Dimensions of State Politics, Economics, and Public Policy," *American Political Science Review* (Sept. 1969): 867–79.

11. Ibid.: 878.

12. Robert Michels, *Political Parties* (1915; reprint New York: Collier Books, 1962).

13. Phyllis Schlafly, public comment made during the 1964 election.

14. Samuel J. Eldersveld, *Political Parties* (Chicago: Rand McNally, 1964), esp. ch. 6.

15. Herbert J. McCloskey, Paul J. Hoffman, and Rosemary O'Hara, "Issue Conflict and Consensus among Leaders and Followers," *American Political Science Review* (June 1960): 406–29.

8
Special Interest Groups

Interest groups use various means to influence political outcomes. Here, labor rallies outside the Minnesota state capitol (1989) against Boise Cascade for using nonunion help to build its new plant in International Falls. One of the signs reads "Union People Vote." St. Paul, Minnesota. *(Michael Siluk/The Image Works)*

On any day in any state during any legislative session one can find the capitol crowded with **lobbyists** — the hired guns of powerful interests, some would say. The hallways, or lobbies, just outside a state's house and senate chambers and near the committee rooms buzz with the talk of lobbyists and lawmakers. Testimony on critical bills is given by lobbyists or by persons they have brought in. Lobbyists trek in and out of legislators' offices all day long. Lawmakers can, if they wish, enjoy meals at the expense of the interest groups that hire the lobbyists. Legislators summon lobbyists routinely to ask for data, or to ask how their group feels about a proposed bill, or even to ask the lobbyist if an amendment to a bill is acceptable to the interest group. Many bills are written by lobbyists or their lawyers.

A large and growing proportion of the money that fuels electoral campaigns comes from **interest groups** — corporations, professional associations, labor unions, educators' organizations, local governments, and other groups that spend some of their time and money trying to influence government. Legislators and legislative leaders solicit money from interest groups directly. Sometimes large checks arrive by mail, unsolicited. Even incumbents with no electoral opposition receive interest group money. Lobbyists maintain ongoing communication with legislators, agency personnel, and members of governors' staffs about their groups' policy preferences. Sometimes lobbyists initiate court action to support their position (as in seeking an order to void a statute or agency rule that they oppose). Often they run radio, television, newspaper, magazine, and billboard advertisements portraying themselves as good citizens whose desires reflect the public good.

What are the effects of interest groups and lobbyists? Bill Schluter, a Republican member of the New Jersey house, cites the candid comments of the director of public relations for that state's Chamber of Commerce: "I have not seen legislators who could be bought, but I met a lot who could be rented, who can be influenced by the need to finance their campaigns."[1] The efforts of interest groups and lobbyists, and their money, have a tremendous impact on government activities. Legislators, governors, and other elected state and local officials obtain their positions by appealing successfully for public support. To continue in public life, they must continue to satisfy enough people to secure reelection. Thus, when a lobbyist who represents a slice of the electorate tells a politician how the people stand on some matter, the lobbyist's comments are influential. In addition, elections cost money, and lawmakers know that interest groups support candidates who support them.

While political self-interest is a powerful motivation to listen to interest groups and their lobbyists, it is not the only one. Lawmakers must make hundreds, even thousands, of choices every year. For legislators, votes must be cast both on the floor and in committee. Governors and other state executives must similarly make decisions constantly. Where can they obtain the information needed to guide their choices? Decision makers come to their jobs with a set of values and at least some information, but none can be fully informed on all matters. Legislative and executive staff personnel provide information to varying degrees, depending on the state or local government involved, but in no cases can staff members provide everything. Lobbyists, then, are an important source of information and voting cues.

In an ideal world of perfect democracy, everyone would be politically equal, for political equality is an important value in democratic theory. In the real world, however, people are not equal politically. In general, though, political inequality is not the result of forceful denial of access to the political process; rather, it is largely due to the fact that some people are active in politics and others are not. Many well-educated and well-to-do business and professional people understand how the political system works and how to exert influence. They organize and spend time and money to advance their own interests. Sometimes political organization and action is triggered by the actions of other groups. But many Americans do not get involved, whether due to a lack of interest or a shortage of time. As a result, they are largely irrelevant to the political process. Yet politicians listen to those who speak out, especially when the comments may be instrumental to their political fortunes. They do not listen to those who fail to speak out. E. E. Schattschneider once remarked that democracy's choir sings with an upper-class accent.[2] Interest groups are in that choir, for the songs they sing speak largely of their own interests.

PARTICIPANTS IN INTEREST GROUPS

W̄ho are the groups in the state political systems and what do they seek to accomplish?[3] To gain a sense of the types of interest groups that operate within any particular state, one needs first to consider what it is that the state does and then to look at the state's economic foundation. What do states do? They establish and fund educational institutions at all levels, from kindergartens to graduate, medical, and law schools. Indeed, education consumes more than one-half, and often two-thirds, of annual state budgets. States also establish local governments — counties, cities, special districts — and control their structures, authority, and limitations. States license professions and businesses, ranging from hairdressers and morticians to taxi companies and boxers. Much of our tort law now exists in state statutes. So do provisions controlling the use of water, timber, and minerals. States tax both businesses and individuals. They promote economic development but discourage and penalize drug use, rape, and murder.

So who are the people who try to influence policy outcomes by lobbying lawmakers, executive branch officials, and even the courts? They are individuals and groups that have stakes in the laws and the budgets that legislatures adopt.

Educators In every state, teachers' organizations are an important and usually effective lobby. The state controls teacher credentials, teacher tenure, and much school funding, so it is to be expected that educators would lobby. Associations of school districts, school board members, and school administrators also lobby the state, often joining forces with the teachers but sometimes opposing them.

Local Governments and Professionals Associations of cities, counties, and special districts are highly visible and effective interest groups and lobbying forces in the states as well. The structures, duties, and resources of local governments are state controlled, so the fact that they form a lobby is not surprising.

Similarly, physicians, lawyers, planners, psychiatrists, social workers, and most other professionals lobby. They donate to campaigns, spend to gloss up their public images, and send lobbyists to the legislature and other decision points in state government. These professions are state-regulated. Why? Because, while regulation may well advance public health and safety, it also helps to limit access into the professions. These lobbyists thus have a stake in convincing lawmakers to maintain regulatory laws.

Business Interests and Volunteer Groups Business interests are important and powerful lobbying groups in the states. Businesspeople often oppose taxes and regulation but favor receipt of government contracts, government spending, and tax breaks. Public officials worry constantly about the economic health of the state, so they are usually receptive to the arguments of businesses. Farmers often lobby, successfully, for tax breaks on farm machinery. Mining operations receive depletion allowances. In recent years businesses have pressed for reductions in the cost of worker compensation taxes and for some freedom from labor unions.

Similarly, realtors lobby to stay free of state regulations establishing health and safety standards for rental properties. Doctors lobby for statutory caps on malpractice damage awards. Trial lawyers oppose damage caps; they make their living in the courts, often through shares of damage awards. And so it goes. Group after group works the political system in search of laws and appropriations that give it an edge, or money, or both.

Professional interest groups are often joined by volunteer groups seeking public policy that advances their ideological positions. The prolife movement wants bans on abortions. Parents seek tougher drunk-driving penalties. Some want certain chemicals outlawed. Still others are interested in reforming the political system.

Table 8.1 lists, in order of prevalence, the various types of interest groups that are active in California and Wyoming, the most and least populated states, respectively, in the nation. As you can see in the table, businesses, governments, and professions are predominant. The reasons are simple. States tax, enact worker compensation laws, and build much of the transportation and educational infrastructure with which businesses operate and on which they depend. Local governments are the legal children of the states, and much of the state political agenda impacts them. Thus, it is no surprise that they lobby their political parent. The states regulate the professions, usually at the request of the professionals themselves.

Similarities and Differences among the States

There are only minor differences between California and Wyoming, as Table 8.1 indicates. Wyoming has significant oil and mineral reserves, so the energy and mining interests are politically active. Agricultural lobbies appear to rank higher in California, which is understandable given the extensive irrigated and publicly subsidized farming in the southern region of that state and the vineyards in the northern region.

In a recent study of interest groups in the American states, Clive Thomas and Ronald Hrebenar identify the interest groups that are the most active and influential. Their findings place business, educators, professionals, financial institutions, local governments, and farm organizations near the top.[4]

However, many variations exist among states, among localities, and during different periods of time in the kinds of interest groups that engage actively in political lobbying. For example, the automobile industry is large and economically significant in Michigan; thus the major auto manufacturers and the auto

TABLE 8.1
Types of Interest Groups in Two States
(in order of prevalence)

California	Wyoming
Business	Business and industry
Miscellaneous/public interest	Energy and mining
Health	Local government
Local government	Medical, health, and social services
Education	Education
Insurance and finance	Political reform
Agriculture	Professionals
Labor	Police and firefighters
Legal	Seniors
Utilities	Banks and financial institutions
	Environment
	Agriculture

Sources: Adapted from Charles G. Bell and Charles M. Price, *California Government Today*, 3rd ed. (Belmont: Wadsworth, 1988), p. 129; and Tim R. Miller, *State Government: Politics in Wyoming*, 2nd ed. (Dubuque, Iowa: Kendall/Hunt, 1985), p. 62.

workers' unions are politically active in that state. In Arizona and Montana, mining is a major industry and is significant politically. The same is true of farm interests in the Midwest, of the tourist industry in such states as Florida and Arizona, and of oil interests in Oklahoma and Texas.

Single-Issue Noncompromisers

There has been an increase in recent years in the number of **single-issue interest groups** that champion some policy stance on a single issue. These groups are often ideological in nature and press moral rather than economic values, though this is not always the case. Prolife activists, parents against drunk driving, parents in favor of home schooling or school choice, and opponents of gun control are examples. The participants in recent tax-limitation campaigns include some who just don't want to pay taxes and others who are ideologically attracted to minimalist government.

Single-issue groups and their lobbyists are sometimes rigid and therefore difficult for lawmakers to deal with. In the long run this can work to the disadvantage of the groups. For example, those whose stance on abortion or pornography is deeply rooted in moral values often view compromise as an unacceptable breach of moral virtue. But collective choices in democracies are by their nature the product of compromise. It is one thing for an individual or group to live by a particular standard of behavior; it is quite another to insist that that standard be imposed in undiluted form on an entire society.

Public officials who, by definition, represent or work for entire polities thus find it hard to deal with single-issue noncompromisers. For example, legislators who refuse to embrace a group's rigid position risk losing the support of that group. But lawmakers who do support such a position must then forsake compromise with all the others. It is difficult for legislators to muster support for their own bills, and, indeed, even to stay in office, if they are unwilling to compromise with their colleagues. Linda Wagar cites the comment of an Alaska state senator: "Lawmakers who try to adjust their votes to the demands of every special interest group eventually lose the respect of their colleagues and constituency."[5]

Why Interest Groups Are Formed

One could easily gain the impression that politically active interest groups exist solely for the purpose of pressing their positions and preferences on the government. But more often than not, this is not the case. For most interest groups, political action represents just one of their many activities, and generally not even the primary one.

Professional associations of physicians, counselors, lawyers, and teachers, for instance, are formed to share professional information, keep members abreast of professional developments, advance job security, and generate collective insurance or recreational opportunities. These pursuits often lead the groups into the political arena, but political objectives per se do not explain the groups' existence.

THE LOBBYISTS

One need only wander through a state capitol when the legislature is in session to gain a sense of the role of interest groups in the political process. The lobbies just outside house and senate chambers are crowded with lobbyists milling around, often calling legislators off the floor and into the lobby for consultation as debate and voting proceed (hence the term *lobbyist*). The same activity can be seen in the hallways outside committee hearing rooms. Indeed, lobbyists often consult with legislators during hearings and are frequently called on to answer questions about bills that the sponsoring lawmakers themselves cannot answer.

The lobbying business is not easy. Lobbyists must hustle constantly, counting favorable and unfavorable votes by legislators both in committee decisions and on the floor. Sometimes they must combat the pressure from interest groups on the other side of the issue. Lawmakers often request information, and lobbyists must round it up. Increasingly, lobbyists are pressured for campaign donations, or they help in pressuring one lawmaker on behalf of another. But through all of this, it is clear that the door is open for interest groups and their lobbyists to be highly influential, particularly when they judiciously and skillfully use good information and campaign money.

Lobbying, like much of state government, is said to have become more professionalized in recent years. Governors are well educated and capable managers. State legislators enjoy improved staffing, office space, and pay. Similarly, the lobbying game has become less a matter of legislators and lobbyists deciding public policy in local watering holes. The mix of whiskey and political deals, it seems, has given way in some measure to information and larger campaign contributions. Back-room wheeling and dealing may be fading, but the same cannot be said for the impact of interest groups and their lobbyists on public policy.

Just as there are many different types of interest groups that seek to influence the course of public policy in the states, so too are there different types of lobbyists.

Some lobbyists are hired as employees of businesses or industries. Manufacturers, large retail outlets, utility companies, breweries, associations of local governments, and others often maintain their lobbying presence in the capitol through such **employee lobbyists**.

Employee and Contract Lobbyists

--- **FOCUS** ---

8.1   THE LOBBYING INDUSTRY

Some organizations and interest groups use their own employees to do their lobbying. These people are called employee lobbyists, public relations specialists, governmental relations specialists, or legislative liaisons. Other interest groups communicate to lawmakers through contract lobbyists—people who, like other professionals, charge a fee for their services. Some organizations use both their own employees and contract lobbyists, and some lobbyists serve in both capacities.

In Colorado, for example, U.S. West, a telecommunications company, has critical interests in such political issues as deregulation of telecommunications. It maintains a staff of employees who lobby the state legislature and employs the services of several prominent contract lobbyists, especially at critical times during legislative sessions. Danny Tomlinson, a one-time employee of U.S. West who lobbied the state legislature, is now a contract lobbyist who represents the interests of over a half-dozen organizations—from insurance companies and agricultural interests to a land title association and a major state university.

As this example indicates, there is no single pattern of interest group representation; rather, each group chooses one or more methods that it finds most effective. As a result, a veritable lobbying industry has emerged.

Other interests hire **contract lobbyists**, persons who, like attorneys and accountants, represent someone or some organization for a fee. Many contract lobbyists are former legislators who rely on their knowledge of the system as well as on the friendships and political networks they have developed over the years.

Contract lobbyists may represent anywhere from a few to two dozen or more clients. Their tasks are to watch carefully for bills that might affect their clients and to represent their clients' preferences to lawmakers. They do this through ongoing personal conversations, presentations of data, and the orchestration of expert or citizen testimony in committee hearings. Sometimes they testify themselves. They count votes constantly. Sometimes contract lobbyists attempt to secure the passage of legislation; at other times they seek to stop bills. The annual income of an effective contract lobbyist can run into hundreds of thousands of dollars.

Some interest groups' views are represented to lawmakers by way of **volunteer lobbyists**. Environmental, consumer, and good government groups, such as the Sierra Club, Common Cause, and the League of Women Voters, fit this category.

In addition, many lobbyists work for the government itself. One study estimates that from 25 percent to 50 percent of all lobbyists represent some government or government agency.[6] These people are often called **legislative liaisons** because they are state agency employees whose job it is to communicate for their agency with the legislature or another agency or government. They are, nonetheless, lobbyists, for they advocate particular policy positions and do so in statehouse "lobbies."

In recent years statehouse lobbyists or legislative liaisons have become more numerous. The devolution of many responsibilities to the state level has made state policy a high-stakes matter for many interest groups. In addition, with federal deregulation of a number of activities, the states have stepped in with their own regulations, and this has brought out many more lobbyists for professions and businesses (see Focus 8.1). The increased importance of state policy is illustrated by the emergence of Washington, D.C. – based firms whose business it is to maintain lists of recommended lobbyists by state for national organizations or groups seeking lobbying help in a particular state.[7] It should be noted, too, that a significant proportion of modern-day lobbyists are women, unlike the earlier male monopolization of such influence.[8]

TECHNIQUES OF INFLUENCE

Interest groups use a variety of **techniques of influence**.[9] Sometimes their activities involve direct contact with lawmakers; at other times they try to affect the administration of laws that have already passed; and at still other times they attempt to pressure decision makers indirectly through public opinion. Periodically, they may try to determine the outcome of an election or a court decision. Their tactics, in short, are many and varied. Direct communication, building a public image, establishing links, exchanging personnel, role reversals, and PAC money are among the most popular techniques.

A common interest group tactic involves direct communication with decision makers about the concerns of the group. Sometimes it is accomplished through testimony by an interest group spokesperson

at committee hearings, such as when a bill of interest to the group is under consideration. More often, however, it involves personal contact between the group's lobbyist and the lawmaker. As is the case at the national level, professional lobbyists are common in state legislative halls.

The task of the professional lobbyist is not very complicated. Basically it involves vigilance in monitoring the flow of legislation, in keeping track of upcoming administrative appointments, policies, and emerging court cases that affect the group, and making certain that the relevant decision makers are fully aware of the preferences of the group. Lobbying is an informal process that involves extensive direct communication and personal contact.

The successful lobbyist, for example, maintains a close watch on bills introduced into the legislature. When a bill of concern to the interest group is introduced, the lobbyist appraises it in terms of its potential impact on the group's interest. Next the lobbyist conveys the preferences of the group to the lawmakers, especially to those in strategic positions, such as the chairperson of the committee that will hear the bill and the leaders of the majority party. The lobbyist only rarely attempts to twist the arm of a legislator and almost never tries to "buy" a vote with money or gifts. The commodity that the lobbyist peddles is information, and his or her major sources of capital are friendship, trust, and access to decision makers.

Lobbying, then, is largely a matter of good public relations. Lobbyists want the decision makers to be aware of their groups' positions on the issues. They want access to the decision makers so that they can freely communicate with them. They also want to be thought well of so that their preferences and those of the groups they represent will be given serious consideration. Decision makers are more apt to give credence to a lobbyist who has a reputation for honesty, who provides consistently reliable information, and who represents reputable interests.

The success of lobbyists depends in part on the interests they represent and the backgrounds of the lawmakers with whom they deal. Lawmakers, like everyone else, are in part a product of their past, and so their values and preferences are conditioned by their experiences. Thus, a lobbyist representing agricultural interests may have a distinct advantage over his or her counterparts representing organized labor in dealings with lawmakers with a farm background. The spokesperson for labor may have a similar advantage in gaining access to a governor who once served as a union official.

Image Building

In addition to the common tactic of direct communication through paid lobbyists, organized interests often seek to influence the content of public opinion, and thereby exert indirect pressure on decision makers, by creating a positive public image. The behavior of both elected and appointed officials is conditioned by public opinion. Elected officials must concern themselves with public preferences, of course, since their political future is dependent on their ability to win votes. Appointed officials are less directly controlled by the voter, but they too must give some attention to public wants to avoid pressure for their removal. Thus, interest groups frequently devote some of their attention and resources to the creation of a favorable public image of themselves and voter sympathy for their goals.

Public utilities use the mass media to try to convince the public of their critical role in providing valuable public services. Farmers, cattle raisers, and mining companies spend sizable sums to point out how their industry provides jobs, pays taxes, and thereby makes the state a nicer place to live in. Insurance companies, chambers of commerce, teachers, truckers, and laborers do the same. Each group tries to gain favor with the public, hoping that lawmakers will be more receptive to the group's demands if they believe "the public" is on its side.

Interest groups occasionally employ test court cases in their efforts to influence public policy. When a newly passed bill is ambiguous, or when some of its provisions are of questionable constitutionality, a group may file suit to clarify the meaning of the bill or to test its constitutionality.

Common Interests

A common and quite effective interest group activity involves the formation and maintenance of linkages with the government agencies whose functions are of interest to the group. Wildlife enthusiasts, for example, commonly maintain close ties with state game, fish, and parks departments. Local governments maintain close contact with state departments of local government, and teachers' organizations and school districts tend to interact frequently with state departments of education.

Relationships of this sort are natural in some respects, since the interests and activities of the group and agency are similar. But there is mutual advantage in forging and cultivating them. The interest group benefits in that the agency may be charged with the administration of the policies and programs of most concern to the group. Thus, the group has an "inside track" in being able to communicate with the agency and to influence both agency personnel appointments and the vigor with which the policies and programs are implemented. The agency, in turn, benefits in that it can look to the interest group for support in the legislature and with the governor at times of budget review.

Personnel Exchanges

It is not uncommon for interest groups and public agencies to exchange personnel, or for a group to have, in effect, a veto over administrative appointments in the agency. No group has an official veto over administrative appointments, of course. But it is not uncommon for a governor or senate committee to solicit the opinion of the most interested groups informally before making or confirming an administrative appointment.

Only in the most unusual circumstances would someone vigorously opposed by the bar association be appointed and confirmed as a state judge or a person opposed by the wildlife interests be made head of state game, fish, and parks operations.

Much of what state governments do involves regulation. The states license or regulate the insurance industry, teachers, engineers, physicians, lawyers, realtors, and others. Thus, groups and their lobbyists often interact with executive branch officials as agencies develop rules and regulations, or in the instigation of proposals for new legislation. Agencies routinely circulate drafts of proposed rules and regulations to the affected groups. The representatives of these groups testify at hearings. In short, there is much routine interaction between the executive branch regulators and the regulated.

Role Reversals

There are what might be considered role reversals in state politics, particularly in the legislature. We generally think of lobbying as interest group communication and pressure brought to bear on lawmakers. But often it is the other way around. Increasingly, individual legislators, legislative leaders, and the legislative parties lean heavily on groups and their lobbyists for campaign funds. Lawmakers routinely tell lobbyists to sell expensive tickets to fund-raising events, or just straightforwardly demand contributions. Often, too, legislators seek the help of lobbyists in counting the votes of other lawmakers or in stirring up grass-roots support of or opposition to particular bills. The capitol environment is an enormous market in which all participants seek advantages through deals and bargains with each other.

PAC Money

Quite often, mutually supportive relationships develop between interest groups and legislators. Many groups, such as professional associations, unions, businesses, and others, form **political action committees (PACs)**—the political arms of these organizations. PACs pool funds from individual donors and disperse them in small, medium, or large sums to candidates. Gifts of $100 to $5,000 are not unusual. Most PAC campaign contributions go to incumbents, lawmakers chairing critical committees, and legislative leaders. Like seasoned gamblers, interest groups prefer to place their bets on winners.

REGULATION OF INTEREST GROUPS AND LOBBYISTS

Over the past two decades, the states have moved toward placing controls on interest group contributions to candidates for public office. Roughly 20 states now have some controls, though they vary considerably. The southern states, for example, are among the laxest in establishing and enforcing controls on interest groups and lobbying.[10] Some state controls place limits on the size of contributions that can be made, and a few limit the use of corporate funds to support political campaigns. Laws requiring some donors and recipient candidates to report their donations or collections are common.

All states have some form of lobbyist registration and reporting requirements, but they vary considerably. State laws also vary in their definition of a lobbyist. Some states recognize only paid lobbyists while others also include volunteer lobbyists. In addition, many states outlaw **contingency lobbying**, in which the lobbyist is paid by the client only when the lobbying effort is successful.

WHAT MAKES AN INTEREST GROUP EFFECTIVE

Some interest groups are more successful than others, and the success of any particular group can vary with time, place, and the issue at hand. That not all groups make out equally well in the distribution of benefits allocated through public policy is not just a product of accident or chance. To win in the political arena an interest group must do several things successfully. It must draw public attention and concern to what it perceives to be problems. It must be able to place the problem on the agenda of government. It must muster enough support among decision makers to ensure the introduction and passage of legislation favorable to its cause. It must command enough political power to secure both adequate funding and meaningful administration for its programs.

This sort of political success, in turn, requires of interest groups the accumulation and use of several critical elements of political power. These include size, money, votes, leadership, group cohesion, shrewd strategy development and use, symbol manipulation, general public support, and others.[11]

Size

Size is clearly an important determinant of the political effectiveness of an interest group. Except for civil servants and other appointed officials, public officials in the United States are in office because they won elections, and they remain in office only if they can continue to win elections. Thus, since votes are all-important to governors, representatives, and city council members alike, a large interest group with the potential for delivering large numbers of votes for or against a candidate can command that candidate's attention and can usually affect decisions more easily than can a small group.

In terms of sheer numbers, then, teachers and union members are typically more resourceful than physicians or farmers. Insofar as a large group can control and deliver the votes of its membership, it must be reckoned with by candidates for public office.

Money

Another critical political resource is money. Virtually every technique for influencing the political system requires the expenditure of funds, and without at least a minimal budget an interest group is all but powerless. The very organization and maintenance of a group requires funds to rent offices or meeting halls, to pay phone, printing, and postage bills, and to do some traveling. If the organization itself is without funds, the leadership may have to meet the expenses "out of pocket." If the group is to be permanent in nature — which it must strive for to have any sustained impact on politics — it may find it necessary to employ salaried leadership, staff, and lobbyists. It may want to support a periodic publication, such as a weekly newsletter or a monthly bulletin. It may find it desirable to run expensive advertisements in newspapers and magazines in attempts to build sympathetic public opinion. The Sierra Club, public utilities, and major oil companies have done so in the past.

Interest group money has become increasingly important and plentiful in state elections. In Florida, for example, PAC contributions to legislative campaigns rose from $1.1 million in 1976 to $10 million in 1987 — an increase of over 800 percent in only 11 years.[12] In California state legislative campaigns sometimes cost $1 million or more, and in states both large and small, amounts of $50,000 to $250,000 are not at all uncommon. Races for governor can exceed $10 million.

Today, interest groups are expected to contribute generously to candidates' campaigns. Not surprisingly, those that do are often among the most influential groups — including teachers, businesspeople, lawyers, realtors, labor unions, and others.

Cohesion

Generally, an interest group that is tightly knit internally is more effective politically than one that acts as an umbrella for several **factions**, which share some goals but disagree on other matters. A group with diverse membership is not likely to reach agreement frequently or easily on such issues as which candidates or programs to support. As a result, the behavior of members may be difficult to mobilize and control, and members' time, money, and other resources may be hard to obtain or coordinate. Furthermore, internal fragmentation can dissipate the potential power of an interest group as well as confuse its goals. As the various factions of the group push for different issues and in different directions, decision makers may be unable to respond favorably to the group's preferences simply because those preferences cannot be identified. Moreover, decision makers, usually loath to resolve disagreements within interest groups, prefer to be presented with clear-cut preferences. Thus, any type of interest group reduces its political effectiveness when it fails to articulate a united, coherent set of goals.

Group cohesion, then, is critical, though extremely difficult to create and maintain. In the early days of organized labor's fight for legitimacy and better wages, hours, and working conditions (a period that covered roughly the first half of the twentieth century), unions were quite successful in commanding allegiance. Workers had much to gain and comparatively little to lose through collective action. Today, however, the social and economic status of labor has improved tremendously, and the individual worker is much less dependent on the union. Cohesion within the ranks is, as a result, more difficult to maintain.

Cohesion is a problem in other areas as well. Large and small banks may fight over the issue of branch banking. Manufacturers may split on the issue of returnable or nonreturnable beverage containers. Differences between colleges and research-oriented universities may divide the educational community, dissipating the impact of its lobbying efforts. In short, group cohesion is an important political resource but a difficult one to achieve.

Leadership

The politically effective interest group is able to formulate and articulate its goals clearly, identify the points at which it can gain access to decision makers, place its concerns on the agenda of government, and gain the political support necessary to see the programs it favors safely through the legislative and administrative processes. But such a group does not automatically organize itself in these ways; rather, the group does so through its leadership.

Energetic, imaginative, and articulate leadership is critical at every stage of interest group activity. Leadership persuasion is necessary to hold the membership together, whereas lackluster direction or internal wrangling can easily weaken or destroy a group. Organizational skills are required of leaders to keep the group moving effectively over time. Skills in communication are essential to leaders for articulating group goals and ensuring they are known and understood by members and decision makers alike. An uninformed or confused membership can easily drift away, and uninformed or confused decision makers cannot be relied on to consider the preferences of the group. Furthermore, leaders' knowledge of political personalities and of the political system is important in the selection and timely use of political tactics. The use of an untimely tactic or the application of pressure on the wrong person at the wrong time can easily backfire.

Finally, it is the task of leadership to identify and articulate the points of common interest among a group's membership. All groups, regardless of their size, will agree on certain issues but disagree on others. The successful leader stresses the points of agreement and thereby focuses the group's attention on those points, rather than on areas of contention and potential disruption.

Image   The public's image of an interest group can have a significant impact on the group's degree of political effectiveness. When voters and public officials perceive a group as productive, patriotic, and reasonable, as comprised of people of stature and goodwill, and as having roots in the Republic, the group's preferences are likely to be received and considered in a positive and sympathetic way. In contrast, a group perceived as lazy and unproductive or as unreasonable and destructive is likely to have its concerns viewed with skepticism. Indeed, the effectiveness of a lobbyist hinges in large measure on the positive image of his or her client.

Examples of interest groups with a good public image are numerous, although it is important to remember that a group's public image may change as the social and economic situation in the nation evolves. Physicians have historically been viewed as friends of the sick, exemplars of science and wisdom, pillars of the community, and esteemed persons generally, and for good reason. But their image may be changing somewhat, given the dramatic increases in the cost of medical care. Teachers have been viewed as poorly paid but dedicated people concerned with the mental and physical development of the nation's greatest resource—its youth. They have also been portrayed as union members demanding concessions from governments ill equipped to grant them. Business entrepreneurs have been perceived as efficient and hardworking, as risk-takers, and as the backbone of the U.S. economic system; they have also been seen as exploiters of labor. Farmers and veterans have generally enjoyed a favorable public image. Farmers have been viewed as a part of the Jeffersonian tradition so vital to the nation's development, while veterans are given credit and praise for their sacrifices in defense of the country. These and other interest groups devote a lot of money, time, and effort to maintaining a positive public image.

Political Efficacy   Belief in one's **political efficacy**—the conviction that one can have an impact on political decisions—plays a critical role in the propensity of an interest group to seek to influence the political system. Groups that fail even to try to affect the system will have no political influence. Such politically inefficacious groups are subject to a vicious cycle of failure: (1) members fail to see the potential benefits of political action; (2) they remain politically inactive; (3) their political inactivity prohibits them from deriving any benefits from the system; and (4) their initial assumption about the nonresponsive nature of the system is confirmed.

A person's sense of political efficacy is largely a product of the socialization process. If throughout the early formative years both the spoken word and the behavior of friends and family communicate the notion that civic involvement is good and can produce results, an individual is apt to feel politically effective. This person has learned that attempts to influence decisions are proper—even a responsibility or duty—and that actions will lead to results. In addition, the politically efficacious person often has been taught enough about the structures and processes of government to enable effective action. He or she knows something about how and when political decisions are made and who makes them. The result is that persons whose backgrounds have equipped them with both the will and the tools to be politically active tend to have the most impact on the system. In contrast, individuals who have by word and example been taught that political action is futile usually tend to be politically inactive and ineffective.

Similarly, interest groups view the political system and respond to it in different ways. In a related study involving five nations — the United States, Great Britain, Germany, Italy, and Mexico — Almond and Verba identify a variety of "political cultures."[13] They contend that people's expectations of their own ability to affect the decisions of and receive benefits from the government vary according to their nation's political history and their own wealth, education, occupation, and other factors. In rural Mexican towns, for example, Almond and Verba found that some people had little hope of influencing decisions, were not motivated to attempt to do so, and did not expect to receive much in the way of government benefits. In contrast, the researchers found that well-to-do Britons generally considered themselves able to influence decisions and expected the government to pay attention to their concerns. The British, unlike the Mexicans, had what Almond and Verba call "input" expectations (to affect decisions) and "output" expectations (to receive benefits).

Studies of the American voter likewise display correlations between political efficacy and such factors as income, education, race, and occupational status.[14] Well-educated persons, the well-to-do, and those in high-status occupations tend to vote regularly, to be confident in their ability to influence political decisions, and to associate with politically relevant groups (for example, fraternal organizations, labor unions, and professional societies). In general, the poor, unemployed, and undereducated tend to be less confident in their ability to be politically effective and, therefore, tend to be relatively inactive in politics. There are numerous individual exceptions, of course, but as a group the upper class is highly politically active and, as a result, fares better in terms of the output of the political system.

LOBBYISTS IN STATE POLITICS

The structure of the U.S. government system helps to determine the strategies employed by interest groups. Because decision-making authority is widely dispersed, there are many so-called **veto points** at which interest groups have the opportunity to affect government decisions. Federalism, the separation of powers, bicameralism, the plural executive, the existence of a host of boards and commissions, and other structural features of the political system create literally hundreds of points at which authoritative decisions can be made. As a result, interest groups can attempt to influence court decisions, legislative decisions, gubernatorial appointments, agency policies, the operations of boards and commissions, and other official behaviors or decisions.

The Defensive Advantage

Interest groups typically find it easier to stop unfavorable policies from being implemented than to precipitate action. The structure of government, with its host of veto points, makes this possible. Legislative committees can sometimes kill a bill. The governor can often veto entire bills or line items in a budget. State agencies can frequently drag their feet in putting new programs into effect or in implementing old ones. Governors, state senates, and senate committees can halt an administrative appointment.

Thus, because the very structure of the system favors those who seek to stop something from happening, interest groups are in an advantageous position in terms of their ability to thwart action. However, they are much less influential when they attempt to deal with a policy proposal from its inception to its implementation.

Failure and Success

In spite of interest groups' image as powerful and influential entities, they are not always successful. Legislators respond to strong voter preferences regardless of what lobbyists may argue or contend. In addition, interest groups may encounter a number of problems that can weaken their chances of success. For example, they may be frustrated by the opposition of other groups or face hostile public opinion. Politicians may vigorously oppose a group's desires. Members' differences of opinion may fragment a group internally and thus reduce its effectiveness.

Two case studies, one involving an interest group in New Jersey and the other a group in Minnesota, illustrate the factors that lead to group failure or success.

New Jersey Farmers Fail The New Jersey case involved the unsuccessful attempts by an organization of New Jersey farmers in the mid-1960s to stop the state's imposition of regulations requiring farmers to provide hot water for migrant workers.[15] Enforcement of the regulations, which were supported by the governor, was assigned to the Migrant Labor Board.

The growers argued that the costs of compliance would hurt them financially and that the rules were unfair because they would not affect growers in adjacent states. New Jersey farmers attended a public hearing held by the Migrant Labor Board to protest the regulations. The state secretary of agriculture subsequently sought a delay in the enforcement of the regulations, during which time the farmers successfully pushed a bill through the state legislature nullifying the hot-water rule. They were unsuccessful, however, in preventing the governor from vetoing that legislative ruling. After the governor's veto, the farmers appealed the rule in court but lost.

The farmers' group was well organized. It possessed money, able leadership, and a good image. It also knew how to attempt to influence the system. Even so, it failed in its effort to affect the system's decision.

Minnesota Business Interests Succeed   A more recent case in Minnesota produced a different outcome, one in which business interests triumphed after a temporary defeat. In 1981 the Minnesota legislature passed legislation creating a state mini-superfund along with expanded liability for businesses whose hazardous waste discharges cause harm to people. Republican Governor Albert H. Quie vetoed the bill. However, in 1983, with a new governor, Democrat Rudy Perpich, the legislation was passed again and became law. It was characterized politically as protective of the public health and the environment.

The business community opposed the law, arguing that it put companies at excessive and unfair risk of lawsuit and costly damage payments, sometimes for problems that the defendant company may not have created. In their efforts to modify the legislation in 1985, business lobbies sought to change the focus of the political debate from protecting public health and the environment to protecting the health of the Minnesota business climate. Business lobbies thus argued that companies might leave the state because of the increased number and cost of lawsuits. At one point Lloyd's of London declined to offer environmental impairment liability insurance to Minnesota firms.

In 1985 legislation modified the law and the business lobbies won a number of issues. Plaintiffs would now carry a heavier burden to prove that actions by the defendant company actually caused the alleged damage. The breadth of liability was narrowed and a victims' compensation fund was created.

With the protection of the Republican governor's veto gone in 1983, business lobbies had to change their tactics, and they did so successfully. They were able to affect public opinion by altering the political context in which they were viewed—from one of irresponsible handlers of the public health and the environment to that of victims in need of legislative relief.

Strong Parties Weaken Interest Groups

There is some evidence that organized interests are more influential in one-party states than in states with two-party competition. Zeigler and van Dalen argue, for example, that "with regard to political variables, pressure groups are strongest when political parties and legislative cohesion are weakest."[16] When parties are weak and political struggles revolve around factions and personality conflicts, a vacuum of sorts is created. There are no strong, viable parties to recruit and support candidates, forge a well-defined package of policy proposals, or form the legislative majority needed to see the proposals safely through the political process. Instead, candidates are forced to look beyond the party for help, and this often leads them to form ties with and incur obligations to special interests. The absence of a cohesive legislative majority leaves what policy proposals there are to the mercy of the "veto" of the special interests. Politics becomes semi-anarchistic in nature, with each special interest seeking its own agenda.

The interesting question is who will be most influential and under what circumstances. Will strong-willed individual legislators who chair critical committees become one-person dictators on the legislation that passes through their committee? Will the legislative process be plagued with disorganization and ineffective leadership to the extent that affluent lobbies will be able to influence the votes of a majority of legislators? Will the majority party leadership be strong enough to control the power of committee chairs, hold the membership in line in the face of lobby pressures, and thereby push through party programs?

The important issue here is not whether influence is exerted in decision-making bodies but how that influence is distributed and used. Some commentators suggest that the interests of the public are best served by strong political parties in control of decision-making bodies because weak parties cause influence to flow to lobbies, legislative factions, and individuals. Political parties may not be perfectly reflective and representative of the general public, but they are typically more in tune with the public's preferences than are the more narrowly based interest groups and small legislative factions.

INTEREST GROUPS IN A DEMOCRACY

The effects of interest groups on the political system in the United States have long been a focus of political scholars and politicians alike. In 1788 James Madison wrote of "factions" in *The Federalist Papers.*[17] He considered property the source of all political conflict. When people banded together in attempts to influence the decisions of government in ways that would protect the property they had and allow them to acquire even more, Madison viewed this as dangerous. He argued that such groups could influence public decisions in ways that reflected their narrow, selfish preferences at the expense of the public interest. Neither Madison nor any other political writer since has ever come up with a satisfactory definition of the **public interest**. However, most agree on what the public interest in a democracy is not — it is not defined solely on the basis of the preferences of any single interest group, no matter how large or powerful it may be.

While Madison articulated a problem that continues to concern many people today, he was unable to propose a viable remedy. One extreme and unrealistic suggestion is to make illegal the formation and operation of any special interest group. But to outlaw interest groups would be tantamount to making it illegitimate for people to cooperate in the collective articulation of their desires to the government. Moreover, the freedoms of assembly, speech, press, and petition would be seriously compromised.

Another argument suggests that the potential ill effects of interest groups are mitigated somewhat by the competition among the groups. Labor, management, the professions—these and other groups, it is argued, counterbalance one another's impact on the political system. However, not all of the groups are interested in all of the issues. Truckers may be interested in lowering the license tax on large trucks and teachers in policies dealing with educational issues, but not vice versa. As a result, only a few, if any, organized interests may exist to counterbalance the truckers on matters of truck license fees and the teachers on educational issues. Special interests may in this way dominate certain areas of public policy.

While James Madison worried about the potential ill effects of factions on public policy, others have chronicled and lamented some real ones. In a classic work entitled *The Semi-Sovereign People*, E. E. Schattschneider contends that pressure within the American system of politics is dominated mainly by business interests to the exclusion of the bulk of the population.[18] Similarly, Theodore Lowi argues in *The End of Liberalism* that in numerous policy areas relatively small coalitions of interested parties have come to dominate public choices on matters of vital concern to themselves. In addition, Lowi laments what he sees as the tendency of elected lawmakers to relinquish too much public authority and too many public resources to those small coalitions.[19]

On the positive side, interest groups perform a supplementary, or functional, representation role in the political system. The representation schemes employed at all levels of American government define interests geographically. Senators, representatives, mayors, and county commissioners represent people according to where those people reside, not according to their political ideology, occupation, religion, or color. This means that lawmakers are called on to represent a host of diverse interests simultaneously. Any given district is apt to contain physicians, lawyers, merchants, laborers, teachers, and public employees, and it is highly unlikely that these people will agree on most or even many issues. The task of determining the public interest for a district thus falls to the representative. The preferences of a single interest group within a representative's district are unlikely to be fully conveyed to the decision-making arenas themselves.

Interest groups also act as gauges of the intensity of citizens on political issues. As a result of the democratic demand for political equality and the Supreme Court's interpretation of the Fourteenth Amendment relative to legislative apportionment, the vote of every American is equal to that of every other American—regardless of how intense some people may feel about a particular issue or candidate. For example, in a voting situation involving some issue and 9 voters, 5 of whom are mildly in favor of the issue and 4 of whom are vigorously opposed to it, whose preferences should prevail? Given the democratic dictum of majority rule, of course, the desires of the 5 indifferent voters will prevail over those of the 4 intense voters. It would be difficult to have things any other way, for if people were allowed multiple votes on the basis of their intensity on issues, how would it be decided who gets two or more votes? Any deviation from the one person, one vote principle would create many operational and ideological problems. In this sense, then, **interest group intensity** on issues helps to identify the issues about which the members of that group feel most strongly.

SUMMARY

The political landscape of the American states has been changing in recent years and continues to do so. Among the many changes are an increase in the number and diversity of interest groups, a rise in the number of lobbyists, and the growing sophistication of the tactics used by interest groups. The expanded role of government generally, coupled with the devolution of many functions from the national government to the states, means that an increasing number of interest groups have a stake in the decisions made by state and local governments. More interest groups also mean more political pressure as well as more money being spent on state politics. The proliferation of such groups may have rendered the old-time powers of the rich less dominant, for while there is more money being spent, it is more widely distributed.[20]

Interest groups and lobbyists are important players in the political game because they influence to varying degrees the content of public policies. At the same time, they do not control the making of public policy. Lobbyists tend to be most influential when they represent groups that decision makers hold in high esteem and perceive as in tune with the public good. However, elected decision makers defer to voter preferences when these outweigh the desires of an interest group.

Democracy in the states and localities, then, is not a contest that excludes the American voter. Rather, it is more like a game in which those who participate actively, organize themselves, and employ tactics of persuasion can have more influence on the shape of public policy than those who by choice or necessity are relatively inactive in politics.

KEY TERMS

lobbyist	political action committee (PAC)
interest group	contingency lobbying
single-issue interest group	faction
employee lobbyist	political efficacy
contract lobbyist	veto point
volunteer lobbyist	public interest
legislative liaison	interest group intensity
techniques of influence	

ADDITIONAL READINGS

Hrebenar, Ronald J., and Ruth Scott. *Interest Group Politics in America.* 2nd ed. Englewood Cliffs, N.J.: Prentice-Hall, 1990.

Hrebenar, Ronald J., and Clive S. Thomas, eds. *Interest Group Politics in the Southern States.* Tuscaloosa: University of Alabama Press, 1992.

Rosenthal, Alan. *The Third House: Lobbyists and Lobbying in the States.* Washington, D.C.: Congressional Quarterly Press, 1993.

Schattschneider, E. E. *The Semi-Sovereign People: A Realist's View of Democracy in America.* New York: Holt, Rinehart and Winston, 1960.

Thomas, Clive, ed. *Politics and Public Policy in the Contemporary American West.* Albuquerque: University of New Mexico Press, 1991.

Walters, Jonathan. "A Night on the Town Isn't What It Used to Be in Jefferson City." *Governing* (July 1989): 26.

Welch, Randy. "Lobbyists, Lobbyists, All Over the Lot." *State Legislatures* (Feb. 1989): 18.

NOTES

1. Quoted in Bill Schluter, "Contributions Don't Affect Votes? Don't You Believe It," *Governing* (Aug. 1990): 98.

2. E. E. Schattschneider, *The Semi-Sovereign People: A Realist's View of Democracy in America* (New York: Holt, Rinehart and Winston, 1960).

3. For the single best study of lobbying and interest groups in the states, see Alan Rosenthal, *The Third House: Lobbyists and Lobbying in the States* (Washington, D.C.: Congressional Quarterly Press, 1993). See also Ronald J. Hrebenar and Clive S. Thomas, eds., *Interest Group Politics in the Southern States* (Tuscaloosa: University of Alabama Press, 1992).

4. Clive S. Thomas and Ronald J. Hrebenar, "Interest Groups in the States," in *Politics in the American States*, 5th ed., ed. Virginia Gray, Herbert Jacob, and Robert B. Albritton (Glenview, Ill.: Scott, Foresman/Little, Brown Higher Education, 1990), pp. 123–58.

5. Linda Wagar, "Balancing the Demands of Single-Issue Voters," *State Government News* (Nov. 1989): 34.

6. Randy Welch, "Lobbyists, Lobbyists, All Over the Lot," *State Legislatures* (Feb. 1989): 18; and Robert Pear, "Number of Ballot Initiatives Is the Greatest since 1932," *New York Times*, 5 Nov. 1990.

7. Tom Watson, "Dale Florio: A Lobbyist's Middleman Who Helps Business People Navigate State Capitol Halls," *Governing* (Feb. 1989): 32–38.

8. Welch, "Lobbyists," p. 19.

9. See Rosenthal, *Third House*, for more extensive treatment of this subject.

10. Hrebenar and Thomas, *Interest Group Politics*, p. 323.

11. This discussion is drawn from a wide array of sources within the extensive literature on the group basis of politics, including V. O. Key, Jr., *Politics, Parties and Pressure Groups*, 5th ed. (New York: Thomas Y. Crowell, 1964); Schattschneider, *Semi-Sovereign People;* and Harmon Zeigler, *Interest Groups in American Society* (Englewood Cliffs, N.J.: Prentice-Hall, 1964).

12. Anne E. Kelley and Ella L. Thomas, "Florida: The Changing Patterns of Power," in *Interest Group Politics in the Southern States*, ed. Ronald J. Hrebenar and Clive S. Thomas (Tuscaloosa: University of Alabama Press, 1992), pp. 125–51. For more on campaign spending, see Sandra Singer, "The Arms Race

of Campaign Financing," *State Legislatures* (July 1988): 24–28; and Rob Gurwitt, "California, Here We Come: The Professional Legislature and Its Discontents," *Governing* (Aug. 1991): 65–69.

13. Gabriel Almond and Sidney Verba, *The Civic Culture* (Princeton, N.J.: Princeton University Press, 1963).

14. See Paul R. Abramson, *Political Attitudes in America* (San Francisco: W. H. Freeman, 1983).

15. Richard A. Hogarty, *New Jersey Farmers and Migrant Housing Rules* (New York: Bobbs-Merrill, 1966), Interuniversity Case Program no. 94.

16. Harmon Zeigler and Hendrik van Dalen, "Interest Groups in the States," in *Politics in the American States*, 2nd ed., ed. Herbert Jacob and Kenneth Vines (Boston: Little, Brown, 1971), p. 127.

17. Alexander Hamilton, James Madison, and John Jay, *The Federalist Papers* (1788; reprint New York: New American Library, 1961).

18. Schattschneider, *Semi-Sovereign People.*

19. Theodore J. Lowi, *The End of Liberalism*, 2nd ed. (New York: Norton, 1979).

20. Rosenthal, *Third House;* and Hrebenar and Thomas, *Interest Group Politics.*

9

Elections

Candidates for Texas governor participate in a televised debate (1990). The candidates *(from the left)* are Ann Richards (who won the election), Mark White, and Jim Mattox. Dallas, Texas. *(Bob Daemmrich/Stock, Boston)*

In the United States elections are a common occurrence. The prime seasons for elections are late summer, November, and the spring. Partisan (when candidates run under different party labels) primary elections are often held in early spring, though some states hold primaries in August and September. **Primary elections** are nominating elections in which Republican and Democratic voters decide who will represent them in the November general elections. In **general elections** voters elect governors, state legislators, members of Congress, the U.S. president, and many local officials. A large proportion of local governments hold elections in the springtime. Summer and fall primaries and most November general elections are partisan elections. Many local elections, however, are nonpartisan, at least nominally, since candidates do not carry a party label and the parties are not formally involved in the nomination and campaign processes.

It is no mystery why Americans have so many elections, for Americans also have a lot of governments. Voters elect a president, members of the two houses of Congress, members of the state legislatures, governors, secretaries of state, attorney generals, governing boards of universities and school districts, mayors, city council members, boards of county commissioners, sheriffs, coroners, governing boards for sewer, water, recreation, flood, and hospital districts, and many, many more.

Representative democracy in America thus abounds. But how can American voters keep track of all the governments and elections and stay informed as to the issues and candidates? The answer, of course, is that most do not.

ELECTION LAWS

State and local elections are governed by state law and subject to a few U.S. constitutional restrictions. State constitutional and statutory law determines which public offices are elective. It governs the procedures by which candidates are nominated, and it outlines citizen requirements for voting. Some local governments are granted the opportunity to impose additional requirements for voting and holding office, but even in these cases state law still constitutes the basic legal framework for the electoral process.

Historically, state laws imposed voting requirements with respect to age, residency, registration, and, in a few states, literacy. With the 1971 ratification of the Twenty-Sixth Amendment to the Constitution, the minimum voting age was standardized at 18 years across the country. In the past, residency requirements varied among the states, typically requiring an individual to reside from 6 months to 1 year in the state, from 60 to 90 days in the county, and from 10 to 60 days in the district (or precinct) before becoming eligible to vote. Many states have changed these minimum residency requirements, however, recognizing that the high rate of mobility of the American public, combined with residency requirements, often disenfranchises millions of would-be voters. Twenty states now require 30 days' residency, twenty others have no residency requirement, and the remainder have requirements of various lengths.

Voter Registration

Most states require citizens to register to vote around 30 days before an election, though the number of days varies from none to 50. Voters in all states except North Dakota must register. In just over 80 percent of the states, voter registration is permanent; that is, once people register to vote, they do not need to re-register for subsequent elections unless they move or fail to vote for a specified period of time. Those relocating to another precinct or state must register in their new place of residence. If they fail to do so, their names eventually will be purged from the voter registration list.

In nearly three-quarters of the states, voters must identify their partisan preference when they register. They may register as Republicans, Democrats, or Independents. Voters who register as Independents are generally not eligible to vote in party primary elections, whereas those who identify with one of the two major parties may vote only in that party's primary. In addition, there are situations in which voters must register separately for certain elections; for example, in some urban areas voters must register separately for city elections.

The states are also allowed to administer literacy tests to prospective voters, as long as such tests do not discriminate on a racial basis. Until 1965, literacy tests were often used in the South to deny the right to vote to African-Americans. Today, however, no states use literacy tests. Until the 1960s, a poll tax payment was required by some states to register for state and local elections. However, the poll tax was outlawed in 1964 by the Twenty-Fourth Amendment to the Constitution for federal elections, and in 1966 by the U.S. Supreme Court in state and local elections.

The trend in the states has been to make voter registration easier. Fifteen states now provide for registration at state agencies often frequented by citizens, such as motor vehicle departments. In addition, roughly two dozen states now permit voter registration by mail. In 1986 Congress passed the Voting Accessibility for the Elderly and Handicapped Act, which requires the states to make the voting booth accessible to all eligible voters. In 1992 President George Bush vetoed a bill that would have provided for automatic voter registration whenever a person renewed a driver's license. Following the 1992 presidential elections, however, Congress passed a similar bill and President Bill Clinton signed it into law in May 1993. The bill is known as the **motor-voter law**, which allows people to register to vote simply by renewing their driver's license.

Constitutional and Federal Rules

Although state law governs the basic aspects of voter registration and of elections in general, several salient provisions of the U.S. Constitution and federal statutes also affect the conduct of elections in the

United States. The Fourteenth Amendment, for instance, stipulates that no state shall deny to any citizen the equal protection of the laws. It is on the basis of this provision that the Supreme Court has mandated the **one person, one vote** requirement in state and federal elections; it requires, when candidates run for election in districts (such as a state senate election), that the districts contain approximately the same number of people.

In addition, the Fifteenth Amendment makes illegal any discrimination on the basis of race, color, or previous condition of servitude. In 1944, in *Smith v. Allright*, the Supreme Court banned the southern "white" primary, under which southern parties had declared themselves private clubs and barred blacks from participating in primary elections. In a one-party dominant area, where the only meaningful electoral choice is made in the primary, disenfranchisement from the primary is tantamount to complete and total disenfranchisement.

Similarly, the Seventeenth Amendment orders the direct popular election of senators, the Nineteenth Amendment guarantees the right to vote to women, and the Twenty-Sixth Amendment establishes the minimum voting age of 18 years for federal elections. The 1965 Voting Rights Act, renewed several times, empowers the U.S. attorney general to take action under certain conditions to ensure fair and impartial voter registration procedures.

Campaign Financing Rules

In recent years the states have begun to exert some control over various aspects of campaign financing and reporting. Many states have enacted laws governing the amount of money that individuals and organizations may contribute to a single campaign. In addition, some states provide partial public funding of campaigns along with limits on how much may be spent. All states require some form of campaign finance reporting, though the rules are generally lax.

Reporting Finances   Campaign finance reporting requirements vary among the states. Wisconsin, for example, requires such reports from candidates or committees that spend more than $25. In Michigan, Minnesota, North Carolina, North Dakota, and Texas, those who exceed $100 must report. And in California reports are required of candidates and officeholders whose salaries are or will be in excess of $100 per month.

Other states have similar dollar thresholds triggering the need to file financial reports.[1] These reports usually are filed with the secretary of state or the county clerk. In most states it is common for financial reports to be submitted after deadlines have passed, sometimes even after the elections are over, and for the sanctions for such tardiness to be mild.

Contributions   The states impose a variety of limitations on the ability of organizations to make financial contributions to candidate campaigns. Eighteen states prohibit corporations from making any contribution and 14 others restrict the size of contributions. Again, there are wide variations among the states. Michigan disallows corporate contributions to candidate campaigns except for those that are issue-centered. Wisconsin prohibits them except for referenda matters. The states also regulate contributions from labor unions, regulated industries, and political parties. The limits on party contributions are few; those that apply to unions and regulated industries are similar to but slightly less restrictive than the ones for corporations.

Over one-half of the states limit the amount individuals may contribute to candidate campaigns, though these limits also vary widely among the states. Sometimes the ceilings are placed on statewide elections only; other times there are separate limitations on primary and general elections. The interstate variety is enormous.

The attempts to curb election finance abuses, both nationally and in the states, generated a response in the form of political action committees (PACs), which have become a pervasive and an important source of influence in modern-day politics. When the ability of organizations and individuals to contribute generously to campaigns is restricted by the states, those seeking to contribute pool their more limited sums and place them in the hands of PACs, which then act on their behalf. The irony is that the attempts to keep campaign financing honest and at reasonable levels have led to the creation of the PACs, which serve instead to push campaign costs even higher.

Expenditures   While some states seek to limit campaign spending as well as contributions, expenditure limitations are much less prevalent. In large measure this is because of the difficult legal issues associated with spending limits. The Supreme Court has ruled (*Buckley v. Valeo*, 1976) that in the absence of a public election financing system in which candidates voluntarily participate, spending limits constitute impermissible infringements on free speech. For candidates to effectively express themselves and communicate their political views to the voting public they must spend money. Thus, spending limits constitute speech limits.

Incumbent Advantages   Some argue that there is a political problem associated with spending limits — that they constitute an unfair advantage for incumbents. Incumbency, this reasoning goes, creates an advantage in any campaign, and to overcome that edge challengers must spend heavily to advertise themselves to the public. Spending limits, thus, handcuff challengers. Not everyone agrees, of course. Others contend that since challengers receive far less in campaign contributions than do incumbents, spending limitations would help challengers by limiting heavy spending by the already advantaged incumbents.

Variation among the States   Given the political and legal complications of expenditure limitations, it is not surprising that the states do less to limit campaign spending than they do to control campaign contributions. Many states have laws that specify who may authorize expenditures from a campaign fund and what campaign money may be spent for. Currently, only a few states limit the amounts that can be spent in certain elections, and roughly half of the states disallow any spending until an initial financial statement is filed with the state. It is not coincidental that the public officials writing this legislation are the same people who need the money to run for reelection. As a result, serious campaign financial reform has yet to emerge from the legislatures.

Approximately one-half of the states have some form of public campaign financing, but the plans vary widely among the states. Some make it possible for citizens to provide public financing through income tax credits or deductions, or by contributions by way of a check-off on the tax return form. A number of other states appropriate state funds directly. In some instances, taxpayers may specify the party to which their contributions will go. In others, state support is given to both political parties or is available only to candidates for governor. As is the case with all aspects of state election law, the interstate variations are great.

ELECTORAL PARTICIPATION

The American political system is based on a number of normative assumptions, including the belief that the people are sovereign. Authority may be exercised by elected representatives or appointed administrators, but authority rests, ultimately, with the people. Another assumption is that the sovereign citizens exercise their authority by voting.

But do they? The answer is both yes, some do, and no, many don't. In recent decades Americans have become increasingly less interested in voting. They are also showing a weakening attachment to the political parties, which are, after all, major components in the U.S. elective system.

Figure 9.1 tracks voter turnout in presidential elections over a 32-year period, from 1960 to 1992. The trend—until 1992, when the presence of a third candidate, Ross Perot, sparked renewed interest—clearly has been downward. It is important to note further that the data in the figure are for presidential contests, and that voter turnout is lower in almost all other types of elections. Occasionally, a hot local issue stimulates a massive turnout in a community. But voter participation in nonpresidential-year congressional elections, in elections for state offices, in local elections (especially those held in the spring), and in primary elections is often much lower than participation in presidential elections.

Widespread Apathy The apparent lack of interest in self-governance is reflected also in a decline in citizen attachment to the parties. As Table 9.1 demonstrates, Americans' identification with the two major parties has been slipping along with voter turnout.

FIGURE 9.1
Presidential Election Participation by Voters, 1960–1992
(as a percentage of the total voting-age population)

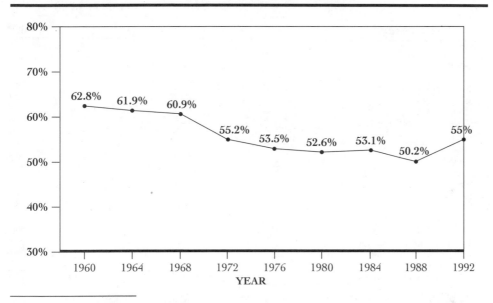

SOURCES: U.S. Bureau of the Census, *Statistical Abstract of the United States, 1990*
(Washington, D.C.: GPO, 1990), p. 264; and Committee for the Study of the
American Electorate, 1992.

Political participation, as measured by voting, varies considerably throughout the electorate. Table 9.2 shows the levels of voter turnout in national elections in two presidential-election years—1976 and 1988. The table also shows how turnout varies with age, gender, ethnicity, education, and employment. As in Figure 9.1, the data indicate a decline in overall voter participation.

TABLE 9.1 Political Party Identification, 1960–1990

Political Party	Percent Identifying				
	1960	*1970*	*1980*	*1988*	*1990*
Strong Democrat	20	20	18	18	20
Weak Democrat	25	24	23	18	19
Strong Republican	16	9	9	14	10
Weak Republican	14	15	14	14	15

Source: U.S. Bureau of the Census, *Statistical Abstract of the United States, 1990* (Washington, D.C.: GPO, 1990), p. 270.

TABLE 9.2
Voter Turnout by Age, Gender, Ethnicity, Education,
and Employment, 1976 and 1988

	Voter Turnout (%)	
Voter Category	*1976*	*1988*
Age		
18–20 years	38.6	33.2
21–24 years	45.6	38.3
25–34 years	55.4	48.6
35–44 years	63.3	61.3
45–64 years	68.7	67.9
65 years and older	62.5	68.8
Gender		
Male	59.6	56.4
Female	58.8	58.3
Ethnicity		
White	60.9	59.1
Black	48.7	51.5
Hispanic	31.8	28.8
Education		
8 years or less of schooling	44.1	36.7
1–3 years of high school	47.2	41.3
Completed high school	59.4	54.7
1–3 years of college	68.1	64.5
4 or more years of college	79.8	77.6
Employment		
Employed	61.8	58.4
Unemployed	41.2	38.6

Source: U.S. Bureau of the Census, *Statistical Abstract of the United States, 1990* (Washington, D.C.: GPO, 1990), p. 262.

Young People Don't Vote   The youngest Americans participate the least. That may be understandable. Most 18-year-olds, as compared to those in their 30s and 40s, for example, are much less likely to be established, employed, and knowledgeable about the workings of government. Rather, they may be transient, as is the case with many college students, and they may have yet to plant roots in a community and perceive personal stakes in political activities. Older voters, by contrast, often have developed habits of participation as a result of years of exposure to the workings and consequences of the system. In general, a mobile 18- or 20-year-old with other preoccupations is less apt to vote than are his or her parents, who realize that they have a personal and economic stake in political outcomes.

Women Voters   Although there was a time when men voted more regularly than did women, that is no longer the case. In the 1988 and 1992 elections, slightly more women voted than did men. Coupled with the fact that women outnumber men, the female vote has become increasingly important. Some studies indicate that men and women tend to differ in their political views and preferences, placing women voters in a position to determine the outcomes of elections.[2]

It is not surprising that women's participation, in relation to voter participation generally, has increased with their expanded role in the work force. Researchers have well documented that the employed, and especially those in professional, prestigious, and high-paying jobs, vote more regularly than the unemployed (see Table 9.2). In recent decades the social and occupational roles of American women have changed, and today more women are part of the work force. As women have assumed many of the roles formerly dominated by men, they too have become more politically active. In addition, national events such as the Clarence Thomas–Anita Hill hearings in 1991 serve to encourage women to become more active politically.

Ethnicity

Voter turnout also varies by ethnicity. As Table 9.2 shows, whites vote more regularly than blacks, though the gap is narrowing. Hispanics are less likely to vote than both whites and blacks. As this very young population comes to political maturity, however, the sheer numbers of America's fastest-growing ethnic group are likely to translate into political power at the polls, and, as the chances of winning increase, so likely will the voter turnout. In the Rio Grande Valley of south Texas, where 80 percent of the population is Spanish-surnamed and where this vote often is seen as the key to a statewide race, it is not unusual for the voting turnout figures to run ahead of the statewide turnout percentages.

Level of Education

In addition, voter participation fluctuates by level of education (see Table 9.2). The more education one has, the more likely one is to vote. Clearly, education is associated with the other factors shown in the table. It takes time to go through school, and thus persons in their 30s are likely to have more schooling than an 18-year-old. A well-educated person is also less likely to be unemployed. Historically, men and whites have had more education than others. These factors can be cumulative and reinforcing. They can, and have, led to broader participation and a more extensive impact on the political system by well-educated, successfully employed middle-aged and older white men. This is changing, though not rapidly.

Women and Minorities in Public Office

The relative growth in voter participation by women and blacks is reflected in Table 9.2. It is also manifest in increased success by women and blacks in winning public office. Table 9.3 shows the increase in the number of African-American elected officials in a variety of positions at the national, state, and local levels. Although persons of

TABLE 9.3
Number of African-American Elected Officials, 1970 and 1990

| | Number of Officials | |
Position	1970	1990
U.S. state legislators and administrators	179	440
City and county officials	719	4,481
Local and state educational governing bodies	368	1,645

Source: U.S. Bureau of the Census, *Statistical Abstract of the United States, 1992* (Washington, D.C.: GPO, 1992), p. 267.

color still do not hold public offices in anywhere near the proportion in which they are represented in the general population, their presence is growing. More specifically, the recent political careers of such mayors as Thomas Bradley of Los Angeles, the late Harold Washington of Chicago, Coleman Young of Detroit, and David Dinkins of New York attest to the growing African-American political presence. There have been increases in the number of Hispanic officeholders as well, but the growth has been more modest.

Women have also been making significant strides in gaining elective offices, such as in state legislatures. Many recent governors have been women, including Christine Todd Whitman in New Jersey, Barbara Roberts in Oregon, Kay Orr in Nebraska, Joan Finney in Kansas, Ann Richards in Texas, Madeleine Kunin in Vermont, and Rose Mofford in Arizona. The 1992 election year was called the "year of the woman" by some observers because of women's role in the electoral arena. In 1992 California, the largest state in the nation, became the first to have two female U.S. senators. Similarly, in 1988 five states had women lieutenant governors, 11 had women secretaries of state, and 9 had women state treasurers.

Legislatures Are Changing

The 1992 elections produced record numbers of women in the state legislatures as well. In 1993 women constituted a record 20 percent of state legislators; 20 years ago that figure was only 5 percent. Over a third of the state legislators in Arizona, Colorado, New Hampshire, and Vermont are women.[3] (See Focus 9.1.)

There have been notable gains at the local level as well. Darcy, Welch, and Clark report that, from 1975 to 1982, the number of women in county offices tripled, the number of women mayors grew from 566 to 1,770, and the count on town and city councils jumped from 5,365 to 12,963.[4] Mayors in 12 of the nation's 100 largest cities have recently been women, including Dallas, Houston, Pittsburgh, Chicago, San Diego, San Francisco, and Spokane. At one point in the late 1980s, five of the ten largest cities in Texas had women mayors. In cities larger than 30,000, over 11 percent had female mayors.[5] Figure 9.2 shows the increase in the number of women officeholders from 1975 to 1991.

--- FOCUS ---

9.1 WOMEN IN THE LEGISLATURE

The 1992 elections produced 125 additional women state legislators, bringing the national total to 20 percent. The distribution is uneven, however. Over 30 percent of the legislative membership is female in Arizona, Colorado, Idaho, Maine, New Hampshire, Vermont, and Washington, whereas the proportion is only 10 percent in Alabama, Kentucky, Louisiana, and Oklahoma.

Does gender diversification make a policy difference? Some researchers suggest that women legislators are more liberal than their male counterparts on many issues; that they are less supportive of abortion restrictions and the death penalty; that they focus on health, child, and family issues more than men; and that their interpersonal and negotiation styles are less confrontational.

There are organizational consequences, too, as women are moving into leadership positions and providing the foundation for bipartisan coalitions. In 1993, for example, the Alaska house elected its first woman speaker; indeed, women took over the entire slate of leadership slots in that state. In the state of Washington, where almost 40 percent of legislators are female, women from the two parties organized the Ladies' Terrorist Society and Sewing Circle, indicating that gender cohesiveness may cross party lines.

SOURCES: Karl T. Kurtz, "The Election in Perspective," *State Legislatures* (Jan. 1993): 16–19; Rob Gurwitt, "Legislatures: The Faces of Change," *Governing* (Feb. 1993): 28–32; and Susan J. Carroll, Debra L. Dodson, and Ruth B. Mandrell, *The Impact of Women in Public Office: An Overview* (New Brunswick: Rutgers University, Center for the American Woman and Politics, 1991).

It is argued that there would be even more women officeholders were it not for a shortage of candidates. A variety of factors, including the presence of children at home and the inflexibility of regular working hours, may restrict the number of available women candidates.[6] If 1992 is any indication, however, the number of candidates is likely to expand.

There is some evidence that the election of minority and women officeholders affects public policy outcomes. Kenneth Mladenka reports that in the cities he studied, the election of minority council members, Hispanics especially, led to more minority municipal employment.[7] Others argue, too, that women are more likely than men to vote Democratic and that this can determine the outcome of elections. In addition, women and men tend to differ in their views on a variety of issues. For example, women are said to be more supportive

FIGURE 9.2

Increase in the Number of Women Officeholders between 1975 and 1991

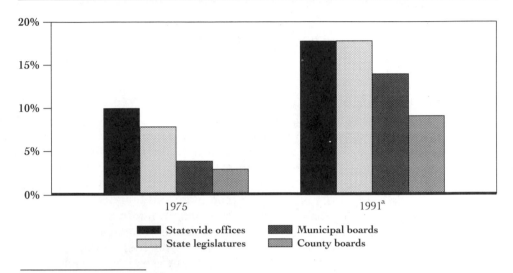

[a]Municipal board figures are for 1985; county board figures are for 1990.

SOURCE: Center for the American Woman and Politics, *Women in Elective Office* (factsheet) (New Brunswick: Eagleton Institute of Politics, Rutgers University, Nov. 1991), p. 2.

of programs assisting the economically disadvantaged and tend to emphasize racial equality, protection of the environment, and control of drugs, pornography, and gambling.[8]

Changes in patterns of political participation and the emerging electoral successes of women and minorities are, thus, far more than symbolic. They have translated into policy differences that are likely to become increasingly important.

THE IMPACT OF INSTITUTIONS ON ELECTORAL PARTICIPATION

In addition to the differences in electoral participation outlined in Table 9.2 (such as those associated with age, gender, and ethnicity), voter participation varies as a result of institutional factors. These include level of government, time of election, presence or absence of political party involvement, and items on the ballot. Consistently, the highest levels of voter turnout occur in presidential elections, which are held every four years in November. Turnout drops in the off-year November elections, when there are congressional contests and state and local races.

Low Turnout in Local Elections

Voter turnout is notoriously low in local elections. Often held in the spring, they include elections for school board members, city council members, and members of special district governing boards. In addition, local elections are generally nonpartisan—that is, candidates do not run as members of a political party—which contributes to the low voter turnout. The impact of these institutional conditions is to reduce the visibility of the elections and thus the interest and participation of the voters. The activities of political parties serve to focus media attention on politics and heighten voters' awareness and interest. When these factors are absent, voter participation falls. Similarly, Americans are conditioned to think of electoral politics in terms of the even-year November elections. The springtime does not seem, to many, a natural time to vote. It is not unusual, then, for nonpartisan elections held in March, April, or May (featuring contests for seats on a school or hospital district governing board, for example) to attract less than 10 percent of the voters.

The blend of individual and institutional factors has a major impact on the results of local elections. As noted earlier, those most likely to vote are well educated, employed, middle aged or older, often white, and holding prestigious and professional jobs. In local elections, when institutional factors such as time of election and absence of party combine with these differential voting patterns, the small sector of the population that actually votes tends to have a distinctive upper-class cast.

Levels of Turnout Affect Outcomes

Elections with extremely low voter turnouts can work to the advantage of particular interest groups. A well-organized group, even though few in number, can often control the outcome.

Turnout Varies among the States

Electoral participation varies among the states. In general, voter turnout in the Midwest is higher than the national average and turnout in the South is lower. Five of the six states with the highest levels of voter turnout are in or adjacent to the Midwest, whereas four of the lowest five are southern states.

History and culture explain some of the state variations in voter turnout. The South, historically, has been so solidly Democratic that most meaningful electoral competition has been in the primaries, and not in the general elections. Thus, the incentive to vote in November has been lacking. The remnants of this heritage can still be seen in some southern states. Although Texas has voted Republican in five of the last seven presidential elections, Democrats still control the state legislature and have an iron grip on most of the races lower on the ballot.

Some features of the moralistic culture of many midwestern states imply a civic responsibility to the community, and thus a moral obligation to participate in civic affairs such as elections. In any case, turnout varies among the states as well as within them, as evidenced by the impact of institutional factors.

MODERN CAMPAIGNS

There are several pronounced characteristics of modern state electoral campaigns. They tend to be candidate-centered rather than party-centered campaigns and are becoming increasingly costly, with political action committees playing an ever-larger role in their funding. In addition, modern campaigns tend to feature incumbents who campaign year-round, who almost always win because they often run unopposed, and who are increasingly sophisticated, often managed by hired professional consultants.[9] In these ways, contemporary state campaigns are similar to those for national office.[10]

The Candidate-Centered Campaign

The decline in the electoral role of the political party in America, the diminished attachment that American voters have to the parties, and the increased importance of campaigning style together have led to the development of the **candidate-centered campaign**, in which the candidates, not the parties, run the electoral campaigns. The candidate works with professional campaign consultants and office staff to raise money, prepare strategy, assemble the campaign agenda, deal with the media, and do the polling and mass mailings. The parties may help with mailing lists and get-out-the-vote efforts, and may provide some technical assistance and a little money, but most activity is undertaken by the candidate and the candidate's advisers.

The Expensive Campaign

State races are increasingly costly. The growth in political ambition and careerism prompts incumbents to raise and spend more to extend their political careers. Serious challengers must then respond in kind with heavy spending. The expanded use of the visual media increases costs as well, especially in statewide races for governor, attorney general, and other executive branch posts. These costs are particularly acute in such states as Texas and California, where there are several television markets.

As noted earlier in the chapter, gubernatorial contests routinely run into the millions of dollars. It is also not unusual for competitive state legislative races, even in small states, to cost each candidate in excess of $50,000. In the 1988 elections in California, for instance, each winning state senate candidate reportedly spent an average of $277,000, and house winners averaged $190,000 each. Incumbents enter races with a major advantage; not only do they enjoy name familiarity with the voters, but they also receive a disproportionate amount of PAC campaign contributions.

In one sense many state-level campaigns are run year-round, just as they are in Congress. The modernization or "professionalization" of state legislatures, the growing importance of the office of governor, and the reduced limitations on the ability of governors to succeed themselves in office together have increased the attractiveness of state elective offices.

Incumbent Self-Promotion: An Endless Campaign

In the legislatures the pay is better than it used to be, the staff help is more abundant, and the physical surroundings are much improved. More state legislators are making elective office a career, or at least a longer-run enterprise, and more governors are seeking reelection.

Not surprisingly, state officeholders use the resources available to them while in office to promote themselves politically and to solidify their base for subsequent elections. Incumbents engage in extensive constituent casework; indeed, they seek it. Newsletters and questionnaires are mailed, each one conveniently pushing the incumbent's name, often a photograph as well, into voters' homes. Notes are mailed by the thousands congratulating constituents and their children on everything from receipt of a scholarship or job promotion to victory in the state wrestling tournament. Each note, too, gets the politician's name into someone's house. Local newspapers carry notices inviting citizens to have coffee and chat with the officeholder in local restaurants on Saturday mornings. Few people may show up, but the notice gains the desired publicity.

The increased desire by incumbents to continue in office is the stimulant for the modern so-called **endless campaign**; the expanded availability of staff, money, and other resources provides the means. These are not, of course, the kinds of things a competent representative should be addressing in the course of representing a constituency; nonetheless, they contribute mightily to an incumbent's advantage.

Similarly, incumbent governors can use the office for political self-promotion, albeit not with exactly the same tactics employed by legislators. As chief executives, governors are positioned to develop and maintain a high public profile. Legislatures, the press, and the attentive public await the unveiling of the governor's policy initiatives. The governor can command statewide attention with a news conference or an announcement at a moment's notice. The governor's activities—public, social, and personal—make news. The ability to stay in the public eye works greatly to the political advantage of the incumbent state chief executive. Thus, it is not surprising that incumbent governors who seek reelection are successful nearly nine times out of ten. Though long in existence at the national level, a career-oriented political class is now emerging at the state level as well.

The Challenger's Dilemma

Given the growth in state-level political careerism, the decline of the political party, and the growth in PAC monies targeted primarily at incumbents, state contests have become increasingly less competitive. Incumbents almost always win, and many legislative seats go uncontested. Alan Rosenthal, a leading authority on state politics, notes that the success rate of incumbents in state legislative races is now well over 90 percent, and that most seats are now safe for one party or the other.[11] In addition, the number of competitive seats continues to decline.

Challengers thus face overwhelming odds. They generally lack name familiarity with the voters. To gain it, they must spend money, but most campaign donations go to incumbents. Challengers need people to help them, but it is generally the incumbent, not the challenger, who has paid staff. State-paid staffers are not supposed to work directly on campaigns, but the act of helping a constituent with a problem or of providing information to someone is, in itself, a boost to the officeholder.

Modern reforms have diminished the political party as a source of support to challengers as well. It is no wonder, then, that many state legislative seats go unchallenged. The minority party in these circumstances often has difficulty even finding a candidate willing to run against an entrenched incumbent.

Hence, the mix of careerism, modernized state legislatures, PAC campaign funding, and weakened political parties makes state contests increasingly less competitive. Some argue that incumbency has replaced political party affiliation as the major cue for voters. This does not mean, however, that incumbent officeholders are completely free of political risk. Some do lose. In 1990, for example, incumbent governors in Florida, Michigan, Nebraska, and Kansas all lost reelection. But these are the exceptions, not the rule.

Sophisticated Campaign Strategies

Modern state campaigns are more sophisticated than ever before. Candidates use polling and focus groups to identify supporters, opponents, and campaign positions. They track, sometimes on a daily basis, voters' feelings on selected issues and then adjust their campaign agendas accordingly. Literature is prepared for various segments of the voting public, with different messages targeted to groups characterized by gender, race, age, or interest in particular issues, for example. Similarly, radio and television advertising is tailored to the voter responses and preferences gauged by polling.

The type, the timing, and the locality of an election may also affect the nature of the campaign strategy that candidates pursue. In a statewide race for governor or attorney general, for instance, candidates have to organize statewide and seek support from party regulars in all or most counties. They need a rather sizable campaign staff. Campaigning is expensive, for candidates have to advertise in newspapers with statewide distribution as well as in local papers. They need expensive spot advertisements on metropolitan radio stations. They have to purchase television time. In their appeals to the voter, candidates seek not only to create an identity for themselves and demonstrate that their platform differs from those of their opponents; they also seek to make clear the distinctions between their own political party and that of the opposition.

The situation differs somewhat in contests for state house and state senate seats. Here, the district may be located in a metropolitan, suburban, or rural area, and this influences choice of campaign strategy. In an urban or metropolitan area, candidates have to pursue strategies similar to those used by candidates for statewide office, such as purchasing the advertising services of the major newspapers, the expensive radio stations, and television. In rural areas, however, candidates find advertisements in major newspapers and on radio and television of limited use. Instead, they concentrate their efforts in the local, less expensive media. Since state legislative contests are partisan in nature (except in Nebraska), candidates work cooperatively with the local county party organizations. Although the candidates cannot depend on the party organizations for extensive help with funding or staffing, they can turn to the parties for relevant information, such as voter registration lists, the names of previous political donors, and the like.

The situation is different still in most local elections. Here, the political party usually is absent. Although a candidate's known affiliation with a party may bring in some votes on election day, the political parties do not play a major or formal role in local elections. In addition, campaign strategies are directly affected by the low voter turnout typical of such elections. Therefore, with the parties absent and voter participation low, the candidate for local office must be careful to target that small group of community influentials who do vote. Media blitzes targeting large areas are not an option—they cost too much and may cover areas the candidate does not need to reach. Some local media coverage is necessary to develop and maintain a presence in the election, and in this radio advertising often plays a key role. Door-to-door campaigning is important, as it is in all elections. Especially critical in local campaigns is careful targeting of the probable voters. In addition, contact with business associations, appearances at service club meetings, block work in communities with high voter participation, and a good public image—that of a community regular and a solid and moderate person—are all essential to a candidate's success in a local election.

The shape of U.S. institutions is reflected in American politics. The system is highly decentralized, with thousands of governments. Most of these jurisdictions conduct elections, but they differ in size, function, political character, and internal organization.

Campaigns Reflect U.S. Institutions and Politics

All 50 states feature partisan, statewide contests for governor, 49 states have partisan races for members of two-house legislatures (Nebraska is the one exception), and over half of the states have elections for judges (some of them are partisan and others are nonpartisan). In addition, the local contests in most states are nonpartisan. Special districts and school districts feature races for policy bodies only, for they hire their chief executive. Some city races may be hotly contested, whereas in some small towns public service is viewed not as a prize but as a public duty.

In terms of competitiveness, partisanship, voter turnout, and many other respects, therefore, extensive variety exists in the American electoral system. (Chapters 11 and 12 examine in greater detail local elections and community power and politics, respectively.)

DIRECT DEMOCRACY

Although the American political system is widely viewed as a **democracy**—one based on the direct participation of voters—in large measure it is really more of a *representative* democracy. Most policy choices are made by representatives, not directly by the citizens. Most ballots cast by voters are for their representatives, rather than direct expressions of voter preferences on specific issues. However, the voters do, in some instances, participate directly in policy choices. The processes that provide for their direct participation include the referendum and the citizen initiative. Such processes are forms of **direct democracy**.

The Referendum

The **referendum** is a measure by which legislation is submitted to the people for their approval. If they vote against the measure, it does not become law. Most referenda are "referred" to voters by their representatives. In some instances, however, a referendum may be initiated by citizens. By way of a petition, citizens may oppose a decision made by some board or legislature by forcing the matter to be referred to voters.

Most referenda are at the local level, in cities and school districts especially, though they occur at the state level as well. Examples include elections on whether to approve city issuance of bonds (borrowing) for building a new stadium, civic center, or park or for resurfacing streets. Communities have held elections to decide such matters as whether to allow eating and drinking establishments to serve mixed drinks, whether to fluoridate municipal water, and whether to preserve environmentally sensitive areas. Recently, there has been a spate of referenda concerning gay rights at both the state and local levels. School districts frequently go directly to the voters, seeking approval of borrowed funds to build additional schools or of increases in the property tax to support annual operating budgets.

Matters may be referred to the voters because a city council or school board wants a showing of public support for a decision that it could by law make on its own. Other times, state law, local ordinances, or local charter provisions require direct voter approval. Borrowing against anticipated tax revenues, for example, often requires direct voter approval. The laws in almost all states provide for the referendum process, but they vary in their applicability as well as to whether they are required by state statutes or local charters and ordinances.[12]

Hardly an American voter will go very long without participating in a referendum. Over the years all of us are sure to be asked to approve, for example, a small municipal tax increase to build a new library, a temporary special district tax to help pay for a new football or baseball stadium, or a slight increase in the property tax to prevent teacher layoffs and school closings.

On occasion, decisions are referred to the voters because councils, boards, or legislatures want to avoid political controversy. Claiming "the right of the citizens to decide," legislatures may avoid taking the blame for approving such controversial measures as abortion, a tax increase, or an ambitious and costly transportation plan. In the 1992 elections, for example, national attention focused on state attempts to restrict gay rights in Oregon and Colorado. The former attempt failed; the success of the latter precipitated a call for a convention boycott in that state. In addition, specific groups that oppose a decision made by a legislature, council, or board can employ the petition process to force the matter onto the ballot.

Many fundamental institutional decisions must, by law, be referred to the voters, including the approval of amendments to state constitutions and city charters. Although such voter involvements are not always characterized as "referenda," they do constitute referrals to the people for direct participation in important decisions.

The Citizen Initiative

The **citizen initiative** is similar to the referendum in that it involves direct voter action. However, unlike most referenda, which begin with a referral by elected officials, the initiative begins with action by citizens. The laws in 21 states provide for the initiative. Although the procedures vary considerably, the basic steps of the process are similar.[13]

Citizens may organize interest groups when they want a law passed or repealed or a state constitution or city charter amended. They may draft their proposal, have it reviewed and approved for proper wording by a specified state body, and secure a certain number of valid signatures on a petition. The number of signatures required varies greatly among the states, ranging from 3 percent to 10 percent of the number of votes cast in some specified preceding election. In Oregon, for example, a number equal to 6 percent or 8 percent of the votes cast in the previous gubernatorial election is required; 6 percent is needed to initiate election on a proposed state statute, and 8 percent for a proposed state constitutional amendment. If the required number of signatures is obtained by a deadline set in law, and the signatures are found to be valid, the measure is then placed on the ballot at the upcoming election.

An Old American Practice

Some form of direct democracy has always played a role in the American political experience. State constitutions, for example, have always been referred to voters for ratification. But the citizen initiative is of more recent origin and is not permitted by all of the states. Its use occurs disproportionately in the West.

The citizen initiative, the referendum, and the **recall** (a process by which voters may remove an elected official from office before the end of his or her term) are in large measure the products of the Populist and Progressive movements of the late nineteenth and early twentieth centuries. Those were decades of extensive and intertwined corruption in both business and government. Unregulated business activity made poor laborers out of millions and multimillionaires of a few. Big money bought and sold politicians and public decisions.

Reformers' Reactions to Bad Government   Populist and Progressive reformists' reactions to the conditions of corrupt government took the form of direct democracy as a means to bypass and recall corrupt elected officials. Hence, there emerged the initiative, the referendum, and the recall. During the Populist and Progressive period, many midwestern and western states were new to the Union or just then seeking statehood. These states picked up the reforms then in vogue and made them a part of their fundamental laws and processes.

The Initiative: A Rediscovered Political Tactic   Although the initiative process was used extensively after its initial development in the early 1900s, it was employed only sparingly for decades thereafter. In the 1970s, however, it was rediscovered as a political tool, by single-issue proponents and tax-limit advocates especially. By the 1990s there was a virtual explosion in the number of citizen-initiated measures facing voters. The number of ballot initiatives had not been as high since 1932.[14] California's tax-limiting Proposition 13, approved by voters in 1978, is the best-known modern-day initiative effort. It inspired similar tax-limiting initiatives in several other states.

By November 1990, while some states continued to receive tax-limit initiatives, many other initiatives were addressing a wide variety of policy areas. There were 67 such measures in all in that year, dealing with pesticide control, prison construction, gambling, abortion, food taxes, marijuana use penalties, term limitations for elected officials, ozone depletion, and other issues.

The recent increase in citizen initiatives is the result of several factors. Single-issue groups have discovered the potential of the initiative. The prolife movement, for example, unable to achieve its policy desires through legislatures, can appeal directly to the voters. Environmentalists interested in instituting controls on chemical use or encouraging glass reuse by means of bottle-deposit incentives do the same. Those who want to reduce the scope of government employ the initiative to try to limit taxes. In addition, a whole industry has emerged to support initiative efforts. Firms can be hired to gather signatures for interest groups and to run the supportive public relations and propaganda campaigns once the measures make it to the ballot.

IS DIRECT DEMOCRACY GOOD GOVERNMENT?

The growth in citizen lawmaking has become a matter of controversy in and of itself. Some argue that, because lawmakers can be insensitive and unresponsive, it is important for citizens to have access to a mechanism through which they can affect public policy directly. Indeed, the initiative, recall, and referendum were developed for precisely this reason. Besides, what could be more democratic than direct citizen control over public choices?

Critics contend, however, that the initiative process can lead to bad and poorly constructed law because citizen input is often uninformed. Virtually all legislation relates to other laws on the books and has complicated repercussions. Limitations on one tax, for example, are likely to have impacts on other taxes. Further, tax limits at the state level have a host of consequences for cities, counties, and schools, as well as for state programs themselves. The campaigns for and against the various initiatives and referenda now take on all the trappings of modern elections, with slick 30-second soundbite commercials that may do less to inform viewers than to appeal to their emotions.

The long-term consequences of direct democracy sometimes are intimidating. In 1992, for instance, Colorado voters approved the so-called Taxpayers' Bill of Rights (TABOR). Although taxing and spending are now limited in Colorado, no one—not the governor nor the legislature nor the people—is sure exactly how or by how much. Under any circumstances, the budgeting process is complicated; but when the normal institutional processes are mixed in with popular control, no one can predict the outcome. It is important, therefore, to explore carefully all potential ramifications of any proposed new law. That is what committee and floor action does in legislative bodies, but that is not what occurs when proposed new laws are placed directly on the ballot. Unfortunately, not all voters may educate themselves fully before voting on ballot questions.

In addition, critics contend that big money interests often outspend opponents in supporting or opposing a measure, and thus the public is further deprived of a balanced view of the issue. Bottle companies and the insurance industry, for example, spend millions to quash initiatives that they believe will hurt them financially. Big money does not always determine the outcome, but it almost always distorts the picture.

California is the leader among the states in the use of the citizen initiative. In 1988 California voters faced 29 such measures on topics ranging from AIDS testing to cigarette taxes and including five separate and somewhat contradictory proposals related to automobile insurance.[15] Neal Pierce comments on the task facing the voters in this blizzard of measures: "If you plan to vote in California this week, you might bring along a sleeping bag—and some rations."[16]

There is, clearly, a trade-off to be made with direct democracy. Ultimately, citizens must retain the authority to structure their governments and choose their policies. But must the exercise of that authority be direct, and, if the answer is yes, must it have the potential to be applied to all policy questions? Does the extensive use of direct democracy invite voters to make mistakes? Does it keep government more in tune with the public? There are no correct answers to these questions. Thomas Cronin expresses the sentiments of some scholars when, in the introduction to his extensive study of direct democracy, he states: "Although my heart tends to side with populism, my head is skeptical about the workability and desirability of direct democracy devices."[17]

Summary

In no area of American politics is the diversity of the states as well represented as in the election systems. Election systems vary from state to state, within states, and from office to office. Elections vary in terms of partisanship, function, and turnout. Statewide races are usually partisan; local races are usually not. Turnout tends to be directly related to ballot position; the higher the office being filled, the higher the turnout. The use of direct democracy methods—the initiative, the referendum and the recall—has added to the number and types of elections held each year.

KEY TERMS

primary election
general election
motor-voter law
one person, one vote
candidate-centered campaign

endless campaign
direct democracy
referendum
citizen initiative
recall

ADDITIONAL READINGS

Dionne, E. J., Jr. *Why Americans Hate Politics.* New York: Simon and Schuster, 1991.

McNitt, Andrew. "The Impact of State Legislation on Political Campaigns." *State Government* (Summer 1980): 135–39.

National Civic League. *A Model Election System.* New York: NCL, 1973.

Salmore, Barbara G., and Stephen A. Salmore. *Candidates, Parties, and Campaigns.* Washington, D.C.: Congressional Quarterly Press, 1989.

NOTES

1. See *The Book of the States, 1990–91* (Lexington, Ky.: Council of State Governments, 1991), pp. 237–60.

2. Center for the American Woman and Politics, "The Gender Gap" (factsheet) (New Brunswick: Eagleton Institute of Politics, Rutgers University, July 1987).

3. Center for the American Woman and Politics, "Women in Elective Office" (factsheet) (New Brunswick: Eagleton Institute of Politics, Rutgers University, July 1988); Karl T. Kurtz, "The Election in Perspective," *State Legislatures* (Jan. 1993): 16–19; and Rob Gurwitt, "Legislatures: The Faces of Change," *Governing* (Feb. 1993): 28–32.

4. R. Darcy, Susan Welch, and Janet Clark, *Women, Elections and Representation* (New York: Longman, 1987).

5. Center for the American Woman and Politics, "Elective Office."

6. Darcy, Welch, and Clark, *Women*; and Karen Beckwith, *American Women and Political Parties* (New York: Greenwood Press, 1986).

7. Kenneth Mladenka, "Blacks and Hispanics in Urban Politics," *American Political Science Review* (March 1989): 165–92.

8. Center for the American Woman and Politics, "Elective Office."

9. Barbara G. Salmore and Stephen A. Salmore, "The Transformation of State Electoral Politics," in *The State of the States*, ed. Carl E. Van Horn (Washington, D.C.: Congressional Quarterly Press, 1989), pp. 175–208; and Alan Rosenthal, "The Legislative Institution—in Transition and at Risk," in *The State of the States*, 2nd ed., ed. Carl E. Van Horn (Washington, D.C.: Congressional Quarterly Press, 1993).

10. Bob Benenson, "Changing Money's Role Is No Easy Task," *Congressional Quarterly Weekly Report* (4 Nov. 1989): 2,987.

11. Rosenthal, "The Legislative Institution."

12. David D. Schmidt, *Citizen Lawmakers* (Philadelphia: Temple University Press, 1989).

13. Schmidt, *Citizen Lawmakers;* Thomas E. Cronin, *Direct Democracy* (Cambridge, Mass.: Harvard University Press, 1989); and *The Book of the States, 1990–91*, pp. 267–76.

14. Robert Pear, "Number of Ballot Initiatives Is the Greatest since 1932," *New York Times*, 5 Nov. 1990.

15. Neal Pierce, "Ballot Initiatives Run Amok: A Warning from California," *Denver Post*, 6 Nov. 1988.

16. Ibid.

17. Cronin, *Direct Democracy*, p. x.

10
The American Metropolis

One of the most famous urban redevelopment projects: the Renaissance Center in Detroit, Michigan. Does the Center improve the city or only emphasize the city's problems? *(John Maher/Stock, Boston)*

POPULATION SHIFTS IN THE UNITED STATES
From Rural to Urban / From Urban to Suburban

SOME CONSEQUENCES OF THE POPULATION SHIFTS
Racial Segregation / Urban Struggles / Economic Segregation /
Fragmented Government / *FOCUS 10.1:* Avoiding Annexation in Portage Township

PROBLEMS ASSOCIATED WITH FRAGMENTATION AND
SUBURBANIZATION
Jurisdictional Inequities / Intergovernmental Conflict / Planning
Difficulties / Financial Trouble for Core Cities / Other Problems

BENEFITS OF SUBURBANIZATION

EXTREME PROPOSALS FOR REFORM
Consolidation / *FOCUS 10.2:* Abolish the Suburbs? / The Metropolitan
Federation

MODEST PROPOSALS FOR REFORM
Annexation / Intergovernmental Service Agreements / The Lakewood
Plan / Metropolitan Councils of Government

THE POLITICS OF METROPOLITAN REFORM
Reform Sounds Rational / People Want a Choice / The Law Favors
the Status Quo / Supporters versus Opponents

THE DOWNSIDE OF THE METROPOLITAN SCHEME
Communities Want Local Control / A Clash of Values

FUTURE TRENDS
Radical Reform Is Unlikely / Urban Villages / A Divided Nation?

SUMMARY

What exactly does it mean when a man who says he is from Dallas meets a woman who claims she lives in Los Angeles? Does the man really live in Dallas, or does he just say that to avoid having to explain where Garland, or Irving, or Grand Prairie, or Arlington, or another Dallas suburb is located? And is the woman from Los Angeles, or is her home really in nearby Inglewood, Burbank, or Santa Monica? It probably doesn't make much difference to the two of them anyway, because they may not at the moment be worrying about zoning restrictions, property taxes, or an upcoming municipal election.

But to many people and in many circumstances it does matter. Dallas is not Garland and Los Angeles is not Burbank. These are separate governments with separate mayors, councils, zoning and taxing laws, and each with its own police, fire, sewer, and water services. Metropolitan America is literally strewn with governments. The Los Angeles, Chicago, New York, and Kansas City areas each sport literally hundreds of individual cities, not to mention scores of school districts and special districts and dozens of counties. This means that a lot of people have the chance to be mayor or to sit on a school board. It also means that the quality and quantity of public services varies from one place to another, and that planning for regionwide transportation, land use, and pollution abatement is hard to accomplish.

POPULATION SHIFTS IN THE UNITED STATES

From Rural to Urban   Both the absolute and proportionate increases in the **urbanization** of the U.S. population over the past two centuries have been astounding. The U.S. population grew from just over 3 million people in 1790 to over 250 million today. In the twentieth century alone it more than doubled. In addition to its absolute growth, the urban population rose from just over 5 percent in 1790 to well over 70 percent in 1990 (see Figure 10.1). The bulk of the populace is now crowded into urban areas, with extremely high concentrations found along the Atlantic and Pacific coasts, along the southern edge of Lake Michigan, and in a few other locations. Over 18 million people reside in the New York metropolitan area, over 13.5 million in the Los Angeles area, 8.1 million in metropolitan Chicago, and almost 6 million in the Philadelphia metropolitan region.[1]

Critical factors underlying the dramatic growth in urbanization include technology and public policy. Modern technology greatly increased economies of scale on the farm, making it possible for fewer people to produce the needed food and fiber and driving the overhead and capital costs of farming upward. In 1840 the average farmer could produce enough food to feed 3.95 people; by 1972 the farmer could grow enough food for 52.4 persons. Similarly, the average farm covered 147 acres in 1920 but 461 acres in 1990. The larger farms generally meant more mechanization to work them, and so the demand for agricultural

FIGURE 10.1
Urban Dwellers as a Percentage of the U.S. Population, 1790–1990

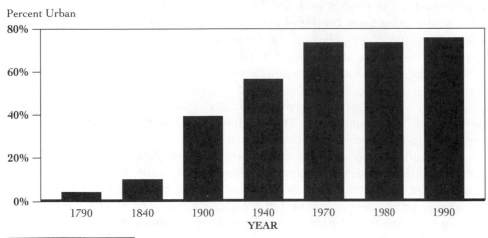

Percent Urban

source: U.S. Bureau of the Census, *Statistical Abstract of the United States* (Washington, D.C.: GPO, various years).

labor was greatly reduced. Thus, large numbers of people moved to the cities in search of work. Whereas in 1920 about 30 percent of the U.S. population lived on farms, only 2 percent resided there in 1987.[2]

Technology Technology produced a **factory-based economy** that served to attract people to the cities. The advancing technology of the nineteenth and twentieth centuries gave rise to an economy based on specialized labor and mass production. Steel mills, automobile plants, shoe factories, and garment mills sprung up in many urban areas. The mass production of the factory, in turn, gave rise to the physical concentration of people. The available transportation systems were such that workers had to live close to their jobs. Thus, the factory also encouraged the growth of urban centers.

Public Policy Certain government policies encouraged the massive migration from farms to cities. For decades, the national and state governments had used public funds to subsidize agricultural research. A number of states supported large agricultural and engineering universities, whose impetus was the early federal land grants. Through the U.S. Department of Agriculture, the federal government supported a network of agricultural experiment stations, an economic research service that focused on agriculture, and a nationwide extension service that disseminated the knowledge of these research-related agencies. Today, these federally supported units are commonly housed within the land grant universities, such as Texas A&M University and the University of California at Davis.

The knowledge produced and disseminated by publicly financed research, in turn, greatly increased the productivity of American agriculture and triggered the trend toward larger, highly mechanized, and more expensive farms. It also contributed to the exodus from the farm.

At the same time, the rapid growth of big business was accelerated by a desire to maintain a viable national economy and the government's refusal to interfere in economic affairs. Giant corporations sprang up in textiles, oil, automobiles, the media, and dozens of other areas. These huge enterprises, based on the mass production and distribution of goods, located in the major urban areas. They provided employment for millions of displaced farm workers as well as newly arrived immigrants. Thus, public policy in regard to the economy helped to initiate and sustain the urban migration.

In addition, publicly built streets, sewers, and water systems, as well as publicly supported services such as police and fire protection and mass transportation, made the big cities livable. The working and living conditions were not always attractive and pleasant in America's growing cities of the nineteenth and early twentieth centuries, but public policy in regard to basic services made them viable.

From Urban to Suburban

No sooner had the nation experienced a massive migration to urban centers than a new migration began—this one from the cities to the suburbs. Whereas in the mid-1800s the United States was a rural nation and by the turn of the century it was well on its way to becoming an industrialized, urbanized nation-state, during the mid-1900s millions of American families were moving to the fringes of the large cities in a move toward **suburbanization**.

The magnitude of the move to suburbia was, and still is, staggering. The rapid growth of the cities began to slacken after World War II, giving way to the growth in suburban areas. Between 1950 and 1960, nine of the nation's ten largest cities, including Baltimore, Boston, and Chicago, lost population despite nationwide population growth. Of the 10 largest cities, only Houston experienced population growth during this decade, largely as a result of extensive annexation of fringe areas.

The data in Figures 10.2 and 10.3 demonstrate the trend toward suburbia. While the national population grew by nearly 20 percent from 1950 to 1960, the suburbs (the portion of the metropolitan statistical area that is outside the central city limits) grew by more than 45 percent, and the central cities grew by just slightly over 10 percent. (A **metropolitan statistical area**, or **MSA**, includes a county with a central city whose population is at least 50,000 and the urbanized area of surrounding counties.) In the following decade, suburban growth slackened somewhat, though the growth ratios remained relatively stable. Looking at the thirty-year period of 1950 to 1980, the data in Figure 10.3 show that the

FIGURE 10.2
U.S. Population by Decade, 1950–1990 (in millions)

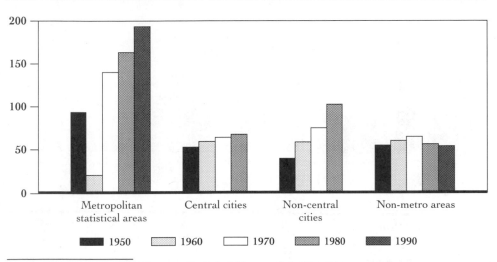

SOURCE: U.S. Bureau of the Census, *Statistical Abstract of the United States, 1981* and *1992* (Washington, D.C.: GPO, 1981, 1992), pp. 16 and 29, respectively.

population grew in central cities by about 14 million and in suburban areas by 60 million. In 1980 suburbanites outnumbered central city dwellers at 101.5 million and 67.9 million, respectively. More recent population estimates indicate a continuation of this trend; the suburban population is still growing and many central cities are still losing population. For example, in 1960, cities of 500,000 or more inhabitants had 24.7 percent of this country's population; in 1990 they had 19.6 percent of the population.

Technology Continues to Advance   While technological advances such as the automobile, radio, telephone, and mass-produced housing made the spread to suburbia possible, a number of public policies encouraged it. The massive state and federal investment in the interstate highway system, with its extensive network of metropolitan expressways, made it possible for millions of workers to commute from outlying suburbs to core cities. Without the expressways it would not have been feasible to travel 20, 30, or even 50 miles to work, as millions began to do.

Public Policy Continues to Broaden   Federal government support of the spread of consumer credit helped make it possible for millions of families to purchase radios and television sets for communication, automobiles for com-

FIGURE 10.3   Percent Change in U.S. Population, 1950–1990

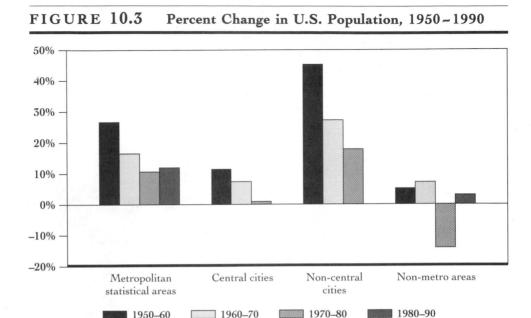

SOURCE: U.S. Bureau of the Census, *Statistical Abstract of the United States, 1981* and *1992* (Washington, D.C.: GPO, 1981, 1992), pp. 16 and 29, respectively.

muting, and, during the 1950s to early 1970s, single-unit suburban homes with small or no down payments. Through Veterans Administration and Federal Housing Administration insurance of home loans, millions of families were able to move into new suburban tract homes for just a few hundred dollars down. The banks were willing to make such loans largely because the federal government agreed to insure them.

The purchase of new suburban homes was made even more attractive to American families because the interest on the loans and the property taxes were deductible on federal income tax returns, as they are today. It was not unusual for middle-income families to have many thousands of dollars in tax deductions. In effect, the tax policies set in place subsidized middle-class homeowners and provided a boon to suburban developers.

Other Factors   Other factors also contributed to the rush to suburbia. While technology made it possible and government policies encouraged it, the more abundant space, the cleaner air, and the newness of suburbia, as well as the traditional American association of virtue with the small community, made it highly attractive. Many people came to associate the large city with high crime rates, dirty streets, dirty air, old housing, and undesirable types of people. The suburb, in contrast, was perceived by many as having clean air, green grass, lower taxes, "nonpolitical" local government, good schools, and a more congenial living environment generally. Of course, sometimes these assessments were accurate and sometimes they were not.

SOME CONSEQUENCES OF THE POPULATION SHIFTS

The consequences of the massive population shifts have been enormous. Urbanization has brought serious problems, including slum housing, a need for land use control, unemployment, sewer and water service difficulties, insufficient police and fire protection, smog, crime, and a host of others. The spread to the suburbs has created difficulties in land use, ethnic distribution, taxation, transportation, and environmental pollution.

Racial Segregation

The movement to the suburbs has contributed significantly to ethnic and economic segregation, for not everyone can afford to live in suburbia. Doing so usually involves home ownership, a down payment to purchase a home, numerous expenses associated with such housing, at least one automobile, and the ability to make steady payments on home and automobile loans. These are obstacles for a large portion of the middle-income class and virtually insurmountable problems for the lower-income class. Since a disproportionate number of ethnic minorities fall in the lower-income category, the practical result is continued segregation of minorities in the core cities and of middle- and upper-class whites in the suburbs.

There have been political consequences of the racial division in the nation's urban areas. As the minority populations grew between the 1960s and the 1980s, many cities came under their political control. As a result, African-Americans gained a political base from which to seek to influence the policies of the states and the national government. Demands for social programs designed to address urban issues such as poverty, education, and employment are expected to continue.

Urban Struggles

The nation's cities are increasingly in trouble. The disproportionately large numbers of city dwellers who fall into the lower categories in terms of income, education, and job status mean that, as the need urban social services and the costs of city government increase, the capacity of the urban population to pay the bill is likely to decline relative to both costs and national wealth.

Given the heavy reliance of local government on the property tax, the cities are likely to continue to face a cost-revenue squeeze, further aggravated by recent cuts in federal funding and in some states, such as California, Colorado, and Massachusetts, by state tax and spending limits as well. Some argue that alterations in the tax base of local governments and continued state and federal assistance are needed to bail the cities out of their financial dilemma.

Economic Segregation

Suburbia also tends to segregate people of all races according to their economic status. Most tract housing developments provide homes in a given price range, with little variation. It is this sort of standardized mass development, however, that made the single-unit structure economically feasible for many in the 1950s and later.

The price of housing in any given suburban area tends to vary only slightly, though there are numerous exceptions. Such standardization, in turn, has led to the development of many communities that are homogeneous in terms of residents' income, occupation, age, and life-style. While this may or may not be good, its impact on ethnic and economic segregation is clear.

Fragmented Government

Suburbanization has had a tremendous impact on the pattern of government organization in metropolitan areas. In particular, the outward expansion has led to the development of new government units. In many metropolitan areas today, there are hundreds of cities, school districts, and special districts. For example, more than 1,000 units of government exist within the Chicago metropolitan area; the San Francisco–Oakland and St. Louis areas each have around 400; Denver, Los Angeles, Detroit, Kansas City, and Newark each have in excess of 300; and the Phoenix and Boston areas each have over 100. These examples represent the norm in most metropolitan areas.

A slight increase in the number of special districts and a dramatic decline in the number of school districts nationwide were observed between 1952 and 1987 (see Figure 10.4). The number of school districts declined due to the massive consolidations promoted by state governments, made possible by increased use of the school bus, road improvements, and more specialized and expensive instruction.

But why, as urban centers spread out into the hinterland, did new cities and special districts emerge? Why didn't the existing core cities extend their legal boundaries outward to include the developing suburbs? And why did the legal boundaries of local governments develop in ways that do not reflect social and economic realities? The answers to these questions are complex, involving the nature of state law, the behavior of central city governments, and the preferences of suburban residents. In terms of state law, for example, in most states it was easier for a new suburban area to secure a charter from the state and thus to **incorporate**—that is, become a new city—than it was for an existing central city to annex the new suburb (see Focus 10.1). As new housing

FIGURE 10.4
Number of Local Governments in the United States, 1952–1987 (in thousands)

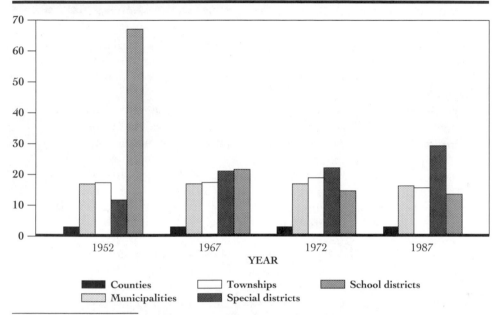

SOURCE: U.S. Bureau of the Census, *Statistical Abstract of the United States* (Washington, D.C.: GPO, various years).

developments sprang up in the suburbs, the existing core cities found it financially impossible to supply the new areas with water, sewer, police, and fire protection services. Therefore, to secure these necessary services, the residents of some suburban areas sought the status of a city, which would permit them to tax, borrow, and spend in order to provide needed services. Once a suburban area gained city status through incorporation, the core city found it virtually impossible to annex it. Most states' laws today require a majority vote at the polls in both the central city and the suburban area for **annexation** (in which a city expands by taking in more territory) or **consolidation** (in which two or more units of government are joined).

However, in many cases developers or residents of suburban areas wanted neither annexation by an existing core city nor the formation of a new municipality—and so they created special districts instead. A **special district** is a single-function unit of local government, established under state law. Examples include fire protection districts, hospital districts, and water districts, among numerous others. Through a special district, residents of an area can create a government and empower it to tax, borrow, and spend in order to provide a service. There has been significant growth in the number of special districts in recent decades, and it has further complicated the fragmented nature of government.

10.1 AVOIDING ANNEXATION IN PORTAGE TOWNSHIP

In states that allow cities to annex unincorporated suburban areas without the consent of those affected, it is not uncommon for suburban residents to seek incorporation for the purpose of avoiding annexation.

In the early 1960s Portage Township, a suburban area located to the south of Kalamazoo, Michigan, took action to gain city status through incorporation and thereby avoid annexation by Kalamazoo. The Upjohn pharmaceutical firm, an extremely large enterprise and a major source of property tax revenues for Kalamazoo, had at that time decided to relocate from downtown Kalamazoo to an area in what was then part of Portage Township. Thus, the city of Kalamazoo acted to annex the suburb so as not to lose the tax revenues generated by Upjohn.

However, the residents of Portage objected and town officials initiated an incorporation campaign, for once Portage obtained city status, an independent majority vote at the polls in both Portage and Kalamazoo would be required for annexation. Portage successfully attained city status before Kalamazoo could annex the area. It also won at the polls, allowing Portage to maintain its independence from Kalamazoo and to capture the valuable tax revenues from the relocated pharmaceutical firm.

PROBLEMS ASSOCIATED WITH FRAGMENTATION AND SUBURBANIZATION

Jurisdictional Inequities   The jurisdictional fragmentation created by suburbanization has led to a number of problems. For example, because the legal boundaries of metropolitan area governments do not reflect the location and distribution of various urban problems, it is increasingly difficult to consolidate solutions to problems in such areas as air and water pollution, mass transit, housing, and land use planning. These problems typically span entire metropolitan areas yet no single government has the jurisdiction or the resources to deal with them adequately.

In addition, considerable inequity exists among the jurisdictions in levels of taxation and quality of services. Some cities and school districts have within their legal boundaries manufacturing plants, shopping centers, or other sources of commercial tax revenue that increase the amount they can spend on public services. Other areas do not have a strong commercial tax base, so they must place a heavier tax burden on the homeowner or offer inferior public services.

Intergovernmental Conflict

Jurisdictional fragmentation often leads to intergovernmental squabbles over various issues, such as the annexation of prime tax-producing property. It is not unusual for two or more cities or school districts to seek the annexation of a piece of land following the construction of a new plant or business. Although each government unit's interest in increasing its tax base is understandable, the wrangling that such battles precipitate can affect intergovernmental relations in other areas of potential cooperation.

In many cases jurisdictional conflicts extend to the state level. For example, suburban and rural coalitions may oppose blocs of urban representatives on issues related to transportation, taxation, natural resources, and other measures.

Planning Difficulties

It is difficult to plan effectively in jurisdictionally atomized areas. In most metropolitan areas, dozens of cities, school districts, county governments, water and sewer districts, and other units all make decisions that can affect transit, housing, or air quality, for example. Yet each government unit must respond to a slightly different constituency, each has a somewhat unique set of functions and problems, and each has its own difficulties in regard to tax resources, the demands placed on it, and state restrictions. Thus, the decision makers in each government unit tend to respond to their immediate and proximate pressures; they have neither the time nor the resources to focus on longer-range, comprehensive problems.

Financial Trouble for Core Cities

Today's core cities are in great financial trouble. The massive movement to the suburbs has eroded the tax base of central cities. In general, the wealthy moved to the suburbs and those in the lower income brackets remained in urban centers. Most new commercial and industrial development also followed the path to suburbia.

While the costs to the central cities for police and fire protection, public assistance, and other public services have increased, the most valuable revenue-producing commercial properties have left. The result is severe financial crisis in most of the largest U.S. cities.

Other Problems

There are other problems associated with fragmented government as well. In some areas inefficiency results from the provision of similar services by multiple small governments. Police and fire protection services, for example, may be provided by a host of amateur departments.

Neil Pierce, an astute scholar of urban America, sums up the problems of fragmented government in this way:

Americans are finding they have more and more governments, special authorities and agencies in their hair, but they are getting less and less governance that ties the problems together, sets priorities and comes up with coherent solutions on the level that counts—the region, our true, new city.[3]

BENEFITS OF SUBURBANIZATION

There are many obvious benefits to the suburban phenomenon. It has provided comfortable housing, good schools, and a pleasant life-style for millions of American families. Small local governments often provide citizens with greater access to their public officials. Jobs for millions of workers are provided by the housing and automobile industries.

However, the proliferation of governments in the suburbs continues to be the object of widespread criticism. Not surprisingly, there have been numerous proposals for jurisdictional reform, some of them extreme and others more modest.

EXTREME PROPOSALS FOR REFORM

Consolidation   Efforts at substantial reform, though psychologically appealing to some, have been unappealing to most and largely unsuccessful. These efforts have involved attempts to reduce the number of metropolitan area governments by consolidation of county government and several cities into a single government unit. Like city limits, however, county boundaries seldom encompass entire metropolitan areas, and thus even consolidation fails to include an entire socioeconomic region within one jurisdiction. Still, counties typically cover sizable portions of metropolitan areas; some argue that city–county consolidation would thus reduce jurisdictional atomization. (See Focus 10.2.)

City–county consolidation has proven ineffective as a means of metropolitan reform in most cases. There were local governmental mergers in New York, New Orleans, Boston, and Philadelphia in the 1800s, but these were accomplished by state legislatures. In the twentieth century, successful mergers included Baton Rouge, Louisiana; Nashville, Tennessee; and Jacksonville, Florida. But the failures far outnumber the successes. Since 1950 consolidation attempts have been frustrated in Newport News and Richmond, Virginia; Knoxville, Memphis, and Chattanooga, Tennessee; Macon and Columbus, Georgia; Albu-

---

FOCUS

10.2 ABOLISH THE SUBURBS?

Given the serious nature of the urban crisis, urbanist David Rusk, ex-mayor of Albuquerque, has proposed an extreme and potentially revolutionary solution—"abolish" the suburbs.

According to Rusk, the basic economic unit of the country is the metropolitan area, including both center city and suburbs. Allowing the suburbs to exist as separate economic units, he argues, denies the center cities the ability to grow and change—to become "elastic." Further, he sees this as the basic problem underlying today's declining center cities and growing suburbs. Rusk's strategy is aimed at bringing suburbs and the center city together as one economic unit, giving the latter some "elasticity." In addition, to overcome the political obstacles, he advises providing some sort of tax incentive to suburbanites. Rusk argues that his plan is a potential solution to the urban crisis.

SOURCE: Reported in Mickey Kaus, "City Limits," *New Republic* (3 May 1993): 6.

---

querque, New Mexico; Durham, North Carolina; St. Louis, Missouri; and Tampa, Florida. Even in Miami and Nashville defeat predated their later successes at city–county consolidation.[4]

A more recent, albeit partial, consolidation involved Indiana's Marion County and the city of Indianapolis; it is referred to as "unigov." But this alteration was put into place by the Indiana state legislature, with no local votes taken on the question. In the Miami area, the structure of Dade County was modernized through the use of a council–manager form of government, and the county's powers were expanded. The existing municipalities, however, remained intact.

Most city–county consolidation efforts have failed because the proposals did not gain a majority vote in both the core city and the outlying area. Often, the proposals were passed by urban dwellers but rejected by suburbanites. The factors contributing to this failure likely include many of the same factors that led to the exodus to suburbia initially—a desire to escape the crowds, crime, dirt, and politics of the core city and to gain such real or perceived suburban amenities as cleaner air, more space, lower taxes, better schools, prestige, and greater access to local government. Therefore, in theory consolidation may make sense to academics and planners concerned about symmetry, order, efficiency, and economy in government, but it apparently makes much less sense to the suburban voter.

The Metropolitan Federation   Another extreme approach to reform involves the formation of a metropolitan federation, though it too has been largely unsuccessful. The **metropolitan federation** involves the division of functions between government units. Although proposed for a number of U.S. cities, it has never succeeded in securing adoption. Proposals for the creation of a metropolitan federation failed in the Boston area to gain state legislative approval in 1896 and 1931, as well as in the Oakland, California, and San Francisco areas for various reasons. Federation proposals were either discussed or formally proposed but never adopted for the areas in and around Oakland and San Francisco, California; Pittsburgh, Pennsylvania; Miami, Florida; and St. Louis, Missouri. The best-known example of an operating metropolitan federation is Toronto, Canada.

Most U.S. states today have laws that permit some form of local consolidation, cooperation, or modernization. These statutes are intended to allow the voters to choose to form regional service authorities or to modernize county government, thereby better equipping local government to address modern urban-area problems and service needs. However, only in rare instances are such reforms actually instituted. Clearly, both the power of the existing arrangements and the broad public resistance to change are strong.

MODEST PROPOSALS FOR REFORM

Unlike the generally unsuccessful efforts at consolidation and metropolitan federation reform, which aim to alter substantially the shape of government in metropolitan America, there have been some successful reforms of a more modest, though slowly developing, nature. These include municipal annexations, intergovernmental service agreements, such as the Lakewood Plan, and metropolitan councils of government.

Annexation   Although core city annexation of surrounding suburbs does not entirely eliminate fragmentation from metropolitan-area government, it can in some instances provide an alternative to the creation of even more cities or special districts. When a city annexes land, it redraws its boundaries to include the new area. But annexation is not often easy, legally or politically. As noted earlier in the chapter, many states require approval of annexation by a majority of the voters in both the annexing city and the area to be annexed. Other states give the option of initiating the annexation process to the people in the affected outlying area. However, because many U.S. cities are already surrounded by other cities, there are only limited opportunities for annexation.

In a few states annexation may be accomplished without any action by residents of the city or the affected outlying area. For example, in Virginia annexation is done by an annexation court, and in Texas some city councils are empowered to annex territory. In addition, some states' legislation prohibits new incorporation within a certain distance from an existing city. In Arizona, for instance, no new cities may be formed within 6 miles of a city with over 5,000 people.

As observed earlier in the chapter, one of the criticisms of the fragmented organization of government in metropolitan America is the lack of efficiency in the provision of municipal services. Some critics contend that it would be less expensive and more efficient for public services, such as police and fire protection and sewer and water service, to be provided by fewer, but larger, government units. However, others point out that bigger governments may not necessarily lead to lower unit costs. In addition, the optimal size for all government units may not be the same or nearly so, for an efficiently sized government for police protection purposes may be far too small for an efficient water system.

Intergovernmental Service Agreements

The problem of government unit size and, in part, the political problems associated with the extreme reform proposals are mitigated by the more modest approach involving **intergovernmental service agreements**—contractual arrangements made between governments for the performance of public services. One government may sell its water or sewer services to another government. A city may purchase space at a county landfill or beds in a county jail. A city and a fire protection district may enter into a legal arrangement involving shared assistance. The approach permits governments to provide services to areas of various sizes. The area encompassed by a fire protection agreement, for example, may be either larger or smaller than an intergovernmental water-supply area.

Furthermore, intergovernmental service agreements do not entail extensive alteration of the status quo. They can be formed without threatening government employees' jobs, without eliminating some mayors' and council members' governments, and without long, abrasive election campaigns. However, such service agreements can legally complicate intergovernmental arrangements and make government more difficult for the citizen to understand and follow. In addition, they can make one government overly dependent on another, a situation that public officials tend not to favor.

The Lakewood Plan

The most extensive network of intergovernmental contractual arrangements is the so-called **Lakewood plan**, used in southern California to provide a variety of public services effectively and efficiently to more than 70 participating cities. The scheme involves the provision by Los Angeles County of over 40 different types of public services, including animal control, building inspection, fire protection, law enforcement, planning and zoning, street construction and maintenance, tax assessment and collection, and tree trimming. The participating cities can contract with the county for any package of services they desire.

Acquiring its name from the city of Lakewood, which in 1954 was the first city to enter into such an agreement with Los Angeles County, the Lakewood plan now involves contracts with most cities in the county for some or all of the available services. The participating cities benefit from their ability to maintain both their existence and a high level of service without massive capital investments in water, sewer, and other public services.

Although the Lakewood plan represents the most extensive example of intergovernmental service arrangements, such schemes are common throughout the nation. Some 63 percent of all U.S. cities have some type of service agreement with another unit of government, and well over 10 percent of those cities receive packages of services.

In short, extreme reform proposals aimed at dramatically restructuring government in metropolitan America are likely to continue to fail. The more moderate approach involving intergovernmental service agreements is a more politically feasible route to reform.

Metropolitan Councils of Government

Another modest reform proposal focuses on **metropolitan councils of government (COGs)**. These councils are not government units and, technically, do not rearrange the metropolitan government pattern. Further, they are not creatures of the state and they do not provide municipal-type functions (such as police and fire protection). Rather, COGs are composed of representatives from the local governments in an area and provide a forum for communication among governments and public officials. In addition, COG staffs study and report on areawide problems.

Prior to 1983, metropolitan councils of government were also involved in what was called the A-95 review process. Area governments reviewed and commented on applications for federal grants by local governments. The initial purpose of the A-95 process was to promote coordination, and to this end President Lyndon Johnson instructed the Office of Management and Budget (OMB) in 1965 to coordinate federal grant programs relating to metropolitan areas. OMB subsequently issued a series of circulars, including circular A-95, which required local government applicants for federal grants to have their proposals reviewed by areawide metropolitan planning bodies in order to improve planning and program coordination among local governments. When A-95 was issued, many metropolitan areas had no such areawide planning bodies, so they moved quickly to create councils of government. Some observers in Washington, D.C., in the states, and in the localities viewed the emergence of COGs as a possible first step toward eventual full consolidation of services in metropolitan areas. But this has not happened. COGs remain researching, coordinating, and planning bodies. They are not units of government, nor are they empowered by the states to provide government functions or to impose taxes.

In the summer of 1982, President Ronald Reagan eliminated by executive order the A-95 review process, effective in April 1983. The move was intended to reduce federal regulations and to increase state and local government autonomy. State and local governments are now encouraged to establish their own consultation and review procedures, and federal agencies are ordered to defer to the states' own review processes. Although the elimination of A-95 did not mean the disappearance of COGs, it significantly reduced their potential for becoming regional governments and thereby replacing existing local government units.

THE POLITICS OF METROPOLITAN REFORM

Efforts to reform metropolitan areas by reducing the number of government units have met with very limited success. Why do reform efforts aimed at consolidation consistently fail? Why do most voters favor the existing fragmented metropolis? There are two basic answers to these questions. First, suburbanites value strongly their local autonomy and independence. Second, proponents of metropolitan reform typically have not achieved the level of political organization required to win elections.

Reform Sounds Rational

Proponents of metropolitan consolidation schemes have tried to sell their plans through all sorts of logical and rational arguments. Consolidation, they point out, increases efficiency and economy in government. Why have 20 police departments in a metropolitan area when one can do a better job? Why have 10 water and sewer systems instead of one? Why elect 15 mayors and city councils when one could do the job? Why, in other words, pay to have a host of governments all using public funds to pay salaries to hundreds of semi-skilled public servants? Consolidation, they contend, could bring both tax savings and better-qualified fire fighters, police, planners, and other public employees.

The promises of improved services, lower taxes, more professional public officials, and a greater capacity to wrestle with modern public problems through consolidation have not convinced the average voter that the existing government structure should be replaced by a dramatically different one. Metropolitan reform thus has been repeatedly defeated at the polls.

People Want a Choice

People want to be able to select from among a variety of life-styles and service and tax levels. In the suburbs, they can purchase a home in a neighborhood with tax levels, service levels, school services, and housing costs that suit their needs or budget. They can have an impact on the quality of education, on planning and zoning, and on police and fire protection. They can enjoy relatively easy access to local public officials. They have worked to create and maintain these and other features of suburban life that they value highly.

While proponents of reform measure the costs and benefits against a model of efficiency and economy, opponents measure the costs and benefits against a model of autonomy and choice. Thus, many voters are unwilling to merge their communities with the larger metropolis.

The Law Favors the Status Quo

Metropolitan reform efforts also have not been successful because many consolidation plans require a majority vote at the polls in both the core city and the outlying jurisdictions. Winning a majority vote in a consolidation election, as in any other election, is largely a matter of effective political organization, a task that proponents have generally not done well. Typically, the reform movements are supported by academics, businesspeople, and planners impressed by the neatness and order that the new schemes promise. Their campaign tactics typically involve an appeal to the logic of the voter through mass-media advertising. Only rarely have the reform movements employed the existing party structure or attempted to create new ones that might better penetrate the grass roots.

Political parties in both the central cities and the suburbs, ethnic minorities in the core cities, and suburbanites all resist attempts at reorganization for fear of losing their political power relative to other groups. Suburban Republicans and central city Democrats, for example, may both fear a potential dilution of their power. Similarly, core city blacks and suburban whites may resist mergers for fear of losing control of their locality to the other group. The considerable uncertainty associated with dramatic reform creates widespread resistance.

Supporters versus Opponents

Social scientists have attempted to identify the factors associated with citizen support for or opposition to structural reform of metropolitan political arrangements. In general, some found that people who are dissatisfied with the present level of public services, who are not suspicious of the core city, and who have a relatively high level of formal education are apt to be more supportive of reform than those with the reverse characteristics.

In addition, some social scientists contend that reform is less likely to occur in older areas, presumably because residents have long enjoyed their independence. Furthermore, cities employing the city–manager system were found to engage in annexation more often than other cities. When state law makes it less difficult to alter the status quo, reform is more often successful. Moreover, the least drastic reform proposals are most likely to gain passage. Finally, a state's level of political party competition appears to have little or no effect on the reorganizational propensities of people at the local level.[5]

THE DOWNSIDE OF THE METROPOLITAN SCHEME

Some observers do not support the creation of large metropolitanwide governments, arguing in favor of various other arrangements instead. Vincent Ostrom, Charles M. Tiebout, and Robert Warren, for example, suggest that there are several criteria by which one should measure the effectiveness of a metropolitan organizational scheme.[6] In addition, they argue that an all-encompassing central government may not always be the best choice. Their criteria include "packageability" or control (that is, whether the boundaries are broad enough to cover problem areas), efficiency, political representation (that is, appropriate political interests should not be denied a role in the decision making), and local autonomy or self-determination. They also point out that a very large jurisdiction—or one of any size for that matter—is not necessarily appropriate for meeting all these criteria. For example, a government package for the elimination of air pollution may differ in terms of size than those needed for health and public assistance services. Thus, metropolitan government, like the polycentric arrangement (discussed later in this section), can do some things but not all things well.

Robert Stein suggests that nearly half of the entire service mix provided by local governments is "planned, financed, produced, or delivered with the active participation of an entity or entities other than the municipal government."[7] Thus, there is currently a lot of variation in what cities do.

A 1970 publication from the Committee for Economic Development suggests that neither a very small nor a very large jurisdiction is most appropriate.[8] The proliferation of small units—the so-called **polycentric system**—is plagued by the obvious shortcoming of not being able to get a handle on issues that affect entire metropolitan areas (for example, air pollution and transit). But the larger units have two critical shortcomings of their own. First, they simply are not, in most cases, publicly acceptable. Second, they may fail to provide representation for subcommunities within the metropolitan area (such as urban blacks seeking more control over the institutions that affect them). The committee proposes, then, multilevel government with different functions performed at different levels.

Communities Want Local Control

In an interesting essay published in 1971, Francis Piven and Richard Cloward argue that metropolitan-area governments became consolidated to the detriment of urban African-American residents.[9] They contend that consolidation occurred as a result of the federal requirement that areawide planning and coordination precede receipt of federal grant monies. What could not be done at the polls, they argue, was done administratively as a result of federal intervention.

The Department of Housing and Urban Development, for example, through such programs as the Model Cities and Metropolitan Development Act of 1967, forced the creation of metropolitan areawide planning and coordinating agencies. The federal government made it difficult or impossible for local governments to obtain federal grant funds. The result was that a new cadre of bureaucratic planners, in regional and federal agencies, became politically influential. The implications were, according to Piven and Cloward, as follows:

> The black masses are now building to electoral majorities in the larger American cities, but the promise of urban political power will be frustrated, for the new administrative government will be responsive to a majority coalition of suburban and inner-city whites. As blacks rise to power in the city, the city will lose power to the metropolis.[10]

More recently, African-American citizens in a sizable sector of Boston proposed to secede from the city and take control of their own affairs by creating the separate city of Mandela. Among their concerns were the costs of converting neighborhood housing to upscale residences for well-to-do outsiders and the impact on housing availability. In another bid for independence from a metropolitan government, on November 2, 1993, the citizens of the borough of Staten Island voted overwhelmingly in favor of seceding from New York City.

A Clash of Values

Thus, some reformers want to consolidate and centralize metropolitan America, whereas others seek to decentralize it further. On the one hand, the extensive fragmentation of authority creates some loss of efficiency and renders systematic attack on such problems as transportation, housing, and air pollution difficult or impossible. On the other hand, the authorities and power structures in large governments are often out of touch with and insensitive to the needs of neighborhoods. The only way to centralize and decentralize at the same time is through a system of federalism. But even federal systems present problems, such as deciding the authority of the central versus regional units and providing for the resolution of jurisdictional disputes.

FUTURE TRENDS

What are the prospects for metropolitan restructuring in the future? As far as formal redrawing of city, county, and special district lines is concerned, the prospects are slim. The law as it exists today in many **Radical Reform Is Unlikely** states requires an independent majority vote in each incorporated jurisdiction involved in an annexation or consolidation effort, and voters are not likely to change drastically their past voting behaviors. Given the increasing deterioration of U.S. cities and the ongoing migration of whites to the suburbs, the opposition to metropolitan reorganization may grow even stronger. Similarly, the existing cities are not likely to allow secession by unhappy neighborhoods.

In addition, state legislatures are not likely to modify state law in ways that would make reorganization easier to accomplish. The Supreme Court reapportionment decisions of the 1960s, coupled with over 30 years of suburbanization, have thrown enormous political strength in state legislatures to representatives in suburban areas. Suburban representatives have an obligation to represent their constituents' preferences, so they will remain disinclined to make reorganization easier through altering state law.

If any changes in the nature of metropolitan decision making are forthcoming in the future, they are likely to be in the form of coordination and cooperation among existing units of government. COGs may continue to promote communication and some coordination of grant applications. Continued growth in the use of intergovernmental service agreements can be expected, for they provide some increased efficiency without major or politically difficult changes to the status quo. Sweeping reform measures such as consolidation are highly unlikely.

Some observers claim that metropolitan America is experiencing yet another shift in settlement patterns, and one that will only aggravate **Urban Villages** the problems created by the earlier shifts from urban to suburban areas. This movement involves the development of **urban villages**—growing "satellite" cities located on the fringes of the core cities.[11] Urban villages are larger, more complex, and more self-sufficient than traditional suburbs. They may begin with the development of a major regional shopping mall, which is then followed by other retail and service enterprises, office complexes, high-rises, and housing. New airports can spark the development of urban villages. New expressways that loop the core cities can stimulate the development of such satellite communities. Many grow very large and become homes to insurance or financial institutions. Citizens can work, eat, shop, and play without traveling to the older core city.

Urban villages have emerged throughout the nation—in southern California, on the East Coast, in the Atlanta area, and elsewhere. Denver may have one in the making. To the south of that city is a large complex of hotels, office buildings, and service industries called the Denver Tech Center. It even sports its own skyline. To the north, Denver is undertaking the construction of a huge new international airport. A semi-independent public entity is constructing a toll road that will loop Denver to the east, connecting the developments of the south and the north. Although the core city of Denver will likely remain an important part of the economic and political system, in many ways the complexes to the north and the south will themselves become cities.

It is interesting to note that decades ago upper- and middle-class citizens often sought to live some distance from the sites of major economic activity. Those who could afford to do so moved away from factories, away from markets, away from downtown, to cleaner, newer, and more spacious suburban surroundings. The old housing left behind became occupied by the poor and ethnic minorities. In the newer urban villages, however, a different trend is emerging. Workplaces are now offices, small businesses, and clean and light industries. The structures are new and built in less dense, or more spacious, patterns. Parking is available; landscaping is generous. Upscale housing is built in rather close proximity. And it is now the lower-class service personnel, rather than well-to-do businesspeople, who must commute some distance to work. Many executives who formerly drove to downtown from the suburbs now live close to work in the urban village, whereas lower-status workers now struggle to commute to work from the older and somewhat distant core city.

The emergence of these **satellite cities** (urban fringe areas that have developed into centers of significant economic and/or residential activity) has also altered expressway traffic patterns. Increasingly, as business and light industry locate outside the urban core, commuting is from one suburb or fringe city to another. No longer is all the traffic going in the same direction, either into or out of the city.

These developments have benefits and drawbacks. For some, the shift means the pleasure of living near one's place of work and in relatively new and clean surroundings. Yet the trend is also contributing to American urban blight. Most new jobs — some say up to 90 percent — are located in urban villages, as is most new housing and as are many recreational and cultural opportunities.

A Divided Nation?

While cities offer a wealth of diversity and opportunity, they are also beset by many problems. Our core cities have increasingly high concentrations of the poor, the unemployed, the marginally skilled and educated, and individuals and families lacking the means to secure and then travel to well-paying jobs. Large numbers of city dwellers are African-Americans or Hispanics or single mothers. The fancy car, the three-piece suit, the nice house, and the well-paying job characterize many residents of urban villages, whereas poverty, crime, and gangs characterize life in many core cities. Increasingly, the same problems are being faced in the older suburbs by both whites and minorities.

The political dilemma of core city leaders multiplies as they face problems related to housing, social services, and law and order with an inadequate tax base. The urban village continues to divide Americans along such lines as color, opportunity, wealth, and location. If it is true, as some contend, that the redistribution of wealth and opportunity is essential to the long-term viability of American society, then the new urban village may be taking the nation in the wrong direction.

SUMMARY

American metropolitan areas are still growing. Public policy and technological change have supported the growth of urban areas into metropolitan areas and continue to do so. Among the consequences of this expansion are jurisdictional problems and inequities, intergovernmental conflicts, planning difficulties, and in many cases a residual core city in severe fiscal distress. However, metropolitan growth offers opportunities as well. New "urban villages" and other kinds of fringe development offer metropolitan residents a variety of settings in which to live and work. There is little doubt that the immediate future of America is a sprawling metropolitan one.

KEY TERMS

urbanization
factory-based economy
suburbanization
metropolitan statistical area (MSA)
incorporation
annexation
consolidation
special district
metropolitan federation

intergovernmental service
  agreements
Lakewood plan
metropolitan council of government
  (COG)
polycentric system
urban village
satellite city

ADDITIONAL READINGS

Bish, Robert L., and Vincent Ostrom. *Understanding Urban Government.* Washington, D.C.: American Enterprise Institute, 1979.

Kantor, Paul. *The Dependent City: The Changing Political Economy of Urban America.* Glenview, Ill.: Scott, Foresman, 1983.

Lyons, W. E., David Lowery, and Ruth Hoogland DeHoog. *The Politics of Dissatisfaction: Citizens, Services and Urban Institutions.* Armonk, N.Y.: M. E. Sharpe, 1992.

Peterson, Paul. *City Limits.* Chicago: University of Chicago Press, 1980.

Walker, David B. "Snow White and the 17 Dwarfs: From Metro Cooperation to Governance." *National Civic Review* (Jan.–Feb. 1987): 14–28.

NOTES

1. U.S. Bureau of the Census, *Statistical Abstract of the United States, 1975* (Washington, D.C.: GPO, 1975); and *Agricultural Statistics* (Washington, D.C.: GPO, 1991).

2. Ibid.; and Drew A. Dolan, "Local Government Fragmentation: Does It Drive Up the Cost of Government?" *Urban Affairs Quarterly* (Sept. 1990): 28–45.

3. Neil Pierce, "Fragmentation Is the Bane of U.S. Cities," *Denver Post*, 10 Dec. 1989.

4. John C. Bollens and Henry J. Schmandt, *The Metropolis*, 2nd ed. (New York: Harper & Row, 1970), chs. 11–12.

5. "Towns Have Written the Book on Sharing," *Governing* (June 1990): 18. See also Vincent L. Marando and Carl Whitley, "City-County Consolidation: An Overview of Voter Response," *Urban Affairs Quarterly* 8: 181–203; John C. Bollens et al., *Exploring the Metropolitan Community* (Berkeley: University of California Press, 1961).

6. Vincent Ostrom, Charles M. Tiebout, and Robert Warren, "The Organization of Government in Metropolitan Areas: A Theoretical Inquiry," *American Political Science Review* (Dec. 1961): 831–42.

7. Robert M. Stein, *Urban Alternatives: Public and Private Markets in the Provision of Local Services* (Pittsburgh: University of Pittsburgh Press, 1990), p. 54.

8. Committee for Economic Development, *Reshaping Government in Metropolitan Areas* (New York: CED, 1970).

9. Francis Fox Piven and Richard A. Cloward, "Black Control of Cities," in *Black Politics*, ed. E. S. Greenberg, N. Milner, and David J. Olson (New York: Holt, Rinehart and Winston, 1971), pp. 118–30.

10. Ibid., p. 119.

11. Christopher B. Leinberger and Charles Lockwood, "How Business Is Reshaping America," *The Atlantic* (Oct. 1986): 43–52.

11

Local Governments

City Hall, Los Alamos, New Mexico. This modern city hall symbolizes the growth of cities in the so-called Sun Belt. It is at the military base outside Los Alamos that the first atomic bomb was constructed. *(Peter Menzel/Stock, Boston)*

As noted in earlier chapters, the relationship of local governments to the states is quite unlike that which exists between the states and the national government. The state – national relationship is federal in nature; each level of government derives its authority from a source legally superior to both — the U.S. Constitution. Although the states and the national government perform a number of overlapping functions, the states and the national government exist and operate in parallel fashion.

A different relationship exists between local governments and the states. All units of local government, be they cities, counties, school districts, or special districts of some sort, are legally inferior to the state government. They are created by the state through legislative statutes or constitutional provision, they derive authority from the state, the state imposes duties and limitations on the local units, and the state may, if it so chooses, legally abolish local governments. There is, in short, no such thing as an inherent right to local self-rule.

CHARACTERISTICS OF CITY GOVERNMENT

Cities are actually **municipal corporations** — they exist because they possess a charter from the state. Through statutes or constitutional provisions, states classify cities according to size. They may be classified as having one million or more residents, 100,000 to 500,000, or 2,500 to 100,000. In addition, the state may permit the creation of **towns**; that is, municipalities with fewer than 2,500 residents. When a city falls into one of these categories and operates with the charter authorized by the state for that size city, it is termed a **general law city**. These cities operate under the same charter, which, by a general act of the legislature, is authorized for any city that falls into that population classification.

Creatures of the State For each class of city, the state constitution and statutes indicate, in considerable detail, the government structure, the electoral system, and the powers, duties, and limitations of the cities. Cities in the largest population categories may be required to employ a strong mayor form of government, have a city council of nine members, elect both the council and mayor for four-year terms, and employ a partisan ballot when electing council members from wards or districts. Cities in the next class size may be given an option between a council – manager form of government and a weak mayor form of government. They may be required to use a seven-member council, to elect council members to two-year terms of office, and to employ at-large and non-partisan elections. Cities in the smallest class size may be required to do the same.

State constitutions and statutes also prescribe local government powers, duties, and limits, usually in great detail. As mentioned earlier, the statutes may specify the form of government, the length of terms for council members and the mayor, and the time of year when elections can be held. In some cases, even the salaries of such local officials as the fire and police chiefs are specified. The statutes may tell the cities what type of taxes they may levy and at what level. For example, for cities in the smallest population class, the state may permit a property tax up to a certain millage* level and a sales tax up to a certain percentage, but it may bar the imposition of an income tax.

Controlled by the State

State specifications of local government powers and duties can be extremely detailed. The statutory list of duties and functions for Colorado's cities and towns, for example, addresses numerous issues —water facilities, fences and walls, buildings and fire escapes, fire hazards, steam boilers, packing houses, breweries, stables, foundries, mills, ditches, houses of vice, fights and misconduct, riots and disturbances, vagrants and prostitutes, children's play (involving kites, balls, hoops, and other amusements), bail bonds, railroads, peddlers, games, sale of bread, weights and measures, secondhand stores, streets and sewers, utilities, parking facilities, and a host of other minor details. This sort of detail reduces the operational flexibility of local governments and forces the legislatures to focus often on altering state statutes that relate to local government.

Although the powers and duties of local governments are spelled out in great detail by the states, historically the courts have chosen to interpret them conservatively. Whereas the U.S. Supreme Court typically has interpreted the constitutional powers of the nation rather broadly, state courts have held that cities and other units of local government have only those powers that are clearly given to them in state constitutions and statutes. When some question about the intent of the law emerges, and when the courts could conceivably interpret the power of local governments liberally, they have consistently chosen not to do so. This behavior not only keeps tight limits on the activities of local governments, but it is also a powerful and symbolic illustration of the legal inferiority of local governments vis-à-vis the states. The 1872 ruling by Supreme Court Judge John F. Dillon is often cited as illustrative of the legally inferior position of local governments. In Dillon's words:

> It is the general and undisputed proposition of law that a municipal corporation possesses, and can exercise, the following powers, and no others; First, those granted in express words; second, those necessary or fairly implied in, or incident to, the powers expressly granted; third, those essential to the declared objects and

---

*A *millage rate* is a tax rate expressed in terms of tax dollars assessed per $1,000 of the assessed value of real property. For example, a homeowner might be assessed a tax of $1 for every $1,000 his property is worth.

purposes of the corporation—not simply convenient, but indispensable.[1]

Dillon's rule (discussed more fully in Chapter 2) demonstrates that local governments have only those powers expressly granted to them.

Home Rule

States have attempted to loosen the legal shackles that constrain local governments by instituting constitutional or statutory home rule, especially for the largest cities. Simply stated, **home-rule provisions** are intended to allow local governments some freedom to choose the form of government and range of functions they will perform, without interference from the legislature.

However, generally state legislatures and state courts have been reluctant to grant much legal freedom to local governments, even to those with home-rule status. Although a majority of the largest cities in the United States operate with home-rule charters, the use of such charters is not widespread in medium- and small-sized cities.

Incorporation

Just as state law prescribes the powers, duties, and government form of cities, it also specifies the process by which communities can incorporate, obtain a state charter, and thus become a city.

The incorporation process typically goes like this: The residents of an area discover that their need for such services as sewers, water, and police protection cannot be met adequately by the county government. Given their powers, limitations, and government structure, counties usually cannot provide the services that a city can. Thus, in line with the dictates of state law, the residents must secure a given number of signatures on a petition asking for an election to decide whether a majority of those in the community wants to form a city. If the issue passes, a second election is held to elect members to a charter commission, which then draws up a **charter**—or basic law—for the city. The charter, of course, is subject to the confining requirements of state law. (In actual practice, the charter commission election may be held concurrently with the initial election.) Once a charter acceptable to the state is written, the residents vote on it. If it is adopted, as it almost always is, elections are then held to choose city officials.

The Functions of City Government

Cities are multifunctional government units established to provide a wide variety of essential services in areas of high population concentrations. The primary municipal functions are designed to ensure public safety and health. Police and fire departments provide for public safety and water and sewer systems promote public health. Other primary municipal services include street and park maintenance and recreation. Some cities also operate hospitals and schools or administer some aspect of the social service system. It is clear that, for the most part, cities provide those services without which people could not live in highly concentrated fashion.

THE ORGANIZATION OF CITY GOVERNMENT

Cities must be organized with a view to providing citizens with municipal services. While there is almost infinite variety in the shape of city governments nationwide, four major forms exist—the strong mayor–council system, the weak mayor–council system, the commission plan, and the council–manager system.

The **strong mayor–council system**, common in the largest cities, includes a popularly elected mayor and a unicameral city council. Elections are usually partisan, with each of the two major parties running candidates for mayor and council. Council members typically represent wards or districts. The mayor is a full-time politician. Like governors and the president, mayors are highly visible. They have a policy platform and program that they attempt to put into effect; they are the chief administrative officer in that they are situated at the top of the city bureaucracy and are able to hire and fire high-level administrators; they often have the power to veto council action; and they play a major role in preparing the city budget each year. Structurally, the strong mayor–council system resembles the model shown in Figure 11.1.

The Strong Mayor–Council System

FIGURE 11.1   The Strong Mayor–Council System

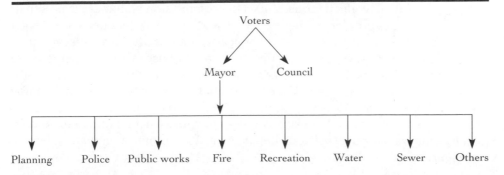

The Weak Mayor–Council System

The **weak mayor–council system** is similar to the strong mayor scheme except that the powers of the mayor in areas of personnel, finance, and political leadership are considerably weaker. The weak mayor plan, typically found in small- and medium-sized cities, is often accompanied by nonpartisan elections. Weak mayors are seldom full-time politicians. Moreover, because the political parties are not as dominant in city politics, the weak mayor seldom receives the public attention that strong mayors enjoy. In addition, the weak mayor may not possess a veto over council action, plays a minor role or no role in budget formation, has little or no power to appoint administrative personnel and does not play a major role in the formation and introduction of a policy platform.

Although the weak mayor plan looks like the strong mayor plan shown in Figure 11.1, the powers of the weak mayor are considerably reduced. In addition to the structural features depicted in the figure, both strong and weak mayor cities may have one or more elective boards or commissions that oversee some city activity.

It is important to note that the weak and strong mayor forms are not pure models. Many cities contain some structural and operational features that strengthen the mayor and other features that weaken the position by forcing the mayor to share power with the council or some semi-independent boards and commissions. The extent of variety among America's cities in this respect is vast.

In mayor–council cities in the United States, the terms of the mayor and council members vary in length. Thirty-one percent of mayors serve two-year terms, and 68 percent serve four-year terms. Council members serve two-year terms in 37 percent of these cities and four-year terms in 61 percent. The shorter council member terms are more common in the Northeast. About one-half of all mayors possess a veto over all council actions, while 91 percent may veto some types of council action but not others. In nearly 80 percent of all mayor–council cities, the council has between 6 and 15 members.[2]

The Commission Plan

The **commission plan** differs considerably from the strong and weak mayor–council forms. Under the commission plan there is no separation of powers, as the legislative and executive functions are merged. The voters elect a city commission (typically composed of five or seven members) that acts as the policy-forming body and whose members serve as the chief administrators for the city administration. Each commissioner, in other words, functions as the head of one of the city departments (for example, public works, police, or fire). Theoretically, the city commission, as a collective entity, supervises the various administrative departments. In actual practice, however, each commissioner oversees one department. The commission plan is depicted in Figure 11.2.

FIGURE 11.2 The Commission Plan

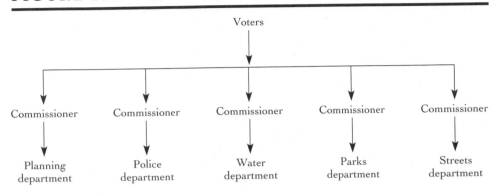

The commission plan differs from the mayor–council systems in several respects. First, there is no directly elected single chief executive, either weak or strong. Second, there is no check on commission action in the form of a veto. Third, there is a built-in incentive for **log-rolling**—the process of accumulating votes in order to build up a majority coalition. At budget time it is in the interests of each commissioner to go along with the budget demands of the other commissioners so as to gain their loyalty in subsequent matters.

The commission plan is not widely employed by cities. It was supposedly invented in Galveston, Texas, in 1901 following a hurricane. In the wake of the disorganization that accompanied the disaster, a committee of "leading citizens" was formed to reinstitute domestic health and safety. Its remedial activities were apparently so exemplary that it was decided to continue under the plan, using it as the permanent form of government. Then, in 1907, the city of Des Moines, Iowa, refined the plan, and it was subsequently adopted by other cities as well. But the commission plan has not gained the widespread acceptance accorded the other plans.

The Council–Manager System

Some cities employ the **council–manager system** of government (see Figure 11.3). Here, the **city council**—which is often composed of five, seven, or nine persons (ten or fewer in 97 percent of all council–manager cities) typically elected in at-large and nonpartisan elections—acts as the legislative or policy-forming body. The council appoints a professional manager to act as the chief administrative officer and, in effect, to run the city. The manager, who is hired and who may be fired by the council, need not be a resident of the city. The office of mayor exists, but the position is filled in various ways. Generally, the mayor is simply "first among equals," and the title serves only a ceremonial function.

FIGURE 11.3   The Council–Manager System

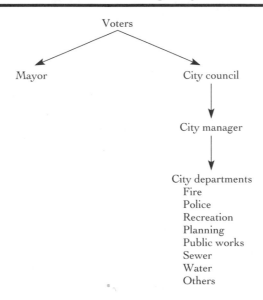

As the chief administrative officer, the **city manager** typically prepares the budget, makes recommendations to the council, appoints administrative personnel who are not under civil service, and, in general, runs the administrative affairs of the city without interference from the city council. In fact, some city charters and state statutes specifically prohibit council members from interfering with the city manager's operations. The council can, of course, fire the manager if it chooses to do so, but council members are not supposed to deal directly with administrative officers in such departments as police and fire. Rather, all communication with the lower ranks of administration is supposed to be through the city manager's office.

A Product of Early-Twentieth-Century Reforms   The council–manager form of government is a product of an early-twentieth-century reform movement that emerged in the context of the larger national Progressive movement. Toward the end of the nineteenth century and into the early twentieth century, many city governments were dominated by corrupt politicians or political machines. These "machines" operated as the key to elaborate exchange systems, wherein they bought the votes of the masses of incoming immigrants in exchange for such favors as jobs, handouts to needy families, the conduct of funerals and wakes, and other commodities desperately needed by immigrants who had recently left their homelands. When necessary, the political machines supplemented the immigrant vote with outright manipulation of elections. Phony votes were cast, deceased people's names were kept on the rolls, and ballot boxes were stolen or "lost" when the situation demanded it.

Muckraking writers such as Lincoln Steffens and business reformers such as Richard Childs (who later became the president of the National Municipal League) led the fight in the early part of the twentieth century to curb the activities of political machines. One of their primary aims was to remove politics and the politician from government and substitute instead efficient businesslike management. Part of their plan involved replacing the mayor–council system with the council–manager form of city government.

A Managerial Model   The council–manager form of government is patterned after the managerial model of the private corporation, as Figure 11.3 shows. The voters are viewed as the functional equivalent of corporate stockholders. While stockholders select a board of directors to oversee the activities of a corporation, voters elect a small city council to guide the affairs of government. In place of the company president, whom the board of directors hires to manage the corporation, the city council employs a city manager, who is supposed to be politically neutral, technically competent, and uniquely qualified to run the affairs of the city within the policy guidelines set forth by the city council. The city manager, then, acts as the chief administrative officer of the city. Supposedly, the manager is politically neutral and only administers the policy handed down by the council. The city manager is empowered to hire and fire administrative subordinates, is generally instructed to prepare the city budget, and, supposedly, operates without daily interference by the council. Rather, the city council grants the city manager the freedom to conduct the job as he or she sees fit, but the council can fire the manager if it is unhappy with performance.

Underlying Assumptions   There are a number of interesting assumptions underlying the council–manager plan. For example, there is the assumption that alterations in both individual behavior and the operations of entire governments can be accomplished by tinkering with organizational structure. The elimination of the position of strong mayor, the substitution of a small city council for a large one, the use of at-large rather than ward elections, and the employment of a city manager as a sort of equivalent to a corporate manager all seek to eliminate graft and to promote a businesslike economy and efficiency. Students of administrative behavior suggest, however, that while government structure is not unimportant, it alone does not govern behavior. Professional norms, ideology, training, working conditions, personal contacts, and opportunities are equally important in affecting both individual behavior and the general tone of government operations. One cannot eliminate greed, the potential for under-the-table payoffs, or communication based on personal acquaintances simply by juggling the lines on an organization chart.

Another assumption underlying the council–manager system is that the operations of government can and should be nonpolitical. The major target of the early reformers was the political machine, controlled by a highly organized political network running from the ward supervisor to the manager. The words *politician* and *politics* became dirty words. Thus, through use of a nonpolitical city manager, at-large rather than ward elections, and the elimination of partisan designations on the ballot, it was assumed that politics could be removed from the operation of government and that many of the evils of the political machine would thus disappear. But the notion that politics could be eliminated from government was based on the narrow assumption that politics involves only those activities undertaken by a partisan party. Hence, it was thought that politics would cease to exist if party labels were omitted from the ballot. In practice, of course, politics involves much more than political parties. It also includes the competitive struggle among individuals and groups to affect the content and implementation of public policy. Politics is partisan combat, carried on according to a set of rules, wherein the competitors seek to place their problems on the public agenda and secure public resources for the services and other benefits they desire; they seek to secure, in short, benefits at public expense. Tax policy, the provision of police and fire protection services, zoning and educational decisions — these and other public services are the outcomes of partisan political struggles.

Yet another assumption of the council–manager plan, and one implicit in the early-twentieth-century reform movement, is that the values of economy and efficiency in government are supreme. Most would agree that economy and efficiency are desirable in government, but not at the expense of effective response to citizen desires. Some would argue that in a democratic system the primary task of government is to respond to the desires of the people, and that, while efficiency and economy in government are important, they are secondary to that primary function.

The political machines that were the object of reformers' attacks were interesting institutions. There is no question that they were corrupt and self-centered and that they made off with large amounts of illicitly obtained funds. At the same time, however, they performed a number of functions, which have since been taken over by government agencies, that provided much-needed aid and much desired upward mobility for many newly arrived immigrants. The old machines helped the widows, the orphans, the unemployed, and those generally in distress. Some critics argue that, because the power of the political machine was partially dependent on the vote of the urban masses, it was much more responsive to their needs than modern-day bureaucracies, which are staffed with people protected by elaborate civil service provisions.

Although the reformers contributed significantly to the demise of the old machines, other factors helped as well. Changes in the national immigration laws reduced the number of new immigrants and eventually dried up the pool of new voters. At the same time, many second- and third-generation immigrant children were so successful — thanks in part to the activities of the political machines — that they no longer had to sell their vote to the ward heelers in order to receive assistance in getting jobs and other aid. Instead, they could afford the luxury of voting as they pleased.

While admitting that the magnitude and character of machine politics have significantly changed since the turn of the century, Raymond Wolfinger argues that the urban machine is not gone from American politics.[3] Given the growing number of urban poor and the proliferation of urban-oriented public programs, the conditions favorable to thriving machine politics are present. In other words, according to Wolfinger, the poor provide the political machine with an electoral base, and new public programs generate opportunities for considerable patronage.

THE DISTRIBUTION OF STRUCTURAL FORMS OF CITY GOVERNMENT

The reform features developed in the early twentieth century—the council–manager system and at-large and nonpartisan elections—are unevenly distributed both geographically and in terms of city size. The mayor–council form of government is the older, more traditional form and is found most often in the East and Midwest. The council–manager plan and nonpartisan elections are especially prevalent in the Midwest, the West, and the South. The explanation for the trend in western states may be simple: western cities were just coming into existence when the early-twentieth-century reforms were in full swing. Western cities thus adopted the structural plans that were popular at the time, and most have maintained them ever since.

As Table 11.1 indicates, the council–manager system is commonest in cities with populations over 25,000, whereas the mayor–council system is predominant in very large cities (those whose population exceeds 500,000) and

TABLE 11.1   Form of City Government by City Size, 1992

City Population	Number of Cities		
	Mayor–Council	Council–Manager	Commission
Over 100,000	77	102	8
25,000–100,000	354	564	37
Less than 25,000	3,369	2,017	127
Total, all cities	3,800	2,683	172

Source: The Municipal Year Book (Washington, D.C.: International City Management Association, 1992), p. xiv.

very small cities. In recent years the council–manager system has gained popularity in every size category and in every region of the country.

Cities employing the council–manager model usually use other reform features, including at-large and nonpartisan elections. Eighty-eight percent of council–manager cities have nonpartisan elections, and 76 percent of those cities employ the at-large model for at least some council seats.[4]

POLITICAL INFLUENCE AND CITY GOVERNMENT STRUCTURE

The structure of a city government helps to determine its internal distribution of political influence. The person or persons who control the formation of the budget, personnel appointments, the flow of information within the administration, and the council's agenda are in an extremely influential position. The governmental structure helps to determine this influence.

Budget Control and Personnel Appointments

In an age when most government budgets are large and complicated, city councils, often composed of part-time politicians who devote a few hours a week to public affairs, seldom have the time or expertise necessary for a complete and careful budget review. As a result, the budget submitted to a council by an administration seldom undergoes extensive modification.

In a *de facto* sense, then, the administrative officials — whether the mayor, the mayor's staff, or the city manager — exercise extensive control over budgetary matters. Their budget control can extend into other forms of influence, for department and agency heads cannot afford to ignore the demands and preferences of those who control the operating budget. In a strictly legal sense, of course, the legislative branches of all American governments control spending, and the problems and political pressures in a community help to structure program and budgetary priorities. But in practice, the people who work out the details of a budget and submit it for review to a city council control in large measure the internal distribution of government dollars.

In addition, the authority to hire and fire personnel contributes to the power of an administrator. The ability to hire employees permits administrators to fill positions with people who are sympathetic with their views and who are likely to accede to their preferences. The power to dismiss an employee is, of course, an effective tool to secure compliance with orders.

The ability to control the flow of information in an organization and the capacity to structure its agenda give an administrator an enormous amount of influence. Policymaking bodies such as city councils spend their time deliberating the items on their agenda, but matters do not get on the public agenda by accident or chance, just as problems do not define themselves. Among the infinite range of possible public issues, some are selected and placed on the public agenda for consideration and others are not placed on the agenda.

Control of Information and the Agenda

Typically, some of the items that do reach the public agenda are those identified as problems by city administrators. Parks departments point to the need for more parks, fire fighters point to the need for more staff and new equipment, and so on. Administrative departments and special interests push constantly for the placement of their problems on the public agenda. Thus, with the abundance of potential issues and agenda items, the person who structures the public agenda is in a position to put some things on it and leave others off — thereby narrowing the range of options. In addition, the person who sits atop the flow of information in a city administration is in a position to choose what the council will hear and what it will not hear.

In strong mayor–council cities, the mayor has an independent constituent base, is empowered to hire and often to fire top administrative personnel (such as department heads), is empowered to veto council action, is the top administrator (with considerable legal administrative authority), and plays major roles in structuring the budget and the public agenda. It is the mayor's program and the problems that the mayor identifies that become the focus of city government.

Strong versus Weak Mayors

In weak mayor–council cities, the situation is different, as political power is somewhat more widely diffused. The weak mayor typically does not have the veto, budget, and appointive powers of the strong mayor. Instead, the council is in a position to control appointments and, in some cases, to put the budget together from the beginning. Likewise, because the weak mayor is not a highly visible figure with the power to structure the public agenda, agenda setting is more apt to be done by the council or individual department heads. In short, power is more broadly shared in the weak mayor–council system than in the strong mayor–council scheme.

In commission plan cities influence is also rather diffused. Executive leadership and, indeed, even coordination of activities may be lacking. Each commissioner may be powerful within his or her own

Commissioners and City Managers

department, but none has the legal authority and political visibility of the strong mayor.

In contrast, influence in council–manager cities is concentrated in the city manager, who is not directly elected. The budget is prepared by the city manager or the manager's staff. The council's agenda is set and top-level administrative appointments are made by the manager. As a full-time chief administrator who generally operates with a council composed of part-time politicians, the city manager has a monopoly on information and technical expertise. Council members' knowledge of the city's problems and alternative solutions tends to reflect that of the manager. This is not to suggest that city managers manipulate the flow of information from their administration to the council, but they do sit in the most critical position in the information process. Thus, even though the early rhetoric regarding the role of city managers suggested that they were nonpolitical administrators, they actually play an extremely influential role in the policymaking process.

CITY GOVERNMENTS DIFFER IN MANY WAYS

For years social scientists have tried to describe and explain the different characteristics and behavior of American cities. While they have been successful in identifying differences in the social, economic, and political realms, the exact causes of these variations are still unknown.

Structural Scheme Variations   Cities with different structural schemes tend to differ in certain other respects as well. According to a 1965 study conducted by Alford and Scoble, council–manager cities, in comparison with mayor–council cities, are likely to have higher growth and higher levels of citizen education, to be more homogeneous (socially, ethnically, and religiously), and to have more mobile populations.[5] In other words, they are more apt to fit the model of a middle-sized, growth- and business-oriented, middle-class community.

Similarly, in a summary of the research findings of a number of 1960s studies, Lewis Froman observes that council–manager cities are most likely to be of medium size, growing, and white collar; to have high-value housing; to contain fewer citizens of foreign-born parentage and fewer nonwhites; to have a higher-educated and wealthier population; and to display more occupant ownership of single-family housing units.[6] In addition, they are likely to spend more money per capita, to have lower municipal debt and higher property taxes, and to hold both at-large and nonpartisan elections. Wolfinger and Field contend that there is a geographic pattern to the distribution of government forms, and that cities with reformed structures are more likely to be found in the West than in any other region.[7]

Council–manager cities differ from council–mayor cities in the behavior of the electorate as well. Voter turnout tends to be lower in cities with the manager plan, in part because the plan is usually accompanied by nonpartisanship and at-large elections.[8]

Differences in Public Policy and Opinion

Just as the structural characteristics of cities tend to correlate with social, economic, and demographic factors, so too differences in the public policies of cities tend to vary with different government structures, as well as with social, economic, and demographic characteristics. In a 1967 study of two hundred randomly selected cities, Lineberry and Fowler examine the relationship between the use of reform features and policy output in cities.[9] Their conclusion is that structure has some impact on policy output, as measured by taxing and spending levels, as well as on the political style of a community. Reformed council–manager cities, they argue, tend to tax less and spend less, with the exception that council–mayor cities with ward elections spend less when their elections are partisan.

However, in a 1980 study involving 22 cities tracked over an 11-year period, David Morgan and John Pelissero conclude that government structure does not affect fiscal behavior.[10] Robert Stein notes in a book published in 1990 that the provision of services by cities is related to the nature of those services, beginning with collective goods and moving to private goods.[11]

In addition, in a 1963 study of the results of local referenda, Edward Banfield and James Q. Wilson argue that some citizens, particularly people of Anglo-Saxon descent and Jews, are most likely to display a so-called "public-regarding" ethos, whereas other citizens, such as ethnic minorities, are more inclined to be "private regarding" in their outlook and electoral behavior.[12] That is, the private-regarding individuals tend to support only those public programs from which they will receive some direct benefit. Banfield and Wilson imply that cities containing a high proportion of public-regarding citizens are more likely than other cities to support the adoption of reformed government structures and new public programs designed to benefit the entire community. In a later study, published in 1971, Wilson and Banfield modify their earlier conclusions but do not abandon the ethos theory of political behavior.[13] In this ethos study, they contend that political ethos is more pronounced among individuals who exhibit so-called leadership qualities and that it likely played a role in cities' initial selection of government forms.

Variations in Political Behavior

A number of studies examine the behavior of city councils in relation to public policy and political processes. In a 1968 study, for instance, Bryan Downes suggests that city council members from high socio-economic backgrounds are inclined to support high city expenditure levels.[14] However, Downes also notes that other factors, such as the wealth of a city and the nature of its political system, affect expenditure patterns as well.

A 1991 study by David Morgan and Sheilah Watson indicates that collaborative policy leadership is most likely to occur in large cities, with mayors the dominant figures in most cases.[15] James Clingermayer and Richard Feiock found, in their 1993 study, that representatives from reformed political structures (at-large elections) tend to focus less on constituency casework and more on the "high politics" of policy formation.[16]

Some Generalizations

What can we conclude from the aforementioned studies? A few generalizations can be made with some confidence. First, government forms are not randomly distributed throughout the nation. Cities with certain economic, educational, ethnic, religious, age, and locational characteristics tend to adopt certain structures. Second, while these factors may be taken as indicators of structures, policies, and styles of political activity, they are not completely reliable. Third, political structures do have some impact on voter behavior and public policies, as indicated by the lower levels of voter turnout and expenditures in reformed cities.

Finally, it appears that, in a sense, the anti-political machine reformers have had their way. If differences in values and policy preferences within a community are muffled (as the preponderance of evidence suggests is the case in the reformed cities), if a wide range of issues are not placed on the public agenda and, therefore, not accommodated by official decision makers, then politics to a degree has been removed from government just as the reformers intended. However, democratic theory demands most of all that governments and public officials be responsive to the people and that community concerns be the primary business of the government.

COUNTIES, SCHOOLS, AND SPECIAL DISTRICTS

Most of the thousands of units of government in the United States are made up of counties, school districts, and other special districts. As with cities, they are all creatures of and legally subordinate to the states. They employ thousands of public servants, perform hundreds of functions, and spend billions of dollars.

County Government

To most Americans the **county** (the largest political subdivision of the state structure) is not among the most visible or salient units of government, but it is important nevertheless.[17] Counties administer the voting system of the states, keep vital records, house the courts and maintain jails, collect local taxes, and run much of the social service system.

There are more than three thousand counties in the United States, and enormous variation exists among them. In Alaska, counties are called boroughs, and in Louisiana, parishes. Connecticut and Rhode Island have no functional county governments. Delaware has just 3 counties, whereas Texas has 254 counties. Eight states have fewer than 20 counties and 7 other states have more than 100. The range of population in the counties is vast. Loving County, Texas, has 154 people; Los Angeles County is home to over 8 million residents. Most counties operate with an antiquated political structure that widely disperses authority; however, a few have adopted modern arrangements that centralize administration.

The existence of counties dates back over a thousand years in Britain. Initially arms of the royal government, through the years counties also became the providers of education, aid to the poor, police protection, roads, courts, and more. In the American colonies and later the states, the county served as the arm of the state. Today, some counties perform only housekeeping functions, such as keeping records, maintaining jails, and holding elections. Other counties perform services much like those performed by the cities. As noted in Chapter 10, under the Lakewood plan, Los Angeles County provides many municipal-type services to cities.

Functions Traditionally, counties typically perform several basic functions. They play a critical record-keeping role. Births, deaths, voter registrations, election returns, property ownership, land transactions, and other information are recorded and kept by the county. In addition, counties exercise a number of police powers. In areas outside of incorporated municipalities, they provide police protection through the sheriff's office. Liquor licenses and building permits may be controlled by the county. Some counties administer zoning and building codes, inspect food-dispensing establishments, and guard against disorderly behavior and houses of ill repute. Many counties have their own court systems and thereby help to administer the business of the state trial courts. The county sheriff often maintains the county jail.

Counties also play an important role in elections by registering voters, preparing ballots, supervising elections, and keeping some election records on behalf of, and as administrative subdivisions of, the state government. Finally, counties provide a range of services. They construct and maintain roads; they assess property and collect taxes for both themselves and other local government units within their boundaries; and they may maintain parks, libraries, airports, hospitals, stray animal kennels, sanitary landfills, and public assistance programs.

As the preceding description of county functions suggests, most activities undertaken by counties tend to be of a housekeeping nature in comparison to the broader range of activities performed by cities. Most county functions are the product of earlier decades when the activities of government were minimal. Those functions are spelled out in detail in state statutes; counties, then, have relatively little freedom of policy choice.

Structure   The structure of county government bears a slight resemblance to the plural executive model employed in state government (see Chapter 5). County government is composed of what some call **row officers** — a directly elected sheriff, coroner, clerk, recorder of deeds, superintendent of schools, and board of supervisors. They are referred to as row officers because on an organizational chart they all line up in a row, and they all have independent constituent bases. In other words, the county lacks elective executive leadership.

The legislative branch of county government is composed of the county board of supervisors, often called county commissioners. The boards typically have three, five, or seven elected officials, though in some states (such as Michigan, Tennessee, and New York) the boards are much larger. Texas is fairly typical in that the voters of each county (by single-member district) vote for four county commissioners and, in a countywide election, for a presiding officer. The chief executive of Texas counties is called the county judge, though the position has only limited judicial functions. Unlike most city and school board elections, those for county officials are by partisan ballot. County board activities may include the formulation of the budget, the enactment of zoning and building codes, the parceling out of liquor licenses, and others. The legislative functions of the board are usually fairly restricted, however, as many of the duties of the county are spelled out in state law.

Other directly elected county officials include the sheriff, coroner, clerk, treasurer, registrar of deeds, and, in some states, the county superintendent of schools. Like the members of the county board of supervisors, these individuals run for office on partisan ballots and serve two- or four-year terms. The duties of the sheriff include the enforcement of law in those parts of the county that are not within municipal boundaries, the maintenance of jails, and the delivery of court summonses. The coroner's job, of course, is to establish death and determine the cause. In some states coroners must have some medical training, but this is not a universal requirement. The duties of the county clerk, in those states in which the office exists, include such clerical activities as issuing marriage and hunting and fishing licenses, registering voters, preparing ballots, and assisting the board of supervisors. County treasurers collect the tax revenues for the various local governments within the boundaries of their county and disperse them to each local government according to the legally established mill levies. The treasurer also keeps financial books and acts as custodian of the funds. The duties of the registrar of deeds involve just what that title implies — to keep an official record of property ownership, including the registration of deeds, property sales, mortgages, and estate titles.

Counties in over one-half of the states elect a superintendent of schools. However, this official performs only minimal duties, as the actual job of running the schools falls to the school districts themselves, not to the county. In addition, the counties in some states elect an assessor, who makes estimates of property values for tax purposes; a highway superintendent; an auditor; and a surveyor.

There is some limited structural variety among the American counties. County executives (similar to mayors) are elected in 388 counties; another 786 counties operate with a chief administrative officer (similar to a city manager). Some 27 of the 3,042 counties have merged with other local governmental units.[18]

Criticisms   County government has been the object of intense criticism in recent decades. The most common complaints are that the county is structurally incapable of generating effective political leadership and of attacking problems successfully; that it lacks the legal authority to provide the broad range of services that people now demand; and that it is plagued by other dysfunctions, such as a lack of a civil service system and of skilled personnel. With the multimember board of supervisors, plus the sheriff, the clerk, the assessor, the treasurer, and others all directly elected at the polls, and each possessing an independent constituent base, it is argued that the county is without an individual executive capable of identifying problems, leading a ticket, pushing a platform, and bearing the responsibility for the administration of the affairs of the county.

Similarly, since state law largely deprives the county of anything other than housekeeping powers and duties, it has limited ability to tax, spend, and act so as to deal effectively with such modern issues as public assistance, police protection, housing, pollution, and water and sewer service. In addition, because most counties use the spoils system of employment rather than a civil service system, it is argued that they lack skilled personnel.

Reform Proposals   Not surprisingly, county government reforms have been proposed. Proponents of reform suggest that the row officers be replaced by a structural arrangement involving an elective or appointive chief executive, that a civil service system be adopted to replace the spoils system, that steps be taken to ensure that certain officials (such as the coroner, the treasurer, and the assessor) receive adequate training for their job, and that state law be modified so as to broaden the powers of the county, especially in the areas of taxation and zoning.

Several counties, including Cook County in Illinois and Milwaukee County in Wisconsin, have adopted reforms instituting a chief executive. Dade County in Florida's Miami area and California's Los Angeles County have assumed broad municipal-type functions in order to serve millions of people as a city would. Although there have been other attempts to merge governments or update structures in order to allow counties to meet the growing demands of an urban and suburban society, county government in twentieth-century America still resembles that of the nineteenth century in many respects.

Many state governments have acted to make it possible for counties to modernize their structures. Thirty-six states now allow some form of county home rule, but voters in the counties themselves have been very slow to make changes. In those 36 states, just 4 percent have adopted home-rule charters.[19]

Like America's modern cities, counties today face a variety of challenges. They remain creatures of the state and as such they are subject to the limitations imposed by the states. The states require counties to provide certain services but restrict the types and amounts of taxes that counties may levy and collect to pay for those services. The issue of unfunded or underfunded state mandates is highly controversial in many counties today.

School Districts

With a few exceptions, elementary and secondary education in the United States is administered by local **school districts** — single-function local governments that, like cities and counties, are creatures of and legally subordinate to the state government. As of 1987 there were 14,721 school districts in the United States, less than one-quarter the number that existed in 1920. The decrease in the number of school districts is the result of widespread district consolidation, made possible by improvements in roads and bus transportation, encouraged by rising costs and the savings associated with consolidation, and required by state legislation.

As single-function units of local government, school districts operate independently of other local units. The only exceptions are that the counties help school districts collect the property tax on which the latter largely depend and that the local schools are subject to oversight by state departments of education. Like cities and counties, school districts have their own legal boundaries, which may or may not parallel those of other local governments. In some communities in the eastern part of the United States, elementary and secondary education is provided by municipalities.

Structure   In many ways the government structure of school districts resembles that of the council–manager plan in city government. In what are nominally nonpartisan elections, voters elect a multimember school board that, like the council in city government, acts as the policymaking body. The school board, in turn, hires a school superintendent, the school district's counterpart to the city manager. The superintendent, who acts as the chief administrative officer for the district, is supposed to have purely administrative-type duties and, theoretically, is nonpolitical. The superintendent is hired on the basis of administrative abilities and may be dismissed by the school board, which often involves a contract buy-out.

The rest of the school district government is structured hierarchically under the direction of the superintendent. Each school is headed by a principal, though in large school systems there may be an intermediate level of organization between the superintendent and the individual school principals. In

---

FOCUS

11.1   POLITICS IN THE NEW YORK CITY SCHOOLS

One recent example of politics in the educational system is the experience of the former chancellor of the New York City school system. In 1993, Chancellor Joseph A. Fernandez was deemed responsible for an alteration in the curriculum of some New York City schools that included the incorporation of materials designed to foster tolerance for alternative life-styles. The reading materials selected for young children shocked many traditional-minded parents and church leaders in the New York City area. Given the public response, it was soon apparent that the New York City school system had crossed a political boundary and, regardless of the appropriateness of the curriculum changes, Chancellor Fernandez, as leader of the system, had to go. He resigned early in 1993. Schools and school leaders are subject to political pressures.

addition, school districts, like other government units, may employ a staff organization including offices for budgeting, planning, and purchasing.

Are Schools Political?   There is an old, staunchly defended myth about American schools, which holds that they are nonpartisan and nonpolitical entities. For most Americans, education is an extremely important business, and this is reflected in the fact that more is spent on education than on any other single state or local function. Since education is so important, many believe that it is crucial that it is kept out of the hands of politicians and that local control be maintained. Thus, Americans hold strongly to the notion that schools should be controlled locally, that they should be kept nonpolitical, and that district elections should be nonpartisan.

However, in school district government as in anything else, politics involves much more than simply keeping party labels on or off the ballot (see Focus 11.1). Politics involves interpersonal and intergroup competition to control the content and implementation of public policy. It involves the authoritative resolution of conflict among individuals and groups that have different values and images of the public good. Questions having to do with the property tax rate, the establishment of expenditure priorities and item-by-item allocations in the school budget, the content of the curriculum, segregation and busing, as well as contests for seats on the school board are competitive and political in nature. The schools employ most state and local employees, spend most state and local tax dollars, and are a part of the political process.

Financial Problems   Schools in the United States are facing an increasingly serious financial crisis. The financial position of the schools and, indeed, of most local governments has been undercut by inflation, by the constant demand for more and better services, and by the decreased propensity of people to hold their wealth in the form of taxable real estate. Inflation and the demand for more and better services have driven the total cost of elementary and secondary schooling up from $103,100,000 in 1960 to $371,900,000 in 1991. However, the property tax — the financial mainstay of the schools — has been increasingly hard pressed to supply the funds. Whereas previously many people may have held their wealth in the form of land and estates, fewer do so today. Instead, the wealthy accumulate stocks and bonds, with the result that the brunt of the property tax burden falls to the elderly, those on fixed incomes, and young, newly married couples with children — persons whose ownership of taxable real property (or payment of rent, which has the property owner's taxes built in) is high relative to their income.

The ability of the schools to escape their current cost–price squeeze is further hampered by rigid state laws limiting the taxing and spending powers of local governments. Some states impose an absolute millage ceiling on the property tax; that is, they limit the extent to which the schools can tax property. Others demand that a popular referendum be held to approve school district borrowing for building or operating purposes or to raise the tax levy beyond a certain level. Popular approval of property tax hikes is increasingly difficult to come by. Almost annually, a few school districts across the country are forced to close their doors for days or even weeks because they are financially destitute. In 1992, for example, the Los Angeles schools were on the verge of bankruptcy. Given today's taxpayers' moods, as reflected in such actions as the passage of California's Proposition 13, and more recent reductions in federal support for schools and educational programs generally, these problems are sure to grow even more severe.

Inequities in Quality of Education   A problem related to school financing results in inequities among school districts. The schools rely heavily on the property tax, and some districts are richer than others. Within the borders of one district there may be industrial or commercial property, such as a shopping center, plus a considerable amount of high-cost housing. But an adjacent district may be poor; it may contain little or no industry and low-cost housing. The result is obvious: The tax bases vary, the incomes of the districts vary, and the quality of education varies. Indeed, the poor districts, where high-cost remedial educational programs may be the most sorely needed, tend to be least able to afford them.

The states have equalization programs designed to counteract the financial imbalances among school districts, whereby the states' share of the cost of elementary and secondary schooling is apportioned so as to benefit the poorer districts. Although equalization formulas help to eliminate some of the worst inequities, they do not solve the problem. There is growing concern that the very use of the property tax to support the schools results in the denial of equal opportunity to the nation's schoolchildren. There have been court cases in several states challenging the property tax as contributing to the "denial of equal protection of the law"—a Fourteenth Amendment guarantee. The Supreme Court, however, has ruled that an absence of dollar equality in district-to-district support of education does not constitute denial of equal protection of the law under the U.S. Constitution (*San Antonio Independent School District v. Rodriguez*, 1973). In some states, challenges under the state constitution have been upheld.

Creatures of the State   Although the relationship between the local school districts and their parent governments, the states, varies considerably, state offices or departments of education typically require periodic reports from the local districts, establish standards for teachers and certify them, and, in some states, select the textbooks and prescribe some of the course curricula for the local schools.

The state seldom involves itself in the daily operations of the local districts. However, it does maintain general surveillance and supervision. (For more on public education, see Chapter 14.)

Special Districts

Like all units of local government, **special districts** are also creatures of the state. State law provides for their existence, outlines the processes by which they may be formed, and specifies their powers, duties, and limitations. Typically, special districts are unifunctional in nature; that is, they perform a single function, such as the creation and maintenance of parks or sewer facilities. They generally have the authority to tax, spend, and borrow money. Some are governed by boards that are popularly elected. Like cities, counties, and school districts, special districts have legal boundaries that seldom parallel those of other governments.

The number of special districts has increased dramatically in recent decades, and by the 1990s the number exceeded 30,000. Almost two-thirds of these were in only 11 states, including over two thousand in both Illinois and California and more than one thousand in Pennsylvania, Kansas, and Texas.

Types   The variety of special districts is extensive. Nearly one-third of them deal with some aspect of natural resources, such as soil conservation, drainage, irrigation, or flood control. Another 17 percent provide fire protection, 10 percent provide urban water supply, and others deal with cemeteries, housing, highways, parks, hospitals, and other such facilities. Figure 11.4 shows the variety of special districts that exist within the state of Florida.

The number of cities in the United States is growing very slowly, the

FIGURE 11.4
**Number and Types of Special Districts in Florida
(as a percentage of all special districts)**

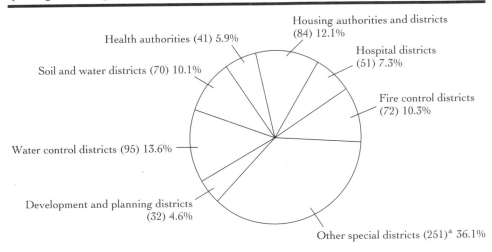

Health authorities (41) 5.9%

Soil and water districts (70) 10.1%

Water control districts (95) 13.6%

Development and planning districts
(32) 4.6%

Housing authorities and districts
(84) 12.1%

Hospital districts
(51) 7.3%

Fire control districts
(72) 10.3%

Other special districts (251)[a] 36.1%

[a]Port and inlet authorities/districts (29)
Housing finance authorities (28)
Library districts (23)
Industrial development authorities (23)
Park and recreation districts (22)
Miscellaneous (20)
Utility authorities/districts (18)
Mosquito control districts (13)
Aviation districts/authorities (13)

Water and sewer districts (12)
Regional planning councils (11)
Road and bridge districts (10)
Improvement districts (10)
Lighting districts (7)
Water management districts (5)
Transit authorities (3)
Community development districts (3)
Mobile home districts (1)

SOURCE: *Special District Accountability in Florida* (Tallahassee: Florida ACIR, Nov. 1987).

number of counties remains stable, and the number of school districts continues to fall due to consolidation efforts; the number of special districts, however, continues to increase. Much of this growth has been in housing and community development districts as well as library districts.

Functions   There are two primary reasons for the fairly recent and dramatic growth in the number of special districts. First, special districts can span an area and "package" a problem with which existing cities and counties cannot cope. For example, as new housing subdivisions spring up in areas adjacent to existing cities, they develop a need for both water and sewerage service. At first, these needs may be adequately provided for by water wells and septic tanks. As the density of the population increases, however, more modern water and sewerage facilities may become mandatory. The city to which the new developments are adjacent may be unable to extend its lines and provide the service.

The city's facilities may already be operating at full capacity, and it may not have the resources with which to expand them. At the same time, the taxing and borrowing powers of the county within which the new developments exist may not be sufficient to permit the construction and maintenance of the needed facilities, or the county may be barred altogether by state law from providing such services. Therefore, in this situation, the formation of a new special district may be the only alternative. The boundaries of the district can be drawn so as to include only the area where the new services are needed, and the district can borrow the funds needed to build the facilities and impose a property tax sufficient to retire the bonds.

Situations similar to the hypothetical case just described are numerous given the rapid, widespread suburban growth in recent decades. Service needs have developed in the areas of sewerage, water, police, fire, parks, hospitals, and dozens of others. Thus, it is not surprising that the number of special districts has increased rapidly.

The other reason for the growth in the number of special districts is related to the fiscal limitations that state laws frequently impose on local governments. It is not unusual for a state to limit local governments as to the kinds of taxes they may impose, the amount of taxes they may levy against property or retail sales, and the amount of debt they may incur. As a result, the formation of another government—a special district—may be an attractive way to get around the limitations. Since special districts can borrow, tax, and spend just like other local governments, they can act as a mechanism for borrowing the money and imposing the taxes that are beyond the legal limits of the existing cities and counties.

Problems   While special districts are obviously critical to the provision of needed public services, they create some problems as well. For example, their mere existence further complicates the problems associated with governmental fragmentation. Comprehensive community planning is difficult when sewerage and water, education, police and fire protection, recreation and land use planning are all handled by different units of government. It is no easy task to generate cooperation among counties, cities, school districts, and a host of special districts. In addition, special districts can add to already widespread citizen confusion about government in that they make its structure and operation more complex.

Special districts can also represent a bonanza for local attorneys and a burden for the already overburdened property taxpayer. Both statutory and case laws regarding local governments are extremely complicated, especially as they relate to finances. As a result, it is imperative that special districts keep an attorney on retainer. The lawyers may or may not earn their wages; nevertheless, the taxpayer pays the retainer tab in literally thousands of special districts.

Finally, in some cases, the growth in the use of special districts has created new financial burdens for citizens. In Colorado, for example, the special district share of the local property tax doubled in the past two decades. In some instances, when special districts were created by developers, bonds were floated to provide improvements and pave the way for massive housing developments, generally just outside metropolitan areas. In Texas, for example, the state legislature authorized the creation of municipal utility districts (MUDs) that allowed developers to buy up open land and, after issuing bonds backed by the MUD, to develop the land. When a city grew close enough to annex the developed land, the city also took over the MUD bonds. However, when a city could not annex the developed area in light of the recent downslide of the real estate market, the few existing taxpayers living in those areas were stuck with astronomical property taxes, and the holders of tens of millions of bonds were in danger of losing their investments.[20]

SUMMARY

The more than 86,000 units of local government that exist in the United States display a rich diversity in institutional design and reflect a variety of historical American perspectives on the nature of politics. U.S. counties feature a highly decentralized form of government organization, and one that largely reflects nineteenth-century Jacksonian notions of democracy. With its long string of directly elected positions — including the commissioners, the sheriff, the coroner, the treasurer, the assessor, the clerk, and the auditor — the county scheme was designed to be highly democratic; that is, to maximize the ability of citizens both to be officeholders themselves and, as voters, to keep officeholders on a short leash.

In contrast, the council–manager form of city government emerged from the early-twentieth-century campaigns for economy and efficiency in government. Whereas the line of row officers in the county scheme decentralized authority, the council–manager system concentrated it in the hands of a small city council and its hired city manager. While today the Jacksonian concern for citizen participation in a democracy is still evident in the county arrangement, the reformed council–manager model employed in many cities reflects the private-sector business preoccupation with a streamlined and centralized government structure that is geared more toward efficiency than representation.

Interestingly, twentieth-century reform movements — whether targeted at state institutions, the fragmented metropolitan scene, or local governments — reflect the tension among different traditions and images of politics. Some observers favor a governing arrangement that is highly representative of the wide range of interests and perspectives in a community. Representation, in this view, overrides concerns about economy and efficiency. Other observers prefer a form of government that emphasizes clarity and simplicity, speed in decision making, and economy and efficiency; for them, these concerns outweigh broad representation, extensive deliberation, and compromise.

Most U.S. institutions reflect some dimension of the different traditions. Many council–manager cities, for example, overlay their otherwise centralized and politically neutral structure with a string of boards and commissions, created incrementally over time and designed to provide a variety of groups with special influence over certain policy areas.

All U.S. institutions are, at any given point in time, a reflection of their political history. That history, which has featured a variety of experiences and ideas, is evident in our local institutions. With ongoing change and growth, the American political landscape will continue to evolve.

KEY TERMS

municipal corporation
town
general law city
home-rule provision
charter
strong mayor–council system
weak mayor–council system
commission plan

log-rolling
council–manager system
city council
city manager
county
row officer
school district
special district

ADDITIONAL READINGS

Fleishman, Arnold, and Joe R. Feagin. "The Politics of Growth-Oriented Urban Alliances: Comparing Old Industrial and New Sunbelt Cities." *Urban Affairs Quarterly* 23 (1987): 207–32.

Judd, Dennis R. *The Politics of American Cities: Private Power and Public Policy.* Glenview, Ill.: Scott, Foresman, 1988.

Swanson, Todd. "Semisovereign Cities: The Politics of Urban Development." *Polity* 21 (1988): 83–110.

Yates, Douglas. *The Ungovernable City.* Cambridge, Mass.: MIT Press, 1977.

NOTES

1. Quoted in Clyde Snyder, *American State and Local Government,* 2nd ed. (New York: Appleton, 1965), p. 353.

2. *Municipal Year Book* (Washington, D.C.: International City Management Association, 1979), pp. 98–101.

3. Raymond E. Wolfinger, "Why Political Machines Have Not Withered Away and Other Revisionist Thoughts," *Journal of Politics* (May 1972): 365–98.

4. *Municipal Year Book,* p. 101.

5. Robert R. Alford and Harry M. Scoble, "Political and Socioeconomic Characteristics of American Cities," in *Municipal Year Book* (Washington, D.C.: International City Management Association, 1965), pp. 82–97.

6. Lewis A. Froman, Jr., "An Analysis of Public Policies in Cities," *Journal of Politics* (Feb. 1967): 94–108.

7. Raymond Wolfinger and John Field, "Political Ethos and the Structure of City Government," *American Political Science Review* 60 (June 1966): 306–20.

8. Robert R. Alford and Eugene C. Lee, "Voting Turnout in American Cities," *American Political Science Review* (Sept. 1968): 796–813.

9. Robert L. Lineberry and Edmund P. Fowler, "Reformism and Public Policies in American Cities," *American Political Science Review* (Sept. 1967): 701–16.

10. David R. Morgan and John P. Pelissero, "Urban Policy: Does Political Structure Matter?" *American Political Science Review* (Dec. 1980): 999–1,005.

11. Robert M. Stein, *Urban Alternatives: Public and Private Markets in the Provision of Local Services* (Pittsburgh: University of Pittsburgh Press, 1990).

12. Edward C. Banfield and James Q. Wilson, *City Politics* (New York: Vantage, 1963).

13. James Q. Wilson and Edward C. Banfield, "Political Ethos Revisited," *American Political Science Review* (Dec. 1971): 1,048–62.

14. Bryan T. Downes, "Suburban Differentiation and Municipal Policy Choices: A Comparative Analysis of Suburban Political Systems," in *Community Structure and Decision-Making: Comparative Analyses*, ed. Terry N. Clark (San Francisco: Chandler, 1968), pp. 243–67.

15. David R. Morgan and Sheilah S. Watson, "Policy Leadership in Council-Manager Cities: Comparing Mayor and Manager," paper prepared for delivery at the annual meeting of the American Political Science Association, Washington, D.C., Aug. 29–Sept. 1, 1991.

16. James C. Clingermayer and Richard C. Feiock, "Constituencies, Campaign Support and Council Member Intervention in City Development Policy," *Social Science Quarterly* 74 (March 1993): 199–215.

17. For articles on U.S. counties, see the Advisory Commission on Intergovernmental Relations' *Intergovernmental Perspectives* 17 (Winter 1991): entire issue.

18. Blake B. Jeffrey, Tanis B. Salant, and Alan L. Boroshok, *County Government Structure* (Washington, D.C.: National Association of Counties, 1989), p. 120.

19. Ibid., pp. 131, 146.

20. See, for example, Michael Mehle, "Crackdown on Special Districts Brewing," *Rocky Mountain News*, 6 March 1991.

12

Community Power and Politics

The Austin, Texas, city council in session. Then-mayor Ron Mullen, at the head of the table, discusses the council's goals for 1983–85. *(Bob Daemmrich/The Image Works)*

POWER IN THE LOCAL COMMUNITY

WHO CARES WHO GOVERNS?

Scholars Care / The Public Cares, Sometimes

DO POWER ELITES GOVERN THE COMMUNITY?

Middletown's Royalty / Atlanta's Elite / Other Perspectives

IS COMMUNITY POWER PLURALISTIC?

Pluralism in New Haven / Pluralism in Florida / Other Perspectives

DO EXPERTS GOVERN THE COMMUNITY?

Full-Time Managers Monopolize Information / Complexity Enhances the Experts' Power

DO LOCAL ELECTION SYSTEMS BENEFIT THE ELITE?

Partisan versus Nonpartisan Elections / Variations in Voter Participation / At-Large Elections / The Effects of Electoral Reform / Recent Gains for the Disenfranchised

DO THE FEDERAL AND STATE GOVERNMENTS RULE THE COMMUNITY?

Federal and State Mandates / *FOCUS 12.1:* The Impact of a Federal Mandate on a Small Town / Who Should Pay for Mandated Programs?

DOES OUTSIDE CAPITAL GOVERN THE COMMUNITY?

The Urge for Economic Development / Does Development Improve the Economic Health of Communities? / Outsiders Limit the Community's Power to Affect Policy

SUMMARY

We often refer to the person or group in control of our communities as "they." They raised our taxes. They failed to patch potholes. They fouled up the traffic light sequence on Main Street. They put too little money into lighting parks. They discriminated in city hiring policies. They run the town to suit their own self-interests.

Who are "they"? Clearly, they are people in positions to exert power and to influence the outcome of community politics. But are they the leaders who occupy positions in the governments described in Chapter 11—the mayors, council members, county commissioners, and school and special district board members?

Over the years social scientists have found these to be interesting and important questions. In representative democracies, citizens are supposed to control the outcomes of community politics through their representatives. But to what extent does this actually happen? What is the role of the citizen and how much influence do elected officials have in the public affairs of the community? In an official sense, of course, these are the people who make and implement all authoritative decisions. Policy proposals do not become law until majorities of school board members or city council members pass them. Proposals that pass are of little impact until city managers, school superintendents, and other chief executive officers, along with the public employees who report to them, put money and effort into implementing the policies. Some of these people, then, have the power of the official vote. Others construct the public agenda and implement policy. They are all influential in important ways. And they all play power roles in governing.

This chapter examines these and other related issues, as well as the relevant perspectives generated by scholars in the field. Does it matter who governs, whether power elites rule, or whether power is pluralistic? Do local election systems bias the choice of local leaders? To what extent do state and federal governments and the financial capital of businesses and industry drive local choices?

POWER IN THE LOCAL COMMUNITY

Many social scientists and others have long suspected that hidden powers lurk behind the scenes of community government—that so-called **power elites** selfishly manipulate community decisions to their own benefit rather than to the public good. However, as Norton Long points out, it is more popular to believe in the existence of power elites than it is to verify their existence:

It is psychologically tempting to envision the local territorial system as a group with a governing "they." This is certainly an existential possibility and one to be investigated. However, frequently, it seems likely, systems are confused with groups, and our primitive need to explain thunder with a theology or a demonology results in the hypostatizing of an angelic or demonic hierarchy. The executive committee of the bourgeoisie and the power elite make the world more comfortable for modern social scientists as the Olympians did for the ancients.[1]

The view of the local community as run by an executive committee of the bourgeoisie is widespread, but it is not universally accepted. Other schools of thought and inquiry hold that community power is distributed in pluralistic, not monolithic, fashion; that it is so widely diffused that, in effect, nobody rules. More recently, some scholars have questioned whether community politics is controlled by anyone within the community itself; they ask whether community events are dictated by outside institutions and forces, and, if so, whether this diminishes the importance of community politics.

It is important to note the manner in which U.S. institutional arrangements affect patterns of community power. Nonpartisan elections held in the spring depress voter participation, which, in turn, can result in an elitist electorate. Some argue that at-large elections diminish the numbers of ethnic minorities on city councils and school boards, and that the use of part-time bodies to govern schools and cities enhances the influence of such hired experts as city managers and school superintendents. In addition, it is argued that the federal system with its unitary local–state ties conditions the way in which local decisions are preempted by other governments and external factors.

WHO CARES WHO GOVERNS?

Theoreticians concerned with democratic thought care who governs **Scholars Care** local communities. From time to time, almost everyone cares who governs in particular situations. However, most citizens are too busy with their jobs, their families, their homes, and their finances to worry much about the morality or virtue associated with elite or democratic political systems. Some people do worry about it. Some argue that elites should rule because, given their special qualifications, they are better equipped than others to make collective choices, or have a moral right or duty to do so, or both. Their membership in the right political party, the right church, and the right race, together with their superior socioeconomic status or intelligence, endow elites, it is argued, with the right or ability to rule.

Advocates of democracy, however, argue that all elitist systems are illegitimate and that decision-making influence should be equally distributed throughout the community. Individuals are the best judges of their own best interests, and they do not need a self-selected elite to tell them what they want or need. People concerned with normative political theory, then, elitists and democrats alike, care who governs.

The Public Cares, Sometimes

From time to time the average citizen becomes aware of or concerned with the distribution of community influence. Government decisions are authoritative in nature; they are coercive; they help to determine who gets what, when, and how much. At the local level, government decisions affect the payment of traffic fines, the value and use of land, the distribution of the tax burden, the location of parks, the effectiveness of police and fire protection, and a host of other aspects of daily life that can affect millions of citizens, their families, and their pocketbooks.

City decision makers decide whether to spend public money to waive utility fees so as to attract, and subsidize, business development, or to use that money to improve parks. Decision makers can see to it that good streets and sewer hookups are available in low-income neighborhoods, or they can respond to citizen needs by the squeaky-wheel principle, thus letting most city investment go to middle- and upper-class areas. School officials also face choices. They can insist that the best teachers work in the schools where the children need the most help, or they can let those teachers transfer to upper-class neighborhood schools and hire inexperienced teachers for what are often the most difficult and least desired positions. School leaders can tailor curricula to the interests of the gifted and talented or focus resources on basic instruction in reading and writing for the entire student body. There are choices to be made that are not without significant consequences.

Thus, in particular situations, the average citizen may become interested in who governs local politics. When property is about to be rezoned to permit the construction of apartment houses or a gasoline station, when a new tax for a new park complex on the other side of town is proposed, when it is decided that students will be bused 10 miles to a school in a different town, when part of a citizen's front yard is taken for a widened four-lane thoroughfare — in these cases citizens care very much who governs. Whereas the theorist cares in the abstract who governs, the question is of vital interest to the bulk of the population only on special occasions, only for short periods of time, and only in reference to specific issues. Although there are both theoretical and utilitarian reasons for people to care who governs, seldom is that concern widespread or intense.

DO POWER ELITES GOVERN THE COMMUNITY?

Some studies conducted by scholars in community politics suggest that business- and economic-oriented power elites govern many local communities in the United States. The studies employ the **reputational** and **stratification approaches** to the question of how power is distributed in a community. Basically, their method proceeds as follows. First, an effort is made to identify persons in the community who are likely to be knowledgeable about important community matters and who are apt to know of the most influential people. Once a list of community knowledgeables is completed, the informants are interviewed and asked to identify the powerful people in the community. A score is kept of the nominations to the influential list, and those receiving the most votes are then presumed to constitute the community's power elite.

The reputational and stratification approaches are, of course, more complicated than this brief description indicates, but basically they amount to a reliance on other people's perception of an individual's influence as a measure of community power. That is, some people are considered to be part of a power elite because other people think they are. Only rarely is the actual behavior of power elites intensely examined.

Middletown's Royalty

A well-known example of a community study involving the reputational and stratification approaches was conducted by Robert and Helen Lynd in 1929.[2] The study focused on Muncie, Indiana, or "Middletown" as the Lynds called it. Gathering their information from personal observation, interviews, and newspaper reports, the researchers concluded that virtually every aspect of community politics and economics in Muncie was controlled by a single family—referred to as the "X" family in the study and meaning the glass-manufacturing Ball family.

According to the Lynds, the Ball family controlled the banks, the churches, the lawyers, the YMCA, the newspapers, the political parties, the chamber of commerce, the mayor, the community meeting halls, the breweries, the dog pounds, the hospitals, the local college—nearly everything, in other words. In the Lynds' words:

> Middletown has, therefore, at present what amounts to a reigning royal family. . . . the Middletown situation may be viewed as epitomizing the American business-class control system. . . . The ownership of banks, factories, colleges, breweries, dog pounds, hospitals, mayors and county chairmen, centered in this millionaire group, has produced an appalling economic pressure on citizens who find themselves in the house of bondage.[3]

Atlanta's Elite   Another well-known community study was conducted in 1963 by Floyd Hunter.[4] It focused on identifying the power elite in Atlanta, Georgia, a "regional city," as Hunter called it. He described his findings in terms of a **power pyramid**; that is, those at the top of the pyramid of power were often nominated as influential and, therefore, they constituted the community power elite. Hunter claimed that they controlled the important decisions in Atlanta, even though others actually carried out the plans and programs.

The following excerpts from Hunter's study convey his conclusions:

The "men of independent decision" are a relatively small group. The "executors of policy" may run into the hundreds. . . .

A group of men have been isolated who are among the most powerful in Regional City. . . .

The pattern of business dominance of civic affairs in Regional City is a fact. . . .

Most institutions and associations are subordinate, however, to the interests of the policymakers who operate in the economic sphere of community life in Regional City.[5]

Other Perspectives   While the investigations of the Lynds, Hunter, and others have led some scholars to conclude that ruling power elites exist in many communities and control decision making, other investigators harshly criticize the power elite school of thought. Among the most severe critics is Nelson Polsby, whose attacks are aimed at researchers' methods of studying the power elite as well as their interpretations of the data.[6] In *Community Power and Political Theory* (1963), Polsby outlines what he perceives to be the basic assertions of the elitist, or stratification, school. First, they contend that the upper class, which is composed of those in the top economic, occupational, and status brackets, rules the local community. Second, they argue that politicians and political decisions are actually subordinate to the economic elite; that is, that the economic big shots pull the decision strings. Third, it is assumed that the elite is a united and all-purpose group that rules in its own self-interest. Finally, community conflict is viewed as essentially class conflict in that lines are drawn on the basis of class status.

The critique of the elite model by both Polsby and Raymond Wolfinger is effective.[7] They note that the information obtained through interviews is based on vaguely worded questions, such as "Who is the most powerful person in town?" In this case, the word *powerful* can mean different things to different people. The reputational approach, according to Polsby and Wolfinger, may produce unreliable data for this reason.

The elitist method is also criticized for failing to distinguish between power in general and power in specific issue areas. In other words, the reputational approach does not distinguish between questions of who governs and who could govern, for in political and social life not every individual or group is interested in every community issue.

Finally, and perhaps most importantly, is the question of whether the existence of a power elite even conveys much about politics in a community. In some cases, the elite may be small, homogeneous, and united in its values. In other cases, the elite may be rendered impotent by conflict among its members. Therefore, in some communities the values of the upper class might coincide with those of most other members of the community, whereas in other communities upper-class values may conflict with those of the rest of the community. The mere reputational existence of an elite group does not guarantee its influence in community affairs.

IS COMMUNITY POWER PLURALISTIC?

Another major school of inquiry and theory holds that, in some communities, power is pluralistic rather than monolithic. In **pluralism**, power is not monopolized by a single elite but is distributed among many groups. In addition, the holders of power often vary with the issue involved. Influence may not be perfectly distributed throughout the community according to some ideal model of political equality, but neither is it monopolized by a small elite.

Pluralism in New Haven

The pluralistic theory of community power is generally associated with Robert A. Dahl and his 1961 study of New Haven, Connecticut.[8] Essentially eclectic in nature, the study relied on a variety of methods and data sources in efforts to discover who governed in New Haven. According to Dahl, the investigation included the following: (1) an examination of the socioeconomic characteristics of city public officeholders to determine if any major changes had occurred as a result of the type of persons in office; (2) the identification of a particular socioeconomic class and observation of the extent of its activity in local politics; (3) the examination of several issue areas to determine who was active and influential in each one; (4) a survey of a random sample of voters to determine what kinds of people were politically active and at what levels of political activity; and (5) an examination of changes in voting patterns among different strata of the population.

Employing a method quite unlike the reputational approach of power elite theorists, Dahl arrived at a very different set of findings. In particular, he found that decision making in New Haven displayed several characteristics. For example, only a few individuals were directly influential on policy matters in the various issue areas. Rather, voters exerted considerable influence on decision making—they selected the public officials and their preferences represented boundaries that those directly involved in decisions could not safely go beyond. In addition, influence tended to be specialized; that is, not everyone was interested in or active on every issue.

According to Dahl, the old families that made up the social elite in New Haven were once dominant in community affairs but their influence had given way to an **executive-centered coalition** formed around the mayor and the mayor's close associates. While political resources were not evenly distributed throughout the community, neither were they totally monopolized by a small elite. Every citizen possessed the vote, and the most influential tended to concentrate their influence in those specialized issue areas of greatest interest to them. In addition, it was found that some people used their political resources more skillfully than others. Political resources took many forms, including money, status, access to decision makers, skill, and time. There were also slack political resources in the community—that is, individuals and groups that had the ability to influence decisions but chose not to much of the time. Finally, Dahl found that the distribution of power changed with time and issue area.

Pluralism in Florida

A major study of a growing south Florida area—Broward County, the second most populous area in that state—was conducted by Ronald Vogel in 1992. Using the reputational method, which commonly leads to the conclusion that elites rule communities, Vogel found a pluralist decision-making system:

> Twenty-six of the leaders described a community that we would commonly label pluralist. . . . Nobody described Broward's decision-making structure as elite, though a few respondents indicated that Broward had an elite.[9]

Vogel noted that "leaders talked of the need to build a new coalition for every decision or issue."[10] His findings appear to fit nicely with an observation made by Nelson Polsby back in 1963:

> If a man's major life work is banking, the pluralist presumes he will spend his time at the bank, and not in manipulating community decisions. This presumption holds until the banker's activities and participation indicate otherwise.[11]

Other Perspectives

The pluralist perspective is not without its critics. Some of them argue that the pluralist's focus on a series of important issue areas is faulty in that it fails to provide a criterion for distinguishing between important and unimportant issues. Critics also consider the pluralist approach unwieldy because it demands that behavior be carefully scrutinized before making generalizations about who has power; ultimately, the behavior of every single individual should be studied, an obviously impossible task.

In addition, the pluralists are criticized for refusing to acknowledge even that an imagined power elite has some impact on human behavior. It is argued that, when people believe a power elite not only exists but also has the power to negatively impact those who refuse to accede to its desires, then decisions may be based on placating the elite—whether the elite is real or not. Potentially influential members of the community, in other words, can affect decisions without even trying, for others' perceptions of their ability to affect decisions may influence actual outcomes. When decision makers assume that a community elite will oppose the imposition of a high income tax, for example, that perception may prevent the imposition of that tax—whether or not the elite would actually oppose it.

Peter Bachrach and Morton Baratz point out that the reputational and pluralist approaches each shed some light on the distribution of community influence.[12] The insights provided by the pluralistic investigation are obvious. Using an eclectic approach, the pluralist can identify in specific terms who was active in which issue areas and with what result. The reputational approach is most useful in providing something the pluralist approach cannot—a view of the prevailing political ethos. Although the reputational approach does not entail a careful and systematic inventory of community attitudes, it does give an indication of the types of people who are perceived as influential in a community, including their socioeconomic characteristics and value systems. This information, in turn, may provide clues to the kinds of issues and alternatives that are most and least likely to reach the public agenda in a given community. According to Bachrach and Baratz:

> . . . Power is exercised when A participates in the making of decisions that affect B. But power is also exercised when A devotes his energies to creating or reinforcing social and political values and institutional practices that limit the scope of the political process to public consideration of only those issues which are comparatively innocuous to A. . . . to the extent that a person or group—consciously or unconsciously—creates or reinforces barriers to the public airing of policy conflicts, that person or group has power.[13]

DO EXPERTS GOVERN THE COMMUNITY?

Another research-based image of decision making in certain kinds of American communities places a considerable amount of community power in the hands of experts—those who operate the executive branches of government. This tendency, it is argued, is particularly pronounced in governments wherein the legislative or policymaking body is composed of part-time lay personnel. City councils, in council–manager cities especially, are composed of persons who do other things for a living, who devote just part of their time to government business and are paid little or nothing for it. The same is true of members of school boards, boards that govern such state agencies as universities and colleges, and special districts. These boards may contain homemakers, bankers, drug-store operators, dentists, and small business owners, for example.

Full-Time Managers Monopolize Information

The effect of these governing arrangements is that, generally, the decision-making power flows to the full-time government employees. For example, when a school board meets, it deals with the agenda brought to it by the superintendent of the school system. The superintendent and his or her administration present recommendations supported by budgetary, legal, technical, and other types of evidence and arguments. Other members of the administration may be present to offer evidence or answer questions. A board member, a nonpaid part-timer, may ask probing questions, make other recommendations, or oppose the recommended course of action. That board member may have been pressured by some person or group or may have alternate information or recommendations from someone within the school system. But this is an unusual situation. Generally, school board members, at a disadvantage in terms of information and time, ask few questions, rarely oppose the superintendent's recommendations, and tend instead to praise the administration's work.

The power of permanent administrators and their bureaucracies should not be underestimated. They work at their jobs full time. They have command of all sorts of data. They are familiar with the problems and issues. They are viewed as the experts. It is no small task for council or board members to challenge successfully the stance of the managers, superintendents, and other chief executive officers. Few members of councils or boards have the time to do the kinds of research needed to challenge the administration. There may be problems, data, or perspectives within the organization that never come to the attention of the councils or boards because the organizational ethic is that council and board members seek data only through the chief executive officer. Furthermore, it may be risky for persons of lower rank within the organization to convey information or questions to council and board members directly. Thus, when university governing boards, city councils, or other such bodies meet, the chief executive officer of the organization and his or her administration generally have their way.

The role of the unelected expert is growing as intergovernmental relations become increasingly complicated and the number of local special districts and intergovernmental contracts continues to multiply. In matters of education, corrections, environmental protection, and virtually all other policy areas today, bureaucrats at all levels of government deal with their counterparts at other levels. And they are all specialists of some sort—engineers, lawyers, planners. Not only is their work complex, but so also are their interactions with other governments. It is becoming ever more difficult for a citizen to follow and understand public affairs.

Complexity Enhances the Experts' Power

With the growth in special districts, there are more decision points and government players in the system; with the growth in intergovernmental contracting, local relations are increasingly complex. When the complexity of public affairs diminishes the role and influence of citizens and of council and governing body members, the full-time expert in control of the daily operation of government becomes the *de facto* political power.

DO LOCAL ELECTION SYSTEMS BENEFIT THE ELITE?

With tens of thousands of local governments in the United States, all holding periodic elections, Americans are surely not lacking in opportunities to participate in self-governance. Most Americans live within the jurisdiction of many governments—a city, a county, a school district, and one or more special districts. Under these circumstances one would expect citizen involvement to be extensive and informed Americans to vote in great numbers. Unfortunately, however, this is not the case. Most local elections are instead characterized by low voter turnout, with the percentage of registered voters often failing even to reach double digits. Turnout rates in the area of 20 percent are common; rates as low as 5 percent are not rare.

As is the case at the state level, numerous elections are held every year at the local level. Indeed, with over 19,000 cities, 3,000 counties, 15,000 school districts, and 30,000 special districts there have to be a lot of elections. Some local officials are elected for 2-year terms, others for 4-year terms, and still others for even longer terms. Some local elections are held in the fall, concurrently with state and national elections; others are held in the spring. Some local elections are partisan, whereas others are nominally nonpartisan, revealing the effects of government reforms.

Partisan versus
Nonpartisan
Elections

Elections for office in U.S. counties are partisan in nature; that is, the candidates run as Republicans, Democrats, Independents, Libertarians, or on some other party label. County government has been less affected by reforms than any other unit of government in the American system. Elections for school board members generally are nonpartisan.

The situation in American cities is mixed. Some cities conduct partisan elections and others nonpartisan ones. The nonpartisan election is an integral part of the municipal reforms developed during the early twentieth century. As a result, it typically is accompanied by at-large rather than ward elections and is often found in council–manager cities. As Table 12.1 indicates, elections in most American cities are conducted with nonpartisan ballots. In addition, cities with one of the two reform-era structures—the council–manager or the commission plan—are more likely than mayor–council cities to eliminate the role of the political party. Like the council–manager form of government, nonpartisan elections tend to be most prevalent in medium-sized cities and in cities in the southern and western United States.[14]

Nonpartisan elections were intended by reformers to reduce or destroy the influence of the political parties in local politics, and to a large extent they have done so. In areas where nonpartisan elections are employed, the parties no longer perform their traditional functions—recruiting candidates, raising funds, conducting campaigns for office, criticizing the policies and behavior of the incumbents' party, and providing voters with a means of identifying those responsible for failures and successes. Instead, candidates in nonpartisan campaigns work independently to raise funds and win office, or rely on special interests for support. (The latter is common in factional politics in one-party-dominant areas.) In addition, the public is deprived of the use of the party label as a means of identifying politicians in and out of office and their stances on issues. Traditionally, the political parties serve as useful sources of political information for voters. According to a study conducted in 1988, as voters gain knowledge of partisan information in nonpartisan contests, this provides voting cues and influences their vote.[15]

TABLE 12.1   City Election and Government Systems

Government System	Election Type	
	Partisan (%)	Nonpartisan (%)
Mayor–council system	39.0	61.0
Council–manager system	18.1	81.9
Commission plan	25.4	74.6
All cities	27.4	72.6

Source: Data from *Municipal Year Book* (Washington, D.C.: International City Management Association, 1988), p. 8.

Most social scientists addressing political partisanship and elections contend that the absence of the party label in local elections works to the advantage of the higher-income, higher-status class in a community. When elections are nonpartisan, voter turnout declines, and it is more difficult for voters to keep track of the candidates or identify the candidates' policy positions. It is argued that less educated, poorer, and lower-status voters are disadvantaged by nonpartisan elections in that they are less likely than other members of the community to be associated with the groups that function as alternate sources of information and voting cues (such as churches, service clubs, and the like). As a result, the upper-class, well-informed, group-joining members of the community may exert a disproportionately high impact on electoral outcomes.[16] In other words, as the level of voter turnout declines in a local election, the elitist character of the voting electorate increases.

In elections with very low turnout (which is generally true of nonpartisan local elections), the elitist cast that characterizes voters tends to be even more pronounced. When voter turnout is in the range of 10 percent to 15 percent, for example, the electorate may be heavily representative of community professionals and businesspeople; of people active in churches, service clubs, and other forms of political activity; of those with high incomes and levels of education; and of those residing in upper-class neighborhoods. As voter turnout declines, the electorate tends to become less representative of the community as a whole and more representative of the elitist minority. So, as a result, do those who are elected.

Variations in Voter Participation

Voter participation, however, varies among localities. In a 1968 study of voter turnout in American cities, Robert Alford and Eugene Lee contend that the form of government employed by a city influences participation levels more than any other single factor.[17] Cities in the study that lacked the council–manager form of government (that is, were unreformed) and that held partisan elections had higher turnouts than cities with other systems. In addition, voter turnout tended to be higher when a race for mayor was held concurrently with other contests than when council races were alone on the ballot.

Alford and Lee also contend that voter turnout varies with the locality and age of a city. Older cities, those located in the eastern part of the country, and cities with a stable population demonstrated higher turnout than cities in the West and South, newer cities, and cities with high levels of in-migration.[18]

Many of these findings can be explained by voting behavior and the impact of government structure on it. People tend to know more about and be more interested in elections, candidates, and issues when institutions exist that operate to inform voters about the elections. In addition, informed and interested voters are more likely to vote. Not surprisingly, then, voter participation is low in reformed cities because nonpartisan elections do not involve the political parties, which in partisan elections act to inform and involve citizens in electoral politics. Voter turnout is higher in eastern cities, proportionately more of which remain unreformed. Finally, the higher levels of participation in stable cities may be explained by the higher levels of citizen knowledge about and identification with the community.

According to Eugene Lee, voter participation fluctuates with the time at which a local election is held, with the highest turnouts occurring when the election is held concurrently with state or national elections.[19] Although the original intent of independently held local elections was not to depress voter turnout, this has been the result. Because national and state elections tend to receive wide publicity, they often attract large numbers of voters to the polls. When a local election is held independently, the lack of publicity results in low voter turnout.

At-Large Elections

One of the main aspects of the municipal reform movement was the institution of the **at-large election**, whereby voters in all parts of a city vote for city council candidates.[20] It was designed to remove what the reformers considered a major problem of the ward system—concentration by each councilmember on one area of the city to the disadvantage of the city as a whole. For many years, at-large elections were the dominant form of municipal election, especially in small to medium-sized cities.

Recently, however, the at-large election system has come under both political and legal attack and, in some cases, the courts have required cities to modify the system so as to provide district representation. The criticism is based on national voting rights legislation, which disallows election system features that discriminate against ethnic minorities. At-large balloting can work to prevent African-American and Hispanic citizens from electing their representatives of choice.[21] As numerical minorities, the effect of their vote can be minimized. Without substantial white voter support, for example, a city with a 35 percent Hispanic population could go indefinitely with absolutely no Hispanic council members. When the courts found that at-large systems prevent fair minority representation, they insisted on modifications in the form of partial or full districting systems.

The Effects of Electoral Reform

Studies of contemporary urban institutional reform—primarily changing election structures from at-large to single-member districts —examine changes beginning in the early 1970s and continuing to the present day. These changes are often motivated by demands for equal representation by minority groups and facilitated by the federal government through the Voting Rights Act. Empirical research, in general, suggests that greater representational equity exists under single-member-district election systems.[22] Some scholars argue that city size, not election structure, is most related to representational equity; and that if election structure ever played a role, its impact has diminished over time.[23]

Most scholarly discussion of representational equity focuses on the election of minority candidates by minority voters. Such descriptive representation, while important, usually does not address the policy consequences for the minority community when representation is enhanced. Exceptions include studies linking district election structures with more equitable minority employment patterns in cities and less discriminatory education policy in schools.[24] Research indicating that institutional structure and representation affect policy challenges other research that indicates cities are limited in their ability to affect local policy or make a difference in the lives of their residents.[25]

Recent Gains for the Disenfranchised

The role of minorities in local politics is changing, particularly in large metropolitan areas. Beginning with the civil rights movement of the 1960s, ethnic minorities, African-Americans especially, have been increasingly active as both candidates and voters. Civil rights legislation has broken down the barriers to participation that existed for decades. In addition, demographics are changing, for a growing number of cities are developing African-American or Hispanic majorities as whites move to the suburbs.

The impact of these changes is manifest in the impressive list of major cities that have or recently have had African-American mayors, including Denver; New York; Los Angeles; Chicago; Atlanta; Philadelphia; Cleveland; Washington, D.C.; and Gary, Indiana. Denver and San Antonio have had Hispanic mayors. The 1991 mayoral contest in Denver featured a white attorney, an African-American city auditor, and an African-American city attorney in a three-way contest to succeed Hispanic Mayor Frederick Pena. None of the three received a majority in the initial balloting, so the two top vote recipients challenged each other in a run-off. Both individuals in the run-off were African-American. Minority membership on county and city councils and on state and local school boards is growing as well, as indicated in Table 12.2. These local

TABLE 12.2
Minority Membership on County and City Councils and on State and Local Education Boards

Unit of Government	African-American		Hispanic	
	1970	1988	1984	1989
County and city councils	719	4,089	1,276	1,724
State and local education boards	368	1,542	1,173	1,341

Source: U.S. Bureau of the Census, *Statistical Abstract of the United States, 1991* (Washington, D.C.: GPO, 1991), pp. 266–67.

minority officeholders make up more than 50 percent of the nation's minority officeholders.

In summary, the institutional form that a community employs has an impact on the distribution of political power and on politics. The use of the at-large election may disadvantage minorities and low-income candidates generally. The nonpartisan ballot takes away a voting stimulus and cue — the political parties — thus depressing turnout and the ability of voters to track decisions and hold representatives accountable. It may also increase the saliency of the candidates' race. Holding elections at times other than when state and national elections occur, which many reformed cities and school and special districts do, can depress voter turnout. Low turnout, in turn, may lead to an electorate that is within the upper class economically, occupationally, and socially. What American communities have by way of representation and leadership, then, may be determined to some extent by institutional arrangements.

DO THE FEDERAL AND STATE GOVERNMENTS RULE THE COMMUNITY?

Several developments in recent years raise questions about the extent to which community politics is still guided from within the communities themselves. As noted in the discussion of federalism in Chapter 2, and in Chapter 13 on finances, the federal government has imposed a variety of mandates on state and local governments in recent years, and the states have done the same to their local units. In addition, with the growth in the mobility of investment capital and the renewed willingness of states and localities to chase after business and industry, some observers now suggest that local politics is becoming less relevant because the major decisions that affect communities are being made by outsiders. They suggest that perhaps local politics has become a series of processes by which community leaders decide how to pander to outside forces such as federal money, state government mandates, and industry in an effort to survive economically. Mark Gottdiener describes the situation in this way:

> Local politics has long since passed over into the hands of
> professional managers, giant multinational corporations, local
> capital caught up in a predatory jungle of fierce small-business
> competition, provincial politicians making do on dwindling party
> resources, and, certainly not least, federal interventions
> promulgated by the long series of crises befalling the country
> since 1960. . . . Local politics is hemmed in presently by the power
> of corporations, programs at higher levels of government, and a

failure to generate enough revenues without the need for finance capital's administration of public budgets.[26]

Local governments have always been the legal creatures of the states, and as such they are legitimately subject to state laws. Thus, state statutes that require counties to conduct elections and keep vital records, that control police officer and fire fighter pension funds, or that set the number of school days for local districts are not new, are not especially burdensome to the local units, and certainly are not inappropriate. Similarly, the national government has long issued requirements along with grants to state and local governments, as in the specification of construction and accounting standards in the use of federal highway money.

Federal and State Mandates

The past couple of decades have witnessed an increase in the number of demands placed by one government on another, and in many instances the nature of the demands has changed. Congress has passed a veritable flood of laws that compel both states and localities to comply with their requirements or risk losses of federal funds (sometimes in program areas not directly related to the mandate), or civil penalties, or both. Mandates have been issued in such areas as clean air standards, wastewater pollution, storm drainage runoffs, Medicaid eligibility, accessibility for the disabled, on-the-job drug use, the speed limit, the drinking age, and so on. However, the mandates are almost never accompanied by the funds needed to pay for and implement the programs required. This has resulted in a redirection of state and locally derived tax monies and federal preemption of state and local priorities and policies. Will a city spend money for parks, open space, and better streets? Or will it first upgrade its sewage treatment facilities and redesign access to its buildings? If resources are inadequate to do it all, the city will do what Congress and federal agency rules dictate, which may or may not be what citizens, local influentials, or the elected council wants.

Similarly, the states have increasingly imposed requirements on their own local units, often without providing the funding that the local units need to comply with the mandates. Some mandates relate to governing procedures, others to programs, and others still to fiscal limitations. From 1981 to 1989, for example, the Florida legislature enacted 326 new mandates on local governments having to do with process, programs, and limits.[27] During the 1980s the state of Illinois placed $148 million in mandated costs on its local governments, but more than two-thirds of the total cost was not reimbursed by the state.[28]

State-imposed mandates affect all sorts of policy areas, including personnel, health, transportation, recreation, public assistance, and the environment. For example, states have required that certain school employees be fingerprinted, that drinking water be tested for lead, that landfills be closed, that school buses undergo certain safety examinations, and that the special educa-

─────────────────── **FOCUS** ───────────────────

12.1   THE IMPACT OF A FEDERAL MANDATE ON A SMALL TOWN

A small Colorado town with 1,200 residents operated a sewage system with an old set of collection lines but a fairly modern double-cell lagoon. The system was run by a sole public works director, who also helped the town's two maintenance people with the streets, parks, and cemetery. The director did most of the bookwork on the sewer system, including filling out reports and forms for the state health department.

During irrigation season, the leaky sewage-collector pipes took in excess water and caused bacterial problems in the lagoons. At times the lagoons overflowed and, due to electric failures or vandalism, the pumping system failed, resulting in unplanned spills into an adjacent creek. The spills violated the rules of the state health department, which was doing the bidding of the Environmental Protection Agency by administering the clean water laws of Congress. The state health department sent letters to the town's officials ordering immediate remedies and threatening fines. The town looked to the public works director to handle it—in addition to his street work, lawn mowing, sewage testing, and work on reports for the state health department. Although the town struggled mightily to comply with the law, the town was poor, was not growing, and just did not have the money or staffing to comply fully with the wishes of Congress as passed down through two huge bureaucracies. The town still struggles.

tional needs of deprived or handicapped children be addressed adequately. Cities and counties are told how to regulate and handle underground storage tanks, asbestos, and hazardous materials generally. Counties are instructed in the handling of foster child care. Local units are told how to recycle materials. (See Focus 12.1.)

As with federal mandates, those imposed by the states on local communities are reasonable and in the public interest. Few would argue with claims that drinking water should not contain lead, that school buses ought to be safety inspected, or that counties should address the special educational needs of handicapped children. Thus, the ends or goals of the mandates are generally not at issue.

The cost of the mandated programs and which government will foot the bill are at issue. With the federal government running large annual budget deficits, it is difficult for Congress to fund new policy initiatives. But by using mandates Congress can appear to be responsive to public concerns without spending much money. That is, Congress can respond to citizen and group demands by mandating programs and requiring states to pay for them. For example, recent legislation requires schools to adopt and enforce laws banning drug use in the workplace. Although the development and administration of this policy are costly, Congress can require schools to fund it but take credit itself for the new antidrug initiatives.

Who Should Pay for Mandated Programs?

The same situation characterizes many state mandates. State lawmakers respond to public calls for safer school buses and drinking water and the local decision makers pay the bill. A 1990 study of state mandates conducted by the Advisory Commission on Intergovernmental Relations describes the political issues involved:

> The major mandate issue for many local governments is whether they can meet the financial demands of state mandates within the financial limits imposed by the state. . . . essentially, a mandate substitutes [state] priorities for local ones.[29]

The changing nature of intergovernmental relations thus has implications for community power and policies, as well as for the question of who governs. Without question some people and some groups are more influential in community affairs than are others. At the same time, some decisional latitude and the ability to set local priorities are slipping from the grasp of the communities themselves. According to Mark Gottdiener, "three decades of change have transformed the city from a formidable engine of growth to a federal and state client dependent on a form of municipal welfare."[30]

DOES OUTSIDE CAPITAL GOVERN THE COMMUNITY?

Gottdiener highlights the interpretation of contemporary community power and politics held by many modern observers. He claims in his book *The Decline of Urban Politics* (1987) that the meaningful decisions impacting the local community are no longer made by popularly rooted representative bodies. Rather, much of the political life of the community is directed by external capital and business interests as well as by state and federal governments and bureaucratically rooted specialists.[31]

Similarly, the external preemption of local politics is addressed in a widely cited 1981 study conducted by Paul Peterson.[32] He argues that the primary political drive of the modern city is to survive economically. To survive, cities must grow. They must attract capital, which is mobile. The search for capital takes the form of local policies designed to enable a city to compete with other communities in attracting new business and residential development. In Peterson's words, "the primary interests of cities [are] the maintenance and enhancement of their economic productivity."[33]

The Urge for Economic Development

The cities' development strategy is to invest in infrastructure, including local investment in roads, utilities, and industrial parks, along with taxing and zoning policies that are attractive to development interests with capital to invest. The underlying assumptions in such policies are that new growth will more than pay back the costs associated with its procurement; and that the city will have jobs and tax revenues adequate to meet its needs. In a 1985 study of Cleveland, Todd Swanstrom notes that "by lowering taxes on mobile wealth, cities will eventually increase tax revenues through an expanding tax base."[34]

According to Peterson, community policies devoted to development and growth come at a price—the neglect of social policies and programs—that has a redistributional impact.[35] That is, money spent to attract more business and industry is money that is not spent on recreational programs, on health and hospitals, or on a variety of other services that would benefit those who do not profit from the aggressive economic growth policies. A variety of potentially redistributive local policies are thus preempted by policies designed to placate the interests of economic enterprises external to the community.

Several urban politics researchers challenge Peterson's model of urban policymaking, arguing that cities have a considerable amount of policy discretion. In other words, they contend that politics does matter and cities can have sufficient resources and authority to make effective public policy.[36] The relevance of election structure and representation is clear; it is linked with the models of urban governance outlined by several scholars.[37]

Does Development Improve the Economic Health of Communities?

Some scholars of urban politics suggest that local communities may be wasting their time chasing business and industry. John Herbers reports that after the expenditure of billions of dollars in public funds over several decades, the extent of economic development remains unclear.[38] Disappointment, Herbers argues, has often overshadowed success.

Mark Schneider argues that the locational decisions of business and industry are based on a host of factors, of which local fiscal policies are just one, and that the latter therefore have but a marginal impact on location choices.[39] In addition, the economic health of a community is the product of a blend of many factors, including the health of the national economy, the regional economy, and national and state decisions. Community growth and development may help to keep taxes low and services high—to enhance the economic health of the community. But it is not at all clear, in the context of state, national, and even international politics and economics, that growth and development can be successfully manipulated with local policies. In Schneider's view, then, decisions by local politicians have relatively little impact on a community's economic fortunes; rather, the locals simply respond to demands originating from outside the community.

A prime example of local response to external demands is the City of Denver's efforts in 1991 to assemble a public subsidy package large enough to lure a huge United Airlines maintenance facility to its new international airport. In an effort to beat out locations in Oklahoma and Virginia, Denver offered United over $200 million in an assortment of facilities and tax breaks. But that wasn't enough for the airline's management. They also wanted a package that would total $600 million over 30 years, include state tax credits of $2,000 per year per new employee, and pay the credits to United from the state treasury should the airline suffer profitless years. The city, in concert with the governor, then pressured the state legislature to meet in special session to enact legislation to give United what it wanted. In this instance, the agendas of both the community and the state were driven by outside economic interests. (In the end, Denver's efforts proved futile; United Airlines received a better offer from Indianapolis and decided to locate its facility there.)

Outsiders Limit the Community's Power to Affect Policy

Clearly, much of the power to affect policies in the modern American community lies well beyond the city or town limits. Clarence Stone puts it this way:

> While local officials enjoy considerable formal authority, they must respond to external inducements and penalties beyond their influence. To a large extent, they must play by rules they have not made.[40]

Stone also notes the inherent constraints under which urban governing coalitions must operate:

> Because centrifugal forces are always strong, achieving cooperation is a major accomplishment and requires constant effort. . . . Cooperation across institutional lines is valuable but far from automatic; and cooperation is more likely to grow under some circumstances than others.[41]

Stone's analysis seems to the point. Communities have to deal daily with the impact of outside forces.

SUMMARY

It is not at all easy to grapple with questions of community power and politics. The local political landscape is extremely diverse. Many of these governments are clustered together in large metropolitan areas where one can travel through a city, a county, and a school district without even noticing. Some of the units are enormous, such as New York City and Los Angeles, whereas others are tiny, such as Elsa, Texas.

Many cities and most counties operate with partisan political systems, whereas schools, special districts, and the majority of municipalities use nonpartisan systems. Some elect representatives from districts, others select them at-large, and a few use both methods. Some old cities have longstanding traditions of ethnicity-based partisan politics. Many new cities use a nonpartisan reformed system of government. The scale, age, histories, and economies of American communities are so varied that it is difficult to generalize much about their power and politics.

Further, the environments in which modern American communities operate are complicated by recent political and economic developments. The states and the national government are increasingly intrusive in local affairs, wrapping the communities in a web of dictates and requirements. The nationalization and internationalization of the economy, as well as the ebb and flow of economic circumstances, leave local communities with a shrinking ability to control their own fortunes.

Still, questions of power, of who governs, fascinate political scholars. Some contend that local communities are still run by elites, whereas others see a more diverse and pluralistic system emerging. None fail to recognize the growing power of fundamental experts—city managers, planners, computer and legal experts, and other professionals who occupy bureaucratic slots. Modern research increasingly focuses on the growing role of external forces in community politics, particularly the state and national governments and external and mobile capital. Finally, scholars are interested in the role of citizens in governing their own communities, and hence election systems and elections remain matters of interest in a representative democracy.

KEY TERMS	power elites	pluralism
	reputational approach	executive-centered coalition
	stratification approach	at-large election
	power pyramid	

ADDITIONAL READINGS

Dahl, Robert. *Who Governs?* New Haven: Yale University Press, 1961.
Hunter, Floyd. *Community Power Structure.* Chapel Hill: University of North Carolina Press, 1953.
Jones, Bryan D., and Lynn W. Bachelor. *The Sustaining Hand: Community Leadership and Corporate Power.* Lawrence: University Press of Kansas, 1986.
Stone, Clarence N. *Regime Politics: Governing Atlanta 1946–1988.* Lawrence: University Press of Kansas, 1989.
Vogel, Ronald K. *Urban Political Economy: Broward County, Florida.* Gainesville: University Press of Florida, 1992.

NOTES

1. Norton Long, "The Local Community as an Ecology of Games," *American Journal of Sociology* (Nov. 1958): 252.
2. Robert Lynd and Helen Lynd, *Middletown* (New York: Harcourt Brace, 1929), cited in Willis D. Hawley and Frederick W. Wirt, *The Search for Community Power* (Englewood Cliffs, N.J.: Prentice-Hall, 1968).
3. Ibid., pp. 43, 50.
4. Floyd Hunter, *Community Power Structure* (New York: Doubleday/Anchor Books, 1963).
5. Ibid., pp. 66, 74, 76, 81.
6. Nelson Polsby, *Community Power and Political Theory* (New Haven: Yale University Press, 1963).
7. Ibid.; and Raymond E. Wolfinger, "Reputation and Reality in the Study of Community Power," *American Sociological Review* (Oct. 1960): 636–44.
8. Robert A. Dahl, *Who Governs?* (New Haven: Yale University Press, 1961), p. 331.
9. Ronald K. Vogel, *Urban Political Economy: Broward County, Florida* (Gainesville: University Press of Florida, 1992), p. 40.
10. Ibid.
11. Polsby, *Community Power*, p. 117.
12. Peter Bachrach and Morton S. Baratz, "Two Faces of Power," *American Political Science Review* (Dec. 1962): 947–62.
13. Ibid.: 948, 949.
14. Raymond E. Wolfinger and John O. Field, "Political Ethos and the Structure of City Government," *American Political Science Review* (Dec. 1962): 948.
15. Perevill Squire and Eric R. A. N. Smith, "The Effects of Partisan Information on Voters in Nonpartisan Elections," *Journal of Politics* (Fall 1988): 169–79.
16. Willis D. Hawley, *Non-Partisan Elections and the Case for Party Politics* (New York: Wiley, 1973).
17. Robert R. Alford and Eugene C. Lee, "Voter Turnout in American Cities," *American Political Science Review* (Sept. 1968): 796–813.
18. Ibid., p. 804.
19. Eugene C. Lee, "City Elections: A Statistical Profile," in *Municipal Yearbook* (Washington, D.C.: ICMA, 1963), pp. 74–84.
20. Susan Welch and Timothy Bledsoe, *Urban Reform and Its Consequences* (Chicago: University of Chicago Press, 1988).
21. Chandler Davidson and George Korbel, "At-Large Elections and Minority-

Group Representation: A Re-Examination of Historical and Contemporary Evidence," *Journal of Politics* (Nov. 1981): 982–1,005; Richard Engstrom and Michael D. McDonald, "The Effect of At-Large versus District Elections on Racial Representation in U.S. Municipalities," in *Electoral Laws and Their Political Consequences*, ed. Bernard Grofman and Arend Lijphart (New York: Agathon Press, 1986), pp. 203–25; and Peggy Heilig and Robert J. Mundt, "Do Districts Make a Difference?" *Urban Interest* (Spring 1981): 62–75.

22. Susan Welch, "The Impact of At-Large Elections on the Representation of Blacks and Hispanics," *Journal of Politics* 52 (Nov. 1990): 1,050–76.

23. Delbert Tabel, "Minority Representation on City Councils: The Impact of Structure on Hispanics and Blacks," *Social Science Quarterly* (March 1978): 142–52; Welch, "The Impact of At-Large Elections"; and C. E. Teasley III, "Minority Vote Dilution: The Impact of Election System and Past Discrimination on Minority Representations," *State and Local Government Review* (Fall 1987): 95–100.

24. Kenneth R. Mladenka, "Barriers to Hispanic Employment Success in 1,200 Cities," *Social Science Quarterly* (June 1989): 391–407; Kenneth R. Mladenka, "Blacks and Hispanics in Urban Politics," *American Political Science Review* (March 1989): 165–92; Kenneth J. Meier and Joseph Stewart, Jr., *The Politics of Hispanic Education: Un Paso Pa'Lante y Dos Pa'tras* (Albany: State University of New York Press, 1991); and Kenneth J. Meier, Joseph Stewart, Jr., and Robert E. England, *Race, Class and Education: The Politics of Second Generation Discrimination* (Madison: University of Wisconsin Press, 1989).

25. Paul Peterson, *City Limits* (Chicago: University of Chicago Press, 1981).

26. Mark Gottdiener, *The Decline of Urban Politics* (Newbury Park, Calif.: Sage Publications, 1987), pp. 14, 16.

27. Advisory Commission on Intergovernmental Relations, *Mandates: Cases in State-Local Relations* (Washington, D.C.: ACIR, 1990), p. 3.

28. *Governing* (May 1991): 14.

29. ACIR, *Mandates*, p. 4.

30. Gottdiener, *Urban Politics*, p. 6.

31. Ibid.

32. Peterson, *City Limits*.

33. Ibid.

34. Todd Swanstrom, *The Crisis of Growth Politics* (Philadelphia: Temple University Press, 1985).

35. Peterson, *City Limits*.

36. Clarence N. Stone and Heywood T. Sanders, eds., *The Politics of Urban Development* (Lawrence: University Press of Kansas, 1987); Vogel, *Urban Political Economy*; and Mark Schneider, *The Competitive City* (Pittsburgh: University of Pittsburgh Press, 1989).

37. Clarence N. Stone, *Regime Politics: Governing Atlanta, 1946–1988* (Lawrence: University Press of Kansas, 1989); and Rufus P. Browning, Dale R. Marshall, and David H. Tabb, *Protest Is Not Enough: The Struggle of Blacks and Hispanics for Equality in Urban Politics* (Berkeley: University of California Press, 1984).

38. John Herbers, "A Third Wave of Economic Development," *Governing* (June 1990): 43.

39. Schneider, *The Competitive City*.

40. Clarence N. Stone, "The Study of the Politics of Urban Development," in *The Politics of Urban Development*, ed. Clarence N. Stone and Heywood T. Sanders (Lawrence: University Press of Kansas, 1987), p. 3.

41. Stone, *Regime Politics*, p. 8.

13
State and Local Fiscal Policy

The soaring federal budget deficit has created fiscal worries for state and local governments, which today tend to receive less federal aid than they did a decade or two ago. Here, U.S. Congressman Maurice Hinchey explains the federal deficit at a town meeting in Kingston, New York. *(D. Ogust/The Image Works)*

THE PUBLIC DEMAND: MORE PUBLIC SERVICES WITHOUT MORE TAXATION

FISCAL POLICY: A COMPLEX SYSTEM OF INSTITUTIONS AND BUDGETS

State and Local Spending / Sources of Revenue / Tax Burdens / Tax-Collection Policies / Borrowing: A Major Source of Financing

TRENDS IN FISCAL POLICY

Reduced Federal Funding / Increased Spending / New Taxes / Other Trends / Tough Times Ahead

THE POLITICS OF MONEY

The Federal Role / Tax Revolts / *FOCUS 13.1:* Colorado's Taxpayers Bill of Rights / Privatization of Public Services / *FOCUS 13.2:* The Return of the Toll Road? / Comparing Regressive and Progressive Tax Systems / Expanding the Tax Base / Tax-Base Disparities / Chasing Industry: A Risky Business? / Earmarking Tax Revenues / Taxation and Public Opinion / Tax Reform

THE PROBLEMS AND POLITICS OF BUDGET MAKING

The Executive Budget Process / Influential Experts / Interest Group Influence / The Uncertainty of Budgeting / Incremental Annual Budget Changes / Failed Methods of Budgeting

SUMMARY

State and local finances are complicated because state and local governments are complicated. State governments spend billions on schools, social services, corrections, and so on. Local governments spend for schools, public safety, parks, and utility services. Major state revenue sources include sales and income taxes; local governments rely heavily on property and sales taxes. All of these taxes, of course, hit the poor harder than the wealthy, though the particular mix of services, taxes, and tax burdens varies extensively among the states and among the localities. Americans generally like to receive government services but are less enthusiastic about paying taxes. Recent years have witnessed many tax revolts and budget crises. The fiscal problems facing state and local officials today are increasingly difficult.

The American public is demanding more services from its governments, and politicians promise to provide them if they win elections. Softball players demand more baseball diamonds, lights, and umpires at City Park. Golfers want better greens. The library is a fire hazard and may be closed unless sprinklers and more exits are installed. The police are angry at the offer of a 4 percent salary increase and the rejection of their staff expansion demands. So are the fire fighters. The federal government, working through the state health department, has found in the city illegal discharge of treated sewage; the state will fine the city unless costly improvements are made. The city council just gave the city manager a 5 percent raise; the flood of mail and phone calls indicates that voters noticed, don't like it, and want the council to stop spending recklessly. They demand a tax cut in place of escalating administrative salaries.

Parents complain bitterly at a school board meeting about the closing of an elementary school due to low enrollment. Some also object to an economy measure that rerouted school buses; others want expanded marching band activities. At the same time, teachers threaten a slowdown unless their 6 percent pay and benefits hike is approved. Yet one month earlier the voters had defeated a measure that would have increased the millage rate (or property tax level) to provide more money for the general operation of the schools. The school board and council members meet with a state senator who lives in the community. They tell the senator that their financial woes are, in part, the fault of the state legislature, for it is not allocating enough money to the schools and is imposing too many duties on the city, most of which are costly and unaccompanied by financial support. The state senator mentions an upcoming statewide vote on a tax-limitation measure, the soaring costs to the state of prisons and health care, and the lack of funds to repair even decaying state buildings and roads.

THE PUBLIC DEMAND: MORE PUBLIC SERVICES WITHOUT MORE TAXATION

The American public has developed an enormous appetite for collectively provided goods and services over the past two centuries, and that appetite continues to grow. Americans have long expected government to protect them against external threat and to see to it that their mail is delivered. The national government, whose job it is to attend to these matters, has done so. But throughout much of U.S. history Americans have also assumed that internal law and order would be maintained; schools would be built, staffed, and heated and children would be educated; roads and bridges would be built and maintained; drinkable water would come out of the faucet; elections would be conducted at the proper times; vital records would be kept in accurate and accessible fashion; and so on. These goods and services, however, do not come from the national government; rather, they are provided by the states and localities.

Today, though, the American public is asking state and local governments for even more. The demands include, for example, libraries in most communities; day-care facilities and public housing for moderate- and low-income citizens; parks with lighted softball diamonds and tennis courts; and skating, basketball, football, and baseball facilities. Feeding this colossal public appetite is expensive and, given the public's collective aversion to taxes, not easily accomplished. Governors, state legislatures, city councils, school boards, and county commissioners struggle mightily to bridge the gap between the public's collective wants and its reluctance to pay for them. State and local governments are successful in providing a wide range of essential services—water, roads, schools, and public safety, for example. However, public officials struggle with Americans' demands for more services without more taxes.

FISCAL POLICY: A COMPLEX SYSTEM OF INSTITUTIONS AND BUDGETS

A knowledge of the structural arrangement of the full American government system is essential to an understanding of state and local finances. The complex and varied character of that system is our focus in this chapter. The elaborate and structurally complicated nature of the American political system is evident in the fiscal systems and policies that are employed to provide services and pay for government. **Fiscal policy** refers to the state and local laws that govern the levying of taxes and the spending of money by state and local governments, respectively. Counties operate social service systems, conduct elections, keep vital records, and maintain jails, rural roads, and bridges. Cities provide streets, police and fire protection, utilities, and so on. States provide road services and operate colleges and universities, state roads and parks, and prisons. Much of what the various levels of government do is intergovernmental. For instance, while local school districts run the elementary and secondary schools, states provide much of the money and exercise some control. States collect fuel taxes and share the revenues with cities and counties. States and counties cooperatively operate social service systems.

Similarly, the fiscal system employed to raise money and pay bills is complicated and intergovernmental in that it tracks a complex array of institutions. Citizens pay property taxes to cities or townships, counties, school districts, and special districts. They pay sales taxes to states, cities, and counties. They pay income taxes to states and sometimes to cities as well. Gasoline is taxed by the federal government and the states, and the revenues are shared with local governments. Many government services carry special user fees, such as fishing and hunting licenses. Charges are levied for driver's licenses, automobile license plates, and teacher certification.

All levels of government levy taxes, though the type and level of tax vary widely. Sales, income, property, and fuel taxes vary among states and among cities. So do levels of spending. And so do methods of budgeting.

State and Local Spending

As Table 13.1 shows, various kinds of services are made available to the American public by the nation's states, cities, townships, counties, schools, and special districts. Education—including elementary, secondary, and higher education—constitutes the largest portion of state and local budgets (or about 29 percent of total expenditures in 1990). Other services that require significant financial support include public assistance (11 percent), health and hospitals (8 percent), roads and highways (6 percent), retirement funds for state and local public employees (4 percent), and police protection (3 percent).

TABLE 13.1   State and Local Expenditures, 1990

Function	Expenditures ($U.S. per capita)	Percent of Total Expenditures
Elementary and secondary education	$812	21%
Higher education	295	8
Highways	245	6
Public assistance	431	11
Health	97	3
Hospitals	203	5
Police protection	123	3
Fire protection	53	1
Natural resources	50	1
Sanitation and sewerage	114	3
Housing and community development	62	2
Parks and recreation	58	2
Financial administration	65	2
General control	92	2
Interest on general debt	200	5
Water supply systems	89	2
Electric power systems	125	3
Transit systems	76	2
Employee retirement	154	4
Unemployment compensation	66	2

Source: U.S. Bureau of the Census, *Statistical Abstract of the United States, 1992* (Washington, D.C.: GPO, 1992), p. 284.

The particular services provided vary by the type of government. In 1990 the leading expenditure categories for the states were education, public assistance, highways, and health and hospitals. Other state services include parks, corrections, police protection, regulation of activities (ranging from hair-cutting to mining), and paying for the courts and legislatures.[1] Cities, counties, schools, and special districts provide different types of services. Local schools provide education and special districts provide sewerage, water, and other services. The major service areas of American cities include police and fire protection, sewers and water supply, streets and roads, education, airports, and parks and recreation programs. Some cities also provide natural gas and electrical services. Counties provide public assistance, education, hospitals, roads, and police, though their spending patterns vary dramatically nationwide.

Sources of Revenue

The revenue sources for all state and local governments are listed in Table 13.2. Although there is a bewildering assortment of user fees and charges, the **sales tax**—applied to the purchase of goods and, sometimes, services—is the single largest source of revenue, accounting for 17 percent of the total in 1990. At 15 percent in 1990, the **property tax**, a tax levied on homes, businesses, and other real estate, is also a major revenue producer; it is used almost exclusively by local governments. Although the federal government is an important revenue source, its contribution is declining—from 15 percent in 1985 to 13 percent in 1990. Other sources of revenue for states and localities include insurance trust funds and the state **income tax**, which is levied on personal and business income.

Just as state and local units vary in the services they provide, so too do they differ in their sources of revenue. For the states, the sales tax is the leading source, accounting for 22 percent of the total in 1990. The sales tax is followed

TABLE 13.2   State and Local Revenues, 1990

Source	Revenue Amount ($U.S. per capita)	Percent of Total Revenues[a]
Federal government	$550	13.2
Property taxes	626	15.1
Sales tax and gross receipts	715	17.2
Individual income tax	425	10.2
Corporate income tax	95	2.3
Miscellaneous user fees and charges	849	20.4
Utility and liquor store fees	226	5.7
Insurance trust funds	498	12.0
Other	849	3.8

[a]Because of rounding, figures do not add up to 100%.

Source: U.S. Bureau of the Census, *Statistical Abstract of the United States, 1992* (Washington, D.C.: GPO, 1992), p. 284.

by federal money derived from a host of different programs, amounting to 18 percent of the total in 1990. The individual income tax is also a major revenue source, accounting for 14 percent of all state revenue in 1990.[2]

Cities, however, derive 22 percent of their money from other governments, another 22 percent from an assortment of fees, 16 percent from utility charges and liquor store revenue, and 17 percent from the property tax.[3] America's 3,042 counties differ still. Nearly one-third of their funds comes from the state, 26 percent is generated by the property tax, and 24 percent comes from fees and charges.[4]

There is considerable variation in both spending and revenue systems across the country. In 1990, for example, total state spending ranged from $1,391 per person in Texas to $7,790 in Alaska. Even within regions of the United States the differences can be significant; Wyoming spent $3,270 in 1990 compared to nearby New Mexico's $1,925.[5]

Moreover, not all states employ all of the traditional taxes. Alaska, Florida, Nevada, South Dakota, Texas, Washington, and Wyoming do not have an individual income tax. Nevada, Texas, Washington, and Wyoming all lack the corporate income tax. Alaska, Delaware, Montana, New Hampshire, and Oregon operate without a general sales tax.[6]

In states that do employ all traditional taxes, the rates of taxation vary greatly. Some states use a graduated income tax similar to that of the federal government; others impose a flat percentage rate irrespective of income. For example, Alabama's individual income tax ranges from 2 percent to 5 percent and Colorado's is a flat 5 percent. Kansas has a 4.25 percent state sales tax, whereas Pennsylvania has set its sales tax at 6 percent.[7] Arizona, Michigan, and New Jersey are among the more than two dozen states that exempt food (except for prepared foods) from the sales tax. Mississippi, Virginia, and a few other states impose a tax on food items. In the tobacco-producing state of North Carolina the tax on cigarettes is just two cents per package; in Connecticut and New Jersey it is 40 cents. Hawaii taxes cigarettes at 40 percent of the wholesale price. State taxes on motor fuels vary as well, ranging from less than 10 cents to 20 cents per gallon.[8]

The amount of money the states collect ranges widely. In 1990 Alaska took in $4,069 per capita, whereas Mississippi averaged just $1,264 for each person. The mean in the states in 1990 was $2,017 (see Figure 13.1). Similar differences prevail among the states for specific taxes. In 1990 Alaska and its local governments collected $1,246 per capita in property taxes; in Wyoming the figure was $901, in New Mexico $219, and in Alabama $163. In the category of the personal income tax, New York and Massachusetts collected over $800 per person in 1990 and two states collected under $100. The state of Washington, which has no income tax, was second among all states in 1990 in per-capita collections of the sales tax at $1,045. Hawaii, which ranks low with respect to the property tax, was first at $1,062 in sales tax collections.[9] Minnesota has a highly progressive income tax. Alaska leans hard on its extractive industries for tax revenue. New Hampshire leads the fifty states in allowing the local units to do the taxing.[10]

FIGURE 13.1
State and Local Per-Capita Tax Collections in Selected States, 1990

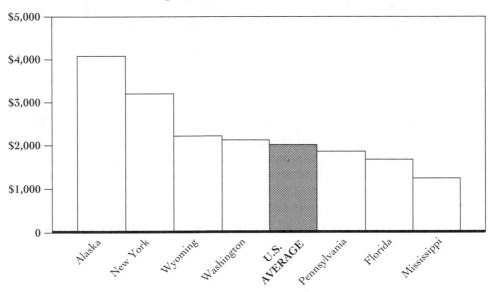

SOURCE: Adapted from Colorado Public Expenditures Council, *State and Local Taxes* (Denver: CPEC, 1992), p. 10.

The variation among the states in total tax collection is to some extent a reflection of their uneven wealth, but other factors also play a role.   **Tax Burdens**

On average, state and local governments collected $115 in taxes per $1,000 of personal income in 1990. But that figure ranged from $196 in Alaska and $155 in New York to just $84 in New Hampshire and $94 in Tennessee and Missouri.[11] Clearly, the desire to provide goods and services collectively varies considerably among the American states.

The relationship between a state's wealth and its taxes can be illustrated by examining the case of New Mexico in 1990. New Mexico ranked thirty-fourth among the states in the total amount of state and local tax collections. It collected $1,690 per capita in 1990, or 16 percent less than the national average. Yet New Mexico ranked eighth among the states in its level of state and local taxes per $1,000 in personal income, the figure being 10 percent above the national average. New Mexico is not a wealthy state, but it has imposed upon itself a state and local tax burden that is higher than the national average in order to provide services for its citizens.[12]

Tax-Collection Policies

There is another important way in which the fiscal policies of the states vary—the extent to which they impose and collect taxes or leave those tasks to the local governments. In some states almost all the money raised to pay for state and local government goods and services is collected by the state, with a substantial portion then allocated to the local governments. As Figure 13.2 shows, that proportion is as high as 82.4 percent in Delaware and as low as 31.7 percent in New Hampshire. The average for all states is 60.2 percent, though that figure has been increasing steadily in recent years. The growth is partly the result of the new federalism, wherein the states have assumed a growing share of program costs and the need, sometimes under court order, to increase and more evenly provide state support for local schools.

State variations with regard to tax-collection methods can have political and economic consequences. A state may have a conservative legislature but some politically liberal cities. If the state does the taxing, public programs are likely to be less well funded than if tax policies and levels were left to the localities. In addition, state-level politicians in states with centralized tax systems are in a better position to exert their will over local priorities and programs

FIGURE 13.2
State Government Share of State and Local Tax Revenue, Selected States, 1990

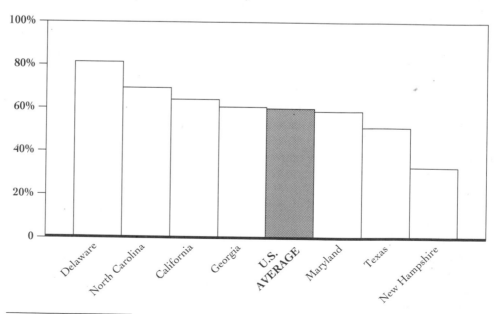

SOURCE: Adapted from Colorado Public Expenditures Council, *How Colorado Compares* (Denver: CPEC, 1992), p. 4.

than are their counterparts in fiscally decentralized states. They can simply set conditions that go along with the distribution of funds. **Fiscal decentralization** —the tendency of some states to give local governments the taxing and spending responsibilities—can lead to wide disparities in the ability of local units to pay for public goods and services. When local units are left to fend for themselves, those located in economically poor sections of a state may simply be unable to raise as much money as their more well-to-do counterparts, and the quality of such services as public education can suffer. Inequities are less likely to occur when the state collects the taxes and supports local schools and other local programs with direct annual state appropriations. However, in this case the state is also in a better position to tell the localities how to run their affairs.

The pattern of taxation has changed significantly over the years. In the early part of the twentieth century, the property tax was the primary source of revenue for the states. Today, sales and individual income taxes generate most state revenue and the property tax is the major revenue source for local governments. In 1989, for example, 49 percent of all state taxes came from the sales tax and 32.4 percent from the individual income tax.[13] At the local level, income and sales taxes are growing in use, as is the employment of user fees. The pattern of taxation tends to change slowly with time.

Borrowing: A Major Source of Financing

Forty-nine of the fifty states (Vermont is the sole exception) prohibit by way of their own constitutional or statutory provisions **deficit spending**—that is, spending more than they take in for the normal yearly operation of their governments.[14] But that does not mean they refrain from borrowing money or that they are without debt. Indeed, borrowing is a major and very important source of money for state and local governments.

Revenue and General Obligation Bonds   When a state or local unit borrows money, it does so by issuing or selling **bonds**—legal instruments in which the government unit promises to repay the bondholder a certain amount of money at a specific time. In effect, a bond is a pledge to pay back what is borrowed, plus interest, at a certain date. Most bonds are issued by investment banks and brokerage houses, which handle the borrowing logistics for government units. Usually the government seeks to raise a large amount of money, and the brokerage house breaks down that amount into smaller denominations. These are then sold to lenders, generally huge financial institutions such as banks, insurance companies, and brokerage houses themselves. Some bonds may then be further broken down into smaller denominations and sold to individuals.

There are two general types of bonds that states and localities employ to borrow money—revenue bonds and general obligation bonds. A **revenue bond** is just what its name implies; that is, a pledge to the lender to be paid off with the revenues from the facility or program built with the borrowed money. For example, a city might issue several million dollars in revenue bonds to obtain the money needed to build a convention center or a sports facility. Those frequenting the facility would then be charged a user fee, which would eventually provide the revenue to pay off the bonded debt.

A city faced with decaying streets may need to embark on an extensive repair program. It might cost millions of dollars that the city just does not have in its annual operating budgets. It might, then, seek to raise the funds for the road repair program by issuing general obligation bonds. A **general obligation bond** involves a pledge by the city to repay lenders with money derived from current revenues or from a small additional tax imposed only until the debt is satisfied. It is called a general obligation bond because the municipality pledges the "full faith and credit" of the taxpayers as security for the payback.

Careful Borrowing Prevents Deficit Spending   State and local governments, like private businesses, would find it difficult to operate without the ability to borrow money. Major capital investments, such as roads, buildings, and land acquisitions, are far too expensive to finance on a cash basis out of any single year's tax revenue. In addition, such investments usually have long-term benefits spanning several generations of citizens. So just as an industry borrows to finance plant expansion and pays off the debt with years of profits, so do cities, schools, utility districts, and states borrow money for capital projects.

State and local governments almost never allow deficit spending—that is, borrowing money to finance the ongoing expenditures of government (for example, employee salaries, as opposed to capital spending on roads, buildings, and the like). They are generally prohibited from doing so by state law, and borrowing for current operations is considered unwise and dangerous, for it just postpones financial trouble and promises to transform current difficulties into future disasters. Many of the past and recent financial difficulties in New York City are the result of deficit spending for ongoing operations.

The Impact of Federal Tax Laws   For years the ability of state and local governments to borrow money was enhanced by provisions in federal tax laws that permitted **tax-exempt bonds**; that is, the interest a lender earned from state and local bonds was exempt from federal taxation. This not only made the bonds easy to sell but also allowed the states and localities to borrow money at interest rates below the then-current level. It was worthwhile for persons in high tax brackets to earn, say, 7 percent rather than 10 percent on their money if in the process they could escape all income tax on the earned interest. In addition, the purchase of state and local bonds was usually a secure investment, especially if the full faith and credit of the taxpayers guaranteed the loans. Indeed, such general obligation bonds could be sold at interest rates below the going rate for the slightly riskier revenue bonds.

In 1986, however, Congress made sweeping changes in the federal tax code, some of which affected state and local borrowing.[15] For example, the tax rates in the top income brackets were lowered considerably, with the result that tax-exempt bonds became less attractive to those with high annual incomes. The tax-free nature of some earned income is less useful if one pays 28 or 33 percent in taxes on the last increment of income than if that last portion is taxed at 50 or even 70 percent. Surely state and local bonds will continue to be attractive to many investors, but clearly a little less so, and the interest rates that those governments will have to pay will be closer to the market for other forms of capital.

Another 1986 congressional change in the federal tax law has placed restrictions on the type of state and local borrowing for which the interest on bonds is tax-free. During the decade preceding the 1986 federal tax law changes, localities sought to promote growth and development by issuing what were called **industrial development bonds (IDBs)**. In doing so, however, the localities were simply lending their name to borrowing by private interests for investments ranging from new golf courses to fast-food outlets. Local officials assumed that such development would strengthen their communities economically. Business and industry leaders liked the IDBs because with the cloak of government backing, the interest paid to lenders was tax-free just as with other state and local bonds, and thus money could be borrowed at a rate a few percentage points below the going market rate. Some argued that the IDB arrangements were thinly disguised and fraudulent schemes to avoid taxes; others touted them as clever ways to help communities. Since 1986, federal tax laws restrict the kinds of bonds that qualify for tax-exempt status, and so IDBs are no longer tax-free.

TRENDS IN FISCAL POLICY

The fiscal policies and financial circumstances of the American states and localities have undergone significant changes over the past decade or so. The most dramatic change has been in the extent to which the federal government has reversed a trend that began some five decades ago and accelerated during the 1960s and 1970s — that of providing an ever-larger proportion of the revenue of state and local governments.

In 1958 funds provided to the states and localities through various federal programs amounted to roughly 11 percent of state and local revenues. By 1978, just 20 years later, that figure had grown to nearly

Reduced Federal Funding

27 percent, following an explosion of new federal support programs during the Great Society era of the 1960s. During the 1980s, however, in the context of the Reagan administration's desire to eliminate much of this fiscal dependency and the tremendous federal deficits, federal aid declined as a proportion of state and local budgets. By 1988 it had dropped to 17 percent; by 1998 it is expected to fall to the 1958 level of 11 percent.[16]

Increased Spending

In spite of public pressure to hold down taxes, and in the face of tax revolts in California, Massachusetts, Michigan, and a host of other states, both state and local spending and tax rates have tended to increase since the late 1970s. From 1979, formal state and local per-capita revenues grew faster than inflation and faster than the growth in federal spending. Indeed, from 1984 to 1988, per-capita revenue growth measured in real dollars grew by just 6 percent at the national level but by 17 percent in the states and localities. As at other times in the past when national spending policy has been conservative, the rate of state and local spending has grown.

New Taxes

In 1978, forty-five of the fifty states employed a sales tax, and that number did not change over the following decade. The tax rates did change, however, with roughly one-half of the states increasing the rate by a penny or so. Similarly, there were major increases in the rate of taxation of cigarettes and gasoline in most states, and marginal jumps in the rate of taxation of alcoholic beverages.[17] Forty-one states taxed individual income in 1978 and forty-three did so in 1990.[18] The changes that transpired during that period were in the form of modifications of rates for various income brackets and, in several states, a reduction of the rates at the higher end. This was done in efforts to hold wealth within the states by keeping high-income people from leaving. At the same time, many states joined the national government in seeking to give full tax relief to the very poorest citizens.

In times of **taxpayer revolt** (when grass-roots movements to limit taxation and spending arise) and public resistance to tax increases, it is easier politically for policymakers to seek additional revenues through the more subtle user fees or small increases in **sin taxes** (that is, cigarette and alcohol taxes) than through more visible and politically costly hikes in income taxes or brand new taxes. It is fair to say that in many, if not most, states the issue of taxation is less an economic issue than a political one.

Other Trends

Other trends in state and local fiscal policies during the past decade or so include an increased reliance on user fees and the institution of state-sponsored, money-making games of chance. More governments have chosen to tax the users of particular services directly, as with park fees, higher gasoline taxes, and college and university tuition rates.[19] And while just 13 states employed lottery systems a decade ago, roughly 30 states do so today.[20]

The clear reason for the increased reliance on such fees and money-making schemes has been to patch together revenues and make ends meet in times of declining federal help and taxpayer resistance.

The 1990s have been a difficult time for the states. The economy has grown slowly, and so have state revenues. But costs keep rising, especially in the area of public health. In 1980 less than 10 percent of the states' budgets was spent on public health; that figure grew to 17 percent by 1992 and is expected to reach 25 percent by 1995. The underlying causes are a combination of generally rising health costs (fees for physician care, hospitals, and medicine) and expanded Medicaid coverage as mandated by Congress. Some states are hit harder than others, including California and states in the Northeast and mid-Atlantic area, as they are also suffering from a decline in the defense industry. **Tough Times Ahead**

THE POLITICS OF MONEY

Fiscal policy and budget making are matters of high-stakes politics, for here it is decided in authoritative fashion who will receive what government has to offer and who will pay for it. Among the most enduring issues is whether taxes should be progressive or regressive; that is, how much should we tax the wealthy in comparison to the poor? In theory, a **progressive tax** means that taxes are tied to personal income; the more a person earns, the more taxes that person must pay. As measured in dollars, a **regressive tax** falls equally on everyone regardless of personal income, so that those who make less pay proportionately higher taxes than those in the upper-income brackets. Other fiscal issues to consider include the role of the federal government in state and local finances,[21] the propriety of taxing services as well as goods, and the morality of state-promoted and state-sponsored gambling.

The role of the federal government in providing financial support for state and local activities grew from a minor one in the early twentieth century to a major role by the 1970s. At the start of the Great Depression in the **The Federal Role** climbed to about 11 percent as a result, largely, of the new programs enacted by Congress during the Depression years to stimulate the economy and provide needed social services.

Federal Programs Grow from the 1950s through the 1970s   The late 1950s and the decades of the 1960s and 1970s witnessed a growth in federal support for education, prompted by the Soviet scientific advances made manifest in the launching of *Sputnik*, the world's first orbiting satellite; by President Lyndon Johnson's Great Society programs, which were enacted in the wake of President John F. Kennedy's death in 1963 and designed to reduce poverty and discrimination, advance education, and clean up cities; and by a national awakening to environmental and consumer protection concerns. Congress passed laws establishing new programs by the hundreds, and by 1978 this assortment of federal programs provided almost 30 percent of all state and local revenue.

By the end of the 1970s, and in many policy areas well before that, federal money was helping states and localities with education, highways, sewer and water systems, airports, an assortment of welfare programs, all sorts of research, law enforcement, mental health, and so on. But there were hitches — and lots of them. As conditions for the receipt of federal money, state and local governments had to meet a bewildering array of federal objectives, ranging from elimination of architectural barriers to the handicapped to certain accounting and personnel practices. As the flow of federal money grew, so too did the paperwork associated with grant application, processing, and reporting. States and localities had difficulty just keeping track of all the federal programs that imposed requirements, or provided funds, or both.

The growth of the federal role in funding state and local programs was accompanied by ideological conflict as well. Some conservatives objected to federal spending for such programs as early education for handicapped children, food stamps for needy persons, and tuition aid, job training, and related support for college students. Others fought the trend for fear that the autonomy of the states and localities would be eroded.

The Reagan Administration Introduces Change in the 1980s   By the 1980s the confusion and paperwork involved in intergovernmental relations were frustrating for almost everyone who had to deal with them. In addition, conservatives, joined by many moderates and liberals, began to worry about the vast federal preemption of state and local political autonomy. Ronald Reagan, a two-term governor of California, was among them; in his quest for the presidency he made it clear that if elected he would seek to diminish state and local dependency on federal money as well as federal strictures on state and local decision making.

Reagan was elected president in 1980 and reelected in 1984. By the end of his second term in office, federal money as a proportion of state and local revenue had declined to approximately 16 percent, from the 1978 high of 28 percent. Although there is disagreement about the causes of the decline, two major factors likely played a role. First, although the Reagan administration had only limited success in convincing Congress to eliminate or combine a host of programs that made funds available to the states and localities, it was able to pressure Congress into either reducing funding levels or holding increases to levels below the annual inflation rate. Second, and perhaps more importantly, beginning early in his first term, President Reagan and Congress teamed up to cut taxes and increase spending, resulting in enormous and precedent-setting federal deficits. The deficits, in turn, precluded the expansion, even the maintenance, of prior federal levels of state and local program support.

The 1980s were a time of heated political arguments. Mayors, governors, and many conservatives called for a reduction of the paperwork and federal dictates that accompanied the flow of federal money to state and local units. Many conservatives wanted the money pipeline to dry up because they opposed the liberal programs that the money funded. Mayors and governors generally wanted the money flow to continue but without the constraints. And everyone wanted less paperwork. Client groups that benefited from federal funds in such areas as education and housing fought hard to keep the money coming.

The issues and arguments surrounding the changed level of federal support were a mixture of philosophy and practicality. Some claimed that the national government had an obligation to provide money to care for all Americans. That is, while the states and localities actually operate education, health, and other programs, the federal government should provide adequate support. Others sidestepped the question of obligation, focusing instead on the sovereignty of the states. The founding fathers, some contended, did not intend for the central government to tell the states how to conduct their business. The issues for still others were much more practical; they did not want to lose the funds for the programs with which they were involved or from which they benefited.

Entitlement Programs   In recent years much of the debate over the federal role has centered around the funding of **entitlement programs** such as Medicaid. (An entitlement is a legally created benefit that is available to all citizens who meet the specified criteria.) The Medicaid program provides medical care for the poor and is jointly funded by the national government and the states. The national government sets the standards and eligibility requirements for the program, however, and thus national decisions translate into fiscal responsibilities for the states. During every year since 1984, the national government has expanded eligibility for Medicaid; as a result, the costs are soaring and squeezing state budgets. From 1991 to 1992, for example, state Medicaid costs rose 12 percent, or nearly three times as fast as overall state budgets.[22] State lawmakers are increasingly frustrated, arguing that federal decisions are controlling state budget choices and, as a result, education, corrections, transportation, and other state-run social programs are being shortchanged.

Many issues and arguments surround the federal role. Which government — federal or state — should take on the financial responsibility to provide health care for all Americans? Or should government be involved at all? Should the federal government be allowed to determine a state's speed limit on highways, a state's legal drinking age, a state's responsibility for indigent health care, or how a tiny rural town cleans its sewage before discharging it into a local stream? Should standards and services be leveled nationally by strings tied to federal money and mandates, or are policy questions best left to the local decision makers?

Tax Revolts   Just as state and local officials were having to adjust to the slowed flow of federal money in the 1980s and later, activists in a number of states took action to cut or limit the ability of the states and localities to raise their own money. An early and spectacular move to limit taxation occurred in California in the form of Proposition 13, a citizen-initiated ballot item.

California's Proposition 13   In the late 1970s property values were soaring in California; property tax rates were growing, too. Homeowners faced rapidly escalating property taxes. Two businessmen, Howard Jarvis and Paul Garn, spearheaded an initiative effort to place on the ballot a measure to roll back and then limit property taxes. They captured the frustration of voters and, in 1978, Proposition 13 passed by a two-to-one margin.

The provisions of Proposition 13 limit property taxes in California to 1 percent of the market value, cap increases at 2 percent of the previous year's level, allow reassessment only when property changes hands, and require a two-thirds vote (both locally and in the state legislature) to levy any new taxes. The impact of the measure has been to cut property tax revenues for California's local governments by more than one-half.

Before Proposition 13, California had been running a sizable budget surplus and was, in the short run, able to provide some relief for the local governments. In the longer run, however, Proposition 13 has placed severe constraints on the budgets of California's local governments and cut deeply into public programs and services. It has led to staffing cutbacks, hiring and pay freezes, and reductions in recreational, library, and cultural programs, and even in public safety. Schools have been especially hard hit. The state is last in per-capita spending for highways. Over time, however, the state and local governments have made up much of the tax losses with hikes in user fees.[23]

Other States Respond to Tax Reformers   Several states followed California's lead with respect to tax reform. In Massachusetts, for example, a measure referred to as Proposition Two and One-Half was designed to hold property taxes to a high of 2.5 percent of assessed valuation. In 1980 Massachusetts voters passed the measure; though taxes did indeed decline, so too did some public services. Other states soon followed with tax-limiting laws, including Arizona, Hawaii, Louisiana, Michigan, Nevada, Oregon, Washington, and Colorado. The specter of such tax revolts has made policymakers in virtually all states more cautious about tax hikes.

Some Unexpected Consequences of Tax-Limiting Measures   There have been some interesting and ironic consequences to the tax-limiting actions (see Focus 13.1). In California, for example, roughly two-thirds of the tax relief went not to the millions of homeowners who had supported Proposition 13 but to owners of commercial and farm properties. And in both California and Massachusetts, as well as in some other states, the limitations placed on local revenue-raising powers have led to more local reliance on state money, which, in turn, has contributed to a diminution of local autonomy. Conservatives, especially, while they generally favor low taxes and small government, also tend to favor local control of policy.

The wrath of some taxpayers has been felt directly at the local level, too. In 1993 in Kalkaska, Michigan, for instance, school officials were forced to end the school year in March instead of June for 2,300 students because the district couldn't afford to remain open. Voters in the district had rejected on three separate occasions a property tax increase to keep the schools open.[24]

The Impact of the Tax Revolt Movement   The impact of the tax revolt movement has gone beyond the actual legal imposition of taxing and spending limits. It has also caused politicians to be extremely cautious in their handling of issues involving tax increases. In the wake of the experiences in California, Michigan, and elsewhere, candidates in both parties regularly run on promises to cut taxes or at least to resist any new ones. Rumblings of grass-roots movements to place tax-limit measures on the ballot still command the attention of decision makers, causing them to assure the public of their dedication to fiscal conservatism. Indeed, the growth in user fees and sin taxes on such items as alcoholic beverages and cigarettes is in part stimulated by a desire to raise more money without broaching the question of increases in the property or income tax. Collected just pennies at a time, these taxes are relatively painless, and tobacco and alcohol are not widely viewed as essentials.

Politicians are wary of tax increases, and for good reason. Larry Sabato, in a book on state governors, notes that after 1960 the tax issue more than any other contributed to the electoral defeat of incumbent governors who lost bids for reelection.[25]

The tax revolt movement, the relative decline in federal financial support, and economic downturns have together made financial survival especially tough for some states and communities. The fall in oil prices hit hard in such states as Texas, Oklahoma, and Louisiana, and tourism-dependent states such as Colorado and Utah are fiscally vulnerable to snow-short winters.

—————————— **FOCUS** ——————————

13.1 COLORADO'S TAXPAYERS BILL OF RIGHTS

On November 3, 1992, voters in Colorado approved a proposed constitutional amendment placing both taxation limits and spending limits on the state and its local governments, including cities, counties, school districts, and special districts. The driving force behind Amendment 1, called the Taxpayers Bill of Rights (TABOR), was Colorado Springs businessman-lawyer Douglas Bruce, an immigrant to the state from southern California. The amendment's passage was unexpected in that Colorado is not a high-tax state and has long had a fiscally conservative legislature. Voter disaffection with America's governments found expression in the TABOR measure.

Now, Colorado's governments may constitutionally increase spending annually by no more than the rate of inflation plus population growth. No taxes may be increased and no new ones enacted without a vote of the people in the affected jurisdiction. Revenues in excess of allowable spending must be rebated to the taxpayers, although TABOR was silent on the matters of which taxpayers and how to refund the money. A vote of the people may authorize the expenditure of extra money.

TABOR has had all sorts of odd and potentially disruptive consequences. If a recessionary economy depresses tax revenues, the spending base for the following year declines; indeed, a ratcheting-down effect could set in and create a downward spiral. Enrollments in colleges and universities beyond projections could produce tuition revenues that may not be spent. Any money not spent in one fiscal year depresses the base for the next year, so there is zero incentive to manage well and carry funds over for difficult times. If property values decline, so do revenues, as the millage rate cannot be raised without a popular vote, and the vote may be taken only at specified times. Officials are not clear as to their ability to enter into such multiyear contracts as lease purchase agreements. Hundreds of attorneys issue advice to state and local officials.

Direct democracy via the citizen-initiative process has Colorado budgeting by ballot. Legislative control, and thus representative government, has been constricted.

In response to the financial squeeze felt by many states and communities, many have considered the **privatization** of public services;
that is, shrinking government by turning over the provision of goods
and services to the private sector. The idea, which is popular among conservatives especially, received a boost during Reagan's presidency in the 1980s.

Privatization of Public Services

In recent years proposals to privatize everything from public hospitals to
the issuance of driver's licenses have been on the agendas of state and local
governments. Indeed, Donna Dudek cites a survey of cities conducted by the
International City Management Association in 1982 that reports that 41 percent
of solid waste collection and 31 percent of residential garbage collection was
being done privately. In addition, private contractors handled 26 percent of
street maintenance, 78 percent of vehicle towing and storage, and 19 percent of
building and grounds maintenance.[26]

Of course, much of what government has done routinely for decades has
involved some reliance on private businesses. Governments purchase vehicles,
equipment, and supplies from private vendors. Huge construction companies
build government buildings and construct roads. At the national level, private
corporations build virtually all the hardware for the defense establishment.
However, the primary assumption underlying the current push for more privatization is that slow, lazy, and inefficient government can become more efficient
through involvement with the lean, ambitious, and innovative private sector. In
addition, many elected officials, conservatives especially, are ideologically committed to the notions of small government, free enterprise, and the private
sector. Of course, many in the private sector support private provision of
government goods and services because it promises to open markets and thus
increase the private sector's profits. In combination, these factors fuel the
ongoing political push toward requiring state and local governments to contract
with private vendors for their goods and services.

Proponents' and Opponents' Views   Privatization is a controversial
political issue that is likely to continue to receive attention. While opponents
such as public employees want to keep their jobs, proponents in the private
sector want profits (see Figure 13.3). Both sides use public-interest rhetoric to
press their particular arguments.

Advocates of privatization contend that the private sector can provide
services of equal or higher value for less money. They often cite a profit-making
fire department in Scottsdale, Arizona, as an example. In addition, the management of some public hospitals in Florida has been turned over to the private
sector, and in New Jersey, Sears, Roebuck and Company issues driver's licenses.
There are many proposals to privatize prisons, and a few are indeed operated
privately.

FIGURE 13.3
The Civil Services Employees Association Opposes Privatization

DON'T LET THE PRIVATEERS' FLAG FLY!

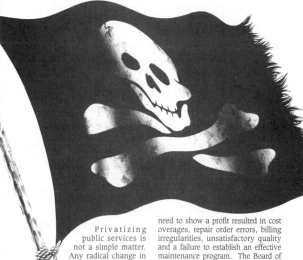

Privatizing public services is not a simple matter. Any radical change in the way things are done includes dangers — so there are important questions that you should ask before you allow any of your services to be privatized. For example:

Why charge the taxpayers to build a facility, then give it to a private company to make a profit from it?

Who'll do the job if private companies move on to more profitable customers when the economy is healthier?

What happens to services that don't return a profit?

Here's what happened when Los Angeles County signed a contract with a private firm to manage and maintain most county vehicles. Their need to show a profit resulted in cost overages, repair order errors, billing irregularities, unsatisfactory quality and a failure to establish an effective maintenance program. The Board of Supervisors voted unanimously to cancel the contract.

The ultimate question: What is really the best way to serve the public?

Capitalize on the experience that's already in place.

No one has more experience than CSEA members – in protecting our neighborhoods and our environment, maintaining our parks and roads, nurturing our children and our elderly, caring for our sick and mentally ill.

Keep that experience. Join CSEA in the drive to keep public services public. For a free copy of *"265,014 Reasons Why New York Shouldn't Be Plundered"*, call toll-free: **1-800-836-CSEA.**

CIVIL SERVICE EMPLOYEES ASSOCIATION
Local 1000, AFSCME, AFL-CIO
Joe McDermott, President

Public employees and their organizations counter with several arguments. One is that private vendors may be unreliable. Often they provide inferior services, experience cost overruns, or simply fail to complete the task for which they are contracted. Indeed, there are numerous instances of problems with private contractors, and public employee unions keep careful records of such failures. Some opponents of privatization point to such failures as the bankruptcy and government bailouts of Penn Central, Chrysler, and Lockheed and the ineptitude and fraud in the savings and loan industry as indications that there is no guarantee of efficiency, honesty, or success in the private sector. Others argue that the protection of civil liberties might be harder in privately run prisons.

In addition, privatization is criticized because its cost savings, when they occur, tend to come at workers' expense. The private vendors are often nonunion, pay substandard wages, and provide little job protection and few if any benefits. These conditions, opponents argue, produce marginal savings or no savings at all by moving the costs elsewhere—either to the workers or the social service budgets when employees who lack benefits are unable to pay for health and other services.

Researchers' Findings A path-breaking 1990 study by Robert Stein of Rice University suggests that privatization, while efficient, does not automatically provide cost savings to municipal governments:

> Research on contracting for goods and services has consistently found this mode of service arrangement to be more cost efficient than direct service provision and production. This, however, has not proven to be sufficient when it comes to reducing the spending levels of municipal governments and the taxes needed to support these levels.[27]

There are some real problems and dangers associated with privatization. Before a city, state, county, or school district moves to abandon public provision of a service, it must be sure that there are competent private vendors available. Unless there are several established and reputable vendors from which to choose, privatization can be risky. If there is only one vendor, problems can emerge down the road. The vendor may raise rates once the government has dismantled its own service provision system. Without private sector competition, the public may find itself gouged rather than saving money. The government also needs to monitor private providers carefully. Cost overruns, shoddy goods or services, or violations of contracts can occur, and vigilance is wise. It is important, too, to know how private vendors treat employees lest other costly problems result from deficient salary, safety, or benefit systems. (See Focus 13.2.)

FOCUS

13.2   THE RETURN OF THE TOLL ROAD?

As America's infrastructure ages and financially strapped states and localities face costly capital construction and repair bills, the notion of private investment is in the midst of a resurgence. In Puerto Rico, a $126 million private toll bridge is being constructed over the San Juan lagoon, which will shorten commuters' trip to the Isla Verde airport. In Orange County, California, plans are in place for using private enterprise to construct four express lanes down the median of crowded Highway 91.

Many other large-scale private ventures are planned or under way across the nation, and they have certain attractions. They relieve government of the need to come up with the cash to fund the capital construction and of the operating and maintenance costs that can dwarf construction costs and last for decades. Sometimes, too, private contractors can complete a job more quickly than the government. The 1991 federal Intermodal Surface Transportation Act, which allows the states to use some federal money to subsidize private projects, has stimulated private or public–private cooperative ventures.

But there are drawbacks to privatization of services as well. Sometimes private outfits have difficulty raising the enormous sums needed to get a project under way. Shifts in the economy and the cost of borrowing money can derail a project. And some politicians and voters alike philosophically oppose public subsidy of private for-profit ventures.

Nevertheless, the nation's aging infrastructure and the public's distress with the size and cost of government are likely to spawn a variety of private experiments similar to those in Puerto Rico and California's Orange County.

SOURCE: Julie C. Olberding, "Paving the Way for Private Roads," *State Government News* (March 1993): 6–9.

Comparing Regressive and Progressive Tax Systems

Who pays a particular tax? Who picks up the tab for public goods and services? The answer to these questions varies from one tax to another.[28] As noted earlier, progressive taxes extract a disproportionately high portion of the income of those in high-income brackets, whereas regressive taxes affect the poor disproportionately relative to their income. The adoption of either tax policy has consequences. Indeed, tax-related politics is a high-stakes, often heated, affair.

The taxes employed by state and local governments are, by and large, regressive, as both the sales tax and the property tax hit the poor harder than the wealthy. The latter pay more in actual dollars, but the former pay much more as a proportion of their income. That is, the poor spend most of their income on essentials — food, clothing, transportation, shelter — so all or most of their money is hit by the sales tax or the property tax. Although the wealthy spend more in dollars on transportation, shelter, and so on, what they spend represents a smaller portion of their income. Certain exemptions help to moderate the impact of regressive taxes. Just over half the states exempt food from the sales tax and all states exempt prescription drugs, for example.

The income tax may or may not be regressive, depending on its structure. A flat-rate income tax, coupled with exemptions that can be taken more readily by the wealthy than by the poor, tends to have a regressive impact. The types of exemptions include capital gains, which are profits from the sale of such items as real property and stocks, and business expenses. In contrast, a graduated income tax, which is based on one's earned income, is progressive. The income tax rate climbs as earned income increases, thus the wealthy pay taxes on a larger proportion of their income than do the poor.

Significant differences of opinion exist as to the best, or fairest, tax system. Proponents of the progressive tax system argue that taxes should be based on one's ability to pay. Those in favor of the regressive tax system adhere to a "benefits received" theory of taxation. That is, they argue that people should be taxed in proportion to the public goods and services they use, and regressive taxes come closer to taxing all people an equal dollar amount. The regressive tax position rests on a conception of government benefits as consisting of such tangibles as streets, sewers, parks, and the like. Thus, people should pay only for what they use and no more, the argument goes.

An alternative perspective that leans toward progressive taxation is based on an expanded view of public goods and services. In this view publicly provided benefits include opportunity as well as tangibles. That is, it holds that certain people who parlay publicly provided educational and occupational opportunities into lucrative arrangements for themselves bear an extraordinary responsibility to reinvest in the system that they have used and from which they have benefited. Professionals in the field of medicine are an example. Physicians may be educated in public institutions — from kindergarten through high school to college and medical school — for which the public pays. The physicians may enjoy public scholarship support, intern in a public hospital, and practice at least some of the time in such a facility. Further, much of the costly equipment that physicians use in school and in private practice is provided by government. Thus, while physicians pay tuition to universities and medical schools, it represents only a small fraction of the total educational cost and of the value of their medical practice, which may generate a six-figure annual income. It is argued, then, that physicians and others in a similar position owe to society what it paid for their educational and occupational opportunities — that they have an obligation to reinvest a substantial amount in the system in order to perpetuate the same opportunities for current and future generations that taxpayers did for them. The theory views the benefits received by wealthy physicians and others rather broadly, for it includes not just streets and parks but career opportunity as well. Therefore, it favors a progressive tax structure—one with a rate that increases with income—as a way to recapture some of the public investment.

Arguments over the systems of taxation are based on both philosophical concerns and self-interest. State and local tax systems are rife with special exemptions wrung politically from state legislators and local government decision makers. Such exemptions include waivers of sales taxes for Sunday supplement newsprint and various types of farm machinery; property tax breaks for church properties (some of which are also used as private day-care centers, counseling centers, and grocery stores); and rebates or delays in the payment of taxes for the elderly. Special interests lean on state and local legislators to provide them with some special service and excuse them from the taxes that others must pay. The decision makers agree to some of their requests and reject others.

In the 1980s the changes in the structure of the federal tax system and the Reagan administration's cutbacks in the flow of federal money to the states and localities helped to create a more regressive tax system. The 1986 changes in the federal law reduced the progressivity of the tax system, with the biggest tax breaks going to the wealthiest taxpayers. At the same time, state and local government replacement of some of the lost federal money with their own has contributed to a more regressive tax structure.

There are some considerations, apart from the philosophical and self-serving arguments, that decision makers must consider. Some taxes are quite stable, providing governments with a steady and predictable flow of revenue, whereas other taxes can be more volatile. The property tax is stable. Should the economy of a community decline for a long period of time, property owners may default on their taxes and lose their homes, businesses, or land. But as this tends not to happen except in the most dire of circumstances, the property tax provides a reliable stream of revenue for local governments.

However, the sales tax can be volatile, and income taxes and mineral extraction taxes can be unsteady. When an economic downturn hits the nation or some region, people cut back on purchases and sales tax collections drop. In boom times they rise. If Utah or Colorado has a warm winter, the ski and tourist business will fall, sales tax revenues will drop, and the state will have difficulty balancing its budget. Similarly, if oil imports rise or national fuel demands fall, the oil extraction tax revenues of Texas, Oklahoma, and Louisiana will drop, unemployment will rise, and the region will face difficult times in terms of state and local budgets and otherwise. Long secure in their reliance on oil and gas revenues, Texas, Oklahoma, and Louisiana had a particularly tough time adjusting to the economic changes of the 1970s and 1980s. Thus, when decision makers establish expenditure habits based on the good times, economic dips can wreak budgetary havoc on the downward side of an economic cycle.

In the current era of tax resistance and unrelenting public pressure for government services, the states and localities are constantly seeking new sources of income as alternatives to tax increases. Their **Expanding the Tax Base** nickel-and-dime efforts include expanded use of user fees and sales of designer license plates. Though some other alternatives hold a promise of considerable revenue-raising potential, they are highly controversial. These include expansion of the sales tax base to include services, taxation of goods sold through mail-order houses located outside a state's boundaries, and the institution of state-sponsored gambling through lotteries.

Sales Taxes on Services Mississippi inaugurated the first sales tax back in 1932. Over the years many other states adopted a tax on sales and today 45 states impose some sort of sales tax. The breadth of the sales taxes varies, with some states taxing goods only and others taxing both goods and some range of services. The use of the sales tax at the local level is expanding, too.

As the U.S. economy has become increasingly service based (76 percent of all employment was in service-producing industries in 1987), the rationale for extending the sales tax to services has grown stronger. But the political opposition to taxing services is stiff. In 1987 the state of Florida, in the context of reenacting laws subject to sunset provisions (which stipulate that programs be reviewed periodically to determine whether they should be continued), and beset with revenue problems, expanded its sales tax to cover a wide range of services, including business and consumer services and services made available from out-of-state vendors.[29] In doing so Florida became only the fifth state (after Hawaii, Massachusetts, New Mexico, and South Dakota) to tax virtually all types of services. The action set off a firestorm of political protest in Florida; five months after its enactment, the state's tax on services was repealed and replaced with a one-cent sales-tax increase on goods. The mass media, concerned with the taxation of television, radio, magazine, and newspaper advertisements, used its considerable resources to try to turn a previously supportive public against the tax. The effort was successful, for the Florida legislature bowed to the public pressure.

As noted earlier in the chapter, state sales tax systems are riddled with special exemptions—ranging from exemptions on food to property tax relief for the elderly—all wrung from state legislatures by various interest groups at one time or another. Proposals to eliminate some exemptions and thereby broaden the tax base often surface when states face tight economic times.

Out-of-State Mail-Order Taxes Struggling to increase their revenues, some states have attempted to tax goods purchased by citizens within their boundaries from mail-order houses located in other states.[30] In a 1967 decision the U.S. Supreme Court ruled that states could not compel out-of-state vendors to collect sales taxes on goods shipped into the state, though they could require the in-state purchaser to pay the tax if the state knew of the purchase (*National Bellas Hess v. Illinois Department of Revenue*). In 1992, however, the Court overturned in part the *National Bellas Hess* ruling. In *Quill Corporation v. North Dakota* (1992), the Court reaffirmed its 1967 ruling that such taxes placed an undue burden on interstate commerce but modified its position by noting that Congress could authorize states to levy such taxes.

The 1992 decision, of course, threatens the booming mail-order catalog business and is likely to result in a fierce battle between the mail-order corporations and the states and local governments over the direction Congress should take. The states and localities lose hundreds of millions of dollars annually as a result of their not being able to require the mail-order firms to collect state and local sales taxes. It is estimated that each year California loses $389 million, Tennessee $62 million, and the state of New York and New York City combined $330 million. Thus far the lobbying efforts by the direct marketing interests have forestalled such action by Congress.

Lotteries and Gambling Systems   An increasing number of states are turning to lottery systems as a means to garner more revenue.[31] Whereas only a couple of states operated lotteries two decades ago, nearly 30 states do so today. However, the revenues generated by state-operated gambling systems are not great, usually representing only a very small percentage of a state's budget. Typically, about 50 cents of each dollar is paid out in prizes. Except for operating costs, the states keep the rest of the money generated by the lotteries, sometimes sharing it with local governments or, more commonly, earmarking it for schools, prisons, economic development, aid for the elderly, and the like.

State-sponsored lotteries are not without controversy, however. Some opponents argue that gambling in general is morally wrong and that states should not sponsor games of chance and thereby encourage citizens to participate. Opponents also argue that lotteries send a bad message to children — that the path to riches is through gambling rather than education and hard work. Still others object because of the alleged regressive impact of lotteries. With the states keeping roughly one-half of the proceeds, they argue, lotteries are simply another form of taxation. Citing studies that indicate lottery players come disproportionately from the middle- and lower-income strata of society, critics contend that the lotteries have a regressive impact.[32]

Opponents' objections, however, have not carried much weight politically, for voters and legislators in an increasing number of states have approved state-sponsored gambling systems as a means to raise revenue, and especially in lieu of the political costs of raising taxes. Educators, state and local officials, the elderly, and others repeatedly contribute to the reservoir of political support for the games, which bring in new money for their budgets and programs.

Researchers who have studied lotteries warn of certain dangers associated with their use.[33] The first is the tendency of decision makers to be optimistic and overestimate expected revenues. Another, related danger is the failure to account for second-year sales slumps, when the novelty of the game has worn off, which appear to affect all lotteries. There is also the danger that decision makers will view the lottery as a fiscal-problem cure-all, giving less attention to the broader and longer-term fiscal needs of state and local governments. Finally, many critics argue that it is inappropriate for government to encourage behavior that is viewed as addictive and destructive.

User Fees   State and local governments have imposed an expanded array of **user fees**, direct charges to citizens for such services as entrance to public parks and golf courses. In the 11-year period of 1976 to 1987, collections from local user fees tripled, from $30 billion to $98 billion. Whereas in 1976 user fees brought in 45 cents for every dollar in taxation, by 1987 the amount increased to 61 cents per dollar. As a percent of total local revenue, user fees rose from 17 percent in 1976 to 21 percent in 1987.[34]

Two primary incentives work to encourage governments to employ user fees. First, the fees represent a nontax method of raising revenues, which is important in the current wake of public hostility to new taxes. Second, for local governments user fees are a way to raise money without having to seek permission of the state legislature.

Tax-Base Disparities

Among the many consequences of the jurisdictionally fragmented government system of the United States is that some governments are rich and others are poor. The per-capita state government revenue in Alaska, for example, is almost three times that of Mississippi. The disparity is in large measure the result of the different levels of wealth in the two states. Similar variations exist among cities, counties, and school districts within the states.

Tax-base disparities lead to chronic political and legal controversy. Central cities generally face high costs for police and fire protection, social services, and maintenance of old utility systems, while they watch their tax-producing property age and newer business, industrial, and residential development move beyond the city limits to the suburbs. Although core cities such as Boston, St. Louis, Detroit, and Denver are the economic, social, and cultural hubs of their respective regions, suburbanites and others benefit from their services and activities generally. Squeezed between high costs and weakened tax bases, core cities look for revenues from the state governments and often resort to taxes designed to get at nonresidents and non–property owners who work in the cities (for example, local sales and income taxes or commuter taxes). Citizens and lawmakers in the suburban and out-of-state areas, in turn, resist what they view as inappropriate subsidization of the core city.

Similarly, the financing of public schools is controversial. In all states except Hawaii the state government pays for some portion of the cost, with the local school districts or municipalities picking up the tab for the rest. The question arises, then, as to how to allocate state funds to the local districts. Some favor skewing the state's per-pupil allocation toward the poorer districts so as to compensate for the local district's difficulty in raising its share from a relatively poor population and poor tax base. Others object and support instead state allocation systems, which reward those districts that show a willingness to reach into their own pockets and pay generously for schooling. Many courts over the past two decades have disallowed state allocation systems, which make some, but inadequate, effort at and progress in moderating extreme disparities among jurisdictions. Indeed, in 1993 nearly half of the states were in litigation concerning the constitutionality of school funding disparities.[35]

Chasing Industry: A Risky Business?

Another political issue that flows in large measure from the jurisdictionally fragmented system of U.S. government involves state and local attempts to develop jobs and promote economic health by attracting new business and industry into the state or town with public money. Some of the public money is used to hire people to recruit new businesses and to advertise the benefits of the state or community. But some of it is spent in the form of straight-out grants or tax breaks. For example, a community may waive a series of sewer, water, curb, and gutter installation fees for an incoming firm, or a state may make land available at cut-rate prices and foot the bill to extend utilities and roads into the area. Many of the debates over tax policy revolve around the question of what an increase or decrease in the property or corporate income tax might do to the attractiveness of the area for new businesses, or what it might do to drive existing ones out.

Attempting to attract business with policy tinkering can be a tricky business. Overly high taxes may keep development out. Excessively low ones may leave a government without the money needed to provide good utility, education, and transportation services and thus leave a community unattractive for the business and its employees. Failure to provide any incentives may mean losing a prospective business. Jumping too quickly can involve giving away public money to a business that might come anyway. And once decision makers begin to reach into the public treasury to help one private enterprise, others line up for their share. In addition, the subsidies can grow when jurisdictions seek to outdo each other in the use of collective resources to benefit private operations.

Still, governments engage in these activities all the time and with increasing frequency. Political leaders in most states consider economic development a prime responsibility; at election time they tout their past successes and promise more. There is little evidence, however, that the use of public money to try to stimulate economic development works, in the short run anyway. Yet many public decision makers argue that quick fixes for deeply rooted economic problems are possible, and their promises of economic development seem to work well at election time.

The practice of **earmarking** certain tax revenues for specified purposes is popular. Gasoline taxes, for example, are typically earmarked — by either statutory or constitutional provision — for use on roads only; the money may not be used, that is, for schools or health care or corrections. Special interest groups tend to favor earmarking because it provides a guaranteed source of money to support the programs they favor.

Earmarking Tax Revenues

However, earmarking restricts a state's flexibility. When funds are earmarked for one purpose, the state cannot use those funds to respond to a crisis in another area. To some extent, every state earmarks some of its revenue — some for roads, some for schools, some for parks, and so forth. Rhode Island law earmarks just 5 percent of the revenue of that state, whereas in Alabama 89 percent of state revenue is designated for specific purposes. Most states fall somewhere in between these two extreme cases, however. California earmarks 12 percent, Illinois earmarks 21 percent, and Texas and Florida each earmark 25 percent of state revenue.[36]

Taxation and Public Opinion

Since the 1970s the American public's view of the value and efficiency of state and local governments has improved. In 1972 the federal government led both states and localities in positive citizen responses to the question "From which level of government do you think you get the most for your money?" (see Figure 13.4). By 1988 the federal government had slipped considerably, local governments had improved slightly, and the states had made a major gain in public opinion.

Several factors may have contributed to the improved image of state and local governments. Under the Carter and then the Reagan administrations, the states and localities had to assume more responsibility for funding their programs. They tightened their fiscal belts and squeezed more out of each tax dollar. At the same time, the flow of rules and regulations from Washington, D.C., increased, and with it irritation and impatience with the federal government spread. Although the public appetite for taxes has certainly not grown, an increased number of citizens are more comfortable than before with the performance of their state and local units.

Tax Reform

The views of many scholars and some legislators on tax policy are reflected in a report published in 1988 by the Lincoln Institute of Land Policy and the National Conference of State Legislatures (NCSL).[37] The report defines a good tax policy as one that (1) generates revenues in a reliable and stable manner, (2) is broadly based and does not result in any single

FIGURE 13.4

A Public Opinion Survey: "From Which Level of Government Do You Think You Get the Most for Your Money?"ᵃ

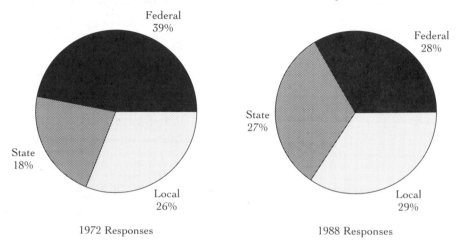

1972 Responses   1988 Responses

SOURCE: ᵃGraphs show percentage of respondents choosing each level; because some did not choose a level, percentages do not add up to 100.

SOURCE: Debra Dean, "Closing the Opinion Gap: State and Local Units Fare Well in ACIR Poll," *Intergovernmental Perspective* (Fall 1988): 24.

excessively high tax, (3) is efficient in collection and easily understood, (4) makes policymakers accountable for the tax, (5) minimizes interjurisdictional competition, and (6) is antiregressive. The tax policies of the states, however, do not meet most of these criteria, nor are they likely to do so anytime soon. Rather, state tax revenues are often unstable, fluctuating with the ups and downs of the economy; they are generally regressive, hitting the poor the hardest; and exemptions for special interests are common.

The political processes that characterize U.S. government today make significant reforms in the direction proposed by the Lincoln Institute of Land Policy and the NCSL highly unlikely. Wealthy Americans, who are much more active politically than those in the lower income brackets, are not apt to support a shift in the tax burden in their own direction. In addition, the special interests that have been so successful in extracting tax exemptions would resist attempts to eliminate their special status.

Tax policy, insofar as it changes at all, tends to change slowly and incrementally. Sweeping tax reform of any sort is difficult to sell politically because it would impact too many interests simultaneously, and their collective resistance to the reforms would likely be too weighty to overcome.

THE PROBLEMS AND POLITICS OF BUDGET MAKING

In addition to having to decide who to tax and for what and how much, governments must devise yearly budgets that outline how they plan to spend the money. This is not a simple or easy task, nor is it without high-stakes controversy. Many parties are involved in the budget-making process — from bureaucrats fighting for more money for their programs and interest groups seeking more public money for private benefits to the governor, mayor, or city manager who may be responsible for drafting budget proposals and the legislature, city council, or school board that ultimately controls the budget. The various participants in the budget process encounter a number of difficulties, many of which are related to the politics of taxation.

The Executive Budget Process

Until early in the twentieth century, government budgets were assembled by legislatures, often through the work of a legislative budget or finance committee. The various bureaus, agencies, or departments in the executive branch submitted requests to the committee, and it would aggregate all requests into one or more budget documents for ultimate approval by the legislature, council, or board. The system worked well in an era of small government. However, as the scope and size of American governments grew, the **legislative budget** process became increasingly less functional.

Thus, beginning with the Budget and Accounting Act of 1921 at the federal level, and in state and local governments in the years and decades that followed, many American governments moved to the **executive budget** process. Under this system, department and agency budget requests are not sent to a legislative committee, council, or board; rather, the requests are first received by the governor, the mayor, the city manager, the school district superintendent, or the special district manager, or their staff members, before going to the legislative body for enactment. The rationale for the executive budget process is to permit chief executives, who are responsible for the administration of public policy, to review and coordinate the host of budget requests and bring them in line with their priorities. Advocates of this method say that, because chief executives must ultimately supervise the administrative apparatus, they should be empowered to assemble a budget that best enables them to get the job done.

However, the task of budget assembly involves much more than simple coordination; indeed, it translates into political power. Legislatures, whether they are state legislatures, city councils, or school boards, control the purse strings of government and thus have the authority to change a chief executive's budget proposal. But authority is not always the same as ability. Government budgets today are huge and complicated. Legislators confront a host of controversial issues, and the budget bill is just one of them. As a result, most legislators do not possess the time or knowledge of detail needed to examine thoroughly a massive and complex budget and to suggest informed major changes. Moreover, because legislatures are multimember bodies composed of legislators with different priorities, it is not always possible to assemble a majority vote to change items in a budget bill.

Considerable variation exists in the extent of budget involvement and budget power among state and local chief executives. In most states the governor and the governor's staff are central to the budget-building process and, as a result, enjoy vast influence in this area. But in some states such as Colorado the legislature still controls the budget-making process; here a joint house-senate budget committee and its staff are the centers of budget power. Similarly, in some cities the council performs the basic work of budget construction, whereas in others, usually the large cities, the mayor and the mayor's staff do the initial budget work. In council–manager cities, school districts, and special districts, the hired chief administrative professionals—the city managers and district superintendents—control the budget-making process and are highly influential as a result.

Influential Experts

Much of the actual detail work on state budgets is performed by full-time, salaried professional staff members. These people are very knowledgeable about budget processes and contents. They analyze agency requests and make recommendations to the committee for which they work. As a result of their full-time status and expert knowledge, these staff members gain influence and power.

In council–manager cities, school districts, and special districts, the experts' power can be controlling. Council and board members are generally part-time politicians and usually serve just one term of office. By the time they learn enough about the contents of a complex budget, their term has expired and other budget novices replace them. Thus, the administrative professionals, with their experience, expertise, and continuity, are the true budget decision makers.

An example of the power of expert staff members comes from a story about Robert L. Mandeville, former chief of the Budget Bureau in Illinois, a state that has had annual budgets in excess of $20 billion. The Budget Bureau served as an arm of the Illinois governor. When Mandeville did not concur with the budget request of an agency, the legislative appropriations staff would kill it. But Mandeville was smart, experienced, knowledgeable about the budget, as well as respected and feared. The governor went with Mandeville's recommendations, and so did the legislative staff. Legally, the Illinois legislature controlled the purse strings, but Mandeville exerted considerable influence.[38]

Interest groups are sometimes very influential participants in the
budget process. Teachers' organizations have a stake in the budget,
as it impacts their salaries and professional working conditions.
Truck and automobile interests have stakes in transportation funding, softball
fans have an interest in parks and recreation budget lines, and so on.

Interest Group Influence

Groups try to influence budget decisions in several ways. They provide
much of the money for legislative campaigns and have access to lawmakers,
which they employ to enlist legislator help to preserve or enhance the appropriations that affect their interests. Groups also seek good relations with and
access to staff members, both in the executive's budget office and in legislative
committees. Good relations can translate into supportive staff recommendations
as well as access to vital information. In addition, interest groups try to create
favorable public images for themselves on the assumption that goodwill may
mean sympathetic and supportive postures by the people's elected representatives.

One tangible result of interest groups' attempts to influence budgets is the
earmarking of certain tax revenues. In all states and in many communities, some
portion of the revenue is earmarked by law for certain purposes. Interest groups
benefit from the earmarking arrangement, as it guarantees their programs a
predictable flow of money. They thus lobby hard for the enactment of statutory
or constitutional earmarking. As discussed earlier in the chapter, however,
earmarking can pose problems for legislatures, states, and localities in that it
prohibits fiscal flexibility even in response to changing problems, needs, and
priorities.

The Uncertainty of Budgeting

Budget making is affected annually by inflationary pressures and the
demands of numerous government and nongovernment interested
parties. Always the agencies want more staff, more supplies, more
equipment, more buildings, and thus more money. Interest groups press for
more money in certain program areas than in others, often with some success.
The public demands more services of higher quality but with fewer taxes. In the
Sun Belt states the size of the public grows each year as immigration increases
the number of people who must be served by that area's governments. And
revenue flows can be fickle, for they track the ups and downs of the economy.

As noted earlier in the chapter, except for borrowing for capital construction purposes, state and local governments may not deficit spend. Instead, they
must balance their budgets each year. A **balanced budget** involves months of
work before the start of a fiscal year. Revenues must be estimated and balanced
against the total expenditures expected to accrue in the fiscal year, which
usually ends 15, 18, or more months later. Revenue forecasting is not an easy
task. Many important sources of state and local revenues—the sales, income,

and extraction taxes, especially — can be volatile, subject to the ups and downs of economic trends that are beyond government's control. In Utah, for example, the legislature cannot predict snowfall on the state's ski slopes, but it will affect revenues collected from sales-tax-paying tourists. Similarly, Texas can do little to control the politics of the Middle East, which affects oil imports and oil prices. Even revenue surpluses can create problems. The expenditure of windfall revenues can inflate the cost of government in subsequent years when the economy is less healthy.

The difficulty of revenue forecasting is reflected in the state budget itself, for most states include in it a reserve of 3 percent to 5 percent to accommodate any unexpected revenue fluctuations. Many states also look to more than one revenue forecast; they may examine the statistics generated in both the legislative and executive branches as well as some independently created estimates. Still, there are years when state and local governments misjudge revenues and are forced to reduce agency budgets midyear. This is a problem, of course, because small budget cuts on an annualized basis become large cuts when less than the full year remains to find the savings, and when clientele groups and the general public are not accustomed to midyear curtailment of services.

Furthermore, revenue forecasting can be politically manipulated. Governors, mayors, legislators, and others are often tempted to overestimate revenues rather than face the political heat of denying some requested increases in order to assemble a fiscally conservative and safe budget. Even though purposeful overestimating is a dangerous practice, elected officials sometimes risk it so as to postpone political controversy.

Incremental Annual Budget Changes

Budget changes from year to year tend to be incremental rather than large or dramatic for several reasons. First, growth in available resources tends to be small each year, so the money is rarely available for a huge increase. Second, political and legal realities preclude large downward adjustments. Buildings must be maintained, utility bills must be paid, hospitals must operate, water and sewage must flow, and police officers and fire fighters must be on the job. Schools have to stay open throughout the school year and forest fires must be extinguished. Big cuts on an annual basis wreak havoc in these and other program areas, which neither decision makers nor citizens are apt to allow. As a result, states and localities add to their budgets, and occasionally subtract, incrementally, a little at a time.

Failed Methods of Budgeting

There have been times in U.S. political history when alternative administrative techniques of budgeting have been attempted in an effort to add rationality to government. In the 1970s, for example, zero-base budgeting (ZBB), popularized by President Jimmy Carter, called for each expenditure item to be reconsidered and rejustified every year, thereby eliminating automatic increments. In the 1960s the planning-programming-budgeting system (PPBS) enjoyed some popularity; here budget categories were tied to programs rather than to administrative units or budget line items.

However, neither ZBB nor PPBS worked very well. The former encouraged the rehashing of old political issues and thereby led to time wasted justifying obviously needed expenditures. The latter generated confusion in general and hindered lawmakers' desire to examine specific budget lines. In essence, neither scheme could remove the human element or the politics inherent in government generally and in budget making in particular.

Summary

American government is a system of multiple, varied, and interrelated institutions made up of from ten to literally hundreds of parts, such as multiple branches, boards and commissions, and semi-independent agencies. As a result, state and local government finance is characterized by multiple, varied, and interrelated patterns of taxation and spending. Revenues come from income taxes, sales taxes, property taxes, user charges, fines and fees, sales and services, lotteries, and other governments. Revenue and expenditure patterns vary among cities, among counties, and among states.

The financial systems and patterns, like the institutions of government themselves, are interrelated. Although state and local units receive some federal funds, those funds come with mandates attached. The state government is the parent of the local units, and as such it sets the parameters for local finance systems. The local units administer many programs on behalf of the state, such as schools and social services, and they often do so in part with state money.

To many Americans the varied and interrelated nature of state and local finance is unclear. Citizens pay property taxes to a city or township, a county, a school district, and possibly many special districts. The county usually collects the property taxes and distributes the funds among the other governments. In April citizens pay income taxes to the national government and, in most states, to their state government. When they go shopping, citizens pay a sales tax, often to the state, a city, and possibly a county all at the same time. Anglers pay the state for a license; so do hunters and drivers. Recipients of social services are helped by people and programs paid for with local, state, and federal government funds. Students attend schools supported largely with local and state money and in part by federal dollars.

Politics also affects state and local finance. Interest groups lobby for tax breaks and funding advantages. The public demands more services of better quality as well as tax relief. Tax reformers seek measures that limit the ability of governments to increase the taxpayers' burden. Indeed, few policy areas more clearly reflect U.S. government institutions and political power than do state and local finance.

KEY TERMS

fiscal policy
sales tax
property tax
income tax
fiscal decentralization
deficit spending
bond
revenue bond
general obligation bond
tax-exempt bond
industrial development bond (IDB)

taxpayer revolt
sin tax
progressive tax
regressive tax
entitlement program
privatization
user fee
earmarking
legislative budget
executive budget
balanced budget

ADDITIONAL READINGS

Anton, Thomas J. *The Politics of State Expenditures in Illinois.* Urbana: University of Illinois Press, 1966.
Gold, Steven D., ed. *The Unfinished Agenda for State Tax Reform.* Denver: National Conference of State Legislatures, 1988.
Wildavsky, Aaron. *The Politics of the Budgetary Process.* 4th ed. Boston: Little, Brown, 1983.

NOTES

1. U.S. Bureau of the Census, *Statistical Abstract of the United States, 1992* (Washington, D.C.: GPO, 1992), p. 280.
2. Ibid., p. 288.
3. Ibid., p. 298.
4. Ibid., p. 297.
5. Ibid.
6. Ibid., p. 290.
7. Ibid., pp. 290–91.
8. Ibid., p. 290.
9. Colorado Public Expenditures Council, *State and Local Taxes* (Denver: CPEC, 1992), pp. 12 and 16.
10. Ibid., pp. 10–11.
11. Ibid., p. 11.
12. Ibid., pp. 10–11.
13. *The Book of the States* (Lexington, Ky.: Council of State Governments, 1992–93), p. 376.
14. Ibid., p. 355.
15. See Jeffrey H. Birnbaum and Alan S. Murray, *Showdown at Gucci Gulch* (New York: Vintage Books, 1987).

16. Advisory Commission on Intergovernmental Relations, *Intergovernmental Perspective* (Spring 1989): 13.

17. *The Book of the States* (Lexington, Ky.: Council of State Governments, 1978–79 and 1990–91), pp. 309 and 316, respectively.

18. Ibid., 1978–79, p. 319; *Book of the States*, 1992–93, pp. 376–77.

19. Penelope Lemov, "User Fees, Once the Answer to City Budget Prayers, May Have Reached Their Peak," *Governing* (March 1989): 24–30.

20. Elaine S. Knapp, "Lotteries No Gamble," *State Government News* (March 1988): 14–16; Marilyn Marks, "Florida Ends Tax Services, Raises Sales Tax," *Governing* (Jan. 1987): 57; and Elder Witt, "States Place Their Bets on a Game of Diminishing Returns," *Governing* (Nov. 1987): 52–55, 57.

21. For more on this topic, see Robert Gleason, "Federalism 1986–87: Signals of a New Era," *Intergovernmental Perspective* (Winter 1988): 9–14; John Shannon, "The Faces of Fiscal Federalism," *Intergovernmental Perspective* (Winter 1988): 15–17; John Shannon, "Federalism's Fiscal Fable," *State Government News* (Oct. 1988): 26–27; and John Shannon, "The Return to Fend-for-Yourself Federalism: The Reagan Mark," *Intergovernmental Perspective* (Summer–Fall 1987): 34–37.

22. Carol S. Weissert, "Medicaid in the 1990s: Trends, Innovations and the Future of the 'PAC-Man' of State Budgets," *Publius* (Summer 1992): 93–109; and Cornia Eck *et al.*, "State Budgets and Tax Actions, 1992," paper presented at the National Conference of State Legislatures, Denver, Colorado, July 1992.

23. John Herberts, "Read My Lips: The Tax Revolt Hasn't Had All That Much Impact," *Governing* (April 1990): 11.

24. "School System Goes Broke," *Denver Post*, 25 March 1993.

25. Larry Sabato, *Goodbye to Goodtime Charlie* (Lexington, Mass.: Lexington Books, 1978), p. 110.

26. Cited in Donna Dudek, "Going Private . . . Paying Less?" *State Legislatures* (March 1987): 26–29.

27. Robert Stein, *Urban Alternatives: Public and Private Markets in the Provision of Local Services* (Pittsburgh: University of Pittsburgh Press, 1990), pp. 187–88.

28. Steven D. Gold, "Wanted: A Good State Tax Policy," *State Legislatures* (April 1988): 24–27; and Steven D. Gold, "Taxing the Poor," *State Legislatures* (April 1987): 24–27.

29. Steven D. Gold, "Florida's Sales Tax on Services: Aberration or Innovation?" *State Legislatures* (Jan. 1988): 10–13.

30. See Michael H. McCabe, "States Eye Mail Order Sales Taxes," *State Government News* (March 1988): 22–23; and William T. Warren, "Closing the Bellas Hess Loophole," *State Legislatures* (Feb. 1989): 10–14.

31. Knapp, "Lotteries"; Marks, "Florida"; and Witt, "Diminishing Returns."

32. See John Mikesell and Kurt Zorn, "State Lotteries for Public Revenue," *Public Budgeting and Finance* (Spring 1988): 38–47; and Daniel Suits, "Gambling Taxes: Regressivity and Revenue Potential," *National Tax Journal* 30 (1978): 19–35.

33. See Jeffrey L. Katz, "Lottery Fatigue," *Governing* (Sept. 1991): 62–66; and Steven D. Gold, "Lotteries: Still Small Change," *State Legislatures* (July 1989): 14–15.

34. Lemov, "User Fees."

35. See Charles Mahtesian, "The Quagmire of Education Finance," *Governing* (Sept. 1993): 43–46.

36. Martha K. Fabricius and Ronald K. Snell, "Earmarking State Taxes," paper presented at the National Conference of State Legislatures, Denver, Colorado, 1990.

37. Steven D. Gold, ed., *The Unfinished Agenda for State Tax Reform* (Denver: National Conference of State Legislatures, 1988); and Gold, "Wanted: A Good Tax Policy."

38. John M. Downing, "The Financial Wizardry of a Fiscal Spin Doctor," *Governing* (Jan. 1989): 42–47.

14

Public Education

Education isn't just textbooks and blackboards anymore. Here, second graders and their teacher work with a computer. As the complexity of the educational process increases, so does the difficulty of managing this policy issue. *(Elizabeth Crews/Stock, Boston)*

As measured by either money or number of employees, public education is the largest policy area with which America's state and local governments are involved. Thomas Jefferson believed that schooling and literacy were essential to democratic governance and, throughout the life of the Republic, most leaders have agreed with Jefferson. In recent years, however, education has become a controversial topic of political debate. This chapter focuses on the development of educational policy, school governance, and contemporary controversies surrounding public education.

A retired teacher who had taught in a major metropolitan public school system wrote the following in 1990:

> The power to discipline is taken away from the teacher, and disruptive children are allowed by administrators, parents and the law to remain in the classroom. Parents excuse students' misbehavior, poor attendance and failure to complete assignments. Children come to school unprepared, unmotivated, undisciplined, hostile, angry, drugged, drunk, emotionally upset, hungry, frightened and/or disruptive.[1]

For years we have heard that the quality of education in America is slipping. Some blame teachers; others fault politicians for inadequate funding; still others target administrators for their failures. Many critics argue that the visual media and a breakdown of the family unit have together robbed students of intellectual curiosity and weakened the influence of home-based motivation, direction, support, and supervision. There is widespread agreement that as a nation we are in trouble because of the problems of the educational system. But there is little agreement on who or what is at fault or on how to fix the situation.

PUBLIC EDUCATION IS BIG BUSINESS

Public education in the United States is an enormous enterprise. It is also a state and local matter and not directly within the province of the national government. In the fall of 1990, nearly 90 percent of all Americans between the ages of 5 and 17 were enrolled in public schools.[2] Total enrollment included more than 46 million students, over 40 million of them enrolled in public institutions. Another 13 million students were enrolled in colleges and universities, with over 10 million of them in public schools. Whereas in 1940 75 percent of all American adults had not completed high school, in 1989 more than 75 percent of adults had at least a high school diploma.

Furthermore, state and local governments spent on education in 1988 almost four times as much as they spent on public assistance, 4.5 times as much as they spent on highways, 14 times as much as they spent on corrections, and 9 times as much as they spent on police. In terms of dollar amounts, city govern-

TABLE 14.1
Number of State and Local Full-Time Employees in Selected Service Areas, 1990

Service Area	Number of Employees	
	Local	State
Education	5,974,000	1,984,000
Police and fire protection	991,000	89,000[a]
Health and hospitals	772,000	730,000
Highways	308,000	261,000
Public assistance	272,000	217,000

[a]Includes police officers only.

Source: U.S. Bureau of the Census, *Statistical Abstract of the United States, 1992* (Washington, D.C.: GPO, 1992), p. 305.

ments in 1988 spent just under $175 billion on education and counties spent over $105 billion. The local school districts together spent almost $167 billion, or nearly as much as all of the nation's cities paid for sewers, water, police and fire protection, and all other public services.[3]

Education in America is big business in terms of number of employees as well. Table 14.1 shows that, at the local level, educators far outnumber highway, police, fire, and welfare employees combined by well over two to one. Even at the state level, there are more employees in education than in all other areas combined. Clearly, then, education is the major policy area for state and local governments.

A DECENTRALIZED SCHOOL SYSTEM

Like the U.S. political system in general, American education is a structurally decentralized enterprise. Although the number of local school districts has declined dramatically, down from well over 100,000 a few decades ago, the educational system is still guided and administered by over 14,000 local elected governing school bodies. Some districts are enormous, with thousands of employees and tens of thousands of students. Others are very small units where, quite literally, almost everyone knows almost everyone else. (Examples are two districts in New York State, Shelter Island and New Suffolk, that have only about 50 students each.) Some school districts are rich because they are located near high-tax-paying businesses, industry, and residential properties. Others, particularly those located in and around core cities or declining rural areas, are poor. Much of the money for education and some curricular, fiscal, and administrative control of the schools come from the states. But as there are 50 states, there are also 50 different sets of arrangements.

American educational policies and problems reflect the nation's institutional arrangements. Decentralization means variety — in school governing arrangements, in school fiscal systems, in state versus local control of schools, in curriculum. It also means that governance and control are shared. School governing boards are, in most of the nation, local and single-functioning governments. Some school systems are run by cities, particularly in the eastern United States. In all states the state government pays some of the cost of public education, and thus the local districts must live with some state controls and mandates. The national government has no direct hand in the establishment or governance of schools, though it does provide a small amount of specialized financial support. However, Congress has the power to pass laws requiring a variety of things of the schools, and U.S. presidents commonly assess the ills of education and share their conclusions with the nation. Public education has become, thus, an intergovernmental enterprise; while it is highly decentralized, all levels of government seek to keep a hand, or at least a finger, on the controls.

THE CHANGING ROLE OF THE SCHOOLS

Public education today looms large in terms of its impact on Americans' lives. Most American citizens spend the single largest portion of their waking hours in school for 13 or more of their first 18 years of life. Regardless of whether a student is gifted or the teaching is sound, the social and intellectual impact of education is enormous. Social norms are transmitted, history and culture are passed along, and tastes or distastes for various subject matters and for learning in general are developed. For students in unstable homes or with troubled backgrounds, school may be the only source of regularity and stability in their lives.

Americans have come to expect much from their schools, and their mounting demands have come with increased costs and some difficulties. Initially, community leaders established schools so as to increase literacy in society and enable people to read the Bible. Others, such as Thomas Jefferson, came to view schools as vehicles for education in civics and, thus, for the development of a public properly suited for democratic government. That is, self-governance could not be achieved by an illiterate citizenry unable to understand public problems and issues, unschooled in its own history and traditions, and unaware of the ways of democracy; rather, a literate and educated population was considered essential to democratic government.

With time, Americans have come to ask more of the schools. In addition to creating a literate and civil society, for example, the schools have the responsibility of preparing students for work. Education in the sciences and mathematics contributes to this goal, as do vocational programs in agriculture, business, engineering, and other subject areas. Before women's entrance into the workplace, the schools emphasized the teaching of home economics for young girls. Similarly, in the age of the automobile, Americans demanded driver's education. With the civil rights movement of the 1960s and 1970s, the courts saw the schools as vehicles for racial integration. As social norms changed, Americans asked the schools to teach sex education, health, and drug prevention. With changes in the structure of the U.S. economy and the family unit, schools came to provide career counseling, hot lunches, and child-care services.

In the 1990s, as high school student test scores continue to fall and the dropout rate continues to rise, educators are being asked simultaneously to toughen educational standards and reduce the number of high school dropouts. And, as always, America's schools are expected to educate children and adolescents and to provide families with musical and athletic entertainment. Today's teachers, then, are not only educators; they also play the roles of coach, counselor, truant officer, and others.

THE DEVELOPMENT OF PUBLIC EDUCATION

P**ublic** elementary and secondary education in America today is tuition-free, universal, and compulsory, but it was not always that way. Initially schools were not public at all; they were run by churches. Slowly support grew first for publicly paid elementary school for the poor and then for universal compulsory elementary education. Later it was extended to the high school level. The first free state public school system was established in 1850 in Connecticut and the last in 1910 in Mississippi. Public funding of education also evolved slowly from partial support to full support.

Elementary and Secondary Schools

In the early years of public schooling, local governments bore most of the financial burden and received only very little help from the state. During the late nineteenth and early twentieth centuries, for example, local governments paid for about 80 percent of the total cost of public education. This pattern has since changed dramatically, however. In 1987 the states' share was larger than the local and federal portions, amounting to roughly one-half of the total elementary and secondary education expenditure (see Figure 14.1).

The level at which the American public supports the schools varies among the states. In 1990, for example, there was a spread of nearly three to one between Alaska and Tennessee, which spent the most and least per capita for elementary and secondary education, respectively (see Table 14.2). The varia-

FIGURE 14.1
Local, State, and National Government Funding of
Elementary and Secondary Education, 1960 – 1987

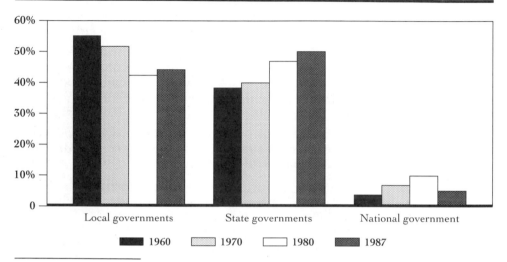

SOURCE: National Center for Education Statistics, *The Condition of Education, 1988* (Washington, D.C.: U.S. Department of Education, 1988).

tions in state spending are in part tied to the relative wealth of a state. For example, comparatively, the wealthy states of Alaska, New Jersey, and New York can spend more on education than the less wealthy states of Arkansas, Alabama, and Mississippi. In addition, the average level of education of a state's residents tends to be related to the variations in state spending. While higher levels of education can explain the greater wealth of certain states, it appears that well-educated Americans value education highly and are willing to spend more on the education of their children.

Higher Education

As with elementary and secondary education, higher education in America has its roots in the churches and has grown enormously as a public enterprise. Today, roughly 13 million people are enrolled in colleges and universities, and approximately 75 percent of them are in public institutions of higher education.[4]

Variety in Type and Mission Although most public colleges and universities stress the importance of both instruction and research, the emphasis given to each varies considerably with the mission of the school. Research universities put research first, as one would surmise from their self-characterization. Their faculty members do some teaching, but not a lot; they,

TABLE 14.2
Per-Capita Public Elementary and Secondary Education
Spending in Selected States, 1991

States Highest in Spending		States Lowest in Spending	
Alaska	$1,626	Tennessee	$618
New Jersey	1,223	Arkansas	668
New York	1,186	Mississippi	671
Wyoming	1,178	South Dakota	716
Connecticut	1,151	North Dakota	719

Source: U.S. Bureau of the Census, *Statistical Abstract of the United States, 1992* (Washington, D.C.: GPO, 1992), p. 154.

and the entire institution for which they work, are judged primarily by the fruits of their research. Other universities value research but direct much more faculty time and institutional resources toward students and the classroom. Properly performed, teaching and research can be complementary and reinforcing regardless of the major emphasis.

An important and growing sector of higher education is the two-year community college. Some of these institutions, which exist throughout the nation, provide the first two years of a liberal arts education and prepare students for transfer to a four-year college or university. Other community colleges are vocational in orientation and train students for various trades or occupations. Many perform both functions. The community college does not have a residential campus like that of most four-year institutions, as it caters to local citizens who commute from their homes. A large proportion of two-year-college students are part-timers seeking to advance their education while holding down full-time jobs. Indeed, an increasing number of students in all colleges and universities —43 percent in 1990—attend on a part-time basis.[5]

Variety in Size, Structure, and Level of Support   Just as there is tremendous variation in the mission and character of America's public colleges and universities, so too do they differ in size, in structure, and in level of government support. Some state systems of higher education are small and relatively simple. Wyoming, for example, has one major university located in Laramie, complete with graduate programs and a law school, that is governed by an elected board. The state also has two junior colleges, each with its own local governing board and the authority to offer some junior- and senior-level courses.

California, in contrast, maintains an enormous three-tier system of higher education. It includes 106 community colleges governed by locally elected boards, 19 state universities offering graduate work at the master's level, and a university system with several campuses (including Berkeley, Davis, Los Angeles, Santa Barbara, Riverside, Irvine, and San Diego), research facilities,

TABLE 14.3
Per-Student State Appropriations for Higher Education, 1989

States Highest in Spending		States Lowest in Spending	
Alaska	$9,879	Vermont	$2,337
Hawaii	7,229	Louisiana	2,634
Connecticut	6,343	New Hampshire	2,782
Wyoming	6,028	North Dakota	2,803
New York	5,934	Colorado	2,853

Source: U.S. Bureau of the Census, *Statistical Abstract of the United States, 1992* (Washington, D.C.: GPO, 1992), p. 168.

and laboratories offering instruction through the doctoral level as well as training for careers in medicine and law. The university systems are each governed by a statewide multimember board.

As with elementary and secondary education, the levels at which the states support higher education vary widely. As Table 14.3 shows, two states provide per-pupil funding at a rate of three or more times that of Vermont, which spends the least per pupil. What the states do not provide in general fund dollars generally comes from user fees — in this case, student tuition.

Higher education in America experienced dramatic growth and some significant changes in character during the 1960s and 1970s. The number of young adults grew, as did the percentage of those attending college. As a result, the institutions of higher education grew, though not only in size; many also changed their names and expanded their missions. For example, many land grant and teacher colleges became state universities, and some two-year schools became four-year institutions. Colorado A&M College became Colorado State University. New York built its multicampus state university system.

In the late 1970s and the 1980s, enrollments in institutions of higher education stabilized and the growth in campus physical plants, in faculty numbers, and in state appropriations leveled off. However, the manifestations of the earlier period of growth remained. Today, higher education is far larger, more expensive, and more bureaucratized than ever before.

THE FEDERAL ROLE IN EDUCATION

The U.S. Constitution does not address the issue of education. Article I, Section 8, which specifies the powers of the national government, is silent on the matter of schooling. The authority of the states in education is implicit rather than explicit. However, when American governments began to provide public education, it was the local and state governments that assumed the task.

Throughout most of U.S. history the national government played almost no role in public education, save for the provision of a very small amount of financial support. The schools themselves were, and indeed still are, local and state institutions. But the federal government did provide modest help; for example, the Northwest Ordinance of 1787 gave land to the states to support schools, the 1862 Morrill Act granted land to the states for establishing and maintaining colleges of agricultural and mechanical arts, and the Smith-Hughes Act of 1917 provided funds for state vocational education and support payments to local schools that taught the children of military personnel located in or near the districts.

Expanded Federal Involvement

Following World War II federal involvement in public education began to expand. In 1958, following the Soviet success in placing the satellite *Sputnik I* into orbit, Congress enacted the National Defense Education Act, which made money available to the states and local schools for improved programs in mathematics, the sciences, and foreign languages. In the 1960s, and in the context of President Lyndon Johnson's Great Society programs, Congress enacted more legislation to support the schools. The 1964 Economic Opportunity Act established Head Start, designed to prepare underprivileged youngsters for elementary schooling, as well as a work-study program for college-level students. The 1965 Elementary and Secondary Education Act made funding available to local schools for programs for students from low-income families, for library resources, for textbooks, and more. In 1944, 1952, and 1966, Congress enacted programs to support higher education for veterans of military service. Other legislation established the guaranteed student loan program, Pell grants, and grants to institutions of higher education for physical facilities and student aid. A variety of laws administered by a host of federal agencies now sponsor university research. The agencies include the National Science Foundation; the departments of Defense, Education, Housing and Urban Development, and Health and Human Services; the U.S. Public Health Service; the Environmental Protection Agency; and others.

The scope of the federal role in public education also includes its impact on the budgets of the states and localities. Federal money rose to over 9 percent of state and local education revenue in 1980 from virtually no support throughout the early part of the twentieth century. It declined to roughly 6 percent in 1988, as a result of the Reagan administration's push to cut federal spending for nonmilitary programs as well as the huge federal deficit, which has dramatically reduced federal spending in many other domestic policy areas.[6]

Federal Impact on the Educational Agenda

State and local schools are affected by educational studies conducted by the federal government as well as by the utterances and behavior of federal officials. A 1983 study entitled **"A Nation at Risk,"** produced by a presidential study commission, indicted the nation's schools for not adequately preparing students to function effectively and competitively in today's world. The study put America's schools in the national spotlight and triggered a rash of legislation and reform efforts in the states.[7] The comments of Reagan's secretary of education, William Bennett, had a similar effect. More recently, the 1989 gathering of state governors at the University of Virginia at the initiative of President George Bush refocused concern about education and the educational agenda, and set into motion more attempts to change the nation's school system.

The federal role in education, then, was modest during the first 150 years of the Republic but has grown considerably during the past 40 to 50 years. The nation's schools remain state and local institutions, and the amount of federal funds that flows to them is still not large. However, the federal government does affect America's schools, largely through regulation and through its influence on public opinion.

SCHOOL GOVERNANCE

Most of America's public elementary and secondary schools are governed by popularly elected boards in roughly 14,000 school districts. These are single-purpose units of government with boundaries that are seldom coterminous with those of any other local government. Although in a few school districts the governing board members are appointed by county officials or the school systems are run directly by city or county governments, the dominant pattern is governance by elected school boards. In higher education, school governance is highly complex and varied. Some states feature single governing boards that control an entire university system; others have nearly as many governing boards as they have colleges and universities. In some cases the board members are elected; in others the governor appoints them.

The State Role in Education

It is important to remember that all local governments are legally the creatures of the states; thus, local school districts and state colleges and universities are as well. As a result, neither local school boards nor the boards that govern institutions of higher education exercise full control. Rather, they operate within the confines of state law. Increasingly, the states are assuming an active role in school governance, particularly at the elementary and secondary levels.

In 1940 there were 108,579 local school districts; by 1952 there were still over 67,000 districts in operation. Today there are fewer than 15,000. Although the local school districts have always been legally subordinate to the states, prior to the 1960s they operated quite independently of state or federal control and influence. Beginning in the 1960s and continuing in the decades that followed, however, school districts lost much of their independence. As schools were consolidated, the number of districts was greatly reduced. As school enrollments grew in the 1960s, so did school faculties, administrations, and budgets. Local district relations with state government began to change as the states assumed a larger portion of school funding. In addition, the civil rights movement focused the nation's attention on the methods of school financing that made some districts wealthy and others poor. The states thus expanded their funding of education and adopted allocation formulas designed to reduce, to some degree, the extreme variations that existed among school districts.

However, with increased state funding came more state controls — from control of teacher qualifications and certification, the school calendar, and local tax and finance systems to demands that teachers be held accountable for the results of teaching and more. State officials argued that their funding of a larger portion of the educational bill gave the state the right to a larger voice in school policy and entitled it to require evidence of what the money was buying. The federal government made similar demands on the schools at this time.

Local Policy Bodies

Today, school boards still constitute the basic policy bodies for local schools. The boards approve budgets, all personnel actions, and academic programs; determine curricula; and hire and fire administrators, including chief executive officers or superintendents. But more so than ever, school boards perform these functions within the context of state-imposed financial, personnel, and curricular policy as well as certain federal controls. The states may decide such matters as the length of the school year, textbook adoption, permissible tax levels, district boundaries, budget forms and processes, teacher certification procedures and standards, accountability systems, and school lunch menus. In 1989, for example, the California legislature passed a bill instructing the State Department of Education to set low recommended fat and cholesterol intake levels for elementary and secondary school lunches.

The states are not always successful in their attempts to control the local schools, however. In 1990 in Colorado, for instance, the state failed in its attempts to postpone the start of the school year until after Labor Day so as to extend the tourist season, and to bar local school boards from giving leave time from the classroom to teachers involved with teachers' associations.

School Administrators

Local Districts   Although the school board represents the formal local depository of policymaking authority, as a practical matter it tends to share that power with the school administrator or district superintendent. Like city council members in council–manager cities, school board members are not professional politicians but laypeople who serve on a voluntary, part-time basis. They thus tend to defer to the expertise and recommendations of the superintendent. It is difficult for school board members, who have occupations of their own and who meet just a few times each month, to do otherwise. The ability of the professional educators, and of the administrators especially, to influence policy is thus substantial.

Still, school board members do play an important, albeit indirect, role in policymaking. As Meier, Stewart, and England remind us, "the first step in influencing policy decisions is gaining access to the school board."[8] In a 1991 study of the minority community, they found that African-American school board members tend to influence the selection of African-American administrators, and that the administrators thus tend to respond to the initiatives of the board members.

College and Universities   The relationship between administrators and boards in colleges and universities is similar to that within local school districts. Whether the governing board members are appointed or elected, whether they oversee one institution or an entire state university system, they find it all but impossible to take a direct hand in the operation of the schools—in part because they are laypeople and in part because the prevailing sentiment in the nation is that they should not do so. Rather, the boards act on an agenda brought to them by college and university presidents. Together with other central administrators, the university president defines and portrays the institution for the board, identifies the problems and priorities it should address, and suggests the actions it should take. Professional administrators thus tend to dominate the policy agenda of higher education in America. Although some degree of decision-making authority is exercised by the faculty with respect to curricula and by the governing board with respect to policy, the career-oriented, often mobile professional administrators (some have called them "carpet-baggers") are at the center of power in colleges and universities.

Constituencies' Competing Demands

Increasingly, local elementary and secondary school boards and district administrators are sharing their power with various constituencies within the community. Teachers have long been politically influential in school district affairs. Through their collective membership in local and state teachers' associations, complete with leadership, dues, and communication structures, teachers can exert influence over the school budget, the school curriculum, and the election of school board members. Teachers' organizations press the interests of their members during contract negotiations over salaries and benefits, are involved in selecting course offerings and determining student requirements, and often recruit and support school board candidates who share their views. Given that school board elections are usually held separately from state and national elections and thus feature low voter turnouts of 5 percent to 10 percent of the voting population (see Chapter 9), a highly interested and well-organized association of educators can exert a tremendous impact on election outcomes. Although there have been efforts to reduce the impact of educators on school elections by conducting them in November along with state and national contests, educators have resisted the change.

In addition to teachers' associations, a variety of citizen-based groups exert pressure on the schools. Beginning about a decade ago, antitax groups across the nation, such as the one behind California's Proposition 13, have increasingly placed financial pressures on the schools in their search for tax relief. Today's school boards and administrators thus find it difficult to secure voter passage of millage rate, or property tax, increases and of capital construction bond proposals. At the same time, education funding from the states is affected in that the taxpayer rebellion makes state lawmakers hesitant about approving significant increases in school budgets and property taxes.

In some communities parent groups seek to help run the schools in an effort to improve the education of their children. In certain schools in Chicago, for example, parent council members are elected and play a major role in school finance and personnel decisions.

All sorts of competing demands for school system money and teacher time and attention are being made by various groups. Some press for a "return to the basics" in the curriculum, which usually means an emphasis on mathematics, science, English, social studies, and foreign languages. Other groups, noting that many high school graduates do not go on to college, press for vocational programs. Still others press for student retention plans or for more stringent academic standards. Schools across the nation are pressured by citizen groups to teach the biblical version of the creation of life in science education, to provide sex education, to eliminate the sex education program, to provide special programs for gifted children, or to address the special needs of disadvantaged and handicapped children. Some schools offer special programs for teenage mothers that involve day-care services for their children.

Local school boards and educational administrators today can no longer formulate policy with relatively little interference from other parties (see Focus 14.1). The federal government, though it contributes only a small amount of money to the schools, exerts more than a little influence. State governors and recent U.S. presidents have brought educational issues to the nation's attention. State legislators and state education departments impose more standards, procedures, and controls on local districts than ever before. And local citizen-based groups are increasingly more active in school politics.

14.1 COMPETING DEMANDS IN THE DENVER SCHOOL SYSTEM

In 1992 the Colorado governor intervened in a protracted conflict between the classroom teachers and the school board in Denver, forcing a negotiated contract that called for site-based collaborative decision making (CDM) involving participation by teachers, parents, and others. Subsequently, tight state appropriations for the schools and a 1992 state constitutional taxation and spending limit triggered substantial cuts in Denver's school budget.

In 1993 the school board, its school administration, and its site-based collaborative teams were all struggling to cope with massive core-city school problems while having to cut over $30 million from the school budget. The site-based collaborative teams felt the need to figure out independently how to spend money in their individual schools. The school board and administrators felt the need to maintain some control in order to abide by state and federal laws and mandates.

The following exchange between Denver's school superintendent, Evie Dennis, and a Rocky Mountain News reporter in 1993 provides a glimpse into one side's version of the difficulties of modern-day local school politics:

News: Some collaborative decision-making teams say they'd like the district to allocate a lump-sum budget to each school and let the teams decide how to spend it.

Dennis: One thing you hear a lot about is, give us our money and we'll do our own purchasing. I have to live with some things—contractual-type things, minority- and women-types of things that this board has approved, and I cannot say to a school, "Here, you can do what you want to do." They could sign a contract that could put this district in bankruptcy. I can't walk over and say, "Here's a hunk of money—do your own thing."

News: CDM members complain that they were ignored in deciding how to cut the budget.

Dennis: I can't cut out bilingual education. I can't cut out magnet schools. I can't cut out transportation. I can't cut out special education. These are all programs mandated by state and federal law. That kind of message goes out there saying you can save all this money without any understanding of what it is the school district has to deal with.

SOURCE: Berny Morson, "School Teams Revolt over Budget Cuts," *Rocky Mountain News*, 25 April 1993.

LONGSTANDING ISSUES IN EDUCATION

Some educational issues have long been addressed by government, school boards, school administrators, and teacher and parent associations alike. Among them are the curriculum, racial desegregation, separation of church and state, school financing, and educator salaries.

The Curriculum

It is generally agreed that English, science, mathematics, and the social sciences should be taught in elementary and secondary schools. But whether these subjects should constitute the exclusive content of the curriculum has long been debated. Some argue that the curriculum should also include course offerings in computer science, human relations, domestic science, human survival, music, and many other areas.

All youngsters will need some level of competence in written and oral communication and mathematics to function as adults in society. Increasingly, skill in the use of computers is becoming important as well. While some argue for an emphasis on the basics — English, mathematics, science, and so forth — others point out that this type of curriculum, because it is geared toward the college-bound student, neglects the needs of the majority of students who do not attend institutions of higher education.

Ideally, school curricula would provide both liberal and vocational education. Coursework would stress literacy, reasoning skills, the basic sciences, the social sciences, the arts, and cultural awareness. In addition, it would prepare students for productive and rewarding employment when they enter the work force. In reality, however, America's schools have neither the time nor the money to provide the ideal curriculum. As a result, communities and school boards struggle with a political battle not over the basic objectives of education but over the division of scarce resources — time and money.

Church and State —How Separate Are They?

The separation of church and state is both an old and a new issue that involves a complex array of related issues. There are political disputes over the propriety of prayer in public schools, the use of public money to support church-related schools, and the teaching of creationism alongside science-based biology. The legal foundation for such disputes is in the First Amendment to the U.S. Constitution; it reads, in part, "Congress shall make no law respecting an establishment of religion, or prohibiting the free exercise thereof." What does this mean? Are prayers in school permissible? May tax dollars purchase textbooks for a Catholic or Lutheran school? May the biblical version of the origins of the earth and humans be taught in public classrooms? Americans have fought over these and similar questions for decades.

Although some of the questions remain unanswered, many have been resolved through the decisions of the U.S. Supreme Court. For example, the Court has interpreted the Constitution as disallowing prayer in public schools, although permitting students to be released for a time to receive religious instruction off the public school premises. In addition, the Court's interpretation of the Constitution prohibits the expenditure of public funds to pay the salaries of teachers in church-based schools. However, it is permissible for government to loan textbooks and cover the cost of busing children to religious-based schools because textbooks and bus rides are considered nonreligious in nature. In a June 1990 decision, the Supreme Court held that school facilities made available for other student groups must also be made available to student groups that meet to study the Bible.

In general, the Court has strictly maintained the separation of church and state, often finding even small efforts to help church-based schools in violation. However, some accommodations have been made so as to avoid construing separation of church and state as discouragement of religion in general.

Since much decision making is within the purview of the nation's 14,000 local school districts, it is inevitable that they will continue to encounter battles over matters of textbook material, prayer, and more. The political struggles, however, must take place within the contexts of Supreme Court decisions and of the policies set by state legislatures, state boards, and state departments of education.

Racial Desegregation

During the early to mid-1900s, most of the nation's schools were racially segregated, in part as a result or public policy and in part because of residential patterns. In *Plessy v. Ferguson* (1896), the Supreme Court held that separate public accommodations for the races were permissible so long as they were "equal" in quality. This view provided the legal basis for segregated public schools throughout the first half of the twentieth century, primarily in the South. But even in northern states, where students attended schools in their neighborhood and where forced segregation did not exist, the schools were racially segregated because of residential patterns. In addition, the racially separate schools were almost never equal, and some blacks had no schools at all.

In 1954, however, the Supreme Court overturned the *Plessy* ruling in its decision in **Brown v. Board of Education**. The Court held that segregated schools were inherently unequal and thereby eliminated the legal foundation of racial segregation. But the Court did not address the segregation resulting from residential patterns and the use of the neighborhood school. Segregation thus persisted well after the *Brown* case. Persons and groups pushing to desegregate the public schools initiated legal action. The result was Court-mandated busing to achieve integration under some conditions. School districts were forced to bus children to schools outside their neighborhoods to achieve integration in areas where segregation had occurred as a result of past, and purposeful, public policy. The Court did not mandate busing in areas where segregation had occurred as a result of residential patterns and the use of the neighborhood school. The Court also did not require busing across school district lines in metropolitan areas.

Busing is a controversial political issue. Most Americans, regardless of race, support the racial integration of schools, and roughly half believe that African-American students perform better in integrated classrooms and want their children in integrated settings. But a majority of whites and almost half of blacks oppose busing. Some object to the longer bus rides to and from school. Others want their children in neighborhood schools, close to home and among residential friends. Forced busing has caused many parents to remove their children from public school and send them to private schools instead. The move to the suburbs contributed to the overwhelming African-American majority in many core-city schools (see Chapter 10).

Given the extremely heavy concentrations of minorities in many American cities and the ongoing patterns of residential segregation, busing has made a dent in segregation, though it has been small and limited primarily to the South. In areas where racial desegregation has been achieved, good educational results have been seen. Whites do no better or worse in integrated settings, and blacks do somewhat better, especially in the early years of schooling.

While other serious educational problems continue to plague the nation's schools, particularly in urban areas, the political controversy over busing has dissipated somewhat. Many schools remain racially segregated to a significant degree, and the Court seems unwilling to expand its busing mandate to include neighborhood schools. Thus, wide-scale integration of America's schools is not likely to occur in the short term.

School Financing: Inequities versus Local Autonomy

A host of related educational issues revolve around the central matter of school financing. Among them are how much society should spend on education, whether the supporting taxes should be progressive or regressive, the size of the state's share in funding, and administrators' and teachers' salaries. In addition, there is the major question of whether the inequities in wealth among states and among school districts are fair or legal.

School districts rely heavily on the property tax to provide education. But the variations in the value of property among school districts are wide, such that some districts are much more wealthy than others. Some have challenged the legality of this situation. In 1971, for example, the California Supreme Court, basing its decision on the state's constitution, rejected the property tax as a means of school funding because of the inequities it creates. Soon after, however, in *San Antonio Independent School District v. Rodriguez* (1973), the U.S. Supreme Court declined to invalidate the school financing scheme in Texas in a challenge based on the U.S. Constitution. In 1989 the state courts in Kentucky and Texas joined many other states in ruling the existing states' financing systems unconstitutional. It is now the responsibility of those state legislatures to devise new allocation schemes. In a federal system, the state courts are free to render decisions that are based on state constitutional and statutory law and that go beyond U.S. Supreme Court rulings. In these states, they did.

Thus, while the Supreme Court accepts the property tax funding system that results in inequities among school districts, some state courts do not. In the latter cases, the usual state response has been to increase the state's proportion of total school funding and to distribute it in a more equitable manner among the various districts. Currently, about half of the funding for elementary and secondary schools comes from the states. While this has somewhat reduced the funding inequities, it has not eliminated them.

Others argue in favor of local autonomy. They want the option of taxing themselves so as to provide some educational extras if they so choose and without being penalized with a parallel loss of state support. They also value highly the independence of the local unit. Opponents counter that educational opportunities should be the same across the nation and for all students regardless of their socioeconomic status. Still others contend that equality in per-pupil funding across districts does not guarantee equal educational quality because excellence rests on more than just money.

The states will continue to struggle with the issue of school financing. New funding schemes, new challenges, and other issues related to equal opportunity, equal protection, and local autonomy are likely to surface in the states. The 1993 decision by the Michigan legislature to scrap the local property tax altogether is powerful testimony to this.

Educators' Salaries

The level of salary paid to elementary and secondary teachers is a longstanding issue in educational finance. Compared to other professions, such as law, engineering, accounting, and medicine, teachers are not well paid. Among the states in 1988, for example, average teacher salaries ranged from a high of $43,200 in Alaska to a low of $21,300 in South Dakota.[9] They also trail behind the salaries paid to educational administrators. The average salary paid to a high school principal in 1990 was $55,722 and that of an elementary school principal was $48,431. School counselors averaged $35,979, and classroom teachers averaged $31,278 in 1990.[10]

A 1989 report by the National Education Association notes that over a half-million teachers hold second jobs during the summer, the academic year, or both. Studies of education, including the 1983 "A Nation at Risk" report, call for better teacher salaries in order to attract persons of high ability to the classroom.[11]

Higher teacher salaries, however, are not easily provided by school districts. With so much of the support for education resting on the property tax, spending and taxing increases of any type often meet with public resistance, especially in a time of taxpayer revolt. In addition, some argue that teachers receive other benefits, such as multiple annual vacations, summers free, and an income protected by tenure. Teachers counter that course preparation, grading, and parent meetings often occur during evenings or on weekends because their daily schedules leave little time for these essential duties.

RECENT ISSUES IN EDUCATION

Many recent educational issues have emerged in the context of the perceived national crisis in education. These include debates over accountability, teacher competency testing, teacher tenure and merit pay plans, voucher systems, schools of choice, early childhood education, the rising dropout rate, violence in the schools, and the special needs of at-risk youngsters.

A National Crisis

The 1983 report by the National Commission on Excellence in Education entitled "A Nation at Risk" established what is now a decade-old concern—that American education is in a crisis condition and desperately in need of improvement. Calls for change, of course, predated the report, but it was not until the 1980s that a deep sense of urgency developed about the quality of schooling, the educational level of the nation's population, and the ultimate effects on the nation's future ability to cope effectively with domestic issues and to compete internationally. Short- and long-term solutions were proposed to address the educational problems. The many proposals for change have included schools of choice, magnet schools, early childhood education, teacher and student competency testing, year-round schooling, elimination of teacher tenure, merit pay systems, and others.

A stream of "bad news" about the nation's schools and students followed issuance of the 1983 "A Nation at Risk" report. Achievement test scores fell steadily between 1962 and 1982, though they have since stabilized somewhat. In a recent study of 13-year-olds in a dozen countries, American students scored at the bottom in math and near the bottom in science. Indeed, 60 percent were unable to complete simple math problems correctly.[12]

Causes The causes of the national crisis in education are numerous, complex, difficult to resolve, and a matter of debate. Some critics argue that the schools are at fault in that fewer students than ever before are required to enroll in math and science courses and that students are instead permitted to study health, recreation, and other elective subjects.[13] In addition, it is argued, students receive less homework than in the past and teachers are less qualified.

Many critics allege that colleges and universities emphasize teaching methods and techniques when training the nation's teachers, rather than the actual subject matter.

Numerous other observers, including many teachers, contend that the major causes of the crisis in education lie not within the schools but within contemporary American society. They see a decline in parental involvement in and support of their children's education, particularly in single-parent and stepparent homes and among other families lacking time and money. These critics also cite such factors as child abuse, teenage pregnancy, drug use, and parental neglect. They argue that many students come to school hungry or exhausted after having to work a late-night job. Some schools now serve breakfast to help remedy the problem of students coming to school hungry. Other students may use drugs, sell drugs, or bring violence into the school. According to former Colorado governor Richard Lamm in 1989:

> No nation has a higher rate of illegitimate children, or drug and alcohol abuse, or child abuse, or crime among children and young adults. . . .
>
> No nation abandons or abuses its children with greater frequency, or murders its children in greater numbers, or abandons its children as often, or subjects them to divorce in greater numbers. Almost as many American children live with a single parent or step-parent as live with both natural parents. . . .
>
> Approximately 2 million thefts, assaults, and robberies are committed in schools every year and more than 5 percent of all secondary school teachers are physically attacked every year. Almost one-third of all school principals report that student possession of weapons is a problem in their schools.[14]

Teachers generally agree with Lamm's observations. They see students from low-income families struggling to fit in with those who are better dressed. They argue that talk of violence is common among students and that violence itself is increasing in frequency. They also see parents of two-income families sending their sick and contagious children to school because they have nowhere else to keep them during working hours.

Hunger, psychological stress, lack of self-esteem, shortage of sleep, limited parental support, violence, drugs, television instead of homework — these and other factors do not add up to a sound learning environment for many American students. Unless society's problems are addressed adequately, some critics argue, student test scores and skills are not likely to improve because the schools will remain limited in what they can teach America's youth.

Improvements   There is some evidence, however, that education in modern-day America is improving. For example, though the dropout rate is still high, 95 percent of school-aged children do attend school. Even the number

FIGURE 14.2
Percentage of Americans Age 25 or Older with
at Least a High School Education, 1970–1991

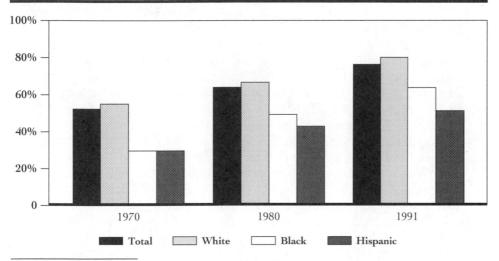

SOURCE: U.S. Bureau of the Census, *Statistical Abstract of the United States* (Washington, D.C.: GPO, 1992), p. 137.

of high school dropouts has declined somewhat—from 12.2 percent in 1970 to 10.7 percent in 1989.[15] However, the dropout rate varies considerably among regions of the nation. For instance, an early 1990s report indicates that 50 percent of all ninth graders in the Chicago school system drop out.

In addition, the overall educational level of the U.S. population has increased (see Figure 14.2). Whereas in 1940 about 75 percent of all Americans had not graduated from high school, that figure fell to 47.7 percent by 1970 and to 23.8 percent by 1991. Among African-Americans, those not completing a high school education fell from 92.7 percent in 1940 to 68.6 percent in 1970 to 36.7 percent in 1988.[16]

The American public's confidence in the school system has weakened only slightly. In a survey conducted by the National Center for Education Statistics, 54 percent of Americans expressed "a great deal" or "quite a bit" of confidence in 1977, and 50 percent conveyed the same opinion in 1987. However, between 1977 and 1987 the percentage of Americans assigning the schools an "A" or "B" grade rose from 37 percent to 43 percent.[17]

Although America is facing a crisis in education, more citizens than ever before are attending school and are graduating from high school. In addition, the schools still enjoy substantial public support. As a result, it is argued that policymakers should approach reform with care so as to affect only those areas in need of improvement (see Focus 14.2).

14.2 SCHOOL REFORM IN KENTUCKY

In 1990 the Kentucky legislature passed a school reform package that significantly restructured governance of, and altered the pattern of state funding for, public education. The action was triggered by a state supreme court decision that found the previous funding system unconstitutional. The Kentucky court is not alone in its action, as the high courts in roughly a dozen states have made similar findings. The Kentucky judges declared illegal the then-existing inequities among the districts in per-pupil funding, teacher salary, instructional material, class size, course offerings, and facilities. In response to the court's decision, the legislature formed a task force to make recommendations for change. The massive 1990 legislative package was based on its recommendations.

The new legislation called for a decentralized system of public education. In Kentucky today significant decision-making powers are given to the local schools and to individual school building councils with parental membership. Financial rewards are provided to districts that show improvement. A preschool program is in operation, as are student support networks providing day care, health care, and counseling. Antinepotism rules are imposed, and district personnel involvement in school elections is restricted. Major new taxes support the reforms in Kentucky. They include hikes in the sales tax and in both the individual and the corporate income tax.

Kentucky's experience is not atypical. In virtually every state educational reform is a major issue; moreover, the problems being addressed and the reforms being proposed are similar. The issues center on funding inequities and inadequacies. The reform proposals emphasize decentralization, more financial help for poor districts, and measurement of student performance (accountability).

Interestingly, within modern school politics most observers see student performance problems as rooted in larger societal conditions, such as the weakening family unit, drug use, teenage pregnancy, and the prevalence of television. However, the reforms target not societal problems but the schools. It may be less difficult to pass laws aimed at teachers, the curriculum, and budgets than to legislate parental care and child behavior.

SOURCE: Tim Storey, "Kentucky Redesigns Its Schools," *State Legislatures* (July 1990): 47–51.

Amid the growing concern with and discussion of public education in **Early Childhood** the 1990s, a host of changes specific to the school systems have been **Education** suggested, many of them highly controversial and political.

As the two-income family continues to be a necessity for many across the nation, working parents seek day-care arrangements for their children. Moreover, preschool education for three- and four-year-olds benefits children later on in terms of their improved educational performance, their reduced susceptibility to public assistance dependency as adults, and in other positive ways. For these reasons local and state policymakers are giving more attention to **early childhood education** programs.

In a 1989 article Penelope Lemov cites the Children's National Defense Fund's estimates that one in five children lives in poverty today and that one in four will do so by the year 2000.[18] Similarly, a *Coloradoan* article cites a 1989 congressional study indicating that nearly 50 percent of all African-American children live in poverty.[19] The same report notes also that the median family income of white families is one and three-quarters that of Hispanics and double that of African-Americans. Under such conditions, then, millions of children are without the means to purchase such basics as paper, scissors, and other supplies or to eat properly balanced meals. Many also spend much of their early childhood years on their own, with little or no parental supervision or support. These children are most likely to experience unemployment, poverty, and public assistance dependency as adults.

Early childhood education appears to have several long-term impacts on the futures of disadvantaged children. Studies suggest that early intervention helps to prevent educational problems later in school. In addition, the children are less apt to experience teenage pregnancy, tend to have lower delinquency and arrest rates, are more likely to graduate from high school, and are less likely to become dependent on public assistance as adults.[20] It is estimated that every dollar spent on early childhood schooling saves the American public between $4 and $5 in later expenditures on other educational, student retention, and public assistance programs as well as on the justice system.[21]

Roughly one-half of the states have instituted some form of early childhood education program. California, Illinois, Louisiana, and South Carolina have adopted programs aimed at low-income and disadvantaged students, commonly referred to as at-risk children. The programs in Massachusetts, New Jersey, Oklahoma, and Pennsylvania are more broadly based.[22]

Whereas early childhood education focuses on the decline of the **Schools of Choice** family unit as related to the educational crisis, **schools of choice** proposals find fault in the public school system. Those advocating schools of choice seek to take from educational administrators the authority to draw and enforce geographic boundaries for neighborhood schools and to allow students to attend the school of their choice within the district.

Some choice advocates favor a **voucher system**; that is, vouchers would be issued to parents, who would "spend" them to pay for tuition at the school of their choice. The assumption is that students would tend to gravitate toward the best schools, insofar as space would allow, thereby forcing the weaker schools to improve themselves or face declining enrollment. In other words, the schools participating in the voucher system would have to compete for students through the revitalization of their teaching staff and curriculum. Advocates of schools of choice allege that the current system is unresponsive to change, and that their proposal represents a cost-free method of improving education.

Controversy and Criticism Although many national and state politicians support schools of choice reform, it is a controversial issue in America. Opponents allege that a series of problems would be created by such reforms, including increased racial segregation, the selection of schools made on the basis of irrelevancies, and planning difficulties. Critics also claim that the system would favor wealthy and well-educated families, as they would tend to be most informed about the available choices and to have the resources needed to transport their children across town to the school of their choice. As a result, critics argue, racial segregation in schools might increase and those students most in need of a sound learning environment—often urban minority-group members unable to make the trek to another school—might be least likely to receive it. In addition, the least politically influential students and parents might be left behind, meaning that the pressure for improvement in schools of poor quality would be diminished.[23]

There are several practical problems associated with the schools of choice system as well, such as the distribution of resources among the district schools and a range of issues related to schools that do not compete successfully. In the latter case, a failed school might have to close its doors, but problems with contracts, the school building, and where to send the affected students would remain.

Although there is much support for schools of choice, thus far the system has not been adopted widely by school districts. Some districts have developed a small-scale version called the **magnet school**, which generally offers some sort of unique programming to interested students.

Minnesota's Schools of Choice In 1987, the Minnesota state legislature mandated open enrollment both within and across school district lines. A cross-district schools of choice system is financially workable in Minnesota because the state pays a high percentage of total school costs. Students are required to give advance notice of their intent to attend a school other than the one they would otherwise attend, though they need not identify the particular school. There have been a few problems related to planning and staffing, though the number of students opting for choice tends to be low—only 440 students did so in the 1987–88 school year and roughly 1,000 in 1988–89.[24] In addition, the St. Paul school district established, in cooperation with a bank, a downtown kindergarten where youngsters can attend school near their parents' place of work, thus combining schooling and day care.[25]

Related legislation in Minnesota allows high school students in grades 10 through 12 to enroll in college courses and to receive both high school and college credits for them. This is a popular program, with thousands of students participating each year.[26]

Another major voice for educational reform is the influential work of John Chubb and Terry Moe, *Politics, Markets, and America's Schools* (1990).[27] They argue that the existing institutional arrangements do **Other Reform Proposals** not address the problems of the nation's schools, in part because the institutions themselves are problematic. Chubb and Moe propose revolutionary changes in the nature and structure of education, responding to what they view as market demands for education. Although the writers see many of the new and innovative reforms as on the right track, they argue that they do not go far enough.

A radical voucher program similar to that proposed by Chubb and Moe was turned down by Colorado voters in 1992. Created by a citizen initiative, it would have permitted parents to collect vouchers from their local districts worth a dollar amount equal to one-half of the state's per-pupil appropriation to the district. The parents would then spend the vouchers in the school of their choice—public, private, or religious. The estimated average voucher would be worth approximately $2,500 in the first year. California voters rejected a similar plan in November 1993.

Critics argued that the plans would cripple public school systems. Although the proposals failed, similar ones are likely to appear in other states. Indeed, if the American public continues to perceive the nation as being at risk due to an educational crisis, other revolutionary proposals are sure to surface. As a result, education at the state and local levels may be radically different in the twenty-first century.

Concern over contemporary education has brought forth calls for various types of **assessment** and **accountability** in an emphasis on **Assessment and Accountability** the schools as the source of the educational crisis. Some want teachers to be assessed in terms of their competency. Others want students to be required to show that they have mastered specific knowledge and skills before they are permitted to graduate. Still others seek to evaluate entire schools or school systems by referring to such aggregate indicators as the dropout rate, the retention rate, and students' post-graduation success.

It is not surprising that pressures for these types of measurement are increasing. In recent years the levels of state educational support have increased dramatically, and with the money has come state-level interest in what the money is buying, fueled in part by the 1980s perception of a crisis in education. Most states now require some type of outcome testing, and some tie the distribution of state aid to the results. In most states the testing of students and teachers began after 1980.

Although competency testing and outcome assessment may seem like reasonable requirements, they are matters of intense political controversy. Teacher competency testing, for example, can be unreliable, as some skills and knowledge are more easily measured than others. It is not difficult to discover the level of a teacher's factual knowledge of subject matter, such as in physics or economics. But many knowledgeable people are behaviorally ill-suited to teach first graders or junior high school teenagers. Over a few semesters or years, administrators and peers can assess a teacher's style, temperament, effectiveness, and suitability for continuous classroom interaction with students. But standardized competency questions cannot judge a teacher's overall teaching ability that well. Rather, the testing may even weed out teachers whose style and rapport with students translate into effective instruction.

Another major concern with competency testing is its potential to have a disproportionate impact on minority teachers. Nelson Dometrius and Lee Sigelman suggest that:

> . . . The imposition of teacher testing will have a homogenizing effect on the racial-ethnic diversity of the . . . educational work force, measurably decreasing the number of black and Hispanic teachers. . . . The conclusion [is] that . . . the drive for quality in public education — a goal that virtually everybody supports — will proceed at the expense of at least one other widely shared goal, that of achieving and maintaining a racially-ethnically representative educational system.[28]

In the context of falling test scores and other educational problems, lawmakers want quick prescriptions. As the political battle continues, those holding the purse strings want immediate results while those in the classroom resist short-term measures such as testing in favor of long-term solutions to complex questions.

Teacher Tenure

Teacher **tenure**, which protects experienced teachers from dismissal except for moral or criminal offenses or severe incompetence, has come into disrepute in recent years. Some critics of the schools call for its abolition as one way to improve education, whereas educators resist moves to abolish tenure. The attacks on tenure seem to emerge from a misunderstanding about its purpose, shared by both critics and defenders, and the failure of the educational establishment to take action against problem employees who are tenured.

The underlying assumption is that tenure protects academic freedom. Students and, indeed, society would suffer if teachers were not free to teach the best information available and to interpret subjects as they see fit. If teachers were subjected to pressures to impart orthodoxies, whether political or religious, or certain scientific findings for fear of losing their jobs, children would receive a poor education. Thus, the states consider it to be in the public interest to afford teachers, after an initial probationary period, substantial protection against arbitrary dismissal. Tenure is a continuous employment contract subject to termination only for incompetence, criminal offenses, certain moral transgressions, or financial exigency; the burden of proof must be carried by the institution.

While tenure is clearly valuable in protecting academic freedom, in adding to the attractiveness of the teaching profession, and in guarding against arbitrary and unfair dismissals, it has also been problematic. The main problem is the reluctance with which institutions seek to remove truly incompetent teachers. For fear of undermining the practice of tenure itself, peer hearing panels and administrators often refuse to revoke tenure even in clear cases of incompetence. Ironically, however, such efforts to protect tenure lead to criticism of the system and, in the long run, weaken the support for tenure by eroding the political support base.

All states have policies that grant teachers either tenure or some other form of due-process protection. Texas has never had a full-blown tenure system, and New Mexico replaced its tenure system in 1986 with an alternate set of due-process protections. Colorado did the same in 1990. Tenure is likely to remain a target of certain interests, especially those who interpret the policy not as preserving academic freedom in the interest of the larger public good, but as providing job guarantees and protection of incompetence.

Merit Pay

The salary system referred to as **merit pay** is based on teachers' performance. Popular among critics of prevailing practices, it does not provide annual salary increases based on teachers' length of service and level of education. Rather, pay increases are determined by administrators, who give the largest increases to the teachers they judge to be the most meritorious, or worthy. Advocates of this system contend that the system used widely today fails to differentiate between the good teacher and the poor teacher in that both receive the same increase in salary each year. The merit pay system rewards teachers whose performance is excellent and, some contend, gives teachers an incentive to perform to the best of their ability.

Although most agree that good teachers should be rewarded, it is difficult to define good teaching. Are good teachers popular teachers, unpopular teachers who still get students to perform, kind and understanding teachers, strict teachers, or teachers who teach large quantities of information or who encourage students to think for themselves? It is the responsibility of educators to determine what constitutes good teaching and the job of administrators to decide which teachers satisfy the criteria. Yet this type of judgment is not easily made, for the results of good teaching are often not evident until years or decades later.

Many educators are opposed to the merit pay system. In addition to maintaining that good teaching is hard to define, they express concern over who will do the judging and the potential impact of the system on teacher morale and cooperation. It is argued that school principals, for example, who spend little time observing teachers in the classroom and whose long-term experience with the consequences of good teaching is limited, cannot make informed and fair judgments. Educators also contend that if teachers themselves lack confidence in the evaluative judgments, the merit pay plan will not increase their performance in the classroom. Since performance is tied to high morale and confidence in the fairness of school administration, they argue, the merit pay system may have unintended effects on teachers.

SHOULD SCHOOLS BE REFORMED OR LEFT ALONE?

In the context of an educational crisis in the 1990s, the issues and debates will persist and changes in education are likely to occur. Some states may attempt more reforms than other states, and some of the changes may lead to more or less improvement than others.

However, there is some feeling that policymakers in America should leave the schools alone, and that much of the attention being given to reform efforts is making matters worse. Most of these critics view the educational crisis as rooted in larger societal problems. To the teaching of basic subjects has been added new subject matter areas. Counseling, feeding, transporting, and caring for the social and psychological needs of students are now on the list of school responsibilities.

According to a 1989 *Washington Post* poll, most Americans want the schools to do even more in the way of social services. Among those participating in the survey, 82 percent wanted the schools to serve breakfast to children from low-income homes, 77 percent said the schools should make birth control information available to students, 69 percent wanted health and nutritional guidance to be given to pregnant students, and 51 percent would have the schools provide psychiatric counseling.[29] Although these services would address many of the societal and family problems that interfere with effective teaching and learning today, they would also further dilute the central educational function of the schools. Can schools and teachers focus only on the basics of learning and ignore the problems of children? Consider this:

> For two days, Josh Austin cried in school because his ear ached. . . . The solution wasn't so simple as sending him home. His mother, Kim Austin, was working up to 10 hours a day at a discount store. A single parent struggling to raise three children on take-home pay of less than $600 a month, she had no transportation and couldn't afford the $600 deductible on her health insurance.[30]

If Josh fails academically, who is to blame? Will schools of choice, accountability testing, merit pay, or abolition of teacher tenure help him succeed in school?

Some social science researchers suggest that factors outside the schools account for student performance differentials. David Morgan and Sheilah Watson report, for example, that "background or environmental characteristics are more potent in accounting for achievement than are school or education system measures."[31] These researchers also allege that children from female-headed households perform less well than others. They conclude that "system changes cannot be expected to overcome the handicaps of educationally and culturally deprived citizens with low incomes."[32]

Some recent reform proposals contain multiple goals and might seem to be at cross-purposes. The plan articulated in 1989 by President George Bush and the governors of the states, for example, included the goals of more rigorous standards and higher student retention rates. In the long run, these two goals may not be mutually exclusive. In the short run and without changes in home life or early childhood schooling, they may work at cross-purposes.

Divorce, employment, health, sex, drugs, and violence are among the many issues with which today's teachers must deal. Educational bureaucracies are larger than ever, and the expanded administrative staffs demand more of teachers' professional time. Politicians — from presidents, governors, and state legislators to school board members and administrators — seek both to advance their personal political ambitions and improve education by conceiving of new ways to operate the schools; their proposals may disrupt ongoing educational routines. Many teachers view increased parental involvement, not changes to the school system, as a key to improved student performance.[33]

Although most critics agree that education in America needs to be improved, those who see the major problems as rooted in societal conditions contend that politically motivated or poorly conceived reform proposals may do more harm than good. They argue that change should be instituted slowly, should be carefully planned, and should be largely determined by those most in touch with students — the teachers. However, since education is a public matter that consumes the largest proportion of local and state money, it is likely to remain an issue of political debate.[34]

SUMMARY

The diverse and decentralized nature of U.S. government institutions in general also characterizes the nation's system of public education. American students are taught in some 14,000 local school districts as well as in many private and religious-based schools. These thousands of school systems are similar in some respects but different in others. They often differ in terms of their size, the needs of their students, the resources available to them, and the extent to which they must either raise their own revenues or rely on state funding.

Local school districts are subordinate to the state and, therefore, are legally under the state's control. Some states fund and control their school districts more than other states. The trend in recent decades is toward increased state funding and control of the local district.

Although the Constitution does not specify a federal role in education, national policymakers seek to press their policy agendas on the educational system by making a limited amount of federal funding available to the schools, accompanied by a growing array of conditions and mandates. The educational system remains local in terms of its daily operation. It is increasingly a state-run system with respect to its funding, legal control, and direction. The federal government continues to find ways to control some school-related policies even though its financial contribution remains small. U.S. presidents, secretaries of education, members of Congress, governors, and state legislators talk extensively about the schools as thousands of locally elected school board members seek to balance budgets and community pressures and as teachers prepare lessons, grade papers, and teach students.

Just as America's schools are plagued by problems ranging from drugs and violence to declining student test scores, so too are they the targets of critics proposing various reforms. Following the 1983 "A Nation at Risk" report, reformers sought to improve education by adding to the curriculum, increasing the requirements for graduation, improving teacher salaries, and hiring more staff. More recently, the reform efforts are in the direction of developing competition among schools, providing school choice, and restructuring top-down forms of governance to allow bottom-up control of curriculum and school management. Some recent reforms include participation by both parents and teachers in site-based management.[35]

Whether the reform efforts will improve education in America is yet to be seen. Some of the problems facing educators today may be rooted in environmental factors beyond the control of the schools but within the control of the family or community. Given the financial investment in the educational system and the importance of its function in society, the schools will likely remain at the center of American politics.

KEY TERMS

"A Nation at Risk"
Brown v. Board of Education
busing
*San Antonio Independent
    School District v. Rodriguez*
early childhood education
schools of choice

voucher system
magnet school
assessment
accountability
tenure
merit pay

ADDITIONAL READINGS

Chubb, John E., and Terry M. Moe. *Politics, Markets and America's Schools.* Washington, D.C.: Brookings Institution, 1990.
Cistone, Peter J., ed. *Understanding School Boards.* Lexington, Mass.: D. C. Heath, 1975.
Meier, Kenneth J., and Joseph Stewart, Jr. *The Politics of Hispanic Education: Un Paso pa'lante y dos pa'tras.* Albany: State University of New York Press, 1991.
Meier, Kenneth J., Joseph Stewart, Jr., and Robert England. *Race, Class, and Education.* Madison: University of Wisconsin Press, 1989.
Ward, James G., and Patricia Anthony, eds. *Who Pays for Student Diversity?* Newbury Park, Calif.: Corwin Press, 1992.

NOTES

1. Sherwood L. Jensen, "School Teachers Fight Education War with Little Ammunition," *Rocky Mountain News*, 19 June 1990, letter to the editor.
2. U.S. Bureau of the Census, *Statistical Abstract of the United States, 1991* (Washington, D.C.: GPO, 1991), pp. 142–43.
3. Ibid., pp. 148, 280, 298, 299.
4. Ibid., p. 160.
5. Ibid.
6. U.S. Bureau of the Census, *Statistical Abstract of the United States, 1989* (Washington, D.C.: GPO, 1989), p. 134.
7. National Commission on Excellence in Education, "A Nation at Risk" (Washington, D.C.: GPO, 1983).
8. Kenneth J. Meier, Joseph Stewart, Jr., and Robert England, "The Politics of Bureaucratic Discretion: Education Access as an Urban Service," *American Journal of Political Science* 35 (Feb. 1991): 165.
9. "Teachers Moonlight Despite Pay Hikes," *Fort Collins Coloradoan*, 23 March 1989.
10. Census Bureau, *Statistical Abstract, 1991*, p. 147.
11. N.E.A. report cited in "Teachers Moonlight Despite Pay Hikes"; and National Commission on Excellence in Education, "A Nation at Risk."
12. "Bush Enlists Governors to Fight Tide of Mediocrity in Education," *Denver Post*, 24 Sept. 1989.

13. Edward D. Fiske, "Impending U.S. Jobs 'Disaster': Work Force Unqualified to Work," *New York Times*, 25 Sept. 1989.

14. Richard Lamm, "Young Americans Don't Measure Up," *Rocky Mountain News*, 24 Sept. 1989.

15. Census Bureau, *Statistical Abstract, 1991*, p. 156.

16. Census Bureau, *Statistical Abstract, 1991*, p. 133.

17. National Center for Education Statistics, *The Condition of Education* (Washington, D.C.: U.S. Department of Education, 1988).

18. Penelope Lemov, "Bringing the Children of the Underclass into the Mainstream," *Governing* (June 1989): 34–39.

19. "Half of Black Children Live in Poverty," *Fort Collins Coloradoan*, 2 Oct. 1989.

20. Colorado Legislative Council Staff, memo on early childhood education, Denver, 3 Nov. 1987.

21. Lemov, "Bringing the Children."

22. Colorado Legislative Council, memo.

23. Kathleen Sylvester, "Schools of Choice: A Path to Educational Quality, or 'Times of Inequity'?" *Governing* (July 1989).

24. Rudy Perpich, "Minnesota School-Choice Program Leads Nation," *Denver Post*, Oct. 1989.

25. "School District, Bank Provide Workplace Kindergarten," *Denver Post*, 3 Dec. 1989.

26. Rudy Perpich, "Minnesota School Choice Program."

27. John E. Chubb and Terry M. Moe, *Politics, Markets, and America's Schools* (Washington, D.C.: Brookings Institution, 1990).

28. Nelson C. Dometrius and Lee Sigelman, "The Cost of Quality: Teacher Testing and Racial-Ethnic Representativeness in Public Education," *Social Science Quarterly* 69 (March 1988): 81.

29. As reported in "Poll: High Schools Should Offer Social Services," *Fort Collins Coloradoan*, 8 Sept. 1989.

30. Janet Bingham, "Schools Take on New Role as Health Go-Between," *Denver Post*, 3 March 1991.

31. David R. Morgan and Sheilah S. Watson, "Comparing Education Performance among the American States," *State and Local Government Review* (Winter 1987): 20.

32. Ibid.

33. "Teachers Want Help from Parents," *Rocky Mountain News*, 10 Sept. 1989.

34. "Educational Improvements Emerge as Priorities for '89," *State Legislatures* (Feb. 1989): 6. See also Theodor Rebarber, "Accountability in Education," paper presented at the National Conference of State Legislatures, Denver, 1991.

35. Theodor Rebarber, "State Policies for School Restructuring," paper presented at the National Conference of State Legislatures, Denver, 1992; and Karen DeWitt, "Education 2000 Goals Lagging, Report Shows," *Denver Post*, 1 Oct. 1992.

15
Social Services

Social services exist to help those who are unable to help themselves. Here, applicants for unemployment compensation wait for the local unemployment office to open. As the local economy—based primarily on leather tanning and glove manufacturing—suffered, many found themselves without work. Gloversville, New York. *(Mitch Wojnarowicz/The Image Works)*

WHAT ARE SOCIAL SERVICES?

WHO NEEDS SOCIAL SERVICES?

AMERICAN INSTITUTIONS ADMINISTER SOCIAL SERVICES

THE DEVELOPMENT OF SOCIAL SERVICES POLICY
British Roots / The Great Depression

MAJOR CONTEMPORARY SOCIAL SERVICES PROGRAMS
Social Security / Aid to Families with Dependent Children (AFDC) /
Supplemental Security Income (SSI) / Medicaid / Food Stamps /
Other Programs

PROGRAM VARIATIONS AMONG THE STATES
The Medicaid Example / Why Policy Differences Exist

THE POLITICS OF SOCIAL SERVICES
The Role of Interest Groups / High-Stakes Politics / Big Money at
Stake / FOCUS 15.1: Women and Public Assistance

CONTEMPORARY SOCIAL PROBLEMS
The Homeless / The AIDS Epidemic

SOCIAL SERVICES: AN ONGOING POLICY PROBLEM
Rising Costs / Administrative Difficulties / Faulty Public Perceptions

SUMMARY

A teenage boy with average intelligence, as it is currently measured, has been expelled from school for the third time. His parents don't know yet, however. His father left home when the teenager was an infant, and his mother is visiting his sister 70 miles away. The youth receives little or no help with his schooling at home. His mother is too busy raising four other children. No one in the household works. Government programs provide the family with money for food and rent.

The expelled teenager has never lived in a home with working parents. His mother wants to work but lacks the skills and time, given her child-rearing responsibilities. The young man does not receive parental support and, together with his peers, has little interest in school. Although he can get part-time work at minimum wage, it is insufficient to make a dent in housing, food, medical, clothing, transportation, and other costs of modern life.

What will become of this young person and the family that he may some-day have? Will he obtain the motivation, education, and skills needed to become gainfully employed? What should the American public, through the agencies of government, do to help him?

A severely handicapped youngster lives with her parents. Her father works at a low-paying job and is not qualified for higher-paying employment. The mother cares for her child around the clock. The family's medical bills are large and frequent, but the family has no way of paying them. What should the government do to help the handicapped girl and her family?

A 15-year-old boy is repeatedly abused by his alcoholic father. The teen-ager is accustomed to the physical abuse; he has learned to take it and is now big enough to fend some of it off. But his schooling has suffered. And he has learned from his prime adult role model that physical violence is the normal approach to interpersonal relations. Experience in thousands of other similar cases suggests that this youngster is likely to encounter problems later on with substance abuse, the law, and family violence, and to need psychiatric help. What should the government do to help the teenager now or later on as an adult?

The city park is decorated with large cardboard boxes and other tempo-rary shelters of the homeless who live there. Many homeless people are tempo-rarily dislocated, but a large and increasing number of them are permanently without a home. Should the city build shelters? Force the homeless out of the park? Pay for the temporary or permanent housing of the homeless? Is housing a panacea or merely a temporary solution?

The preceding four scenarios convey only a small sample of the social issues that spawn political agendas. Should government act to rectify these unfortunate situations or allow them to continue? If action should be taken, what type, at what expense, and by which government? In conditions of limited resources, which group should receive help first? What can be done to help the homeless and some others become responsible and self-sufficient? To what extent are some of these problems the fault of the family or of a society that structures educational, medical, occupational, and other opportunities and hurdles?

American voters elect politicians to address social problems, though many issues remain unresolved. The proposed solutions are often altered as new problems emerge, as new theories and data become available, and as public opinion changes. Collectively, the solutions become social policy. It is made by county commissioners, by state legislators, by members of Congress, and largely by administrators in local, state, and national social service agencies. Indeed, a major attribute of social service policy is the extremely close relationship among the policymaking sectors—local, state, and national.

WHAT ARE SOCIAL SERVICES?

The term **social services** refers to the public policies that address the health-care and assistance needs of the handicapped, children, and others not fully able to care for themselves. Many such policies were once commonly referred to as **welfare** because they involve the transfer of collective public resources to individuals; that is, payments from the public treasury are made to individual recipients. However, the term *welfare* is confusing because subsidized low-interest loans to college students, crop-price support payments to farmers, and the use of public hospitals by fee-collecting physicians are also examples of individual benefits being derived from collective resources. Therefore, it is more appropriate to refer to the health and assistance policies discussed in this chapter as social services policies.

WHO NEEDS SOCIAL SERVICES?

In the early 1990s, over 30 million Americans—half of whom were under the age of 19 or over age 65—lived below the federally established **poverty line**, a measure of about three times what it costs to eat a modest diet. About 10 percent of American whites, over 25 percent of Hispanics, and around 32 percent of African-Americans lived below the poverty line. Well over 10 percent of all American families did so, and nearly half of them were headed by single mothers. In addition, those living in homes headed by people with less than an eighth grade education were roughly eight times more likely to be poor than those living in households headed by people with at least one year of college. The larger the family and the younger the head of household, the higher the incidence of poverty.[1]

A recent report by the National League of Cities paints a rather dismal picture of poverty. The report notes that over the past two decades poverty has become more concentrated in urban areas and certain neighborhoods. The ranks of the poor are increasingly comprised of children, and those caught in poverty are less likely to escape their condition than those of past generations. The poor are more isolated from the rest of society and increasingly trapped in their predicament. "Such conditions are devastating for those caught up in it, especially children."[2]

Those living in poverty are more likely than others to have problems with health and medical services. One-third of America's poor children and poor pregnant women have no health insurance coverage. In families with incomes below the poverty line, 60 percent of the women of child-bearing age are not covered by Medicaid—a joint federal and state program that provides medical coverage to the poor—and over 33 percent have no medical coverage.[3]

People with health and income problems have also had to deal with stereotypical images of themselves as lazy, irresponsible, and the like. In reality, however, the bulk of Americans in need of social services are blind, disabled, elderly, or children or single mothers without financial support. The needy also often lack an education or marketable skills.

AMERICAN INSTITUTIONS ADMINISTER SOCIAL SERVICES

The complex interconnections among American institutions of government are clearly evident in the area of social services. Some programs are federal, others are state, and still others are local. Many programs are jointly funded. A number of federal programs, such as Aid to Families with Dependent Children and Medicaid, are administered by the states and localities, are jointly state and federally funded, and are operated with state criteria, some of which are federally mandated. The programs themselves are connected, with eligibility for one sometimes constituting eligibility for another.

American governments have put into place a bewildering array of policies and programs to deal with the plight of persons with health, income, and self-care problems. In terms of the number of people served and the costs, Aid to Families with Dependent Children (AFDC), Supplemental Security Income (SSI), Medicaid, and the Food Stamp program are the largest programs. However, hundreds of others detect disease; immunize children; inspect foods, water, and waste; collect vital statistics; care for abused or neglected children;

and so on. Annually, a large proportion of state legislative agendas are comprised of bills addressing children, families, hospitals, health facilities, health insurance, and health care provision and regulation. A significant percentage of the lobby corps in the state and national arenas occupies its time with social services issues.

Like public education policies, social services policies are intergovernmental in nature and a reflection of federalism. Unlike education programs, however, a large proportion of the funding for social services comes from the national government. The major social programs are heavily or fully funded by the national government, and SSI and the Food Stamp program are administered in large measure by national authorities. AFDC and Medicaid are state administered; AFDC is mostly nationally funded and Medicaid is run on a blend of state and federal money. Many features of the major American social services are outlined in Table 15.1.

THE DEVELOPMENT OF SOCIAL SERVICES POLICY

As with so much of American public policy, the origins of American   **British Roots**
social service policy are rooted in our country's British heritage. One
critic notes "a consensus about the purpose of welfare that had survived with remarkably little alteration since the Republic was founded and, for that matter, could trace its roots to the Poor Laws of Elizabethan England."[4] The Poor Laws established basic public policy orientations toward poverty and were widely followed in England and the United States from the eighteenth to the early twentieth century.[5] According to one analyst, those charged with the administration of the Poor Laws contended that poverty "was no organic disease, nor 'principally the result of unavoidable distress,' but arose from 'fraud, indolence, or improvidence.' "[6] Public assistance, such as it was, was made a duty of the local government or parish.[7]

TABLE 15.1   Major Social Services Programs

Program	Eligibility	Funding	Administration
Aid to Families with Dependent Children (AFDC)	Families in need	Most federal, some state	State/local
Food Stamp program	Needy	Federal	State/local
Medicaid	Needy	Federal/state	State
Supplemental Security Income (SSI)	Blind, disabled, and elderly in need	Federal	Federal

The American system of poverty relief took on many of the British features.[8] Through the first few decades of the twentieth century, poverty in America was dealt with primarily by the subnational and private components of the government system. Although the national government did operate certain specialized programs for veterans, Native Americans, and a few others, the established notion was that the national government should not take an active role in the provision of social services.[9]

The Great Depression
The Great Depression of the 1930s began the process of changing the established attitude toward social services and drew the national government into their provision in a much larger way.[10] The then-existing poverty relief systems were not equipped to deal with the increased pressure brought about by the Depression. State and local agencies were not in a position to deal with the problems it created. As a result, lasting changes to the system were made.

As Charles Murray notes, Franklin Roosevelt's **New Deal** introduced four lasting changes to the welfare system: Social Security, Aid to Families with Dependent Children (AFDC), Worker's Compensation, and Unemployment Insurance.[11] Thus, at the end of the New Deal, the national government was firmly in the public assistance business.

MAJOR CONTEMPORARY SOCIAL SERVICES PROGRAMS

Social Security
The foundation for contemporary social services policy was the 1935 **Social Security Act**. The retirement section of the act was designed as an insurance and entitlement program, not as a social service. Enacted in the wake of the Great Depression, the underlying rationale of the Social Security Act was that Americans would pay into a central national fund during their working years and then draw from the fund in retirement, thereby avoiding late-life poverty. Benefits were and still are considered entitlements because the recipients pay in advance for their retirement benefits through a payroll tax shared by workers and employers. In practice, however, general tax revenues are used to augment contributions. The act also contains provisions to help the disabled and dependent children. Since 1935 the basic Social Security Act has been amended and expanded repeatedly. In 1965, for example, came the inclusion of Medicaid, which provides health care for the poor.

The Social Security Act includes a provision for **Aid to Families with Dependent Children (AFDC)** as a result of subsequent changes in the law. AFDC is administered by the states and remains today their major aid program. The states individually establish eligibility criteria for AFDC, though under certain federal guidelines. The national government funds the program payments, no matter the cost.

Aid to Families with Dependent Children (AFDC)

In establishing eligibility criteria each state determines a need standard, or the income required to meet basic family needs. A family qualifies for AFDC if its gross income is less than 185 percent of the state's need standard or if its net income is less than 100 percent of that number. In addition, the states set payment standards, which are what a state will pay. The payment standard, which may be the same as or less than the need standard, is the maximum payment allowed. The need standards and payment standards vary among the states, as is to be expected in a federal system comprised of one central government and a host of semiautonomous states.

Eligibility for AFDC is also tied to family circumstances. A family must be needy, as judged by the relationship of its income to the need standard, and be absent one parent by way of death, divorce, or abandonment. Under recent federal law, however, states have the option of covering two-parent families when both parents are unemployed. Roughly two-thirds of the states exercise this option, and the costs are paid by the national government.

The **Supplemental Security Income (SSI)** program is intended to help poor people generally, though only those in certain specified categories. Established in the 1935 Social Security Act as separate programs for the blind, aged, and disabled, the law was amended by Congress in 1972, when the programs were combined into one SSI program.

Supplemental Security Income (SSI)

The national government is responsible for funding and administering the SSI program. However, the states are allowed to supplement SSI payments; roughly half of the states exercise this option, but the level of supplementation varies widely among them and only a few provide a significant supplementary amount. Unlike AFDC, moreover, the SSI payments provided by the federal government are uniform in terms of amount among the states.

The **Medicaid** program provides payment for the medical care of the poor. Authorized in amendments to the Social Security Act and established in 1965, the program has been altered several times since. In general, those who qualify for AFDC or SSI also qualify automatically for Medicaid. In addition, the states may expand coverage to include the so-called "medically indigent" — people who have incomes below the federal poverty line but do not

Medicaid

qualify for AFDC or SSI, such as working couples or families with low earned incomes. Roughly 37 percent of families below the poverty line do not qualify for AFDC or SSI, and only 14 states provide Medicaid coverage for them. Among all Medicaid recipients, 68 percent qualify by virtue of their eligibility for AFDC and 25 percent through their receipt of SSI help.

Funding   Medicaid is jointly funded by the national government and the states, with the former covering from 50 percent to 80 percent of the cost. The program is the most costly of the various social services. The largest proportion of Medicaid payments goes to cover patient co-payments and premiums under **Medicare** — a federal program that covers partial medical costs for the elderly. The federal share of medical costs varies among the states according to average per-capita income, such that the least wealthy states receive the highest proportions. However, no state receives less than 50 percent. The national government also provides its share to states that choose to extend coverage to the medically indigent.

Coverage   Medicaid generally covers hospital costs and primary physician fees. States determine coverage within the bounds of federal rules. However, the state-determined criteria mean large gaps in coverage nationwide. Texas, for example, extends coverage to only one-fourth of those living in poverty and offers less than one-half of the optional services.[12] Federal guidelines require coverage of certain services, including nursing home care, X-rays, family planning, health screening for children, and others. The states may extend coverage beyond these federal minimums; for eyeglasses, for example. The federal government also requires coverage for certain groups, such as the blind, the elderly, the disabled, and single-parent families in need. Since 1989 and 1990, federal rules also mandate coverage for pregnant women and for children under age 1, initially, and under age 8 later for families whose income is less than 75 percent of the federal poverty line.

Most Medicaid recipients are children, adults with dependent children, or the elderly poor. Indeed, the aged constitute 15 percent of the recipients and account for 60 percent of the costs. Demographic trends showing growth in the elderly population are expected to put upward financial pressure on Medicaid budgets.

Costs and Effectiveness   Medicaid is a costly and politically controversial social service in the states. The costs of the program grew rapidly in its early years. Although in recent years the expenditure growth rate has leveled off, Medicaid constitutes a large state budget item. Since 1986, for example, Medicaid costs have increased an average of 13 percent per year, or two to three times the growth rate of state budgets generally.

Most states have initiated a variety of cost-containment efforts, including a tightening of the eligibility requirements for AFDC. In Missouri, in 1991,

5 percent across-the-board cuts in state agencies were implemented to pay the costs of new federal Medicaid mandates. Other approaches include primary care systems, wherein one physician is designated to determine a patient's needs, rather than allowing a string of specialists to do so serially and independently; mandatory family contributions to nursing home costs; the establishment of medical service rate-setting commissions; the use of health maintenance organizations (HMOs) for Medicaid patients, which pool patients under the care of a predetermined set of physicians; requiring hospitals that treat federally covered Medicare and Medicaid patients to donate certain services to the medically indigent; and limiting the number of covered in-patient hospital days in particular circumstances.

In 1991 Oregon was the first state to attempt to ration health care. Although the U.S. Department of Health and Human Services rejected the original version of the plan, a modified version gained federal approval as an experiment under the Clinton administration. Under the state's plan, a primary list of treatments is identified and the coverage base is broadened so as to provide medical coverage for all poor people in Oregon. The plan also emphasizes prenatal care at the expense of high-cost specialized treatments.

Over the years the Medicaid system has been the victim of physician and laboratory fraud, which also has driven up its costs. For example, in some instances pharmacies provided kickbacks to nursing homes in exchange for channeling patients their way, or deals were rigged to send blood work to certain laboratories. One physician billed Medicaid for six tonsillectomies on the same person, and a chiropractor submitted eleven bills for a patient seen only once. More generally, the number of surgeries has increased, raising the question of whether all of the operations were necessary. Physicians convicted of fraud tended to receive light sentences.[13]

However, the Medicaid program is an effective one. One analysis of the impact of both Medicaid and the **Women, Infants, and Children (WIC)** program (which provides health and nutrition benefits for pregnant women and young children) suggests that both have a "significant negative impact on the infant-mortality rate for all infants. . . . [The] federal programs [have] saved [the lives of] between 20,000 and 35,000 infants per year."[14]

Food Stamps

The **Food Stamp program** is a major source of assistance for needy persons. First created in 1940, it was temporarily terminated when the nation entered World War II and then reestablished in 1965 as a part of President Lyndon Johnson's Great Society agenda.

The Food Stamp program provides stamps for the purchase of food, though some items such as prepared foods available in grocery stores are not covered. It is operated by the states for the U.S. Department of Agriculture. Before 1978 the recipients had to spend some of their own money to obtain the stamps. The

Food Stamp program has the effect of evening out some of the variations among the states in other public assistance programs, for those who receive less from other sources can as a result receive more food stamps. The poorer and larger a family, the more food stamps it may receive. Unlike AFDC, the Food Stamp program is available to both the nonworking and the working poor.

Other Programs   Although AFDC, SSI, Medicaid, and the Food Stamp program constitute the foundation of the social service assistance system and are perhaps the best known, they are by no means the only programs. Some states operate general assistance programs for those in need, including people who find the benefits of the other programs inadequate. However, not all states have such programs, and those that do generally fund only small amounts, though this varies considerably among the states. The national government sponsors a program to provide help to the poor for home heating and cooling. Need is based on the recipients' eligibility for AFDC, SSI, food stamps, certain veterans' benefits, or some other standard.

The states operate literally hundreds of programs designed to help those in need. The laws adopted or modified in the states in 1988 alone covered the following subjects: foster child care; adoption assistance; termination of parental rights; child abuse and child neglect detention, prevention, reporting, treatment, investigation, and victim assistance; child care and early education programs, including facilities, licensing, training, support, work programs, and employer support; physical and mental health care for children; child custody; domestic violence; drug abuse and prevention; nursing homes; home care; health insurance; employee health plans; health maintenance organizations; hospital finance, building, and regulation; the medically indigent; unemployment insurance; worker's compensation; child support enforcement; tax relief for the elderly; tax credits for dependents; job training; nutrition programs; low-income child care; licensing of health care professions; and employer tax incentives for the support of day-care programs. It is clear that a very large part of the state agenda involves social services.[15]

PROGRAM VARIATIONS AMONG THE STATES

The social services programs most subject to state-determined policy are the programs that differ considerably among the states. Each state establishes AFDC eligibility requirements for recipients, and half of the states determine the size of the support payments by establishing payment standards. Although the states may extend coverage beyond the federal requirements, most do not exercise this option. The national government's Medicaid contribution to the states ranges from 50 percent to 80 percent of the total cost, depending on each state's average per-capita income.[16]

The policy variations result in differences in the average monthly AFDC payment (see Table 15.2) and in the percentage of a state's population receiving AFDC or SSI (see Table 15.3). Table 15.2 lists the average monthly AFDC payments in 1991 in 10 states. The highest amount was paid in California at $620 per month, whereas Alabama paid the least at $114 a month. In addition, state-established need or payment standards and the economic circumstances of a state's population result in variations in the proportion of people receiving aid. As Table 15.3 indicates, 11 percent of those residing in Mississippi but only 1.8 percent of the New Hampshire population received AFDC or SSI in 1991.

The interstate differences can be substantial. Two states may establish similar AFDC need standards, but one may have many more poor families than the other, so that a higher percentage of its population qualifies for aid. Moreover, two states with similar need standards and economic circumstances may set very different payment standards, so that the proportion of qualifying families may be the same but the size of the payments differs. In a state with high need and payment standards and a high proportion of poor families, the number of recipients and the size of the payments are both large.

The Medicaid Example

The detailed aspects of social policies in the states reveal the bewildering array of interstate differences. For example, only 19 states have laws that limit the number of inpatient hospital days paid by Medicaid in a single year, and the law in each of those states differs from those of the others. In Mississippi the limit is 30 days; in Texas there is a per-illness limit; in Alabama there are exceptions to the stipulated limit for persons under age 18; and in Maryland the limit is set at 120 percent of the average stay for all persons in the same "diagnosis-related group."[17]

TABLE 15.2
Average Monthly AFDC Payment per Family, Selected States, 1991

States with Highest Payments		States with Lowest Payments	
California	$620	Alabama	$114
Alaska	619	Mississippi	118
Maine	559	Louisiana	167
Hawaii	546	Texas	168
Connecticut	534	Tennessee	170

Source: U.S. Bureau of the Census, *Statistical Abstract of the United States, 1991* (Washington, D.C.: GPO, 1991), p. 373.

TABLE 15.3
AFDC and SSI Recipients in Selected States, 1991
(as a percentage of the state's total population)

States with Highest Percentages		States with Lowest Percentages	
Mississippi	11.0%	New Hampshire	1.8%
Louisiana	9.2	Idaho	2.6
California	8.8	Nevada	2.8
Michigan	8.3	Utah	3.2
Maine	8.3	North Dakota	3.4

Source: U.S. Bureau of the Census, *Statistical Abstract of the United States, 1991* (Washington, D.C.: GPO, 1991), p. 372.

Why Policy Differences Exist

Some social service policy variations among the states are explained by social and economic conditions as well as by attitudes, values, and political traditions. Wealthy states, such as New York and California, have more money to contribute to their aid programs; other states, such as Louisiana and Mississippi, have less to contribute. Traditions and attitudes also help to determine the relative generosity of state legislatures. Public attitudes in some states tend to be relatively supportive of public assistance, whereas other states have attitudes and traditions that are less favorable toward public assistance. These attitudes and values are part of the political culture of the state. Highly industrialized and urbanized states tend to be more generous, which may be explained in terms of the relationship of social and economic factors to a state's politics. Industrialized and urbanized states have diverse populations, in terms of employment and life-styles, providing the base for political strength for both major parties. Competitive politics appears to produce conditions in which there is support for social service policies.

THE POLITICS OF SOCIAL SERVICES

The politics of social services is evident in the special interest groups that support them and that spend millions to influence state legislatures. Listed in Table 15.4, for example, are some of the interest groups in Colorado that are registered with the House of Representatives and that lobby on social policies.

The Role of Interest Groups

The energies of many interest groups are directed toward state budgets. Church groups, social workers, reform organizations (for example, the League of Women Voters), and organizations representing

TABLE 15.4
Selected Lobbying Groups in Colorado with an Interest in Social Policies, 1989

Acupuncture Association of Colorado
Advisory Commission on Family Medicine
Alliance of American Insurers
American Academy of Pediatrics
American Association of Physical Therapists
American College of Emergency Physicians
American Medicine International
American Mobile Home Association
Blue Cross and Blue Shield
Colorado Academy of Family Physicians
Colorado Association of Commerce and
  Industry
Colorado Association of Community Mental
  Health Centers
Colorado Association of Home Health Agencies
Colorado Association of Homes and Services
  for the Aging
Colorado Association of Marriage and Family
  Therapists
Colorado Catholic Conference
Colorado Chiropractic Association
Colorado Chiropractic Society
Colorado Coalition of Legal Services Programs
Colorado Dental Association
Colorado Dental Hygienist Association
Colorado Dietetic Association
Colorado Domestic Violence Coalition
Colorado Health Care Association
Colorado Hospital Association
Colorado Medical Society
Colorado Neurosurgical Society
Colorado Nurses Association
Colorado Ob/Gyn Society
Colorado Ophthalmological Association
Colorado Optometric Association
Colorado Orthopedic Society

Colorado Pharmacal Association
Colorado Podiatry Association
Colorado Psychiatric Society
Colorado Psychological Association
Colorado Public Health Association
Colorado Radiological Society
Colorado Society for Clinical Social Work
Colorado Society of Anesthesiologists
Colorado Society of Osteopathic Medicine
Colorado Trial Lawyers Association
COMPRECARE
Denver Medical Society
Doctors Company
Eli Lilly and Company
Evangelical Lutheran Church in America
Grand Avenue Drug
Health Insurance Association of America
HMO Colorado
Jefferson County Community Center for
  Developmental Disabilities
Kaiser Foundation Health Plan
League of Women Voters of Colorado
Mental Health Association of Colorado
Mesa Drug Store
Mile High United Way
National Association of Social Workers
National Federation of Independent Business
Peak Health Plan, Ltd.
Pfizer Pharmaceuticals
Pharmaceutical Manufacturers Association
Rocky Mountain Health Care Corporation
Rocky Mountain HMO
Rose Medical Center
Schering Corporation
Upjohn Company
Walker Drug Company

Source: House of Representatives, State of Colorado, *Registered Lobbyists* (Denver: Colorado House of Representatives, 1989).

children, the elderly, and families lobby in favor of high allocations for medical care and health maintenance programs, for tax breaks and other forms of assistance for the elderly, and for legislation that protects, cares for, and educates children. Much of the politics of social services in the states revolves around the problems of funding increasingly costly programs in the context of tight budgets and of meeting the expanding federal mandates related to AFDC, Medicaid, and a host of other programs.

The professions are often at odds with each other. In recent years professional insurance for doctors has become extremely costly as a result of increases in the number of malpractice lawsuits. As a result, physicians have sought tort reform legislation restricting the size of jury awards to successful plaintiffs. They have been opposed by trial lawyers, who argue that patients who have been hurt should have the right to seek large awards.

Similarly, dentists and dental hygienists, and ophthalmologists (physicians) and optometrists (who measure vision and prescribe glasses), often confront each other on the range of functions that the law should permit dental hygienists and optometrists to perform (for example, whether optometrists should be allowed to write prescriptions for certain kinds of eye medications). The dentists and ophthalmologists argue that their lengthy medical training is critical to a wide range of health care provisions and thus restrictions on the allowable activities of the hygienists and optometrists are reasonable. The hygienists and optometrists counter with the contention that they are qualified to provide a wider range of services, and that more liberal laws would help control the rapidly escalating costs of health care in the United States.

High-Stakes Politics

Lobbying by professionals is heavy indeed, for there is much at stake. Although the political rhetoric focuses on matters of what is allegedly best for patients and the public, the bottom line is how much of the enormous and growing health care market each group can capture through state laws that favor them.

General business organizations are concerned with the overall costs of doing business. Their lobbyists often oppose bills that would mandate coverage of certain medical procedures (for example, mammograms for women) in employee health insurance benefits because of the increased costs, or favor bills that would reduce the extent and costs of worker's compensation for injured and disabled employees. American physicians, who for years fought bitterly against what they called "socialized medicine," now support increased government spending for health care. In 1989 the American Medical Association (AMA) led a coalition of groups in a push for broader and more generous Medicaid coverage, relaxed eligibility requirements for AFDC and Medicaid, and expanded Medicaid reimbursements to doctors.[18]

Big Money at Stake

In 1988 the states and the national government together spent over $54 billion on Medicaid alone. SSI, food stamps, care for the medically indigent, direct support of hospitals, foster care, medical education, indirect support of various groups by way of tax breaks, and scores of other programs bring the total cost of social services into the hundreds of billions of dollars annually. It is no wonder, then, that so many professional, business, and other interest groups remain politically active in the formation of policy. The poor and needy themselves are absent from much of the action because they do not tend to involve themselves in politics.

Some politically active interests see the solution of many of the nation's social services problems in less, not more, government money. Charles Murray, for example, argues that some programs are counterproductive because they allow certain people to avoid the search for self-sufficiency in the private sector. While self-help may not be possible for some of the disabled or for children, Murray contends that a solution to the poverty problem lies in weaning the capable away from looking to government for help.[19]

Since January 1990, federal law has required job training and volunteer work of public assistance recipients. However, a recent study suggests that for poor women with children, the cost of transportation and day care, combined with the low or moderate pay and impermanence of the available jobs, makes the transition from public assistance to self-sufficiency difficult.[20] Focus 15.1 describes some other factors that affect women's ability to achieve self-sufficiency.

CONTEMPORARY SOCIAL PROBLEMS

The Homeless

Among the newest problems to make the urban political agenda is **homelessness**. Cities, suburbs, and even rural areas have inhabitants with no fixed place of residence. Their "home" might be a park bench, a heating grate on the sidewalk, or a small wooded grove. Their "showers" might be city fire hydrants, public faucets, or standing pools of water.

The term *homeless* seems itself to indicate a solution to the problem — provide a home, or some sort of shelter, to the homeless. However, Alice Baum and Don Burnes suggest that the plight of the homeless is much more complex. They claim that between 65 percent and 85 percent of the homeless are afflicted by alcoholism, drug abuse, mental illness, or a combination of those maladies.[21] Providing a shelter, they say, will not "cure" the problems of the homeless. At the same time, the homeless are very visible in most urban areas, forcing many communities to adopt policies to deal with the problem. In some communities the policy is simply to move the homeless along; in others a combination of public and private efforts at providing temporary shelters has been tried. Neither solution has been particularly effective. The cities are forced to deal with the complex problems that the homeless face without any real assistance from national or state governments.

The AIDS Epidemic

Another social problem that has emerged recently in this country is AIDS (acquired immunodeficiency syndrome). Local governments — cities, schools, hospital districts, and counties — are all in the forefront of the battle against AIDS. Although the national government, through the Centers for Disease Control in Georgia and the National Institutes of Health in

15.1 WOMEN AND PUBLIC ASSISTANCE

In an effort to help lawmakers generate well-informed public policy and make good decisions on how best to help public assistance-dependent women gain employment, the Washington state legislature commissioned a study in 1993 of the characteristics of women who do and those who do not successfully make the transition. The study indicates that successful emancipation is most likely to occur among women who receive social services for short periods of time, who are married, who have a high school or an equivalent education, and who live with other adults. The women least likely to make the transition are heavily dependent on public assistance for long periods of time, have a child under age 1, and gave birth to a child before age 18.

The study suggests that teenage pregnancy, dropping out of high school, and isolation from the adult world can mean long-term poverty for women on public assistance.

SOURCE: Sheri Steisel, "Study Tracks Welfare Trends in Washington," *State Legislatures* (May 1993): 24.

Maryland, strives to find a cure for the AIDS virus, it is the local hospitals and other health care agencies that daily face the problem of dealing with AIDS patients.

The long-term care of an AIDS patient is expensive. The Agency for Health Care Policy and Research estimates that the total lifetime cost for an AIDS patient is now $102,000, and that the total national medical costs for HIV and AIDS will amount to $15 billion a year by 1995.[22] Often private resources—both individual and insurance—are not sufficient to handle the health care costs. Many of the costs may be paid by local taxpayers in their support of medical care facilities.

SOCIAL SERVICES: AN ONGOING POLICY PROBLEM

Rising Costs Social services have become an ever larger political problem for America's state and local governments in recent years. The costs are soaring, primarily due to expanded coverage, rising medical costs, and changes

Homelessness in the United States has led to the appearance of "spontaneous settlements" in many American cities. This is "Bushville" on the Lower East Side of Manhattan in New York City. *(Margaret Morton © 1993)*

in the nature of the American family. More children than ever before are in single-parent homes and more single mothers are without financial support. Many such families, and others, qualify for AFDC or SSI, as well as for Medicaid. Many of the poor who do not so qualify are part of the medically indigent category. When the costs of treating the medically indigent are not covered fully, hospitals and doctors pass some of the shortfall on to those who can and do pay—through higher bills, which lead to higher insurance rates. At the same time, new medical discoveries and equipment also lead to more costly health care.

In addition to the various techniques that have been used to contain costs—second opinions for surgery, HMOs, co-payments by patients, and requiring some free indigent care from hospitals that receive Medicare and Medicaid payments—there is talk of health care rationing.[23] For example, the government is wondering whether it should pay tens of thousands of dollars for heart bypass surgery on an elderly man or woman, how much should be spent from the public treasury for medication for people who contracted a deadly disease through the use and abuse of illegal drugs, and whether public expenditures on health care should be limited and spending priorities established. In the face of rapidly rising costs and competition for public money by programs in corrections, education, transportation, and more, the states are increasingly forced to make difficult choices.

Rising health care costs are impacting all Americans alike through the diminishing quality of health care insurance. As medical costs rise, so do insurance rates, placing many state and local governments in a difficult dilemma. Growing insurance costs take away from funds that could otherwise provide raises for employees. As states and localities face this problem they often come into political conflict with their employees, especially when the employees are unionized. The Clinton administration has made health-care reform a high-profile issue.

Administrative Difficulties

The social services system is beset with administrative problems as well. Some administrative features of the AFDC program, for example, can create difficulties for the poor. It is more difficult for a family to qualify for aid if the father is in the household or if the mother is married. If the father remains in the home but is unemployed, the question arises why he is not working. Often he is simply unable to find work. If the mother is married she must prove that she is not receiving support from the father and explain why. If the parents find work and become self-sufficient, then encounter a setback later on, they must go through the procedures of qualifying for help all over again. Since requalification takes time, it is often tempting to decline employment in the first place unless it promises to be permanent and well-paid.

There are no simple solutions to fiscal and administrative problems, and the tasks of examining and modifying social service programs are made even more difficult politically by public attitudes and misinformation with respect to the poor. The stereotypical image of the poor as able-bodied but lazy people makes it difficult politically to support budget increases sufficient even to keep pace with inflation, and it makes it hard for politicians to associate themselves with social policy. It is simply easier to get reelected as an advocate of business interests than as a representative who struggles with the problems of the politically inert poor.

Faulty Public Perceptions

Facts and statistics belie much of the public image of the needy. Those who receive SSI are blind, aged, or disabled, as well as poor. Roughly two-thirds of the needy are disabled or are single mothers whose ability to work is complicated by such factors as lack of education, skills, or transportation, as well as the need to care for their children. Studies also contradict the images of the poor moving from state to state to find the most generous aid programs and of poor women having more children simply to receive more public aid. Even so, public perceptions of the poor remain largely negative.

SUMMARY

The U.S. system of social services reflects the nation's system of government and politics, for it is substantially decentralized and intergovernmental in nature and, thus, a reflection of federalism. Some social services policies come from Congress, others come from the states, and still others, such as AFDC and Medicaid, are a blend of both national and state policy and money. Some states are more generous than others in funding their programs, which is tied in part to localized values and politics as well as to state wealth. Congress and state legislatures confront lobbyists concerned about the needy, about the professions, or about both.

It is important to remember that public policies — social service policies and others — do not arise independently of government institutions and political processes; rather, they emerge from the legislative process, are implemented by large and decentralized bureaucracies, are impacted by the decisions of judges, and change according to public opinion. The arrival of new agenda items, such as AIDS and homelessness, is an indication of the ongoing development of social services policy at the state and local levels. As state and local governments continue to struggle with the issues of AIDS and homelessness, policies must be constructed to address these new issues.

KEY TERMS

social services
welfare
poverty line
New Deal
Social Security Act
Aid to Families with Dependent
  Children (AFDC)

Supplemental Security Income (SSI)
Medicaid
Medicare
Women, Infants, and Children (WIC)
Food Stamp program
homelessness

ADDITIONAL READINGS

Albritton, Robert. "Social Services: Welfare and Health." In *Politics in the American States*, edited by Virginia Gray, Herb Jacob, and Robert Albritton. New York: HarperCollins, 1990.

Greer, Ann, and Scott Greer. *Cities and Sickness*. Newbury Park, Calif.: Sage Publications, 1983.

MacLeod, Celeste. "Street People: The New Migrants." *The Nation* (22 Oct. 1973): 395–97.

Murray, Charles. *Losing Ground: American Social Policy, 1950–1980*. New York: Basic Books, 1984.

Romo, Harriet D., ed. *Latinos and Blacks in the Cities*. Austin, Tex.: Lyndon B. Johnson School of Public Affairs, 1990.

NOTES

1. U.S. Bureau of the Census, *Statistical Abstract of the United States, 1992* (Washington, D.C.: GPO, 1992), pp. 456, 457, 460.

2. Reported in "Poverty Worse since 1970, Report Says," *Rocky Mountain News*, 12 March 1989.

3. National Conference of State Legislatures, *Medicaid Eligibility: New State Options* (Denver: NCSL, 1987), p. 8.

4. Charles Murray, *Losing Ground: American Social Policy, 1950–1980* (New York: Basic Books, 1984), p. 16.

5. Jack W. Peltason and J. M. Burns, *Functions and Policies of American Government*, 3rd ed. (Englewood Cliffs, N.J.: Prentice-Hall, 1967); Sar A. Levitan, *The Great Society's Poor Law: A New Approach to Poverty* (Baltimore: Johns Hopkins University Press, 1969); and E. M. Leonard, *The Early History of English Poor Relief* (Cambridge, Mass.: University Press, 1900).

6. Pauline Gregg, *A Social and Economic History of Britain, 1760–1912* (London: Harrap, 1950), p. 186.

7. Asa Briggs, *A Social History of England* (New York: Viking Press, 1983), p. 114.

8. This discussion is drawn from Peltason and Burns, *Functions and Policies*. See also Frances Fox Piven and Richard Cloward, *Regulating the Poor: The Functions of Social Welfare* (New York: Pantheon Books, 1971); and Joel F. Handler and Ellen Jane Hollingsworth, *The "Deserving Poor:" A Study in Welfare Administration* (New York: Academic Press, 1971).

9. Handler and Hollingsworth, *"Deserving Poor,"* is an excellent study on welfare administration in the states.

10. This discussion draws heavily from William E. Leuchtenburg, *Franklin D. Roosevelt and the New Deal* (New York: Harper Torchbooks, 1963). See also Henry Hopkins, *Spending to Save: The Complete Story of Relief* (New York: Norton, 1936); Arthur M. Schlesinger, Jr., *The Age of Roosevelt*, vol. 2, *The Coming of the New Deal* (Boston: Houghton-Mifflin, 1958); and ibid., vol. 3, *The Politics of Upheaval* (Boston: Houghton-Mifflin, 1960).

11. Murray, *Losing Ground*, p. 17.

12. Gary W. Copeland and Kenneth J. Meier, "Gaining Ground: The Impact of Medicaid and WIC on Infant Mortality," *American Politics Quarterly* (15 April 1987): 258.

13. See Nicholas Henry, *Governing at the Grassroots* (Englewood Cliffs, N.J.: Prentice-Hall, 1980), pp. 456–58.

14. Copeland and Meier, "Gaining Ground," p. 268.

15. Catherine Sonnier, *Public/Private Partnerships in Child Care* (Denver: National Conference of State Legislatures, State Legislative Report, Oct. 1988).

16. National Conference of State Legislatures, *1988 State Legislative Summary: Children, Youth, and Family Issues* (Denver: NCSL, 1988); ibid., *Medical Eligibility: New State Options* (Denver: NCSL, 1987); and ibid., *Medical Indigency and Uncompensated Health Care Costs* (Denver: NCSL, 1989).

17. National Conference of State Legislatures, *State Efforts at Health Care Cost Containment: 1986 Update* (Denver: NCSL, 1986).

18. "AMA-Led Coalition Proposes Health Care Overhaul for Poor," *Rocky Mountain News*, 17 Feb. 1989.

19. Murray, *Losing Ground*.

20. Carol Kleiman, "New Job Act Fails Welfare Mothers," *Denver Post*, 4 June 1990.

21. Alice Baum and Don Burnes, *A Nation in Denial* (Denver: Westview Press, 1993); and James Bock, "Homeless," *Houston Chronicle*, 18 May 1993, p. 1D. Our discussion of the homeless draws heavily from Bock's analysis.

22. *State Legislatures* (April 1993): 12.

23. National Conference of State Legislatures, *State Efforts at Health Care Cost Containment* (Denver: NCSL, 1986).

16

Crime and Corrections

The criminal justice system in states, counties, and cities is meant to protect the public, even those who are accused of crimes. Here, a suspect is informed of his rights (as provided under the *Miranda* ruling by the U.S. Supreme Court) while being booked in Lynn, Massachusetts. *(John Coletti/The Picture Cube)*

431

What should happen to the young girl who shoplifts, to the young boy who steals, to the executive who earns a million dollars per year in salary from a savings and loan that he or she helps to ruin, or to the prostitute who is caught soliciting and using cocaine? Should they all go to jail? Which government should be responsible for controlling shoplifting, theft, white-collar crime, or sex and drugs—Congress, the state legislature, the city council? These are political questions with political answers.

The U.S. Constitution makes trade, defense, currency, and certain other matters the province of the national government. Most of the rest is left to the states and their local governments. Choices about what, if anything, to do about theft, illegal drugs, and so on are then allocated to the national or state/local policy bodies—that is, to their legislatures.

Sometimes the public and thus lawmakers grow impatient with certain kinds of behavior and decide to become "tough on crime," particularly at election time. As a result, significant increases in the costs of government— more police, judges, prisons, and guards—are needed. The increased spending is a political issue, and the laws, the penalties, and the costs all become political questions that can change from year to year.

American local and state governments pass laws by the thousands, hire people by the tens of thousands, and spend money by the millions or billions to try to keep the public safe. The reserved powers in the Constitution, which are reserved to the states, include what are commonly known as **police powers**— the authority of the states and their political subdivisions to provide for the public health, welfare, morality, and safety of the citizenry. Health, welfare, and morality are important issues, but the largest slice of this local and state government effort to keep the public safe involves crime and corrections.

The public mood has made crime a major political issue for the 1990s. In 1993 George Allen in Virginia and Rudolph Giuliani in New York rode a tough stance on crime to victory in their races for governor and mayor, respectively. Texas voters overwhelmingly supported propositions to deny bail to violent offenders and to spend $1 billion to build new prisons. Colorado and Utah approved tougher laws dealing with juvenile offenders.

State legislatures and city councils enact thousands of laws every year that declare various sorts of behavior illegal. Penalties are prescribed, courts are created and staffed, prisons are built, and rehabilitation and probation programs are established—all intended to make America's cities and neighborhoods safe places to live.

CRIME AND CORRECTIONS ARE STATE AND LOCAL MATTERS

Most of what goes on in crime and corrections in the United States is the business of state and local government units, not of the national government.

Indeed, over 95 percent of all crimes committed are violations of local or state laws. Laws against murder, rape, assault, robbery, or littering are enacted by state legislators or city councils. The same is true of statutes that prohibit illegal drug use or sale, fraudulent representation of mileage on used vehicles, prostitution, speeding, and disorderly conduct.

Most law-enforcement officials in the United States are employees of state and local governments. Although the national government has the Federal Bureau of Investigation (FBI), Treasury Department, Border Patrol, and Bureau of Prisons, the size of the national government law officer contingent pales in comparison to that of municipal police departments. Most jails and prisons are local and state, and so are most of the guards and occupants. A person may be sentenced to do time in a federal prison for conviction under a federal law against racketeering or deprivation of the civil rights of a fellow citizen, but that person is much more likely to be incarcerated in a state prison for running afoul of state laws against rape, robbery, assault, drug dealing, or arson.

American public policies regarding crime and corrections, both in the formation of those policies and in their execution, reflect the U.S. federal system. Thus there are both state and national legislatures, state and national laws, state and national law-enforcement units, state and national courts, and state and national prisoners. All of this means, of course, that the criminal justice system is highly decentralized and that the laws and the structure of law enforcement vary considerably from one jurisdiction to another. Even so, the business of crime and corrections is mostly state and local.

Crime and corrections are also intergovernmental matters, involving local, state, and national institutions. The Constitution and the Supreme Court impact the state and local units in important ways. The high court sets the parameters with respect to the rights of the accused and plays an important role in determining the acceptability of prison conditions in the states. Similarly, state criminal laws and corrections funding policies have dramatic impacts on the local units. When states become "tough on crime," the state jails fill up. In the early stages of the criminal justice process, prisoners are held in local jails, which are usually county facilities. When state criminal justice systems become jammed, it is the local units that initially feel the pressure. And if the states are slow to expand the courts and the prisons, local facilities are overloaded. In the structurally complicated and interrelated system of U.S. government, then, what one institution does has an impact on the others.

WHAT IS CRIME?

Decisions about what behavior is to be classified as criminal are policy choices. They are also political decisions in that they embody the values dominant in society at a given point in time. They reflect the concerns and pressures of the dominant organized political groups and, to some extent, the preferences of lawmakers. Prostitution is against the law in most but not all states. Guns must be registered in some jurisdictions, but not in most. The laws on drugs vary across the nation. Until recently, 18- to 21-year-olds could legally purchase beer in some states; now they may not.

The penalties for crimes vary, too. During the early 1980s, sentences for felonies were increased to the point of being doubled or tripled in many states. The public is in the mood to be "tough on crime," and policies have quickly changed to reflect that mood.[1] But public opinion changes, and so too does the law. What is illegal in one state may be legal in another. Behavior that is considered criminal at one time may be permissible later on.

American legislators adopt policies designed to protect a variety of things. Some laws are enacted to protect human beings themselves; thus, murder and assault are considered to be crimes. Other laws, such as those against theft or arson, are designed to protect property. Still other laws are intended to protect dominant social values; thus prostitution, indecent exposure, certain forms of sexual relations, and substance abuse are outlawed. What is legal or illegal at any given point in time may hinge on the values of the public, of the politically influential, and of the policymakers. These factors can vary by region and change with time. They can also have a direct impact on the volume of business in the courts, on the size of the prison population, and on the cost of the correctional programs.

THE CORRECTIONS CRISIS

Although the states have always had criminal laws on the books and the nation has always had criminals and prisons, in the 1980s and early 1990s the American states faced an exploding prison population and mushrooming corrections costs. According to a 1989 National Conference of State Legislatures publication:

> Across the country, in state after state, legislators and corrections officials are trying to manage correctional systems that to many seem out of control. Prisons are overcrowded, incarceration rates in most jurisdictions are climbing, and state and local corrections budgets are swallowing up more and more dollars. Sentencing practices have come under increasing attack for being inequitable and inconsistent, and for making inefficient use of limited correctional resources. Both institutional and community-based correctional administrators are handling more and more offenders without concomitant increases in resources.[2]

The serious prison problems facing the states in the early 1990s were not simply the products of increasing crime in America. After declining for several

FIGURE 16.1
Selected Crime Rates, 1980–1990 (per 100,000 population)

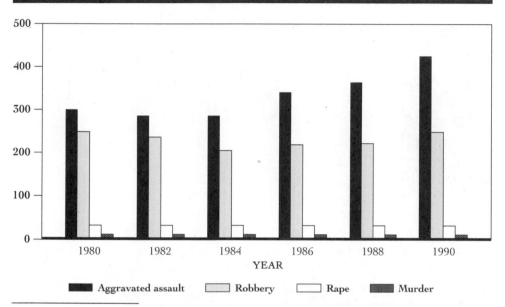

SOURCE: U.S. Bureau of the Census, *Statistical Abstract of the United States* (Washington, D.C.: GPO, 1992).

years, the crime rate appeared to swing upward beginning in about 1984, but by 1988 the rate of serious crimes per 100,000 people was still lower in most categories than it had been in 1980.[3] (See Figures 16.1 and 16.2.) It should be noted, however, that studies on crime rate trends often produce different findings. In addition, simple improvements in the reporting of crimes can falsely suggest a rising crime rate.

The Growing Prison Population

The size of the prison population has increased steadily since 1980. In the 1970s there were roughly 200,000 persons in American state prisons; by 1990 that number rose to about 700,000 (see Fig. 16.3). The states added to their prison population by 35,000 to 40,000 per year between 1970 and 1990. While the states added an average of 800 prisoner beds per week in 1988, the figure was 1,800 per week in the first six months of 1989.[4] The prison population grew by almost 90 percent in the 1980s alone. One out of every 420 Americans was in jail or prison, the highest rate in the world.[5] In California in 1980 there were fewer than 25,000 state prisoners; by the early 1990s that number was 100,000.[6] It is estimated that the total number of people nationwide on probation, on parole, or still in prison exceeds 4 million; in other words, it is higher than the individual populations of 27 states.

FIGURE 16.2
Selected Property Crime Rates, 1980–1990 (per 100,000 population)

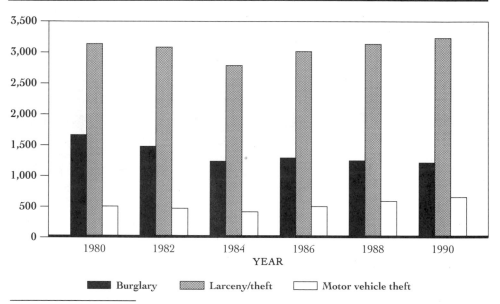

SOURCE: U.S. Bureau of the Census, *Statistical Abstract of the United States* (Washington, D.C.: GPO, 1992), p. 180.

The explosion in the prison population despite a slowly rising crime rate is related to a series of widespread policy changes in the states. Stimulated in part by growing discomfort with the longstanding and widespread discrepancies between sentences for serious crimes and actual time served, in part by the impact on public and legislative opinion of a "tough on crime" stance taken by President Ronald Reagan, and in part by a growing concern with the spread of drugs, state legislatures joined in a collective stampede to get tough on crime.

Longer Sentences   The simplest but most consequential action was to lengthen sentences for felony offenses such as murder, assault, rape, and robbery. In 1978 California enacted across-the-board extensions for 43 major felonies. New Mexico tripled the length of many sentences in 1979. Alabama legislated 30-year sentences with no probation for persons convicted the third time for felony theft of property. Maine eliminated parole, with the result that the average length of prison stays doubled. In the early 1980s Colorado doubled sentence lengths for a host of felonies.

The process continued into the next decade. In 1993 Texas modified its criminal code to lengthen the time required in prison before one could be eligible for release for selected crimes. These were not, then, uncommon strategies.[7]

FIGURE 16.3
Number of Federal and State Prisoners, 1970–1990 (in thousands)

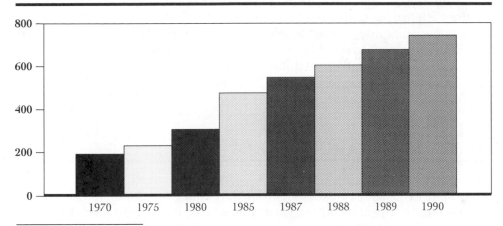

SOURCE: U.S. Bureau of the Census, *Statistical Abstract of the United States* (Washington, D.C.: GPO, 1992), p. 197.

Less Latitude for Judges and Parole Boards   Many states modified sentencing policies wherein judges previously had wide sentencing latitude and could consider a variety of factors in each case in setting sentences. Such systems often led to wide sentencing discrepancies among judges in similar cases and left the time of prisoner release up to parole boards. Policy changes constricted judicial latitude by more precisely specifying sentences or setting forth sentencing guidelines. The changes also curtailed the powers of parole boards.

Other Factors   The combination of these various factors—longer sentences and reduced judicial and parole board latitude—explain in large measure the explosion in the size of the prison population. It took place not as a result of dramatic changes in the crime rate but as a function of policy changes. The states, however, in their tough stance on crime, did not calculate the impact on the size of the prison population.

Other factors also contributed to the increased number of prisoners. The widening of drug trafficking led to more arrests and convictions. The movement of the children of the baby-boomers into their late teens and early twenties— the time of highest crime propensity—pushed the crime rate up.

The "get tough on crime" decade was fueled by the widespread public desire to "make America's streets safe." Grotesque and highly publicized crimes often boosted already existing political pressure to put more people behind bars and to keep them there longer. Some critics argue

The Impact of Public Opinion

that the public's interest in tough policies was stimulated by the media's decisions to highlight crime, such as the victimization of the elderly.

The damage done to the presidential campaign of Michael Dukakis in 1988 by the then-famous GOP ad linking him to rapist **Willie Horton** attests to the impact that an aroused public opinion can have on political outcomes. Horton was out on furlough from a Massachusetts prison while Dukakis was governor, and while out he committed additional crimes. The advertisement implied, with devastating results, that Dukakis was to blame.

WHO IS INCARCERATED?

Prisoners in the states are disproportionately young, male, and nonwhite. They also tend to be repeat offenders. On any given day, one in every 300 Americans is in a jail or prison. Most are men. Indeed, in 1988 the number of prisoners per 100,000 population in the states was 462 for men and just 23 for women. For black men in their twenties the number is 1 in 12. Most prisoners are men under 30 years of age. For burglars the peak age for crime is 16 years of age and then the frequency tails off. For robbers the peak ages are 17 and 18, and by 23 the frequency of crime drops to one-half of the high point. The peak age for crimes of assault is 18 to 21, but the drop-off that accompanies aging here is slower.[8]

Much crime is now tied to drugs. Roughly 20 percent of all crimes today involve drugs or alcohol directly; another quarter are crimes against people, and just under one-half are crimes involving property.[9] But many of the crimes against people or property are connected in some way to drugs, and thus estimates are that between one-half and three-quarters of all street crimes are somehow related to drugs.

TABLE 16.1

Number of Violent Crimes Reported to Police in Selected States, 1990 (per 100,000 population)[a]

States with Highest Crime Rates		States with Lowest Crime Rates	
Florida	1,244	North Dakota	74
New York	1,181	Vermont	127
California	1,045	New Hampshire	132
South Carolina	977	Maine	143
Illinois	967	Montana	159

[a]Includes murder, rape, robbery, and aggravated assault.

Source: U.S. Bureau of the Census, *Statistical Abstract of the United States* (Washington, D.C.: GPO, 1992), p. 181.

TABLE 16.2
Number of Violent Crimes Reported to Police in Selected Cities, 1990 (per 100,000 population)

Miami	4,353	Tampa	3,326
Atlanta	4,085	Detroit	2,699
Newark	3,882	Kansas City	2,550
St. Louis	3,449		

Source: U.S. Bureau of the Census, *Statistical Abstract of the United States* (Washington, D.C.: GPO, 1992), p. 198.

Crime in America, then, tends to be a young man's enterprise, tends to center around drugs, and frequently involves repeat offenders. Furthermore, crime is not evenly distributed across the nation geographically. The number of violent crimes and crimes against property reported per 100,000 people is highest in urban areas, lower in small cities, and lowest in rural America. The rates of crime vary considerably by state and city as well. (See Tables 16.1 and 16.2.)

It is instructive to contrast Tables 16.1 and 16.2, both of which report the number of violent crimes known to police per 100,000 people. The crime rates in California, Florida, and New York are among the highest in the nation, but the rates in the largest cities within each of those states is double or triple the statewide rates. The crime rate in Atlanta is almost 60 times as high as it is in the sparsely populated state of North Dakota.

The rates of imprisonment vary across the states, too, though not as widely as the crime rates (see Table 16.3). The crime rates do not necessarily track with the level of incarceration, suggesting that the particular types of crimes, the rates of arrest and conviction, and policies with respect to sentencing also vary among the states.

TABLE 16.3
Number of Prisoners in Selected States, 1990 (per 100,000 population)

States with the Highest Number of Prisoners		States with the Lowest Number of Prisoners	
South Carolina	451	West Virginia	85
Nevada	444	New Hampshire	117
Missouri	366	Vermont	117
Florida	336	Maine	118
Maryland	323	Rhode Island	132

Source: U.S. Bureau of the Census, *Statistical Abstract of the United States* (Washington, D.C.: GPO, 1992), p. 198.

THE COST OF CORRECTIONS

The lengthening of prison sentences, the reduction of judicial and parole board discretion, and the increase in drug-related convictions together helped to increase not only the size of the prison population but the cost of corrections as well. The increasingly crowded conditions led to more double-bunking, more noise, more violence (including physical attacks and homosexual rape), and deteriorating health conditions. By 1989 more than three-fourths of the states were under court order to reduce prison overcrowding or to otherwise improve prison conditions. The orders were in response to lawsuits brought by or on behalf of prisoners. Some court orders targeted specific facilities, whereas others directed action in entire state systems.[10]

Virtually all states have had to embark on expensive prison expansion programs, as a result of court decisions on prison conditions or because of the states' own strict corrections policies. The cost figures vary, but one 1987 estimate judged the cost of each new prison bed from as low as $42,000 to as high as $116,000, depending on the level of security required. The annual cost of maintaining each inmate in 1987 was estimated in the range of $14,000 to $36,500.[11]

After Michigan embarked on a program to construct 19 new prisons, a state senator commented that "there's no bigger growth industry in the last two years in Michigan than the corrections department."[12] In a recent five-year period Alabama spent $90 million on the construction of new prisons alone, or a total of $1,000 per family in that state. The problems of covering the costs, which were estimated in Alabama at $10,000 to $14,000 per inmate per year, come later. In 1988 the Ohio corrections budget grew by 16.5 percent, but the overall general state budget increased by only 4 percent. In Texas in the same year the figures were 33.8 percent for corrections and only 6.8 percent for the overall state budget.[13] For all states the cost of corrections rose from 1 percent of state budgets to nearly 5 percent between 1980 and 1991.[14]

Like the rates of crime and incarceration, the levels and patterns of spending for corrections also vary significantly among the states. Table 16.4 illustrates the tremendous range in the amount of state spending on corrections. In 1987, for example, Alaska spent over eight times as much on corrections per capita as did West Virginia and 2.5 times as much as the national average. Many factors explain the differences in state spending. There are, for example, differences in the cost of living among the states, such that across-the-board costs are higher in Alaska, New York, and California than in West Virginia and Arkansas. State policies also contribute to the spending variations, for many states differ in the types of behavior considered criminal, in the types of crimes for which conviction carries a prison term, in the length of prison terms, and in the conditions of release. In addition, the frequency of arrest and conviction can affect the size of a state's prison population and, therefore, its corrections budget.

TABLE 16.4
Per-Capita Spending on Corrections in Selected States, 1987

States Highest in Spending		States Lowest in Spending	
Alaska	$171.27	West Virginia	$20.98
Nevada	124.70	North Dakota	23.27
New York	119.79	Mississippi	29.34
California	111.33	Arkansas	29.43
Maryland	99.99	Idaho	32.04
U.S. average: $69.19			

Source: National Conference of State Legislatures, *State Aid to Local Governments for Corrections Programs*, criminal justice paper no. 1 (Denver: NCSL, April 1989).

The states also differ with respect to the level of government that must bear the costs of corrections. As Table 16.5 shows, five states fund most or all of their corrections budgets. The local governments of 19 other states receive no state aid for corrections.

MANAGING CORRECTIONS COSTS

The recent developments in the criminal justice process have created difficult financial problems for the states. One commentator remarks that "getting tough on crime has come to mean getting tough on taxpayers."[15] Similarly, Oregon's former governor Neil Goldschmidt laments that "imprisonment rates are rolling toward numbers that will eat our budgets whole."[16] As a result, the states

TABLE 16.5
State Spending on Corrections as a Percentage of the State/Local Total, 1987

Five Highest		Five Lowest	
Delaware	100%	Pennsylvania	51.2%
Hawaii	100	California	53.1
Rhode Island	100	Oregon	53.9
Connecticut	99.9	New York	54.6
Vermont	99.8	Florida	56.8
U.S. average: 64.7%			

Source: National Conference of State Legislatures, *Opportunities in Community Corrections*, criminal justice paper no. 5 (Denver: NCSL, July 1989).

FOCUS

16.1 THE POLITICAL DEBATE ON PRIVATIZING CORRECTIONS

In 1984 President Ronald Reagan sanctioned private sector incarceration of illegal aliens and triggered a movement to privatize America's prisons. Since then the privatization of corrections has been a popular political issue.

Proponents of private prisons claim that in the area of corrections, as in other public service areas, private facilities and programs can be more efficient than public ones. There is some evidence in support of their claim; in Louisiana, for example, where two identical facilities operate, the private prison's costs are 8 percent less than the public prison's costs.

However, money and efficiency are not the only issues. Opponents worry about how the costs are reduced and whether prisoners may be harmed or have their rights violated in the process. Will the private facilities skimp on food, clothing, health care, recreational opportunities, and more? Will guards and other employees be adequately compensated? Will other long-term problems emerge if costs are cut in the short run? Will the state be liable for acts of negligence or brutality by privateers? Is it morally acceptable to farm out human punishment and to employ mercenaries to do the public's work?

The privatization of corrections is an issue that is likely to remain on states' agendas, especially as they face financial trouble.

SOURCE: Penelope Lemov, "Jailhouse Inc.," *Governing* (May 1993): 44–48.

---

are attempting a variety of approaches to control corrections costs. (See Focus 16.1.)

The cost-control efforts run the gamut from **early release programs** to wholesale sentencing reform and expanded community-based correctional programs. In addition, several states have **emergency release systems** in place, so that when the prison population reaches institutional capacity, the governor can activate a provision that increases, on paper, the time already served by some prisoners and thereby makes those prisoners ready for immediate release. The states that employ emergency release systems include Arizona, Connecticut, Florida, Iowa, Michigan, New Jersey, Ohio, South Carolina, and Washington. In Florida the practice is referred to as "administrative gain time" in that it results in an across-the-board reduction of prisoner sentence time.[17]

Minnesota and Washington have adopted a series of reforms that, among other things, links sentencing to prison capacity. **Sentencing guidelines** are established for each type of crime. Related to the criminal history of the individual involved, the guidelines reduce the discretion of judges and are designed to ensure that similar offenses carry similar penalties. In addition, the sentencing guidelines are strict on violent and repeat offenders and provide nonprison, community-based penalties for those convicted of nonviolent crimes.

Sentencing Guidelines and Commissions

In practice, however, the reforms in Washington and Minnesota have not always worked out as intended, as judges can deviate from the guidelines for stipulated reasons and prosecutors can undercut the system through plea bargaining and manipulation of the charge or charges filed. Such arrangements are also perceived as unfair to prisoners sentenced under previous and harsher laws.[18] Oregon recently adopted sentencing guidelines as well. The guidelines, especially as an alternative to mandatory sentencing, which deprives judges of discretion and latitude, help to stabilize the size of prison populations.[19]

The Minnesota and Washington reforms also feature **sentencing commissions**, which monitor crime patterns for the purpose of recommending modifications in the sentencing guidelines. Sentencing commissions provide some political cover for legislators when the sentences for certain crimes are changed. Political survival for lawmakers today often requires an unyielding tough-on-crime stance, despite the skyrocketing costs of corrections and the taxpayer rebellion. Sentencing commissions, thus, make recommendations based on study and analysis, and legislators can support their own decisions with the objective work of the commissions.

The states rely heavily on **community-based corrections** in an attempt to keep costs under control. Roughly three-quarters of those convicted of crimes are not inside prisons but are on parole or probation in the community. Critics disagree about which offenders should be kept in prison, and for how long; still, not all prisoners behind bars are violent or present a physical danger to others. The National Conference of State Legislatures notes that only 30 percent of prisoners today have been convicted of violent crimes.[20]

Community-Based Programs

There are several ways for the convicted to serve sentences outside of prison itself, or in the community-based programs. One is **intensive probation**, whereby the offender meets with a probation officer as often as five times a week and participates in work and drug or alcohol rehabilitation. Roughly 40 states have some type of intensive probation program. Another community-based program is called **house arrest** because the prisoner stays home; **electronic monitoring**, which involves an electronic device attached to the body, is used to track the prisoner's whereabouts. Texas, Florida, North Carolina, and Wyoming use electronic monitoring.[21] In the fall of 1992 one Texas high school football player wore his court-ordered electronic monitoring device while playing in a football game.

Although community-based corrections programs involve costly equipment and personnel expenses for monitoring and probation, they are much less expensive to run than prisons. A 1989 report indicated the following cost comparisons per prisoner per year:[22]

- Routine probation: $300–$2,000
- Intensive probation: $1,500–$7,000
- House arrest: $4,500–$8,500
- State prison: $9,000–$20,000

The states are beginning to monitor the costs of new sentencing proposals as they are introduced in the legislature. As corrections costs rise, the states are giving more attention to the potential consequences of their decisions.

POLITICAL ISSUES

Although at one level crime and corrections may seem to be technical problems—find the lawbreakers, convict them, and put them in jail—the issues are far more complicated and more political than they appear. Various political issues center on what should be considered a criminal act, why people violate the law, what to do with those who break the law, how much to spend on prisons, and what rights to extend to the accused.

There is wide disagreement on the issue of whether certain human acts should be classified as criminal. Although such acts as armed robbery, burglary, rape, and assault have always been considered criminal and still account for most arrests, convictions, and jailings, the criminal nature of other human acts is less clear. For example, some critics question whether taxpayer money should be spent on chasing down, prosecuting, and imprisoning thousands of individual drug users or those involved with prostitution. Others point out that drug use impairs a person's ability to drive a vehicle and thus puts other motorists in danger. Still others suggest that an individual's use of drugs or involvement with prostitution is criminal because it can indirectly cause harm to others, such as through the destruction of families or the spread of AIDS.

Other political issues focus on what government should do to control **white-collar crime**, such as when managers of savings and loan associations knowingly make economically risky decisions that will benefit their family members or political friends but lead to devastating losses for depositors. Is the fraudulent operation of a financial institution and its effects on both depositors and the American taxpayer (who pays for the losses) a more or less serious crime than the theft of a car or a television set? Which crime should receive the longer prison sentence?

Drug use, drunken driving, greedy or careless savings and loan management—should legislatures treat these and other behaviors as illegal? And if so, should all convicted offenders go to jail? The dollar, or property, damage done by the financial manager may well be thousands of times greater than that done by the petty thief who steals a car. It is estimated that business-related crimes, such as embezzlement, fraud, theft, and arson, cost society ten times as much as the losses suffered through street crimes.[23] But critics disagree on the criteria to employ when deciding whether an act is criminal or the seriousness of a crime. Should the criteria be based on the nature and extent of the actual damage done to oneself, to others, or to both self and others? On the potential for damage to self or others? On the general public's views of morality and good citizenship? Obviously, there are no correct answers to these difficult questions, for they are subject to differences of opinion. Thus Americans dispatch their representatives in government to answer them politically.

Just as representatives decide these questions politically, so too do they change their answers on the basis of political concerns, such as when the costs of the initial decisions become too high. The decision to get tough on crime, for example, has led to overcrowded prisons and skyrocketing corrections costs. Most of those currently incarcerated in American prisons are not guilty of violent crimes and an increasing number of them are there for drug-related offenses. Many other prisoners are thieves whose annual robbery yield is just a fraction of a state's annual cost of keeping them in jail.

The creation of criminal laws often involves trade-offs. Consider again, for example, the recent controversy surrounding drugs and prostitution. Some observers suggest that drug use should be made legal and that drug sales, like those of alcohol and tobacco, could be licensed and taxed. If this were done, they claim, drug-related violence would decrease, states would reap tax revenues from the sale of drugs, the reduced market value of drugs would lead to fewer crimes against property to support costly drug habits, the health-care costs associated with the use of impure drugs and contaminated paraphernalia would decrease, the number of courtroom cases and thus judicial delays would shrink, and prisons would have an abundance of space in which to house those convicted of violent crimes. Some also advocate the legalization, taxation, and regulation of prostitution, claiming similar health benefits and financial savings, to lesser degrees, as would result from the legalization of drugs.

Critics of legalized drug use and prostitution, however, argue that drug addiction would become an even greater problem and result in the loss of productive human beings. In addition, they argue that such efforts would condone, even support, the widespread violation of American values and beliefs.

Clearly, then, trade-offs are a necessary part of criminal law formation. Differences of opinion about what should or should not be outlawed are inevitable. As a result, an act that was legal in 1900 may have been made illegal by 1950, or an illegal act today may be considered legal by the year 2000. Similarly, what is legal in one state may lead to imprisonment in another. The sentence set by one state legislature for a crime may be very different from the sentence set by another legislature for the same crime. In most cases, therefore, determinations of what is illegal or legal are based on a variety of factors — crime statistics, state budgets, and the current values and beliefs held by the public and politically influential lawmakers.

What Causes Crime?

Although the causes of crime are difficult to identify precisely, the effectiveness of the policies designed to reduce or eliminate crime depends on this information. Much is known about the characteristics of lawbreakers. As was noted earlier in the chapter, disproportionate numbers of them are young male nonwhites with a below-average level of education. In addition, we know that the crime rate is higher in large cities than in small cities and rural areas. We know that a very high proportion of street crime is linked to drug trafficking and the support of drug-related habits. We know that inner-city locales, characterized by a high crime rate, high minority populations, and high drug use, are also areas of widespread disintegration of the family structure and consistently high unemployment. In some areas a majority of children and adolescents are without a two-parent family, reside in poverty-level households, lack extensive parental supervision, and are not likely to qualify as adults for most well-paying jobs. But they do know how to earn money through crime. The December 1989 murder of a 14-year-old drug dealer in the New York City borough of the Bronx elicited this comment in a newspaper report: "The legacy of despair he [has] left behind provides little hope of a better life for the next generation."[24]

All that we know about criminals, crime rates, and crime in general, however, does not tell us much about why one inner-city child gravitates toward a life of crime while another does not, or why one savings and loan executive is dishonest while others are honest. Given that crime is concentrated in certain geographical areas and with persons in certain circumstances and demographic groupings, though, there is reason to believe that advances in education and employment opportunities and a strengthening of family support might together help to reduce crime. But how much public money should be spent on this effort and would the government programs alter such conditions? Or should government take on any role at all? While government could perhaps provide education and job training and thereby help stimulate economies, its potential impact on the family, on sex offenders, on crimes of passion, or on drug-trafficking profits is unclear. The wide differences of opinion on these issues are thus negotiated in the political arena.

Another political issue focuses on what to do with convicted law-breakers and on the reasons for administering punishment.[25] Some observers view the prison sentence as a punishment only; that is, as a state-dispensed retribution for harm inflicted on someone else. Others view the prison as a correctional institution designed to teach those incarcerated the skills, attitudes, and behaviors that they will need to become productive and law-abiding citizens later on. Still others see sentencing and incarceration as primarily deterrents to criminal activity or as performing multiple functions—to punish, to deter, and to correct.

Reasons for Punishment

To Deter   Many studies of crime and corrections suggest that imprisonment does not function as a deterrent to crime. It is argued, for example, that as the prison population has increased the crime rate has not decreased, a sign that no correlation exists between the two factors. Similarly, a 1992 survey of Colorado's correctional system found no relationship between the rates of incarceration and crime.[26]

Researchers often draw the same conclusion with respect to capital punishment. For capital punishment to function as a deterrent, it is argued, the potential murderer must first think about the consequences of the criminal act, and this is unlikely with crimes of passion. However, experts contend that some deterrent effect is achieved when justice is administered quickly and consistently. Therefore, while the speed and certainty of punishment may work as deterrents, it is not clear whether severity of punishment, length of prison term, and capital punishment do the same.

To Rehabilitate   Most criminologists are skeptical about the rehabilitative effect of prison on inmates, arguing that prison conditions work against it. The educational and job training opportunities are few or not adequate to provide inmates with skills for gainful employment upon their release. Moreover, while prisons clearly are not intended to be "schools for crime," the inmates' separation from society and their daily interaction with other law-breakers does little to foster their potential for a crime-free life on the outside. Recidivism is thus high.[27]

To Get Even   One currently popular rationale for sending lawbreakers to prison focuses on giving them their just deserts for criminal behavior and protecting the public from further criminal acts. Thus, imprisonment is viewed as a way to get even and to keep violent criminals out of society. However, while those in prison cannot victimize persons on the outside, studies indicate that imprisonment does not always prevent the commission of more crimes later. By the time the offenders are through the system and in jail, most tend to be in their 20s, when the general propensity to commit crime is decreasing. In addition, many crimes are committed by groups, so the incarceration of one member of a group does not necessarily stop the others from engaging in criminal activity. A 1982 study suggests that it takes a very large increase in the number of imprisonments to produce a slight reduction in the crime rate.[28]

Public Opinion and Legislative Action

In a 1988 article entitled "Prisons Can Cost Less," Stephen Carter notes that:

> Not since the National Defense Highway System was built in the 1950s has there been a capital construction program to equal the present effort to construct and upgrade America's prisons. No state has escaped the need for more and better space.[29]

Perhaps no area of public policy better illustrates the public's desire for more public services and less taxation than crime and corrections. Highly publicized reports of hideous crimes bring renewed cries to get tough on crime, to lengthen sentences, and to restrict parole. But the public's aversion to paying for the consequences of the longer sentences and the greater number of convicts remains strong in the tax revolt movement.

Thus, legislative politics regarding corrections is complex and controversial. Sentencing commissions can help to deflect away from elected officials some of the political controversy associated with sentence reductions and early releases. The requirement of financial impact analyses on bills that may increase the prison population can do the same. But the public pressure remains intense. Some observers contend that the public views crime as America's single most important problem. A 1990 poll reported that 71 percent of the respondents said that jail or prison time was needed for offenders convicted of any of 24 crimes ranging from rape and robbery to drunk driving and property offenses. In addition, 92 percent of those polled wanted prison time of 10 years or more for crimes involving the use of a gun.[30] In the 1980s and 1990s several states had items on the ballot designed to eliminate parole or restrict the use of bail.

When constituents call for a tough stance on crime, legislators comply with the public's preferences. The results, however, are crowded correctional facilities, court orders to improve and expand prisons, and mushrooming corrections budgets.

Prison Location

Since the 1950s, prison building has been one of the largest capital construction projects in the nation, and as such it inevitably has become the focus of political decisions. Many communities do not want prisons located nearby. Like toxic waste dumps, prisons are subject to the phenomenon known as **NIMBY** ("not in my backyard"). However, a prison in a small or medium-sized community can have a significant economic impact. In the short run, the local economy is infused with a large dose of construction spending; in the long run, the institution provides employment for the local population.

Since large cities are the locales of most crimes, the homes of most criminals and their families, and the locations of most large police departments and courts, one might assume that prisons ought to be placed there, too. Locating prisons in large urban centers, furthermore, might increase the convenience and minimize the transportation costs of families, police officers, and convicts as they travel among homes, courtrooms, police stations, and prisons. In addition, it might be argued that prisons ideally should be located close to areas with training and counseling facilities that can provide opportunities for future employment upon inmates' release into the community.

However, most prisons are not located in urban areas. In times of economic lags, legislators often fight to have new corrections facilities located within their districts and base their arguments on the anticipated economic impacts. In 1988 the Colorado legislature approved a statewide lottery game, a portion of which was earmarked for new prison construction. The first facility was to be built in the district of the powerful speaker of the state house. In prison construction, location, and other areas of correctional policy, then, legislative decisions are ultimately political.

Gun Control

Whether stricter **gun control** would help curb crime in America is another controversial political issue.[31] The U.S. homicide rate is among the highest for all nations, and most murders involve the use of a gun. Moreover, states with gun-control laws have lower homicide rates than do those without such controls. But some critics argue that people, not guns, kill, and thus would-be murderers would simply obtain a gun illegally or use another type of weapon. Gun-control proponents counter that the additional time required to procure a gun illegally or to find another weapon would allow some potential killers acting out of passion to cool down. Proponents also note that those most at risk from guns kept in the home for self-protection are the gun owners and their families. (See Focus 16.2.)

The legal status of gun-control laws is at issue, too. The National Rifle Association (NRA) argues that the Second Amendment to the Constitution guarantees Americans the right to bear arms. Others counter that the Second Amendment was written to restrict Congress, not the states, and was intended to preserve the rights of state militia, not individual citizens.

The disagreements over gun control are widespread and strongly debated. The NRA continues to oppose all proposed controls and is a powerful lobby

---

FOCUS

16.2 SELF-PROTECTION OR UNJUSTIFIED HOMICIDE?

In October 1992 an exchange student from Japan who was living in Louisiana lost his way while looking for a Halloween party. He mistakenly approached a house, thinking it was the site of the party. The owner of the house, seeing a stranger in his driveway, took his revolver and shouted, "Freeze!" The Japanese student apparently misunderstood and continued approaching the homeowner, who then fired the revolver and killed the student.

A jury acquitted the homeowner in May 1993, in a trial that attracted nationwide attention as well as the attention of the Japanese. Considerable mention was made of the cultural differences with respect to gun ownership. Virtually no private citizens in Japan possess firearms, and in 1992 fewer than 100 Japanese were killed by guns.

Doonesbury   BY GARRY TRUDEAU

nationally and in the states. Given the politically contentious nature of the issue, broad-based gun control is not likely to gain approval in the short term. However, in November 1993 Congress finally enacted the Brady Bill, which requires would-be handgun purchasers to undergo a background check and a five-day waiting period before they can claim their weapon. While the broader consequences of this legislation remain to be seen, it will certainly affect the administration of gun control legislation in states that have such legislation.

There is a widespread belief among the public that criminals gener- **Innocent until** ally have too many rights and that they too often go free because of **Proven Guilty** legal technicalities. Although this view characterizes criminals as the beneficiaries of rights and technicalities, in a democratic system that values due process of law and individual freedoms, the rights and technicalities attach not to criminals but to the accused. Those who have not yet been convicted of the offense of which they have been accused, who like all Americans are presumed to be innocent until proven guilty, are protected by presumptions, procedures, and rights.

In the early part of the twentieth century, the Supreme Court began to interpret the Fourteenth Amendment to the Constitution in a manner that provided citizens protection in state cases, paralleling what was already operative in federal cases. The Fourteenth Amendment addresses the states, whereas the Bill of Rights limits only Congress. As the Court began to give meaning to the Fourteenth Amendment's requirement that states shall not deprive persons of life, liberty, or property without due process of law, it gave persons rights in state criminal cases similar to those already in place in the national Bill of Rights. The Court held that state authorities could not require self-incrimination by the accused. Thus, today the accused has the right to confront hostile witnesses. Once a general criminal investigation focuses on an individual, and that person is to be questioned, the person must be informed of his or her right to counsel. When arrested, persons must be warned that they need not speak and that if they do, what they say may be used against them. Evidence seized through illegal means may not be used against someone; this is called the **exclusionary doctrine**. The courts have recently allowed some leeway in the use of such evidence, however.

Due process rights, then, are designed to protect those accused but not yet found guilty. Since these rights are employed in the daily fight against crime and in court actions, they have generated much political conflict. Sometimes persons with long and well-established criminal records are not convicted for other alleged crimes because the police neglected to warn them of their rights or seized evidence by illegal means. Stories abound of career criminals thumbing their noses at the authorities as their lawyers secure their release from jail very shortly after arrest. Such incidents anger the public, and understandably so. They lead to a view that rights and procedural requirements designed to safeguard the highly valued presumption of innocence in the absence of conviction amount only to a tangle of rules that help criminals stay out of jail.

This is a difficult and politically volatile issue. On the one hand, if precedents were established that would permit procedural shortcuts in the gathering of evidence and the processing of criminal cases, many innocent citizens might wrongly end up with fines or jail sentences. On the other hand, the rules that keep evidence gathering and judicial procedures complex may be misused to the benefit of some of the guilty. When a rogue who has evaded justice by taking advantage of procedures and rights designed to protect the innocent proceeds to commit more crime, the public grows impatient. But many citizens find the same procedures and rights indispensable when they are personally targeted in an investigation on the basis of circumstantial evidence or suffer rough treatment by the authorities.

SUMMARY

Crime and corrections are a politically difficult policy area. While anything less than a tough stance on crime is quickly targeted by both a hostile public and political opposition, so is anything that sounds like higher taxes. Lawmakers are thus in a bind. A public that better understands the costs and limitations of expanded incarceration might well be more sympathetic to alternatives to the one-dimensional policies that simply add to prison time. Leadership is needed if elected officials are to educate, rather than only pursue, contemporary public opinion.

The entire criminal justice system is organizationally complex in that the institutions are intertwined. Supreme Court decisions establish the parameters for state and local law enforcement and corrections facilities. States enact most criminal laws. They also determine much of the workload of local law-enforcement authorities, locally housed courts, and local jails. State-level decisions with respect to sentencing and parole set the workload for locally based community corrections workers. The success of local law-enforcement personnel determines the ultimate success of state corrections policies.

Although the U.S. crime rate has increased somewhat over the past decade, changes in public policy have contributed most to the prison overcrowding crisis. States have lengthened prison sentences, cut down on early releases for good behavior, and cut back on parole. Now both state corrections institutions and state budgets are bursting. Corrections spending is consuming funds that might otherwise go to education, roads, or parks.

Yet as more criminals have been sent to prison for longer stays, the crime rate has not declined. Experts contend that the specter of prison time does not deter crime and, therefore, cannot solve the overcrowding crisis in prisons. Rather, U.S. prisons continue to fill to capacity as fast as they are built.

The nation's jails and prisons hold all sorts of offenders, from murderers and rapists to barroom brawlers and petty thieves. Even though most crimes are committed by teenagers and by those in their early 20s, inmates are often incarcerated well beyond that age. In addition, often inmates in prisons are not segregated by type of offense, and thus someone serving a sentence for burglary may be subject to assault or rape by other inmates serving time for violent criminal offenses.

During the past two decades public policy has sought to reduce some of the disparities in the length of sentence received by persons convicted of similar offenses, to deter crime, and to get even with criminals. Thus, judicial and parole board discretion has been reduced or curtailed. Elected legislators have taken a tougher stance on crime as their constituents have demanded it. At the same time, however, the costs of corrections have risen dramatically, causing some observers to rethink the strict crime policies. The states are now attempting to get corrections costs under control through such methods as emergency release systems, community-based corrections, sentencing guidelines, and sentencing commissions. Some states are also considering the revision of previously lengthened prison sentences.

KEY TERMS

police powers
Willie Horton
early release program
emergency release system
sentencing guidelines
sentencing commission
community-based corrections

intensive probation
house arrest
electronic monitoring
white-collar crime
NIMBY
gun control
exclusionary doctrine

ADDITIONAL READINGS

Anderson, David. *Crimes of Justice: Improving the Police, Courts, the Prisons.* New York: Times Books, 1988.

Byrne, James, and Robert Sampson. *The Social Ecology of Crime.* New York: Springer-Verlag, 1985.

Duffee, David. *Corrections: Practice and Policy.* New York: Random House, 1989.

Federal Bureau of Investigation. *Crime in the United States, 1990.* Washington, D.C.: GPO, 1991.

Greenberg, David. "Age, Crime, and Social Explanation." *American Journal of Sociology* 91 (July 1985): 1–21.

Johnson, Robert. *Hard Time: Understanding and Reforming the Prison.* Monterey, Calif.: Brooks/Cole, 1987.

NOTES

1. In 1988, six states had items on the ballot designed to eliminate parole. See National Conference of State Legislatures, *State Legislatures and Corrections Policies: An Overview*, criminal justice paper no. 2 (Denver: NCSL, May 1989).

2. Ibid., p. 1.

3. Ibid.

4. "Record Jump in Prison Population," *Rocky Mountain News*, 11 Sept. 1989.

5. Julie Lays, "The Complex Case of Costly Corrections," *State Legislatures* (Feb. 1989): 15–17.

6. National Council on Crime and Delinquency, *Crime and Punishment in the Year 2000: What Kind of Future?* (San Francisco: NCCD, 1988), p. 22.

7. Fred Strasser, "Go to Jail," *Governing* (Jan. 1989): 36–41; and NCSL, *State Legislatures*, paper no. 2.

8. NCCD, *Crime and Punishment*, pp. 13–15.

9. NCSL, *State Legislatures*, paper no. 2.

10. Ibid.; and National Conference of State Legislatures, *State Legislatures and Corrections Policies: An Overview,* criminal justice paper no. 2 (Denver: NCSL, July 1989).

11. Ibid.

12. Lays, "Costly Corrections."

13. Ibid.

14. National Conference of State Legislatures, *Bringing Corrections into the 1990s* (Denver: NCSL, 1992).

15. Sharon Randall, "Sensible Sentencing," *State Legislatures* (Jan. 1989): 14–18.

16. Quoted in NCCD, *Crime and Punishment*, p. iii.

17. Strasser, "Go to Jail."

18. NCSL, paper no. 2.

19. Donna Huzaker, "Can States Make Sentencing a Science?" *State Legislatures* (Oct. 1992): 19–22.

20. Ibid., p. 4.

21. Lays, "Costly Corrections."

22. Ibid.

23. Clark Cochran et al., *American Public Policy*, 3rd ed. (New York: St. Martin's Press, 1990), p. 162.

24. "Teen's Slaying Oft-Heard-Tale Today," *Denver Post*, 3 Dec. 1989.

25. NCSL, *State Legislatures*, paper no. 5.

26. NCSL, *Bringing Corrections.*

27. See, for example, Samuel Walker, *Sense and Nonsense about Crime: A Policy Guide*, 2nd ed. (Belmont, Ca.: Brooks-Cole, 1989), pp. 201–34.

28. Kevin Krajik, *Overcrowded Time: Why Prisons Are So Crowded and What Can Be Done* (New York: Edna McConnell Clark foundation, 1982), pp. 15–16.

29. Stephen Carter, "Prisons Can Cost Less," *State Legislatures* (Feb. 1988): 22.

30. Cochran et al., *American Public Policy*, pp. 191–97.

31. Ibid.

17

State and Local Government: Our Past and Our Future

The skyline of Albany, New York. The tall buildings are the Empire State Plaza, which includes the state capitol. The plaza symbolizes the complexity of governing a populous state. *(Joseph Schuyler/Stock, Boston)*

PUBLIC SERVICES: THE DOMAIN OF STATE AND LOCAL GOVERNMENT

Despite the wide media coverage of government in Washington, D.C., it should be clear from the preceding chapters that the government action affecting us daily takes place in state legislatures, in county courthouses, in city halls, and at local school board meetings. New drinking and driving laws come from Albany, Austin, Sacramento, and the other state capitals. If you register to vote, apply for a marriage license, or pay a traffic ticket, you'll probably visit a county courthouse. To apply for a zoning change to build a small apartment building, you'll likely go to city or town hall. Parents and others opposed to the textbooks used in a local elementary school attend school board meetings to voice their concerns.

As the preceding chapters demonstrate, most public services are provided by state and local government units. Police and fire protection; sewer and water services; public health and social services programs; parks, streets, curbs, and drainages; and schools—these are all administered by the states and their political subunits, the counties, cities, townships, school districts, and special districts.

THE POLITICS OF PROVIDING SERVICES

Although matters of public service provision may at first glance seem relatively straightforward, we have seen in the preceding chapters that, in a pluralistic society, they are actually matters of great political controversy. What is controversial and political about police protection? Some citizens want to spend more to increase police patrols; others want to spend those funds on parks or other programs; and still others want to spend less generally in order to lower taxes. What is controversial and political about educating America's youngsters? Some citizens advocate higher school taxes to support programs aimed at helping students from troubled and neglectful home environments get good meals and psychological counseling. Others contend that the function of schools is to educate, not to perform the role of parent, counselor, or child psychologist. And what is controversial and political about reducing the crime rate and maintaining a safe environment for the American public? Legislators and their constituents disagree on how to achieve these goals and on how much to spend in the process.

Taxation for all types of public services is increasingly controversial because of the taxpayer revolt. Thus, ongoing debates center on how much to spend, and tax, in order to educate America's young, maintain green grass in parks, and put criminals in jail. These and numerous other issues are debated through political processes by those representing political institutions.

DECENTRALIZED INSTITUTIONS OF GOVERNMENT

A complex and decentralized set of government institutions exists to provide the various public services and to resolve political disputes. As noted in earlier chapters, through federalism we have two main levels of government — national and state — that operate side by side and whose authority and limitations are established by the people through the Constitution. The nation's founders devised the federalism scheme to address such central problems as national defense, the regulation of interstate commerce, and the establishment of a common currency, while leaving most other public functions (schooling, public health, and public safety, for example) to the preexisting states and their local units. The system was later decentralized even further through the establishment of the separation of powers, bicameralism, the state plural executive, tens of thousands of local governments, complex and labor-divided court systems, and a host of boards and commissions at all levels of government.

In the twentieth century especially, the institutional arrangements characterizing the nation's system of government have changed dramatically. The scope of government operations has expanded at all levels. The state and local units, for example, currently regulate scores of professions; operate thousands of schools, stores, and hospitals; promote economic development; and engage in numerous other activities. The dual nation – state arrangement set up by the nation's founders has evolved into one that today features a tangled web of intergovernmental ties in which the national government preempts much state autonomy in decision making and the states do the same in their relations with the local units. Unlike the system of government in operation just eight decades ago, today's system is run by a far greater number of institutions that are both larger and more dependent on each other than ever before. As noted in Chapter 15, for instance, the contemporary Medicaid program is established in national law, is funded partly by the national government and partly by the states, is subject to some state-determined eligibility provisions, is administered by local units, and uses both public and private health care providers. The tangled, confused, centralized, and decentralized features of Medicaid also characterize scores of other modern-day government functions and programs.

THE 1990s: IS THE STATE/LOCAL SYSTEM IN CRISIS?

Some observers, ranging from Ross Perot to columnist George Will, contend that today's system of state and local government is in the midst of a crisis as it attempts to deal with the growing costs of service demands, insufficient resources, eroding public confidence in government, and a declining sense of community. Increasing public demands for state and local services have had many consequences. The task of the schools, for instance, has been enlarged to include functions related to the decline of the family unit and other social conditions, so that schools now counsel and feed students as well as educate them. Illegal drugs, guns, gangs, AIDS, and homelessness are among the many other societal problems that local law-enforcement and social services agencies must address. As a result, the cost of operating the government system has risen considerably.

The states are forced by federal mandates to administer necessary but costly public services, and often without any significant financial support from the national government. Expanded Medicaid coverage and programs aimed at addressing the needs of the disabled, the special educational needs of handicapped children, the reduction of automobile emissions, the cleaning of wastewater, and the closing of landfills are a few examples of federally mandated programs that are carried out and funded by the states. As members of Congress enact these policies, however, the costs are increasingly being taken on by the states and localities because the enormous national deficit precludes any significantly expanded federal spending. To some extent, the states are doing the same to their local units. Cities, counties, townships, and school districts must abide by state-imposed service mandates, sometimes without any state money for implementation.

At the same time, the American public is demanding tax relief. Increases in the property, sales, and state income tax as well as in user fees (such as for college tuition, automobile license plates, hospital bills, and fishing licenses) are met with public opposition. State and local officials are thus in a difficult dilemma as they feel the need to raise more revenue to meet the dictates of Congress but have an obligation to represent the public's preferences regarding level of taxation. They must deal with social problems, federal mandates, and public demands for more services on the one hand, and with the antitax movement on the other.

In addition, a general decline in the public's confidence in government and politics is a problem for state and local units. However, much of the public disaffection is tied to the national government's role in the enormous federal deficit, in the unpopular combination of Social Security and income taxes, in the 1991 savings and loan scandal, in the housing programs of the Department of Housing and Urban Development, in the 1986 Iran-Contra affair, in the 1991 U.S.

House check-bouncing shenanigans, and in the 1992 Clarence Thomas–Anita Hill hearings. Moreover, the complex political system in operation today makes it difficult for voters to sort out the respective functions of the national, state, and local units. As a result, the public's frustration over income taxes due on April 15 might affect the vote on a local school bond election held in the spring. Voters in a growing number of states are approving term limits for state legislators, even in states with an average tenure that is shorter than the newly imposed limits.

The American public's disaffection with government and politics generally may be tied in part to the nation's declining sense of community. States and communities compete for new industry, often by promising tax giveaways or other benefits. Communities battle each other in their efforts to drive away the homeless and to keep public housing out. In communities with aging populations, there is often reluctance among voters to fund public schools. Proposals to move public money from public to private schools are common on modern state legislative agendas.

A reciprocal relationship may exist between the growing size and complexity of the U.S. political system and the public's declining confidence in government and decreasing sense of community. As all levels of government have grown in size and function, and as state and local activities have become increasingly directed from Washington, the American public has found it more difficult to sort out the vast complexities of the system and, therefore, has come to view its relationship with government as remote and distant. For example, the consolidation of the 130,000 school districts that existed in the 1930s into the roughly 14,000 districts in operation today means that schools are much larger and more impersonal.

FUTURE TRENDS

Observers who contend that the state/local system of government is facing a crisis in citizen confidence in and support for public institutions—one born, at least in part, of excessive institutional size, centralization, and distance—propose the rethinking of the evolutionary direction of the federal system. Perhaps smaller and closer governing is better than larger and distant, they argue. Rather than seeking efficiency through municipal consolidations, perhaps government should focus on fostering a sense of community by way of limitations on city size. Perhaps the largest school districts should be split up and community-based schools re-created. And perhaps it is time to resurrect the states' rights debate, not to retreat to a discriminatory society but to give back some decision-making power to the localities and to reduce the number of federal mandates.

If a heightened sense of community and a restoration of public confidence in government are tied to increased local control and citizen proximity to decision-making centers, then the nation's political future may rest with the localities and the states. It is these government units that provide what Americans need daily—water, streets, safety, schools, and the like. Moreover, unlike members of Congress, state and local officials are neighbors with whom community residents can enjoy direct, personal contact. In conclusion, it is interesting to note that the American revolutionaries, viewing their enemy as a large, distant, remote, and illegitimate government, fought to replace that distant authority with local units of government and local control.

Glossary

accountability The degree to which public agencies, public officials, and individuals are responsible for their actions.

Aid to Families with Dependent Children (AFDC) A major social services program that provides aid to needy families and is funded primarily with federal funds and administered by the states and their local governments.

alternative dispute resolution (ADR) Methods, such as arbitration, for resolving civil disputes. The purpose is to reduce the case load of the courts.

amendment A modification made to an existing or proposed law or bill, such as a state constitution, a statute, or a proposal for a new law. See also *amendment process.*

amendment process The procedures used to amend state statutes or constitutions, such as legislative or citizen proposal of a change and ratification by voters at the polls. See also *amendment.*

annexation Expansion of the boundaries of a city to take in new territory.

apportionment Apportioning, or allocating, the seats in a legislative assembly. As a result of U.S. Supreme Court decisions, apportionment must be based primarily upon population.

appropriation A legislative act authorizing the expenditure of public money for some specified purpose.

Articles of Confederation The document that, prior to the adoption of the U.S. Constitution, established a loose union of the original thirteen states.

assessment The determination of the value of property for the purpose of taxation.

at-large election An election without districts; rather, the candidates are voted on by all electors within a jurisdiction, and voters may vote for any of the candidates. Such elections are common in local government.

balanced budget A budget that authorizes the expenditure of only as much revenue as is expected to come in. State constitutions or statutes require the states to balance their budget — to balance spending and revenue at year's end.

bargain justice The practice by prosecuting attorneys of striking plea-bargaining deals with defendants.

bicameral legislature A two-house legislature, with a house and a senate. The U.S. Congress and 49 states have bicameral legislatures. See also *unicameral legislature.*

bipartisan coalition An alliance of legislators, voters, and local officials from various political parties who join together to support or oppose a bill or issue of special interest to them.

block grant Federal money granted to a state or locality with a certain amount of flexibility as to the purposes for which it can be used. Block grants developed when, during the Reagan presidency, a number of categorical grant programs were "blocked" together into more broadly defined categories.

bond The legal pledge of a government to repay what it borrows from a lender plus interest by a specified date. See also *general obligation bond* and *revenue bond.*

broker role The view of the representative in government as one who bargains, trades, and compromises with other lawmakers to accomplish what is necessary to serve a district's needs. See also *mirror role* and *oracle role.*

Brown v. Board of Education The landmark 1954 Supreme Court case that outlawed racially "separate but equal" public facilities, including separate schools.

busing A method of racial desegregation often used under court order that involves transporting children to schools outside the immediate community in order to improve racial balance in the classroom.

calendar committee A legislative agenda-setting, or scheduling, committee. See *rules committee.*

candidate-centered campaign With the decline in

the political party as a support base for candidates, and with the increasing cost of campaigning, the task of organizing and funding political campaigns falls more and more upon the candidate and his or her own organization.

categorical grant A federal grant-in-aid to a state or locality that must be used for a specific and narrowly defined purpose (in other words, for a specified "category" of activity).

caucus A meeting of party members—for example, of all Republicans or Democrats in a state house of representatives. Caucuses meet to discuss issues, take policy positions, and elect their own leadership.

centralized (or unitary) system A political system in which authority is concentrated, or centralized, in one place. In the states, for example, authority resides with the state and is not decentralized to local governments except insofar as the state allows.

charter A basic foundational document that sets forth the powers, duties, limits, and organizational structure of city government.

citizen initiative A form of direct democracy whereby a proposed law may be placed on the ballot through the gathering of citizen signatures on a petition. See also *direct democracy*.

citizen legislature A legislature whose members serve part-time as representatives, and hold other jobs. Unlike members of the U.S. Congress, they are not full-time professional lawmakers.

city council The "legislature" or policy body of a city, usually composed of five to nine members.

city manager The chief executive or administrative officer in a city that employs the council–manager system. The manager is hired by the city council, rather than elected by voters, and is accountable to the city council. See also *council–manager system*.

civil liberties Freedom to function as a citizen without undue restraint from government. Civil liberties include freedom of expression through speech and press, along with other freedoms such as those contained in the U.S. Constitution's Bill of Rights and the bills of rights in state constitutions.

clientele group An interest group or organized segment of the public that interacts with government agencies in order to gain benefits from agency programs.

coercive federalism A national–state relationship, typical of today's United States, in which the national government employs its spending, regulatory, and other powers to place restraints and mandates on states and localities, thereby reducing the range of state and local decision-making latitude.

commission plan A form of city government in which usually five persons are elected to function both as members of the policy body and as administrators of one or more city departments.

committee on committees A legislative committee that either appoints legislators to standing committees or recommends appointments to party caucuses.

community-based corrections Community-based methods of dealing with persons convicted of crimes without incarcerating them. These include parole, probation, intensive probation, and electronic monitoring.

conference committee A small group of representatives and senators that meets to resolve differences in a bill that has passed the two legislative houses in different versions.

consolidation A merger of government units.

constitution The foundational document of a government that sets forth its basic structure, powers, duties, and limitations. The federal government has the U.S. Constitution and each state has its own constitution. Many state constitutions are long and contain outdated provisions, although this is not always the case.

constitutional convention A convention held in the state or nation for the purpose of drafting a new national or state constitution or revising the current one.

constitutional politics The high-stakes political activity associated with creating new constitutions or amending existing ones.

contingency lobbying An arrangement in which a lobbyist is paid by his client only if he succeeds in doing the job the employer wants, such as getting a bill passed or discarded. Some states forbid contingency lobbying.

contract lobbyist A person who represents, or lobbies for, many clients on a paid contractual basis.

core city The central city of a large metropolitan area, such as Detroit, Chicago, and Los Angeles.

council–manager system A form of city government that emerged from an early-twentieth-century reform movement and features a hired full-time city manager who administers city affairs for the city council. See also *city manager.*

county A unit of local government that performs many administrative functions for the state, such as administering local tax systems, maintaining vital records, and administering elections. Counties typically have elected sheriffs, clerks and recorders, assessors, treasurers, and other officials.

crossover sanction A national law, rule, or regulation contained in one program area and imposed on a state or locality that also "crosses over" to apply in other program areas. For example, failure to comply with the dictates of a particular program might lead to penalties or loss of federal funds in other program areas.

cult of the robe The myth that judges shed all biases and prejudices when dispensing justice, and that judges are not political.

decentralized system One in which most major political decisions are made by regional units and the central government is weak. A confederation is an example of a decentralized system.

deficit spending Occurs when a government spends more than it takes in within a fiscal year. States prohibit deficit spending and require balanced budgeting. See also *balanced budget.*

Dillon's rule The notion that local governments are empowered to perform only those functions clearly authorized by state law. Local governments do not possess "implied" powers.

direct democracy The creation or ratification of law directly by the voters at the polls. The *citizen initiative*, the *referendum*, and the *recall* are methods of direct democracy.

direct primary The selection of candidates for government office by way of direct election by a political party's voters.

due process The notion that established procedures must be used in administrative or judicial proceedings and that shortcuts and violations of rights must be avoided.

early childhood education Schooling for youngsters, often from poor or "at-risk" environments, in advance of regular schooling, which generally begins with kindergarten. Early childhood education is based on the premise that such education increases chances for success and reduces the prospects for an unproductive and troubled adult life.

early release program A corrections program in which convicted persons are released, often for good behavior or to relieve prison overcrowding, before their prison sentence has expired.

earmarking The specification that certain tax revenues are to be used only for a specific and identified purpose. Gasoline taxes, for example, are generally used only to maintain roads.

educational crisis A view held since the 1980s by some observers who believe that America's schools are not teaching students the skills they need to function as productive adults. While some critics blame the schools themselves for the crisis, others target social conditions, such as the breakdown of the traditional two-parent family unit.

electronic monitoring This procedure, often used in intensive probation, involves attaching to the offender's person an electronic device that records his or her whereabouts. See also *intensive probation.*

elementary school Schooling from kindergarten through grade 6. See also *secondary school.*

emergency release system A procedure in some states that triggers early release of convicts so as to make room for those newly convicted. It is a response to the prison overcrowding problem.

employee lobbyist Someone who lobbies for the organization for which he or she works, as contrasted to those who lobby for many clients on a contract basis, or those who lobby as volunteers.

endless campaign A modern phenomenon in which career politicians never stop campaigning, but begin working for reelection the day they are elected.

entitlement program A public program that guarantees benefits for anyone who meets legally specified criteria. Social Security and Medicaid are examples. By meeting the criteria, one is "entitled" to the benefits.

exclusionary doctrine   The prohibition of the use in a trial of evidence that was obtained through illegal means.

executive branch   One of the three branches of American government. The executive branch is headed by governors and other elected officials and is responsible for executing, or implementing, legislatively made policy.

executive budget   A state's budget proposal, assembled by the governor and the governor's staff and submitted to the state legislature for approval.

executive-centered coalition   First identified in New Haven, Connecticut, by the researcher Robert Dahl, this is a political coalition centered around the mayor.

expressed powers   The authority of the national government, as expressed in the U.S. Constitution's Article I, Section 8. The expressed powers are those explicitly enumerated and include, among others, the authority to regulate interstate commerce, coin money, and establish an army.

faction   A term for *interest group* as used by James Madison in Federalist Paper No. 10. See *interest group.*

factory-based economy   An early U.S. economic system in effect when the major industries and employers were large manufacturers of automobiles, steel, and chemicals, for example. Today the United States has a more service-based economy. See also *service-based economy.*

federalism   A governmental arrangement in which the central unit has the authority to make some decisions whereas regional units are authorized to make others. The U.S. Constitution creates a federal system.

fiscal decentralization   The tendency of some states to give local governments much of the responsibility for raising and collecting taxes and spending, rather than the state collecting the taxes and distributing the funds among its local units.

fiscal policy   The political budgetary decisions that affect government spending, programs, and services.

Food Stamp program   A federal social services program that distributes to needy people stamps that can be used to buy food.

formal powers   The legal authority of the state governor, including the power to appoint people to certain positions, prepare budget proposals, and veto legislation. See also *gubernatorial roles* and *informal powers.*

full faith and credit   The U.S. Constitution stipulates that each state is to give "full faith and credit" to the public acts, records, and judicial proceedings of the other states. This stipulation is meant to prevent legal chaos among the states and to help citizens by providing some degree of consistency among the laws of the many states.

general election   A group of local, state, and national elections held in November in which voters elect candidates to office. See also *primary election.*

general law city   A city that is established and operates under the provisions of a state statute that governs all cities of that size category. This is in contrast to a *home rule* city, which, under a different provision of a state's laws, is given the flexibility to design its own structure and processes and, sometimes, to define its own powers as well.

general obligation bond   A form of government borrowing that involves a legal document and a government's pledge to repay a loan by a specified date with general revenues derived from taxes. General obligation bonds are used, for example, to repave city streets. See also *bond* and *revenue bond.*

gerrymander   The configuration of legislative districts in ways that benefit one political party or group of voters and leave others at a disadvantage.

grand jury   A body of citizens that convenes to review a prosecutor's evidence and to decide whether there are grounds for a trial. If there are, it issues an indictment.

grants-in-aid   Funds made available to states and localities by the national government and under federal laws to support specified public programs, such as schools, highways, and utility systems.

Great Society   The proliferation of national programs and funding to address domestic problems and improve the quality of life in the United States during the presidency of Lyndon Johnson. Great Society programs targeted areas such as poverty, urban blight, education, and unemployment.

gubernatorial power   Governors' powers come

from formal, legal grants of power embodied in state constitutions and statutes, as well as from informal influence gained through media exposure and prominence in the political party. See also *gubernatorial roles.*

gubernatorial roles The many activities and responsibilities of the state governor, including both formal responsibilities and informal activities. See also *formal powers* and *informal powers.*

gubernatorial veto The authority of a state governor to stop, or veto, a bill passed by the state legislature.

gun control Laws regulating the purchase, possession, and use of firearms.

habeas corpus A court order directing that reasons be shown for detaining someone.

home-rule provision A provision in a state's constitution or statutes that authorizes cities (and sometimes counties) to design their own unique governmental structure and processes and, sometimes, powers as well.

homelessness A contemporary social problem involving a growing number of Americans who lack permanent homes and face unemployment, illness, and other problems.

house arrest Confinement of a convicted person to his or her home. House arrest often involves monitoring the offender's movements via an electronic device attached to that person.

implied powers Powers of the national government that have emerged from U.S. Supreme Court decisions. The Court, in a succession of individual cases, found that the existence of certain powers was "implied" by other powers explicitly stated. The authority to regulate interstate commerce, for example, was found to imply that the national government could regulate a variety of the activities of corporations engaged in interstate commerce. First established in 1819 in *McCulloch v. Maryland.*

income tax A tax based on the amount of earned income or salary. See also *progressive tax* and *regressive tax.*

incorporation The formation of a city government by residents of a particular area.

incorporation theory Constitutional doctrine applying U.S. Bill of Rights freedoms to states and localities.

incumbent The current, or sitting, holder of political office.

individualistic political culture One of three political cultures posited by Daniel Elazar, the individualistic political culture values self-advancement without governmental interference. It was introduced by immigrants who initially settled in New England and later migrated to the Midwest.

industrial development bond (IDB) Government-backed borrowing by a private party to establish or expand a business enterprise.

informal powers The extralegal political clout of a state governor; may include influence within the political party or the ability to affect public opinion. See also *gubernatorial roles* and *formal powers.*

inherent powers Powers of the national government that, the U.S. Supreme Court has said, are "inherent" in the nature of a central, or national, government—for example, the power to conduct a variety of activities in international relations.

initiative A form of direct democracy developed during the Progressive era. The initiative allows citizens to use the petition method to place proposals for new laws directly before the voters. See also *direct democracy.*

integrated executive A reformed model of state executive branch organization in which departments and agencies performing similar functions are consolidated or coordinated.

intensive probation Heavily monitored probation for persons convicted of crimes. See also *electronic monitoring.*

interest group A group of people with similar interests who band together to pursue activities of benefit to themselves or their cause, including political activities. See also *interest group intensity* and *techniques of influence.*

interest group intensity The degree of sentiment that an interest group possesses on a particular issue. See also *interest group.*

intergovernmental service agreement A legal cooperative deal made between two governments to provide collectively, or cooperatively, public services such as trash collection, or in which one government leases, purchases, or rents a service from the other. See also *Lakewood plan.*

intermediate appellate court   In the U.S. state judicial system, a court that sits below the state supreme court but above the major trial courts. These courts hear appeals from lower courts and reduce the case load burden on state supreme courts.

iron triangle   A term used to describe the close and powerful political relationship that frequently exists among legislative committees, executive agencies, and interest groups. These three form a triangle that is politically strong enough to win legislation and funding for programs that benefit the three parties.

joint committee   A joint house–senate committee in a state legislature. Many states have a joint appropriations or budget committee, for example, on which members from both houses sit together. Some states have many joint committees.

judicial activism and restraint   The tendency of judges to allow themselves liberties in interpreting law or legal precedent, or to deny themselves such flexibility by exercising restraint.

judicial branch   One of the three branches of American government. The judiciary, or the courts, are responsible for interpreting laws and for applying the law in specific criminal and civil cases.

judicial restraint   See *judicial activism and restraint.*

judicial review   An activity of a court in which the court is asked to review the constitutionality or legality of an action by a legislature or an executive official. Generally, the question before the court is whether legal authority exists for the action in question.

jurisdiction   The purview that a court or some other government entity has with respect to policy or legal matters.

Lakewood plan   An intergovernmental service agreement plan, initially developed in Lakewood, California, in which participating cities purchase an extensive range of services from another government instead of assembling the administrative systems needed to provide these services themselves. See also *intergovernmental service agreement.*

latent functions   Secondary and sometimes unintended results. Political parties, for example, work to win elections, but in the process their activities have the "latent" function of informing the public about politics.

leadership powers   The authority and responsibilities of leaders, such as those possessed by the house speaker and the senate president.

legal precedent   Occurs when decisions made in prior court cases guide decisions in similar subsequent cases.

legislative branch   One of the three branches of American government. Legislatures are charged with representing citizens and forming policy. They also control the purse strings.

legislative budget   The name for a budget-making process in which the legislature itself, and not the governor, prepares the state budget proposal, which is then examined and ultimately adopted by the state legislature.

legislative committee   One of the subgroups of state legislators that conduct hearings and examine bills before they are considered by the full state house or senate.

legislative liaison   A lobbyist employed by government agencies or other governments. See also *lobbyist.*

legislative override   A vote by the legislature to pass a bill over the veto of the governor.

legislative process   The procedures by which bills become laws. They include both formal stages and informal bargaining, lobbying, and compromising.

legislative turnover   The election of new members (nonincumbents) to a legislature.

legislative veto   Action taken by a legislature to cancel a decision made by the executive branch.

levy   The imposition of a tax.

limited government   The notion that government may perform only those functions authorized by law.

line-item veto   The veto of a part (or line) of a bill, usually an appropriations bill, rather than the entire bill.

lobbyist   A person who represents the interests of an individual, a group, or an organization before a decision-making body such as a legislature or commission.

logjam   A backlog of bills, common near the end of a legislative session.

log-rolling   Gaining the support of legislators for bills that contain benefits for all involved.

lower court These courts constitute the lowest level of the state judicial system. They hear cases involving minor crimes and relatively low-stakes civil cases, and they do not have appellate jurisdiction. Often they are not courts of record (in which a full recording of the procedures occurs).

magnet school A school that is set up to provide some special form or style of instruction for those within the district who prefer it to the usual program.

malapportionment A representative districting system in which some districts have many more people than others. Outlawed by the Supreme Court in 1962, malapportionment allowed a numerical minority of voters to elect legislative majorities.

marble-cake federalism A term used to describe the state-national relationship in which the federal government makes funds available to states and localities to support state and local programs. The system can be said to resemble a layer cake, with the three sets of government stacked atop one another and federal funds running vertically throughout the system.

McCulloch v. Maryland An 1819 U.S. Supreme Court case in which the implied powers were first established. See also *implied powers.*

Medicaid A major social services program jointly funded by federal and state governments that provides medical care for the poor.

Medicare A national government program created by amendments to the 1935 Social Security Act that provides medical care for elderly Americans and certain others adjudged to have disabilities.

merit pay A salary based on a supervisor's estimate of a worker's merit, rather than on seniority.

merit plan A public employment system in which the initial hiring of an employee is based upon the quality or "merit" of his or her education, experience, and prior performance, and in which pay raises and promotions are similarly based on merit as determined by administrative superiors.

metropolitan council of government (COG) A cooperative organization of local governments in metropolitan areas, generally employed to do planning and conduct studies of areawide needs and problems.

metropolitan federation A reform proposal entailing a government arrangement in which a central unit performs some functions for an entire area and smaller units do the rest.

metropolitan statistical area (MSA) A metropolitan area as defined by the U.S. Bureau of the Census.

mirror role A view of the representative in government as one whose actions reflect constituents' views rather than the lawmaker's own judgments. See also *broker role* and *oracle role.*

Missouri plan A method of judge selection, sometimes called a *merit plan*, in which a panel of lawyers and laypeople nominate several candidates for openings on the bench and the governor appoints one of them.

moralistic political culture One of three political subcultures posited by Daniel Elazar, the moralistic political culture is community-oriented and emphasizes the collective good. It has been embodied by settlers in the Great Lakes and upper Midwest regions.

motor-voter law Permits voter registration at driver's license bureaus and other state offices.

mud-slinging Political campaign tactics involving the levying of personal, questionable, "dirty" accusations against an opponent.

municipal annexation The expansion of the legal boundaries of a city in order for it to take in new territory.

municipal bond A legal pledge issued by cities to lenders to repay borrowed money.

municipal corporation The legal term used to describe a city.

municipality A city or municipal corporation.

"A Nation at Risk" A 1983 report by the National Commission on Educational Excellence that concluded that graduates of American schools were not performing as well as they should and that, as a result, the nation was at risk.

national supremacy Article VI of the U.S. Constitution provides that the Constitution itself and laws and treaties made under its authority are the supreme law of the land. State constitutions are thus subordinate to the U.S. Constitution.

New Deal National government programs of the 1930s, associated with President Franklin D. Roosevelt and designed to stimulate the economy, put people back to work, and rescue the United States from the economic depression.

new federalism   A term used to describe a series of efforts by presidents Richard Nixon and Ronald Reagan, for example, to reassert the place of the states in the federal system; in other words, to decentralize the nation's system of government.

new judicial federalism   A recent pattern of state supreme court decisions in which civil rights and liberties are asserted on the basis of state constitutional provisions.

NIMBY   This acronym for "not in my backyard" refers to community reluctance to have prisons, group homes, drug rehabilitation centers, and the like located nearby.

nonpartisan election   An election in which the candidates do not run on political party labels. See also *partisan election.*

one person, one vote   Equal protection of the law; in other words, all Congressional districts must contain approximately the same number of inhabitants.

oracle role   A view of the representative in government as one whose best judgment, rather than constituents' views, guides decisions. Sometimes called a "trustee" role. See also *broker role* and *mirror role.*

partisan election   An election in which candidates run for office on political party labels. See also *nonpartisan election.*

party caucus   A gathering of members of one political party in a legislative chamber, usually to select leaders, discuss party positions on bills, or plot legislative strategy.

patronage   Occurs when the criterion for filling government jobs is political party loyalty.

petit jury   A trial jury that determines guilt or innocence. A petit jury may consist of up to 12 people.

plea bargaining   A form of bargain justice, employed by prosecutors in criminal cases, in which the defendant agrees to plead guilty to a lesser offense. See also *bargain justice.*

plural executive   An organizational scheme, common within the executive branch of state government, in which voters directly elect many officials; authority is thereby decentralized and the governor's powers are lessened.

pluralism   Exists where a society or polity is composed of multiple groups and centers of influence. See also *power pyramid.*

pocket veto   The refusal of a governor to sign a bill within a specified period of time. The term is also used to describe a similar practice of legislative committee chairs when they decline to schedule a bill for a hearing.

police powers   Those powers exercised by local and state governments to protect and promote public health, safety, welfare, and morality.

political action committee (PAC)   A group that collects funds from members and contributes the money to political campaigns.

political efficacy   One's ability to affect the political decisions of government.

political machine   A term used to describe the tightly organized and disciplined political party organizations that operated in American cities in the early 1900s.

politics   The resolution of conflicts over collective matters.

polycentric system   A locality, state, or nation in which political power is neither concentrated or evenly distributed, but is instead shared by a number of influential groups or parties.

poverty line   A federally defined level of income below which a person or family is defined as eligible for various categories of public assistance. The actual level depends on the size of the household and is adjusted from time to time.

power elites   Those few individuals who may monopolize political power in a locality.

power pocket   A point in the legislative process at which an individual or group with power (a house speaker, a committee chair, or a rules committee, for example) can determine the fate of a bill.

power pyramid   A visual conception of political power as existing in a hierarchial, or nonpluralistic, form. See also *pluralism.*

powers denied   Besides allocating certain authority, or powers, to both the national government and the states, the U.S. Constitution specifically denies to both powers in certain areas—for example, in the establishment of *ex post facto* laws.

precinct   A portion of a political jurisdiction

geographically delineated for purposes of holding elections. People register to vote by precinct, they vote in their precinct at a designated location, and political parties use precincts (precinct committee members) as their organizational base.

primary election An election held to select political party nominees for an upcoming general election. Normally, registered Democrats and Republicans can vote only for candidates in their respective parties. Independents cannot vote in primaries. See also *general election.*

privatization The practice of using private contractors or firms to perform functions traditionally provided by governments, such as trash collection and custodial care of public buildings.

progressive tax A levy that taxes larger incomes at a higher percentage than smaller ones, thereby affecting the wealthy more than the poor. Most taxes, however, are not progressive. See also *regressive tax.*

Progressives Those who, in the late 1800s and early 1900s, pressed for political reforms to counter corruption in government. The reforms included the initiative, the referendum, the recall, the civil service, and a variety of municipal government reforms.

property tax A levy, or tax, applied against property, most commonly real estate.

Proposition 13 This tax limitation measure was passed in California in 1978 and is considered to have triggered similar "tax revolts" in other states.

public entity A government or an organizational creation of a government, such as a park or stadium authority.

public interest A term that is variously defined on the basis of individual values but that most agree is something larger than the interests of one group or individual. Also referred to as "the public good."

public services Services provided to the public by government, rather than sold privately.

Reaganomics The conservative and decentralized approach to public programs and economic policy characteristic of the presidency of Ronald Reagan.

reapportionment The redrawing of legislative district boundaries on the basis of new census data.

recall A Progressive-era invention that, in many states and localities, permits citizens to use petitions to force elections designed to remove a public official from office.

referendum A popular yes-or-no vote by the people on a measure or proposal placed on the ballot, usually by the legislature, for voter consideration. A form of direct democracy. See also *direct democracy.*

reformed legislature A state legislature featuring upgraded legislative staffing, facilities, and pay, as well as lengthened and annual legislative sessions.

regressive tax A tax that affects the poor more than the wealthy. Most state and local taxes (for example, sales taxes) are regressive. See also *progressive tax.*

reputational approach A method of identifying the distribution of community power, and the members of the local elite, by asking knowledgeable community members who the "influentials" are. See also *stratification approach.*

reserved powers Powers reserved for the states by the Tenth Amendment of the U.S. Constitution. The original intention was to reserve to the states and the people all governmental powers not given to the national government. Recent U.S. Supreme Court decisions seem to indicate that the reserved powers may not do much to protect state authority from national mandates.

revenue bond A government-issued pledge to repay a lender with funds generated by the activity or facility created with the borrowed money (for example, a stadium). See also *bond* and *general obligation bond.*

San Antonio Independent School v. Rodriguez A 1973 U.S. Supreme Court decision in which the property tax as a way of funding public schools was judged constitutional despite the funding disparities among school districts.

row-officers A term used to describe the organizational structure of county governments in which several officials are directly elected by voters, and on an organizational chart line up in a row, rather than hierarchically.

rule of law The assumption in our representative democracy that the activities of government and of public officials should be guided and constrained by what is in the written law, and not by the views and preferences of government personnel.

rules committee Exists in many state legislative

chambers. Its task is to schedule bills for consideration by its members. Also called *calendar committee*.

safe seat A legislative seat held by someone who is not likely to be defeated in upcoming elections.

sales tax Applied to the purchase of most nonfood items and some services, the sales tax is a major source of revenue for all states and some cities.

satellite city A concentration of new business and commercial activities and residential housing that develops on the fringe of an existing core city. Often the development of a satellite city is triggered by a new airport or the juncture of major highways.

school board The elected policymaking body in a local school district. See also *school districts*.

school district The organizational government unit for public education in the United States.

schools of choice Refers to state policies that allow parents some degree of choice in school selection so that their children may attend schools other than the ones in the immediate neighborhood. See also *voucher system*.

secondary school Schooling from grade 7 through grade 12. See also *elementary school*.

selective incorporation U.S. Supreme Court decisions that have selectively read into the meaning of the Fourteenth Amendment (which applies to state and local governments) many freedoms contained in the first nine amendments (which apply to the national government).

sentencing commission A commission existing in a few states that studies the patterns of criminal sentencing and makes recommendations for modifications to the state legislature.

sentencing guidelines Provisions in state criminal codes that instruct judges on the range of required penalties for those convicted of particular crimes. See also *sentencing commission*.

service-based economy An economy, such as that of the United States in the late twentieth century, in which most businesses and jobs provide services, as opposed to an economy dominated by manufacturing.

sin tax A tax applied to the purchase of such products as beer, wine, hard liquor, and cigarettes.

single-issue interest group An interest group that presses its views on one or just a few issues. Both

pro- and antiabortion groups are examples. Sometimes these groups present difficulties for legislatures in that they are reluctant to compromise on an issue, whereas legislative politics involves constant compromise.

Social Security Act The 1935 federal legislation that established the social security system. This legislation has been amended many times (for example, with the addition of Medicare).

social services A term used to describe what we commonly call our welfare system. Social services include aid to families with dependent children, Medicaid health services for the poor, food stamps, and more. They are jointly funded by all levels of government but are administered primarily by county governments.

sovereignty The independence or autonomy of a government to make decisions affecting its fate.

special court One of a variety of state courts that handle specific types of cases, such as juvenile courts (for those below the legal age of adulthood), and probate courts (which settle questions of wills and estates).

special district A unit of local government established to provide one service for a designated area, such as water, sewerage, or recreation.

spin doctor A term given to political spokespeople who try to put a particular, usually positive, twist or "spin" on a political statement or event.

state bill of rights Each state constitution contains a bill of rights. These are similar in many but not all respects.

state constitution The most basic, or fundamental, legal document in a state. State constitutions establish the structure and processes of the state government. They vary considerably in their length and detail. Some states have had several constitutions.

statute A state's statutes are its laws, passed by the legislature and signed by the governor. They provide the structural and procedural detail for state government, establish local governments, define criminal behavior, and so forth.

stratification approach A way of identifying a community's power elite by associating those at the top of the social and economic strata with the holders of political clout. See also *reputational approach*.

strong mayor–council system A form of city government in which the mayor possesses significant budgetary, personnel, and agenda-setting powers. See also *weak mayor–council system*.

suburbanization The move to areas that lie within metropolitan areas but outside the boundaries of core cities.

sunk costs The results of prior decisions and investments that restrict the latitude of current decision makers.

sunset provisions Provisions in a law that establish a government program or agency (a regulatory agency, for example) and stipulate that the program or agency shall expire after a certain date (seven years after creation, for example) unless it is renewed by the legislature.

Supplemental Security Income (SSI) A major federal social services program that provides assistance to the blind, disabled, and elderly poor.

supreme court This is the top court, or the court of last resort, in a state's judicial system. Supreme courts deal mostly with appeals from lower courts but may have original jurisdiction in special cases.

tax base The value of all property within the boundaries of a local government upon which taxes can be levied.

tax-exempt bond A bond held by those who lend money to local governments. By federal law, the interest earned on such loans is not subject to the federal income tax.

taxpayer revolt Actions in several states, starting in California in 1978 with Proposition 13, in which the electorate has voted to change the constitution or statutes to limit either taxes or the permissible level of spending, or both.

Taxpayers Bill of Rights (TABOR) A 1992 constitutional amendment passed in Colorado that restricts the ability of the state and local governments to tax and spend.

techniques of influence Methods employed by interest groups, such as donating to candidate campaigns, seeking to influence public opinion, and lobbying in legislatures. See also *interest group*.

tenure A guarantee of job security given to teachers after a probationary period. It is intended to provide educators with academic freedom and with freedom from community pressures to speak, write, and think in certain ways.

third party One of a number of small political parties other than the Democratic and Republican parties. There are many third parties in American politics, but they rarely succeed in electing their candidates.

ticket-splitting Occurs when voters cast some votes for Democrats and others for Republicans rather than supporting a straight one-party ticket.

tort reform Changes in state laws that make it more difficult for persons to sue each other for alleged damages, or "wrongs."

town A form of municipal corporation, similar to a city, but generally very small.

township A unit of local government found in some eastern and midwestern states.

traditionalistic political culture One of three political subcultures posited by Daniel Elazar. In the traditionalistic political culture, the status quo is the norm, while change is not, and those who head the social hierarchy also dominate government and politics. This subculture was introduced by settlers in the South.

trial court Trial courts are the major courts in state judicial systems. They sit above the lower courts, which hear minor matters, and below supreme courts or intermediate appellate courts. Major trial courts hear felony criminal cases, domestic cases involving matters such as divorce and child custody, and civil cases where money or property of substantial value is at stake. State statutes define the jurisdiction of these and all other state courts.

two-party system A system such as the American political system, which is generally characterized by the existence of two major political parties. However, the two parties do not operate in all localities. See also *third party*.

U.S. Constitution See *constitution*.

unicameral legislature A one-house legislature. Nebraska is the only state with a unicameral legislature, though most cities, school districts, special districts, and counties have one-chamber policy bodies. See also *bicameral legislature*.

unified court system A neatly configured and hierarchial state court system in which jurisdictions are clearly defined. This is in contrast to court systems that have developed in incremental fashion, and where neither boundaries nor jurisdictional lines of appeal are always clear.

unitary system See *centralized system.*

urban village A residential and commercial development on the fringes of a core city, the hub of which is often a large shopping center, a new airport, or an office complex.

urbanization The movement of large numbers of people from rural areas to cities.

user fees A payment that citizens must make to use a public facility, such as a city swimming pool, a toll road, a park, or even a school.

veto point A point in the legislative process at which strategically placed legislators can kill bills (a rules committee, for example).

volunteer lobbyist Someone who lobbies legislative and other government decision makers on a volunteer, rather than a paid, basis. Representatives of leagues of women voters, parent-teacher organizations, and churches often lobby on a volunteer basis.

vote broker A local political organization, other than the party, that can deliver a bloc of votes for those seeking the party nomination.

voucher system A method of funding public education in which the state provides vouchers to parents that are used to pay for their children's education in schools of their choice. See also *schools of choice.*

weak mayor-council system A form of local government in which the city council is dominant and the mayor generally lacks the power to control the public agenda, the budget, and major administrative appointments. See also *strong mayor-council system.*

welfare A term formerly used to refer to public assistance programs. See *social services.*

white-collar crime Illegal behavior by businesspeople and professionals, such as embezzlement, income tax evasion, or the fraudulent operation of a savings and loan organization.

white flight The movement of large numbers of white citizens out of the core cities to the suburbs. See also *urbanization* and *suburbanization.*

Willie Horton A violent criminal released early from a Massachusetts prison who subsequently committed other violent crimes. Former Massachusetts governor and 1988 presidential candidate Michael Dukakis was politically damaged by the public's association of him with Horton's early release and subsequent crimes.

Women, Infants, and Children (WIC) A federal social services program.

yellow-dog Democrat One so loyal to the Democratic party as to vote Democratic even if the candidate were a yellow dog.

Index

About the Authors

JOHN A. STRAAYER is professor of political science and past department chair at Colorado State University. He is director of the department's legislative internship program and has served as a lobbyist for the university. He has published *The Colorado General Assembly* (1990); *American State and Local Government* (1973, 1977, 1983); *The Study and Teaching of Political Science* (1980); *Introduction to American Government*, with Robert D. Wrinkle (1975); *American Government: Policy and Non-Decisions*, with Robert D. Wrinkle (1972); and *The Politics of Neglect: The Environmental Crisis*, with R. L. Meek (1971).

ROBERT D. WRINKLE is professor of political science at the University of Texas–Pan American, where he teaches in the Master of Public Administration program. He is the editor of *Politics in the Urban Southwest* and has published articles in *State and Local Government Review, Urban Law Review, Western Political Quarterly, Social Science Journal,* and *Social Science Quarterly*. He is author of *Introduction to American Government*, with John A. Straayer (1975); *American Government: Policy and Non-Decisions*, with John A. Straayer (1972); and the forthcoming *Electoral Reform and Urban Policy: The Impact on Mexican American Communities*, with J. L. Polinard.

J. L. POLINARD is professor of political science at the University of Texas–Pan American, where he teaches public law and minority politics. He served for many years as chair of the Department of Political Science. He is a past chair of the Pre-Law Advisors National Council and serves as a lay member of a panel of the State Bar of Texas. He has published articles in journals such as *Publius, State and Local Government Review, Western Political Quarterly, Social Science Journal,* and *Social Science Quarterly*. He is author, with Robert D. Wrinkle, of the forthcoming *Electoral Reform and Urban Policy: The Impact on Mexican American Communities*.